Reforms at the United Nations:
Contextualising the Annan Agenda

Reforms at the United Nations:
Contextualising the Annan Agenda

Gambhir Bhatta
Assistant Professor
Department of Political Science
National University of Singapore

SINGAPORE UNIVERSITY PRESS
NATIONAL UNIVERSITY OF SINGAPORE

© 2000 Singapore University Press

Yusof Ishak House, NUS
31 Lower Kent Ridge Road
Singapore 119078

Fax (65) 774-0652
E-mail: supbooks@nus.edu.sg
Website: http://www.nus.edu.sg/SUP

ISBN 9971-69-235-X (Paper)

Printed by Photoplates Pte Ltd

Dedicated to the memory of my departed uncle, Lava Dev Bhatta, but for whom I would not be here today doing what I am doing.

Table of Contents

List of Figures

List of Tables

Abbreviations

ACABQ	Advisory Committee on Administrative and Budgetary Questions
ACC	Administrative Committee on Coordination
ASEAN	Association of Southeast Asian Nations
ASG	Assistant Secretary-General
BWDC	Bretton Woods Development Committee
BWI	Bretton Woods Institutions
CC	Code of Conduct
CGG	Commission on Global Governance
CSD	Commission on Sustainable Development
DA	Development Account
DHA	Department of Humanitarian Affairs
DPA	Department of Political Affairs
DPI	Department of Public Information
DSG	Deputy Secretary-General
ECE	Economic Commission for Europe
ECLAC	Economic Commission for Latin America and the Caribbean
ECOSOC	Economic and Social Council
EEC	European Economic Community
ERC	Emergency Relief Coordinator
ESCAP	Economic and Social Commission for Asia and the Pacific
EU	European Union
EXCOM	Executive Committee
FAO	Food and Agriculture Organisation
GA	General Assembly
GATT	General Agreement on Trade and Tariffs
GDP	Gross Domestic Product
GNP	Gross National Product
HRM	Human Resource Management
IAEA	International Atomic Energy Agency
ICAO	International Civil Aviation Organisation
ICC	International Criminal Court
ICJ	International Court of Justice
ICS	International Civil Service
ICSC	International Civil Service Commission
IDA	International Development Association

IFAD	International Fund for Agricultural Development
IFC	International Finance Corporation
IIP	International Institute of Peace
ILO	International Labour Organisation
IMF	International Monetary Fund
IMO	International Maritime Organisation
IO	International Organisation
IR	International Relations
ITO	International Trade Organisation
ITS	International Trusteeship System
ITU	International Telecommunications Union
JIU	Joint Inspection Unit
JSPB	Joint Staff Pension Board
JSPF	Joint Staff Pension Fund
MNCs	Multinational Companies
MRG	Management Reform Group
MSC	Military Staff Committee
MTP	Management Training Programme
MUNS	Multilateralism and the United Nations System
NATO	North Atlantic Treaty Organisation
NGO	Non-governmental Organisation
NIEO	New International Economic Order
OAS	Organisation of American States
OAU	Organisation for African Unity
ODF	Office of Development Financing
OECD	Organisation for Economic Cooperation and Development
OHRM	Office of Human Resource Management
OIOS	Office of Internal Oversight Services
OL	Organisational Learning
OPEC	Organisation of Petroleum Exporting Countries
OT	Organisation Theory
PAR	Performance Appraisal Review
PCG	Policy Coordination Group
PEF	Peace Endowment Fund
PLO	Palestine Liberation Organisation
RC	Resident Coordinator
RCF	Revolving Credit Fund
RCM	Rational-Choice Model
SAP	Structural Adjustment Programme
SC	Security Council

SG	Secretary-General
SMG	Senior Management Group
SPU	Strategic Planning Unit
SWAPO	South-West Africa People's Organisation
TC	Trusteeship Council
TOKTEN	Transfer of Knowledge through Expatriate Nationals
UN	United Nations
UNA-USA	United Nations Association, USA
UNCDF	United Nations Capital Development Fund
UNCHS	United Nations Centre for Human Settlements (Habitat)
UNHCHR	United Nations High Commission for Human Rights
UNCTAD	United Nations Conference on Trade and Development
UNDAF	United Nations Development Assistance Framework
UNDCP	United Nations Drug Control Programme
UNDG	United Nations Development Group
UNDP	United Nations Development Programme
UNEP	United Nations Environment Programme
UNESCO	United Nations Educational, Scientific, and Cultural Organisation
UNFPA	United Nations Population Fund
UNHCR	United Nations High Commissioner for Refugees
UNICEF	United Nations Children's Fund
UNIDO	United Nations Industrial Development Organisation
UNISTAR	United Nations Short-Term Advisory Resources
UNITAR	United Nations Institute for Training and Research
UNO	United Nations Organisation
UNU	United Nations University
UNV	United Nations Volunteers
UPU	Universal Postal Union
USAID	United States Agency for International Development
USG	Under Secretary-General
WCF	Working Capital Fund
WFP	World Food Programme
WHO	World Health Organisation
WIPO	World Intellectual Property Organisation
WTO	World Trade Organisation

Foreword

This new contribution to an understanding of the United Nations and its prospects for change comes from an observer who knows the institution from many different points of view. The author was born in a country that is both a substantial recipient of UN assistance and an important participant in its peacekeeping and development activities; he has worked within the United Nations in various capacities and in different countries; and he is currently teaching management, which is among the major issues of concern to the institution and its members today. This background provides the author a unique perspective of the United Nations, and grounds his analysis in reality.

The author – in an unusual approach – takes a familiar nursery rhyme and its simple phrases as a backdrop to the daunting complexities of this global bureaucracy. That very juxtaposition highlights the challenges that the institution faces. By bringing together theory and practical applications, previous analysis and fresh insights, he reminds us of the many parameters of the actual context of the UN today. In the process, he makes new comparisons, raises new questions, offers a new synthesis, and outlines various options for the future.

Reading this broad overview encourages us all to draw our own conclusions about the future of the United Nations, and perhaps to influence the forces at play and thereby the ultimate outcome of those forces. It is perhaps appropriate that a children's nursery rhyme is the basis for the book's outline, for one of the earliest and most positive aspects of the UN's work has been its concern for the world's children. A reminder of that lever for global progress may offer a subtle note of encouragement for all those – like the author – who hope to contribute to the future of the UN.

Carroll Long
UNICEF Regional Office for Asia
Bangkok, Thailand
February 2000

Preface

At the time of this book going to press, Secretary-General Kofi Annan has finished three very stabilising years at the helm of the United Nations (UN). And while his critics continue to be unimpressed with what Annan has been able to do in particular, or the UN in general, there is a sense among UN-watchers around the world that Annan has indeed been able to slowly bring the public image of the UN around. He started off on the right foot by making a high-profile trip to Washington, DC, upon assuming office in January 1997 and making his own case in front of some of his staunchest critics. In 1998, he played a key role in defusing a showdown between Iraq and the US on the matter of weapons inspection, and followed that with a successful trip to Nigeria to convince the military leaders there about the utility of reverting to civilian rule. Whether or not he will be able to parlay these soft victories into something sustainable for the goodwill of the UN still remains to be seen in the remaining years of Annan's tenure.

But his efforts at revamping the image of the UN come at a critical time for the organisation. Morale never seemed lower at the time that he took over in early 1997, and world opinion, particularly in the US, and specifically among the legislative leadership, was very negative. While Annan still has not been able to convince the American legislators that they should pay their arrears and get the UN on a sound financial footing again, he has probably done more for the UN's image than what he has been given credit for. Annan's reform agenda that was prepared under such pressure in the early part of 1997, and which continues to be the source of much discussion in capitals around the world, is extensive but the critics are right to argue that it does not go far enough. On the other hand, the agenda is probably the best that could be put up given the charged conditions of 1997 and is probably the only source of salvation that the organisation has. For that, Annan deserves much praise.

The main argument in this book is that the UN is an organisation that is constrained by its external environment, and given that it has little control over its external environment, a product of the very principles that were espoused in 1945, the organisation can only muddle through in its operations. No amount of reform is going to reverse that trend. This has already been in evidence in the almost three years since Annan presented his Track I reform proposals.

On the other hand, this study agrees with several authors, and the Secretary-General himself, that given the dynamics of the state-interstate relations, it will not be possible for the UN to be radically altered at this point in time. The global powers, particularly the US, are not yet ready for such a radical transformation. The fact that even in the seventh year an open-ended working group set up to study possibilities for reforms in the Security Council cannot agree even on what to table for discussions in the plenary is symptomatic of this.

The overarching intellectual underpinnings that this study focuses on to assess the UN are theories in International Relations and in Organisation Learning and Change. The former has tended to be the dominant stream in the available literature (and for good reason since it is assumed that any organisation operating in the international arena must of necessity be amenable to analysis using frameworks derived from International Relations Theory). International Relations Theory also helps in understanding relationships among nations and the primacy of national interests. But using International Relations theories alone is not adequate, which is where the available literature on the UN is rather weak. It is just as important to understand how the organisation functions and what scope there exists for its reforms. For, in many ways, it is not possible to understand the UN reform movement without understanding how it functions as an organisation. Much of what was proposed by Kofi Annan makes sense only when looked at from the various rich perspectives offered by Organisation Theory and Practice.

RELEVANCE OF THE ORGANISATION

Interest in the United Nations in the 1990s and in the millennium has waxed and waned. Whereas the period immediately preceding the Gulf War, and during it, world attention was focused on the body in a positive manner, the leadership of Boutros-Ghali, who took over from Perez de Cuellar in 1992, was marked by incessant barbs first at what was perceived by the US as an increasingly militant attitude, and later at the slow pace of reforms. It ultimately ended in a concerted US attack on the integrity of the Secretary-General to lead the international organisation. Now that there is a new leader at the helm, and that he has been able to stabilise the organisation – and along with it begin to alter world opinion – the world is watching the UN again.

Its relevance has never been questioned. With the end of the Cold War, and the world in the throes of a globalisation phenomenon, the relevance of the UN as the only institution where all the nations can talk and hammer out issues is important for global governance. Speaking at the signing of the Milano Charter in Milan in April 1997, Ingvar Carlsson, the former Prime Minister of Sweden, and Chairman of the Commission on Global Governance, said that for the world at the moment there are three possible choices: (a) global democratic leadership based on the UN, (b) a superpower (i.e., the US) to take responsibility and leadership, or (c) anarchy, with no leadership and no democratic mechanism at all. His vote is for the first option, and that is why how the UN is strengthened is a very important concern.

Probably at no other time in the comparatively brief history of the United Nations did the organisation come under such searing scrutiny and criticism as it did during late 1995 and all of 1996 just prior to the selection of Kofi Annan as the seventh Secretary-General. Even after the unceremonious departure of Boutros-Ghali, the new Secretary-General's tenure during the first year did not really spark the kind of enthusiasm that was hoped for to get the reform process jump-started. In the time since though, Annan has been able to quietly take the initiative and has begun to put the UN in a more favourable light.

But even while the organisation is getting some respect, discussions on reforming it are still hopelessly mired in needless bickering among member states not only in the General Assembly but also outside that forum. A few argue that the organisation is for all practical purposes defunct and clawless since it cannot even sustain itself. Yet a vast majority of those who observe the UN differ, gaining solace from the fact that while the US may not be so enthused with the organisation, there is a feeling that states will not just let the only true global organisation wither away.

Critics have castigated the UN as being unresponsive, bureaucratic, wasteful, generally inefficient, and, by and large, ill-suited and, therefore, not completely relevant to these changed times. In response to this, Kofi Annan, within seven months of assuming the post, tabled some rather ambitious reform plans – ambitious at least by historical UN standards – and vigorous debate on them has started. To UN-watchers, there is a drama ongoing in New York at present, one that highlights the plight of the UN in stark terms. For it has become increasingly clear that unless changes are made in the way the UN is structured, is managed, and functions, it will cease to play the kind of role that its Charter envisions.

But the term "reform" itself has been viewed differently by different people. To some, it is a way to enhance the organisation's capabilities to meet its objectives, and to others it is an attempt to change the methodology of redeploying resources for economic and social development programmes. Yet others see it as symbolising, first and foremost, a cut in expenses. Even the disagreements that are evident in the approach towards changing the organisation point out how onerous the task will be for Kofi Annan to push through his Agenda in the remaining years of his tenure.

CENTRAL THESIS AND ASSUMPTIONS

These questions then form the core of this book. The central thesis of the book is that the UN – given the inherent nature of its composition and orientation – cannot but muddle through in its operations. The book is structured in such a manner that while it puts previous reform efforts in the backdrop, it brings to the fore critical analysis on the perceived ills of the UN, and how the Annan Agenda seeks to address them. In particular, the focus is on the following themes:

(1) the nature of the paradox inherent in the UN (i.e., between national interests and multilateralism and the concomitant lack of political will among member states to subsume the former to the latter),

(2) the UN as an organisation that is caught between adaptation and learning,

(3) the structural, functional, and managerial weaknesses of the organisation that have brought it such disrepute,

(4) the leadership issue and the lack of transparency of the selection process of the Secretary-General,

(5) the Track I and Track II components of the Annan Agenda, and their implications,

(6) the US ambivalence towards the UN manifest in the funding crisis, and

(7) the inevitable phenomenon of "muddling through" as a result of the lack of members' political will.

In the process of arguing for the Annan Agenda, the book also makes certain assumptions:

(1) First, the UN – despite all its critics – will continue to operate. The world cannot do without an institution such as the UN and no country – despite the strident rhetoric – is willing to re-create a similar organisation.

(2) Second, as an organisation created by nation states that paradoxically wish to subsume to its authority while at the same time seek to reassert their national sovereignties, the UN will always be constrained by external forces and precisely for this reason, its work will continue to muddle along.

(3) Third, for all the guts that the Annan Agenda has shown, there have been some sacred cows that have clearly been spared. Staff welfare, for example, continues to be an area that critics have zeroed in on over the last five years or so but there is no UN official who is willing to tackle that.

(4) Fourth, the UN – while constituting one organisation to the lay-person – is in actuality a combination of several powerful organisations that exert considerable influence in their particular spheres of expertise and there is not necessarily unanimity among these organisations about how to proceed with reforms in general.

(5) Finally, what is mentioned in New York is not necessarily what is practised in the Country Offices of the UN. The UN has a field presence in practically every country and the manner in which reforms are practised versus how they are formulated are rather instructive.

Since the focus of the book is on UN reforms but more specifically, on the Annan Agenda of reforms, it will necessarily focus upon the UN Secretariat and associated UN agencies. The UN specialised agencies, such as UNESCO, ILO, UNIDO, etc., are not covered because the UN Secretary-General has little control over these agencies, and as such his reform efforts do not extend to their realms. For excellent analyses of the UN specialised agencies, see, for example, Harrod (1988), Williams (1987), Wells (1991), Ameri (1982), and a bit dated but still very useful Cox and Jacobson (1973).

STRUCTURE OF THE BOOK

The book is not meant to be an academic exercise on the behaviour of international organisations, just as it is not meant to be devoid of application of the rich theoretical framework that exists that contextualises and describes how externally-constrained organisations behave. It hopes to be located somewhere in the middle. With that in mind, it has been divided into six chapters. It starts with a review of the literature on the UN and with a search for uniformity and divergence of analysis. It also posits a framework of analysis of the UN within the intellectual underpinnings of Organisation Theory and of International Relations. This is important in order to contextualise the functions and structure of the organisation. It looks at issues of sovereignty, and the organisation caught between fostering learning as opposed to merely adapting to the ever-changing (and apparently rather hostile) environment. Of particular significance is the discussion on Organisational Learning (à la Haas (1990)), on "muddling through" (à la Lindblom (1959)), and on the Realist School of International Relations (à la Morgenthau (1948, 1951)).

The first chapter also describes the UN in all its complexity and reach. This is done through focus on 12 elements of the organisation that range from origins to the Charter to stages of transformation of the UN. This discussion of the organisation will then provide the backdrop to the subsequent analysis to follow. At this point, it needs to be pointed out that no serious scholar of the UN can do without a careful and detailed review of the UN Charter. It is a rather complex document, not so much in the formulation of methods and relationships among the various organs but in the assumptions it makes about how nation states will behave and view international interactions. It is for this purpose that in Annex One of the book, the complete Charter with detailed comments on each Article is included. The readers are encouraged to refer to the Annex often to get an idea of the complexity of the organisation.

Chapter Two details the structural, functional, and managerial weaknesses of the UN. Structurally, the UN, it is argued, is not in tune with the new realities of the post-Cold War; functionally, it attempts to do too much and in too many parts of the world thus overstretching itself; and managerially, whatever it is supposed to do, it is not doing too well (with some notable exceptions). There is a myriad of sub-organisations within the UN and keeping track of all of them is a nightmare. There exists very little coordination among these UN agencies – a charge made even by present and former UN officials. The UN is asked to do more with less, and to top it, it does not have a reliable resource base such that it can readily tap a steady revenue source.

Reform efforts to address these shortcomings are not new. Every Secretary-General has had to contend with these issues to some degree or other. It is only in recent years (as a matter of fact, since 1986 when the issue of financial constraints first publicly burst onto the scene) that the issue of UN reforms has so occupied the minds of the UN leadership as well as its detractors and supporters.

In Chapter Three, an attempt is made to analyse all the reform efforts that have been made up until the end of Boutros-Ghali's tenure. Since much of what Kofi Annan inherited is a product of what his predecessors (especially his immediate one) were not able to do, they merit considerable treatment here. It was during Boutros-Ghali's tenure that the UN underwent frequent spasms of introspection and there was considerable animosity and ill will exhibited when it came time to discuss the renewal of Boutros-Ghali's tenure. While the US argued that it was Boutros-Ghali that had come to symbolise the major stumbling block that was hindering genuine UN reforms, he did indeed make a strong effort to renew the UN, and some of his proposals (such as linkages with regional multilateral organisations for maintenance of regional security) merit further focus. During Boutros-Ghali's tenure, there was also considerable external focus on the UN (primarily related to UN financing), and this chapter puts these proposals in proper perspective.

Chapter Four focuses on the period after early 1997 when Kofi Annan became Secretary-General after protracted negotiations in the Security Council. It did not help matters that Annan had been seen as someone the US was hoisting on the world body but such are the internal processes of the UN. On the other hand, Annan seemed to be the ideal choice – he was low-key and was an eternal UN bureaucrat with a background in peacekeeping and finance (two areas that are at the forefront of the UN at present). His high-profile trip to Washington, DC, in January 1997 to drum up support for his reform agenda was touted as bridge-building, and the chapter will put the visit in its proper context. By July 1997, Annan had come up with comprehensive reform proposals that he dubbed Track I and Track II, and by September, he had submitted them to the General Assembly for debate. This chapter then also looks closely at the two-track proposals and highlights their components.

At the present moment, the UN is undergoing intense scrutiny, and there appears to be considerable apprehension among the UN leadership, the staff, and associated partners about the fate of the Annan Agenda as well as the capability of the UN to deal with any eventuality of the rejection – or watering down – of the reform proposals. The Republican-controlled US Congress has thrown cold water on Annan's proposals and many argue that the General Assembly is merely going through the motions of discussing the proposals, for without US support, nothing much is going to happen to the proposals. In Chapter Five, a comparison and analysis is done of the practicality of all the proposals that have been made.

The final chapter is devoted to looking at the way forward. How will the organisation deal with some key issues that have emerged recently? Primary among them is that of reforms of the Security Council since that is the core organ in the UN and also one that has been extremely resistant to change. There is also the big debate about how powerful member states are not willing to exhibit political will to alter the status quo in the organisation, and this has effectively meant that the UN will not be in a position to do anything constructive as long as that attitude persists. Will the organisation then be able to put together a realistic reform package – one accepted by all in its minimum components – so that it may play a greater role in international governance? It will be argued in this chapter that given the nature of the UN, there is no other option but to muddle through. The chapter also revisits the intellectual underpinnings specified in Chapter One, and discusses the utility of juxtaposing them with what is assumed for the UN in the years to come.

While there is much that has been published in the UN, there is precious little on the ramifications of the Annan Agenda that was presented in 1997. More importantly, what is needed now is to take stock of what has happened to the dramatic and far-reaching proposals that were made amid considerable anticipation by the world community. This is where this book seeks to add to the body of knowledge on the UN.

All the views expressed in this book are the author's own and he takes full responsibility for any errors and omissions.

Acknowledgements

I wish to thank many individuals and organisations that have made this book possible. First and foremost, Ms. Carroll Long, the former UN Resident Coordinator in Nepal (and now at UNICEF, Bangkok) deserves special mention for all her help and guidance for meticulously reviewing the earlier draft, and for agreeing to write the foreword to this book. In many ways, my inspiration for writing this book has come from her. I would also like to thank Dr. Ralph Gerald-Haag, former top UN official, diplomat, and academic, for all the moral support and concern that he has displayed for my own work within the UN. For putting trust in my abilities to contribute to the organisation, I am grateful to Prof. Babatunde Thomas, the former UN Resident Coordinator in Uganda.

Others in the UN system who have had considerable input in helping me understand the organisation include: Lars Sylvan, Mohamed Salem, Matloteng Motlana, Haruna Kyamanywa, Joseph Opio-Odongo, and others too numerous to mention here by name. I would also like to thank Mr. Salvatore Schiavo-Campo at the Asian Development Bank for sharing with me his views on the UN. At NUS, I have to single out my colleague, Dr. Ishtiaq Hossain, who gave me the International Relations perspective to the organisation. I also wish to thank the anonymous reviewers for making extensive and very helpful comments on the draft of the manuscript.

For all the bad press that the UN gets over the waste, and the inefficiency – some of which is actually justified – there are indeed dedicated people in remote and dangerous parts of the world doing work that most of us would shun without a moment's hesitation. Their work conditions may be appalling but the UN is richer for the work that they do. For giving me an opportunity to be involved in one such area, I should remain thankful to the UN Volunteer Programme and to UNDP.

I would also like to thank Mr Dileep Nair, Head of the Office of Internal Oversight Services at the UN, for making time to exchange views on various issues related to the world organisation.

For being patient with the manuscript, I wish to thank Singapore University Press, and particularly Ms. Patricia Tay. Finally, I have to apologise to Bhawana and Ashwin for often paying more attention to this project than to them these past three years.

Chapter One
"Humpty Dumpty sat on a wall...": The Organisation

Much has been written about the United Nations (UN) since it was established in 1945. The spate of literature has been greater since the 1980s, when it can be said that in many ways the current crisis had its genesis. In order to begin to take a holistic look at the organisation, the first task is to see how it is conceptualised.

In taking a closer look at the UN as an international organisation, focus is laid on various issues, including approaching the study of international organisations from the functionalist, idealist, and realist perspectives; of the usage of the UN as an actor, tool or arena; and of the organisation caught between fostering learning as opposed to merely adapting to the ever-changing – and apparently rather hostile – environment. This chapter aims to focus on three things:

(1) conceptualising the UN as an international organisation,
(2) reviewing the appropriate literature on the UN and its reforms, and
(3) describing the UN as it exists today.

1.1 CONCEPTUALISING THE UNITED NATIONS

A review of the literature reveals that there are two principal intellectual underpinnings of the UN as an international organisation: International Relations (IR) and Theory and Organisational Theory (OT) (see Figure 1.1).

The utility of the IR stream is understandable because the UN is operational in the international arena, dealing as it does with global issues and consisting as it does of member states from around the world. The latter (i.e., OT) has tended to be the lesser prevailing of the two philosophical bases[1] but is important nonetheless to understand how the organisation functions and what scope there exists for its reforms. For, in many ways, it is not possible to understand the UN reform movement without first understanding how it functions as an organisation.

1

Figure 1.1
Conceptualising the UN: Intellectual Underpinnings

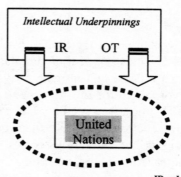

IR = International Relations
OT = Organisation Theory

Source: author.

The conceptual progression of the UN as an organisation can then be taken along the lines presented below. Against the intellectual underpinnings of the UN (i.e., IR and OT) can be juxtaposed the mandates and constraints of the organisation. As is evident in Figure 1.2, from the two main bases come the following key ideas that have been the subject of debates over the years. In the field of International Relations, three strands of thought emerge: sovereignty, interdependence, and the debate between idealism and realism (with inputs from functionalism as well). On the other hand, in the field of Organisation Theory, it is evident that the main strand of thought is the focus on a constrained organisation. This set of constraints is evident both internally (i.e., contained within the UN itself) and externally (i.e., imposed from outside).

Figure 1.2 shows how the conceptual progression of the UN can be framed and how the relationship that exists among the various strands can be expressed. Two key conclusions emerge from the diagram that merit some discussion. First, it is evident that three key fields of study in the social sciences are implied in the three strands of ideas under International Relations (Political Science for the debate between idealism versus realism; Economics for internationalism; and Law for sovereignty). The second conclusion is that it is clear that sovereignty forms the bridge between the ideas inherent in the IR and OT blocks. It is also the element of sovereignty that impinges on the issue of political will, or the lack thereof, that has been pointed out as being the key problem with the UN. This particular problem is discussed later on in the book.

Figure 1.2
Conceptual Progression of the UN as an Organisation

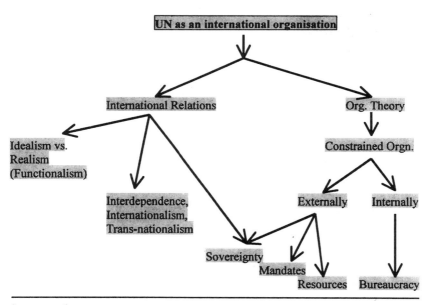

Source: author.

As an international organisation, the UN is but bound to have an element of international politics. So, in order to get an idea of the UN as an international organisation, it is necessary first to get some idea about the theories behind international politics. Here, this study draws from Bennett (1995(b): 15-22) since his work on international organisation is so well-known. Before World War II, many studies of international policies tended to be descriptive and legalistic, which was followed by what is known as geographic determinism (e.g., the focus on naval power as an element of national power). With the emergence of the League of Nations, a move to the philosophy of idealism was signalled, which focused on world order through the subsuming of national interest to international ones. By the early 1950s, the debate had shifted to one of idealism versus realism where the latter included notions of national power, national interests, and balance of power (Hans Morgenthau was the most noted of these realists in the 1950s[2]). A subset of the realist philosophy is the functionalist approach to international politics, which takes a gradualist approach to world order and believes in focusing on functional issues of international organisations so that there are very few conflicts inherent in them (noted proponents of the functionalist aspect to international organisations include David Mitrany and Ernst Haas).

Bennett (1997(b)) points out that of late, however, there is interest in Systems Theory wherein the focus is on inputs, outputs and feedback. Leading proponents of the Systems Theory include David Easton (1992, 1965), Karl Deutsch (1988), Morton Kaplan (1957), etc. But in Systems Theory the problems of defining the parameters of the system are not predictable (i.e., are subjective) and so total reliance on this theory to understand international politics (and consequently international organisation) is not entirely appealing.

The International Relations Blocks

For purposes of describing the context of the UN, it is relevant here to delve further into the idealist, realist, and functionalist aspects of IR, for these three encapsulate best what various people have proposed to reform the organisation.

The realist versus idealist debate as it relates to international organisations is contained in some basic premises of how people and countries (manifest through the organisations) behave in the course of their dealings with others. Since the idealists believe in the Lockian philosophy that man is inherently good and cooperative, and therefore will tend to create structures that further that notion, they have more faith in the manner in which organisations such as the UN can be able to impact in a positive manner things that matter most (such as disarmament, environmental protection, etc.). Idealists include Marvin Soroos (1986) and others who argue that power politics (the hallmark of the realist paradigm) has largely been counter-productive in the present-day interdependent world. Non-realists such as Soroos play themes of cooperation over prerogatives of state sovereignty.

One particular variant of the idealist philosophy is what is known as the Legalist-Moralist School of Political Science that focuses on international law and organisation and that continues to see the international organisations in a positive light although not necessarily as a forum for exercise of national power and self-interest. One of the more well-known idealists in this group is Maurice Bertrand who has seen the UN from the inside and who feels that there is much more scope for enhancing the role of the UN as a constitutional body. Other critics of the realist paradigm in relation to international organisations include Francis Boyle (1985) who has unabashedly called for a greater role for institutions such as the UN.

A subset of idealism is functionalism. Those believing in functionalism argue that international cooperation is possible through organisations that are involved in specific purposes (or functions) and only through regular interaction with these organisations as a basis will something more general as a UN be able to be established. Developed in the 1930s by David Mitrany (1933), and furthered by such intellectual giants as Ernst Haas later on (1964), functionalism, as applied in the context of the UN, assumes that cooperation in narrowly defined technical areas (such as health, aviation, telecommunications, agriculture, etc.) will make the states more amenable to mutual cooperation. This is the underlying premise behind the growth of UN specialised agencies that are quite independent of the main United Nations which serves more as a political body.[3]

On the other hand, the realists believe in the Hobbesian philosophy that man is not inherently good and, therefore, structures and institutions such as international organisations will tend to behave in a manner wherein each nation will try to maximise its own national interests, however the term may be defined. Realists further claim that given the disparities in the balance of power in the world (not only militarily but also economically), nations are apt to use institutions such as the UN to tilt the balance in their favour. This assertion was obviously very evident in the Cold War days when the bipolarity in international relations manifested itself in the workings of the UN. However, it continues to be relevant even in the post-Cold War days since unipolarity has not necessarily meant that nations other than the United States – the dominant power in the international arena at the moment – have not been able to exercise their own rights on to the UN.

The Realist School has intellectual roots in the miseries of the 1930s' Great Depression, the horrors of the Second World War, and the political tensions and international stalemate of the Cold War. Also known as the Power Politics School (Archer (1983: 75)), it has many adherents (Hans Morgenthau being one of the most noted) (for a review, see among others, Archer (*ibid*: 74-82)). The Realist School believes that a nation's sovereignty is the ultimate point that matters in international relations and that there is no common authority over and above that. Realists thus tend to be dismissive about international organisations and give precedence to the capability of the nation state to produce the same results as would be possible from the international organisations. Thus, for example, instead of aid being channelled through the multilateral source of the United Nations, it is diverted through bilateral aid agencies such as USAID. The conservative US Senator, Jesse Helms, is probably the most ardent realist in the mainstream of national politics and in a similar position to significantly impact the fate of the UN.

No discussion of the Realist School of International Relations would be complete without mentioning Hans Morgenthau who until the late 1970s was a fervent proponent of this paradigm. Yet, in 1978, he qualified his support for the realist paradigm, preferring to abandon the notion of power politics (a central tenet of the realist paradigm) in favour of a more amenable world government that could arrest better the malaise contained in the superpower rivalries at its apex then. He had no way of knowing then, but there was indeed a meltdown in the animosity between the superpowers from the mid-1980s on and this gave more hope to the proponents of the UN.

Yet, with the demise of the Cold War, and the resurgence – for what turned out to be for a brief period only, however – of superpower cooperation for some time followed by a unipolar world with the decline of the Soviet Union, has more or less led to a diminishing of the relevance of the realist paradigm. In the early 1990s, there appeared to be an unravelling of the basic tenets of the realist paradigm evident in the lack of superpower rivalry, decline of hegemons (superpowers), and increasing globalisation. This led to a firm belief among many scholars of international studies that the realist paradigm was finally falling apart and that international cooperation would replace the previous tensions that existed during the Cold War period.

Hedley Bull (1977), on the other hand, continues to be a strong proponent of the Realist School and his 1977 work is said to be the "leading British study of international relations from a realist perspective" (Baratta (1995: 11)). Bull argues that there is only a limited role for the UN since even in the anarchy that is present, there is still potential for some order even without international law or international organisation. The realist paradigm of International Relations focuses on a struggle for power among sovereign nations. In this case, the struggle is manifest in the international institutions as well, and the balance of power struggles that were taking place outside the UN arena during the Cold War days were just as evident inside the organisation as well.

The second strand of ideas under IR in Figure 1.2 deals with issues of internationalism, interdependence, and trans-nationalism. Drawing from the notion of interconnectedness and linkages inherent in the Systems Theory, there was great interest in the 1970s in the ideas of interdependence. This is a particularly useful concept to incorporate in national and international governance given the cross-boundary linkages among nation states as a result of, for example, movements in international finance and capital, cross-boundary migrations, rapid information networks, etc. So the notion of interdependence assumes considerable significance for this study. Contained in the strand on internationalism and interdependence is also the global system concept and the world order point of view (see, for example, Boulding (1985), Falk (1977), Miller (1985), etc.) since the systemic component would have to be inter-linked with that of interactions between and among nations.

Proponents of internationalism include Shridath Ramphal, the erstwhile Secretary-General of the Commonwealth, and Willy Brandt, the former Chancellor of the-then West Germany. The focus here is on the superiority of the role of international cooperation (within the context naturally of international organisations given their structures, mandates, etc.) over national sovereignty. The ideas inherent in internationalism are the forerunners of the current fad on globalisation. The rapid pace at which such globalisation has taken place has lent credence to the arguments and exhortations put forward by visionaries such as Ramphal and Brandt in the 1970s and 1980s.

In relation to the UN, the issue of sovereignty is key. Given the specific mention of the application of sovereignty in Article 2(7),[4] a fundamental interpretation of that specific Article leads to the question: when and how can international action be reconciled with the principle of non-interference in matters deemed to be essentially within the domestic jurisdiction of states? There is no cut-and-dry answer to this since sovereignty is a relative concept, and given the rising trend of globalisation in the world today, its utility as a powerful base on which to build individual state action has tended to be somewhat eroded. There is one line of argument that the Charter also asserts the preponderance of individuals over and above the sovereignty issue (after all, the Charter of the UN does start off by referring to "We the peoples of the UN..."). It is largely this notion of going-beyond-sovereignty that has led to the calls from many sources of UN reforms (including the Secretary-General himself) based also on the existence of a Parliamentary Assembly consisting of elected representatives. But the UN is an association of states and as such, it can be argued that the rights of states come first.[5]

The issue of sovereignty can be extended to that of national interests versus international authority. There are numerous examples where nation states, instead of succumbing to the implied greater authority of the UN, have pushed through with policies and stands that safeguard, if not enhance, their own national interests. The refusal of the United States to yield to the International Court of Justice on the claim filed by Nicaragua is a case in point (Simons (1995: 238-39)).[6]

The Organisational Theory Blocks

Merely looking at the organisation from the IR perspective does not give the whole picture. The UN has, after all, been in operation for over 54 years and it has been able to do many good things around the world. It is an organism and it does have peculiarities as an organisation. The reform efforts that are currently being debated can be understood in their entirety only if the organisational perspective is also included in the analytical framework.

However, while Organisation Theory has much to offer to the understanding of the UN, there has not always tended to be the one-to-one direct linkage evident between general Organisation Theory and the study of international organisations.[7] This is because those in the latter category were believed to be better explained by the application of International Relations and politics than by general theory. But this logic suffers from a key weakness that it subsumes the internal characteristics of the organisation also under the IR arena. By arguing that the international organisation can be analysed merely by taking an IR-centric focus, analysts then neglect the rich body of knowledge that exists in Organisation Theory (OT) to help explain many purely bureaucratic phenomena and also help in the understanding of the specific organisation in question. Trends such as creeping bureaucratisation, organisational turf battles, internal and external constraints, resource mobilisation and utilisation, etc., are all ideas that germinate from OT and play an important role in helping understand organisations such as the UN.

No less extensively analysed than IR, but not applied as much to the UN, OT and the general linkages between it and international organisations have also been documented, albeit not so thoroughly (see, for example, Gordenker and Saunders (1978)). In general, that body of literature can be divided into three related categories: (a) behaviour of staff members within organisations, (b) organisational structures and functions themselves, and (c) relationship of organisations to their environments. The latter relationship is important to note vis-à-vis the UN since so much of its existence as an international organisation is based on the constraints imposed by a rather hostile environment.

Under OT, the ideas behind the UN can be viewed as being contained in Organisational Learning (which includes those on change and development)[8] and on the notion of what Charles Lindblom (1959) has called "muddling through". Organisational Learning includes notions of Organisational Development and Organisational Change. The latter includes in its analysis the notion of an organisation constrained by its external environment and since unlike other organisations it can do very little about it, the only possible outcome – organisationally speaking – is what is described as "muddling through". This then is the second strand of intellectual base that Organisational Theory provides in the analysis of the UN. "Muddling through" – or the more appropriate descriptor, incrementalism – is the natural outcome in an organisation that has so much of its resources constrained by externalities (this includes funding, human resources, mandates, etc.).

Of particular concern here is the range of internal and external constraints that an organisation faces and the manner in which it goes about dealing with the constraints in the fulfilment of its organisational goals. One of the main theses of the book is that the UN is unable to take much independent action since its resources and mandates come from external sources (i.e., originally from the Charter, and on a periodic basis from the member states through the General Assembly). As it is not empowered to take any action on its own (including generate resources), the UN has had to operate in conditions of external constraints but over which it has no operational control. The frustrations exhibited by various Secretaries-General (but particularly Javier Perez de Cuellar, Boutros-Ghali, and Annan) attest to this.

Organisations (even those as constrained as the UN) do not exist in a vacuum and are continually forced to interact with their environment in order to be able to fulfil determined mandates. There has been a considerable amount of work done on this basic theoretical construct and the OT literature is rich in explaining the domain of relationships that organisations have with their external environment (see, for example, Aldrich (1979), Bedeian (1984), Morgan (1986), etc.). There is much that can be derived from these works on conceptualising how organisations such as the UN behave in such conditions. This then acts as a proper backdrop to understanding the various reform efforts that have been made at the United Nations.

One particular model that might provide insights into how the UN behaves as an externally-constrained organisation can be found in the Rational-Choice Model (RCM) (see, for example, Hall (1987)). RCM explains that the purpose of organisations is to maximise outcomes and minimise costs when interacting with the environment. They will take advantage of opportunities and attempt to overcome challenges posed by the environment.[9] One such challenge that the UN has continued to face is that of resources. This dependence on external sources of revenue is best conceptualised in the Resource-Dependence element of the RCM (see, for example, Pfeffer and Salancik (1978)). The Resource-Dependence element is crucial in the understanding of the UN as an organisation since so much of the problem-set of the UN at present has its genesis in the resource constraint.

The study of the UN as an organisation constrained by its external environment is also best put in the context of a learning environment, and for this, use must be made of the notion of Organisational Learning (OL). OL depends upon two fundamental foundations (Bedeian (*op cit*: 261)): the notion of rational calculation (that organisations use expectations about future outcomes as a basis for selecting among current alternatives),[10] and that of experiential learning (wherein it is assumed that organisations adjust their activities based on past experiences in an effort to increase their competence). With particular regard to the latter foundation, it is quite clear that the UN has not really practised experiential learning since the very problems that had beset the organisation (that is, the internal ones over which the organisation had had control, for example, bureaucratisation, red-tape, politicisation of recruitment, etc.) continue to be in evidence even at present. Bedeian says that according to experiential learning, "organisations become more competent in activities through experience" (*ibid*). In many cases, this has been quite the reverse in the case of the UN.

Probably no other study has had quite the impact on the issue of international organisations and Organisation Learning as Ernst Haas' *When Knowledge is Power* which was published in 1990.[11] Haas, whose earlier works on functionalism had already shaped the nature of the discourse on specialised agencies in the international system, distinguished between organisations that merely adapt and those that learn. He argued that the focus of learning is then a function of new knowledge and the application of that new knowledge.[12] Going by the tenets that he has put forth, it is obvious that the UN, as opposed to, for example, the World Bank (Haas' own example) has merely adapted and not learned.[13]

The final element of the conceptual block that has been presented in Figure 1.2 is that of a bureaucracy that is part of the internal constraint of the UN. There has not been a lot written about the analytical aspect of the UN bureaucracy primarily since it is such a closed subject, but the available evidence, as well as personal experiences of the author, shows that in many respects the rapid bureaucratisation of the UN has also inhibited the organisation from engaging in OL. The primary strand of literature on this subject has tended to be towards that of international civil service (which is appropriate because the UN Charter alludes to this in Chapter XV, Article 101) (see, for example, Ameri (1996), Bulkeley (1997), Childers and Urquhart (1994), and Lemoine (1995)).

The secondary strand in the area of bureaucratisation, as a subset of the overall internal management environ, is discussed extensively by comparatively fewer people and it is this strand that highlights the reasons why the UN has not engaged in OL. While all studies that focus on the problems of the UN have tended to include some component on the nature of the bureaucracy, there are only a few that attach due criticality to the issue of bureaucratisation in the overall context of internal management. Some of the best work in this area[14] has come from Beigbeder (1987, 1988, 1997(b)) and Bertrand (1997) both of who have had personal experiences with the organisation. The focus of their work is on the macro processes that have impinged on the effective functioning of the bureaucracy (for example, lengthy procedures that have been institutionalised, the need for extensive documentation as a way of ensuring accountability to the member states (through the General Assembly), etc.). An unspecified, yet very much evident, component of their analysis rests on the work done by such intellectual giants as Anthony Downs (1966) and Herbert Simon (1961) whose works on bureaucracy and, *inter alia*, the behavioural patterns of bureaucrats, has conditioned much of the research in recent years on how bureaucracies in organisations (both general and international) function and are constrained by various forces.

The second direction of the conceptual progression of the UN takes into consideration its mandates and its contexts, and can be taken in a logical progression in the manner described next. As evident in Figure 1.1, if the organisation were to be placed at the centre of a schema, the two intellectual underpinnings mentioned above (i.e., IR and OT) form the first level. The next step of the progression is to situate the mandates of the organisation (see Figure 1.3).

In Figure 1.3, it can be seen that there are several mandates (core missions) that the organisation has been given as conceived during the time of the establishment of the organisation. These include: peace and security, economic and social affairs, development cooperation, human rights, and humanitarian affairs. Other selected mandates that the UN has been involved in as part of the core five missions include: narcotics (epitomised by the establishment of the UN Drugs Control Programme (UNDCP) in 1974 and headquartered in Vienna); environment (contained in the creation of the UN Environment Programme (UNEP) in 1974 and headquartered in Nairobi, Kenya); AIDS (leading to the creation of the UN Programme on HIV/AIDS Office in Geneva in 1994); and trade (which in 1995 resulted in the formation of the World Trade Organisation (WTO) taking over from GATT (General Agreement on Trade and Tariff)).

Figure 1.3
Conceptualising the UN: Intellectual Underpinnings and Mandates

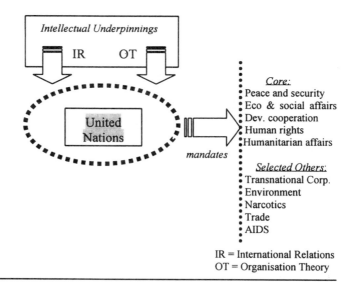

Source: author.

It is important to note here that the mandate of the UN is indeed enormous. Practically all areas that can possibly interact in any form and that impact any groups of countries have now been given to the UN to look after. The UN is considered to be an ideal dumping ground for the world's intractable problems and a forum for airing long-held grievances. It is also important to look at these mandates because there are several elements in them that have been said to have hobbled the UN in its tasks. Some have even called the mandates too broad and too vague and have instead urged that the organisation focus on more narrowly-defined objectives.

What exactly then are the constraints that have made it well-nigh impossible for the UN to fulfil its mandates? The constraints that have been mentioned are numerous, and the set of these forms the fourth conceptual block (see Figure 1.4).

Figure 1.4
Conceptualising the UN:
Intellectual Underpinnings, Mandates, and Constraints

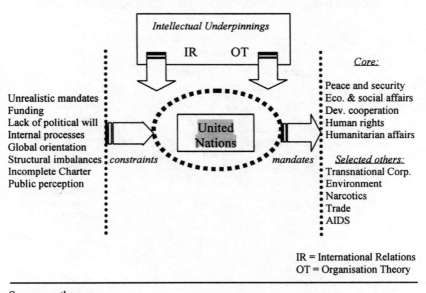

Source: author.

It is clear from Figure 1.4 that the constraints that are mentioned are of a severe nature and it could be said that some of them have their genesis in the manner in which the organisation was formed and others in the manner in which the organisation went about fulfilling them (these are discussed further in the subsequent chapter). In particular, mention needs to be made of the constraint of funding as well as of internal processes (i.e., of management) since these two issues have dominated the debate in terms of UN reforms.

The final building block of this conceptualisation of the UN as an international organisation has to do with its structure. When Figure 1.4 is then expanded to include the several structural components of the UN, the conceptual framework of the UN is more or less complete (see Figure 1.5).

Figure 1.5
Conceptualising the UN:
Intellectual Underpinnings, Mandates, Constraints, and Structures

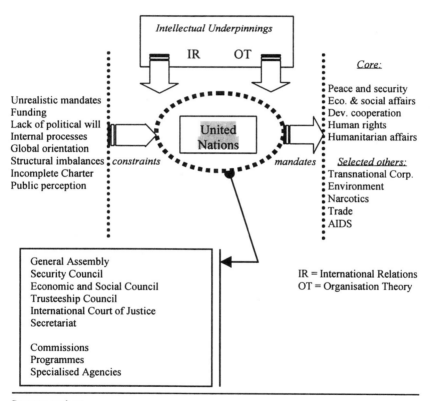

Source: author.

The picture one gets when critiquing the bottom portion of Figure 1.5 is that the UN is indeed a very complex organisation with literally hundreds of sub-organisations, agencies, committees, commissions, programmes, and other bodies. All of them were justified at the time of their formation, but to a lay-person, the entire network of sub-organisations is daunting. Even people long familiar with the work of the UN are not clear on what exactly each subset of the organisation does in relation to the others. As will be shown later on, this very network of sub-organisations in the UN system has created a situation whereby there is very little coordination and there is considerable duplication of work and mandates.

Figure 1.5 also gives a snapshot of how the UN might be viewed while studying various facets of the reform efforts that were – and are being – made. Considerations of the structural aspects (i.e., institutions) cannot be divorced from the functional (i.e., mandates) and neither can the constraints that actually contextualise how the UN operates be set aside. And as has been shown earlier, the intellectual base of the UN should also be kept in mind while reviewing the reform proposals since it acts as a guide to the assessment not only of the internal methods of the organisation but also its interaction in the International Relations field.

The UN as an Actor, Arena, and Tool

In order to better understand the nature of the reform process in the UN, it is also essential to go beyond the conceptual blocks presented above and take the conceptualisation of the UN from a different angle. In this regard, it can be noted that the organisation can be looked at in three different lights: as an instrument, as an actor, and as an arena (Archer (1983); see also Inoguchi (1995)).

As an instrument, the UN is used as a tool by member states (or one such member state) to effectuate some policy goals in the area of international security and peace. Examples of the UN being used as a tool would be the UN presence in Korea in the 1950s and Kuwait in the early 1990s wherein the US used the UN to mount an offensive against individual countries. As an arena, the UN has been used as a forum where all grievances are aired and discussed. Discussions preceding the call for a New International Economic Order in the mid-1970s are examples of the UN being used as an arena for member states to air their views and grievances. As an actor, the UN itself takes the lead role in coming up with policies or with programmes of action. Its role in the development of the new paradigm of Sustainable Human Development in the 1990s is an example of the role of actor that the UN has taken on recently.

Depending upon which one of these is considered desirable for an international organisation, that will delineate what reform efforts need to be pushed through.[15] It appears that proposals submitted by the West, particularly the USA, tend to revolve around viewing the UN as an arena (and in a few occasions, when it suits its purpose, as a tool); on the other hand, proposals submitted by the Third World countries tend to view the role of the UN as an actor and an arena not only actively involved in eradicating poverty, and increasing the general condition of life in the poor countries, but also acting as a forum for them to air their views on various matters. In this dichotomy of views of the UN partly lies the genesis of the divergences in opinions of how the UN should be reformed.

1.2 LITERATURE REVIEW

The literature on the UN is extremely rich. Since practically every country in the world is a member, and also since many groups and regional and international blocs have come forth to present reform proposals, the academic and non-academic work on the UN is phenomenal. Having said that, if one were to critically analyse these materials, it is quite obvious that they can be classified into only a handful of categories. What is attempted here is one such taxonomy of the work that has been done on the UN and with particular reference to materials that are of fairly recent origin. Readers who are interested in the detailed accounts of previous efforts are encouraged to review the collation of materials in Baratta (1987, 1995)[16] for extensive sources on rich accounts of the organisation.

There is a considerable amount of scholarly material on the subject of the UN and its various activities. While it is not possible to list – and review – each and every one (the reader is directed to the bibliography at the end of the book for further appropriate reading), an attempt has been made to cite some of the most relevant ones. The purpose of mentioning the available literature here is not only to put the materials in this book in proper perspective, but also to guide the interested reader to appropriate sources.

A review of the existing literature shows that work on the UN and the reform efforts in it can be categorised as being contained in five key areas. These are detailed below.

The UN in International Relations (including Politics and International Security)

This is probably the most often evident aspect of the UN. There are many streams to this aspect but for purposes of this study, the focus is specifically on the interplay of politics and the relevance of international law, primarily the UN Charter (the basis of International Law in the context of the global body).

No study of the UN should start without a review of its Charter. As a document that governs how the UN is to be structured, and function, it is important that the reader get a feel for the intricacies, strengths, and the weaknesses of that document. Probably the most comprehensive attempt at bringing out the genesis, explanation, and prognostication of the Charter and its Articles is the edited book by Bruno Simma (1994). A voluminous book, it details each and every Article, and comments on the legislative history (with appropriate references to the League of Nations and the 1945 San Francisco Conference), analysis, textual interpretation, practice, and select bibliography of each Article. It is a must reading for all scholars that are interested in looking at any aspect of the UN.

Complementing the work done by Simma is that of Benedetto Conforti (1997). The predominant focus of Conforti's book is on the legal aspects of the Charter but is backed by practical applications of its provisions. Sorted by subject matter (such as membership, functions, etc.) rather than by Charter Articles, the book puts into perspective all key issues. These two books should form the very first reference point for all scholars interested in the UN. For other work on the UN Charter, see, for example, Goodrich, Hambro, and Simons (1969), and Cot and Pellet (1991) in French.

On the application of politics in the context of the UN, there are several outstanding studies done to date. Herbert Nicholas's 1975 work on the *United Nations as a Political Institution* deserves special consideration by the serious scholar. Equally interesting is Yeselson and Gaglione's *A Dangerous Place: The United Nations as a Weapon in World Politics* (1974) not to be confused with Senator Daniel Moynihan's *A Dangerous Place* published four years later. The latter work is based on Senator Moynihan's tumultuous experiences with the UN as the US Ambassador in the mid-1970s. Moynihan did not have a good time at the UN and became very dejected about the organisation towards the end of his tenure. In the charged atmosphere of super-power rivalry, and more importantly, Third World militancy (actively supported by the-then Soviet Union), it is no surprise that Moynihan came out feeling very hopeless about the UN. In many ways, it can be said that it was this experience of a very widely respected American that effectively turned off the appeal of the UN to the American establishment. For more on the politics within the UN, see, for example, Finkelstein (1988).

In the mid-1990s, there was considerable work done in the context of the UN along two specific lines: the first was on reforms (which is discussed later), and the second was on the placement of the UN in the emerging global order given the demise of the Cold War. In the case of the latter, the literature is fairly rich and the avid scholar should have no problem getting hold of some excellent material on the UN and the emerging international relations and world politics scenarios. Roberts and Kingsbury's 1993 work, for instance, is a must reading if one is to gauge the prevailing mood that existed regarding the UN.[17] A year later, the publication of Weiss, Forsythe and Coate's *The United Nations and Changing World Politics* put the emerging organisation in its proper context given the breakdown in the cooperation within the UN. For materials on security and UN intervention, see, for example, Galen (1997) which focuses on the limitations of UN interventions.

Final mention must be made of the MUNS (Multilateralism and the United Nations System) programme which evolved in the first half of the 1990s at the University of Toronto and which was supported by the United Nations University. The edited book by Schechter (1999) – itself a product of a MUNS symposium at the University of Lausanne, Switzerland, in May 1994 – consists of several hard-hitting essays that contextualise the UN in terms of the evolving global structure and in terms of issues related to reforms.

The UN as an International Organisation and Bureaucracy

Much of the academic literature on the UN that does not take a Political Science or an International Relations angle is contained in this heading. This forms one of the two key intellectual streams of this study as well. Within this category, there are three groups of writings that can be identified: (a) one that talks of the organisational aspect in terms of its learning, knowledge, change, etc., (b) the second on the systems notion of the organisation, and (c) the third on the various functional areas of the UN including economic and social development, security, peacekeeping, etc. It is this branch of UN study that provides the bulk of the impetus for the organisational perspective being used in the analytical framework here.

In the context of studying the UN as an international organisation, it needs to be realised that while in some key respects it is no different than a regular organisation (e.g., constrained by externalities, behaviour of bureaucrats, conditions of resource generation, etc.), in many others, it goes much beyond a standard organisation. The fact that the UN's mandate now extends the boundaries – and, therefore, the laws of an individual state – give it a different character altogether. The staffing patterns also then become different as recruitment, career development, compensation, and other personnel administration-related matters take on a different hue.

The study of international organisations (IOs) will not remain complete without first starting to dissect what David Mitrany has put forward in his classics (1933, 1943). Those explanations of IOs are still, to date, considered one of the most influential explanations of the various facets of IOs and many authors have made continual references to the ideas contained in them. Mitrany, a functionalist, argued that IOs are a result of two basic trends: the growth in technology, and the greater desire for higher levels of material well-being that eventually brought people together which necessitated organisational forms that went beyond the nation-state. Mitrany's work has been carried further by various noted scholars; suffice it to mention here the work done by Ernst Haas (1960, 1964, 1986, 1990, and 1995 with Peter Haas) for over four decades now that focuses on the international organisation as a unit of analysis (with particular focus on the UN in his 1986 and 1990 works).

In his 1990 work, in particular, on the UN as an international organisation (*When Knowledge is Power*) his underlying argument is that all international organisations are designed to solve problems but the nature of these problems is ever-changing. This redefinition of problems is possible through two different processes (known as adaptation and learning) and they differ in their dependence on new knowledge in the decision-making process. This emphasis on knowledge is an important one, and many times in the past UN organisations have attempted to re-define their own work along knowledge-based mechanisms (UNDP's attempt in the early 1990s along these lines is symptomatic of this; also symptomatic – and relevant to this study – is the present Secretary-General's efforts to focus on knowledge and its generation and usage in the decision-making process). In that context, Haas' work takes on added significance.

Haas' work is also significant for the purposes here because one of his models of adaptation is what he terms "incremental growth" (1990: 97-108) and by all accounts and evidence the UN – over the past five decades – has tended to lurch incrementally from one issue to the next. Whether Annan's reform efforts towards a more knowledge-driven decision-making process and inclusion of new mandates commensurate with the intent of the Charter will succeed remains to be seen but its genesis of analysis can be situated in large part in Haas' 1990 work.

In the mid-1990s, Ernst Haas teamed up with Peter Haas to further propound on this theme of adaptation and learning vis-à-vis the UN organisation. Writing for the Commission on Global Governance, they argue that "only flexible institutions with an expanding organisational vision can effectively respond to these problems, and help to guide their member states towards more productive governance..." (1995: 296). They conclude that of all the UN agencies, in the main only UNEP and the World Bank have practised organisation learning rather than adaptation.[18] They further conclude that "learning is rare" (*op cit*: 303), and that "learning and institutional reform must come from within"[19] (*op cit*: 324).

In a different context, a superb analysis of the UN as a system of organisations was provided by Mahdi Elmandjra in 1973. A former official of UNESCO, the author had intimate knowledge of the UN and his analysis of the organisation is very revealing. By focusing on the issue of coordination and on the placement of the UN in the international system, he is able to bring out the context in which the UN and its specialised agencies go about doing their work. The work may be dated, but it is very informative.

In the study of the UN as an international organisation, some key literature is contained in, among others: Bertrand (1989) whose *The Third Generation World Organisation* is considered by many to be the most lucid explanation of what kind of an organisation should evolve in order to ensure that the UN fulfils its mandates. Bertrand is very influential among scholars and practitioners on the UN and this book is a must reading. His knowledge base is partly derived from his association with the UN's Joint Inspection Unit, the all-powerful watchdog agency that is at the centre of the reform debate in the UN, hence its utility to the purpose at hand here. LeRoy Bennett's work on international organisations (1995(b)) is also used by various other authors who continue to make use of it as basic reference material. The 1995 version is the sixth edition and perusal of the previous ones gives the reader an insight into how the issues have evolved over the years. Bennett also in 1995 came out with *the Historical Dictionary of the United Nations* (1995(a)) which is a very useful reference material for scholars of UN research. Mention should also be made of Georges Abi-Saab (1981) when referring to the topic of international organisation. His edited book *The Concept of International Organisation* (published by UNESCO) is an excellent choice for researchers.

Going back earlier than the 1980s, mention has to be made of the work done by the political scientist Inis Claude who has inspired many scholars to be involved in the subject of international organisations. His *Swords into Plowshares* (1971) is still considered classic reading on the subject. Implicit in this progress of international organisations is the notion of change and how these IOs go about managing the change process. All scholars of IOs have tended to focus on this issue to some or extent or other. In that context, Lawrence Farley's *Change Process in International Organisations* (1981) is useful reading since it contextualises this facet of the IOs with examples of specific UN agencies. Farley also analyses succinctly the various internal and external sources of change in IOs. Also on the theoretical level, Clive Archer's *International Organisations* (1983) is compelling reading. The author gives a very lucid description of the history of international organisations and also charts the various views on such organisations. Of relevance to the study here is the fact that Archer brings out very clearly the need for political will and visionary leadership in order for these organisations to succeed. What is indeed missing in the UN at present is both (the first was brought out forcefully by, among others, Razali Ismail, the President of the 1997 General Assembly, and the latter by Urquhart and Childers (1996)).

Another strand of literature evident on the UN in relation to its status as an international organisation deals with the issue of bureaucracy and the intricacies inherent within them. Weiss (1975, 1982), Michelmann (1978), and Pitt and Weiss (1986) are some of the key publications on this issue. The underlying focus in their writings is the issue of multinational bureaucracy with heavy reference to the international civil service (this latter element has spawned an entirely new branch of literature on the UN, and is mentioned later in this study).

One of the latest writing on the subject of international organisations is Dennis Dijkzeul (1997) who focuses on the management aspect of multilateral organisations. A superbly written book, it contextualises the discussion of multilateral organisations not only within relevant theories (of governance, management, and coordination) but also exemplifies them with the work of UNICEF and UNFPA.

The UN's Staffing and Internal Management

Houshang Ameri's (1996) work on the politics of staffing of the UN Secretariat is powerful reading and should be taken into consideration while talking of UN reforms. Much of what Annan wants to do in the UN at the moment revolves around getting a cadre of change-oriented people who are also committed to the ideals of the UN and who do not mind working in an organisation that is less than ideal even by the admission of some of its staunchest supporters. While Ameri's work revolves around the Secretariat, many of the lessons are applicable just as well across the spectrum of UN system of agencies. Others that have come up with very useful materials on laws governing international civil service include: Akehurst (1967), Amerasinghe (1988), and Behanan (1952) although much of this is dated material.

Beigbeder's (1987) work on the management problems of the UN is very useful reading and gives a clear picture of what actually happens within the agencies. Beigbeder followed that with his 1988 book on *Threats to the International Civil Service* which is a must reading for any scholar that wishes to assess how international civil service systems work. His most recent addition to this particular body of knowledge is a 1997 book on the internal management of the UN in which Beigbeder (1997(b)) talks of a triple challenge to the organisation: (a) do away with outdated objectives and strategies, (b) shore up the financial base, and (c) reform the management process. Beigbeder sends a dire warning to the leaders of the UN that if the UN bodies do not adapt, they may be financially asphyxiated.

As mentioned earlier, there is also a growing focus on the issue of international civil service (ICS). Lemoine's (1995) book on this subject (suitably sub-titled *An Endangered Species*) is one of the latest additions to this rather-neglected field of management study in the context of the UN. Lemoine's book has been included in the study materials for UNITAR and the author, based on his over four decades of service in the ILO, has come up with a very influential piece on the ICS. The author is rather critical of the ICS and takes the member states to task for attempting to impinge on the staffing processes in the organisation.

Earlier works on the ICS include Graham and Jordan (1980), Meron (1976), and Mailick (1970). Mailick later followed the 1970 study with one in 1985 with Henri Reymond on international personnel policies and practices. Meron, for his part, had focused on the UN Secretariat which is where the bulk of the staffing concerns are evident. For a very well-rounded argument and discussion about the ICS and UN personnel policies, mention has also to be made of Fromuth and Raymond (1987) which was based on a study done by the influential United Nations Association of the USA (UNA-USA) as part of its UN Management and Decision-Making Project. There were other reports that resulted from the project and there are some references – some extensive – to personnel policies and problems (see Fromuth (1986, 1988)). The 1988 study has been well-cited by researchers given the extensive nature of its research and the impact it has had on the working of the UN. Finally, Chris de Cooker's edited work on *International Administration* (1990) is also pertinent material on international civil service and presents several writings on various aspects of the issue.

UN and United States

A fourth strand of literature on the UN and the reform debate is evident in the writings of various authors who have focused on the bilateral relationship between the US and the UN. This is an important element of the focus here primarily because so much of the UN's problem set is tied inextricably with what has been happening inside the US.[20]

Recent material on this subject is capped by that of historian Gary Ostrower (1998) who has analysed the relationships between the UN and the US by using the administrations of ten American presidents as his chronological framework. He lists all the points of disagreements that have plagued these two entities. Maynes and Williamson (1996), on the other hand, contains several essays on the American foreign policy and the UN system. Assessing the diverse issues that surround the American policy toward the UN, various contributors from a diverse field argue that a critical search for elements of a sound and long-lasting US policy toward the UN needs to be done urgently. The consensus is that the UN needs to carefully examine its budgetary processes and underlying assumptions so that everything is transparent to an increasingly sceptical American Congress.

In the early part of the 1990s, when President Bush's New World Order ideas were still prevalent and the Clinton Administration was still under the illusion that it could first of all get Boutros-Ghali to reform dramatically and then to convince the Congress (which at that time was not so overwhelmingly controlled by Republicans) to pay the US's arrears, there was a flurry of research activity in the area of UN reform and how it could be re-aligned so as to satisfy deep-rooted American concerns about its efficacy and about the US's role in it. Robert Gregg (1993) as also Finger (1992) were cases in point as was the report by the United States Commission on Improving the Effectiveness of the United Nations (1993). The latter, in particular, drew from the feedback of average Americans in six cities and reflected the common view of the UN in the United States.

Much of the critical work on the UN from the US obviously comes from the Heritage Foundation, the conservative American think-tank that has over the years been quite successful in presenting the negative sides of the UN to anybody willing to listen. Its 1984 report, edited by Burton Pines, and dramatically titled *A World Without the United Nations: What Would Happen if the United Nations Shut Down*, seems to have so moved then President Reagan that the US increasingly took a more militant attitude to the world body. In the early 1980s, the Foundation also came up with several extremely damaging stories and reports on the UN[21] and followed that up with its 1986 lecture series on how the UN could be reformed. Four former US ambassadors to the UN were approached for their ideas and the 1986 publication brings out their recommendations.[22] Around the same time, other scholarly materials came out that also added to the growing body of disenchantment with the UN, including Gati (1983), Franck (1985), and Ruggie (1985). The Heritage Foundation has not stopped its attack on the UN and has kept up the tempo in various newsletters and reports particularly after Annan's Track I and Track II proposals were made known.

Finally, mention has to be made of Daniel Moynihan's *A Dangerous Place* (1978). The author had been an American Ambassador to the UN in the 1970s at a time when the tide of anti-US sentiment in the body was probably at its peak. He came away from that experience very bitter about the UN and his book crystallised many of the deep-rooted concerns that he had had over how the organisation operated. In many ways – and ironically (considering that Moynihan is hardly the conservative that the Heritage Foundation is) – his work pre-dated that of the Foundation's that used his material as a crutch.

On Reforms and Restructuring in the UN

There are various sources of well-detailed bibliographic entries on matters related not only to the United Nations as a whole but also to the specific issue of UN reform. Readers are recommended to tap into two key sources for this: the Dag Hammarskjold Library in Uppsala, Sweden, and the United Nations Studies Programme at Yale University. In addition, the compendium that was prepared by Joseph Baratta for Transaction Publishers' International Organisation Series in 1995 is an excellent source of information on the literature on various facets related to the UN, including International Law, Organisation Theory, and UN functions.

Taking the lead role on this issue of the UN are several authors who have at one time been practitioners in the organisation and which has thus given them considerable insight into how things get done in the organisation. Maurice Bertrand (1989) is one such individual. A former member of the JIU as also of the Group of 18 experts on the restructuring of the UN (in 1986), Bertrand's ideas come from seeing the UN first-hand. Others at the forefront of writing on the UN and its reforms include Erskine Childers and Brian Urquhart (1994) (whose *Renewing the United Nations System*, which was prepared under the aegis of the Dag Hammarskjold Foundation in Sweden is important material for any work on the UN and its reforms). Urquhart himself (1989(a), 1989(b), 1992) has come up with several analyses of how the UN can be reformed based upon his personal experiences as a high-level official of the organisation.

The 1996 work by Urquhart and Childers on *A World in Need of Leadership* is compulsory reading for gaining an insight into various issues related to the leadership issues in the UN, in particular the role of the Secretary-General (SG). The authors, who between them have a superb level of experience with, and insight of, the UN focus on issues related, among other things, to the selection of the Secretary-General and other leaders of UN specialised agencies (at the time that this book came out in 1996, it was very topical what with Boutros-Ghali going through the throes of a warped selection process). Childers and Urquhart have come up with several recommendations on how to select the leaders of the UN. Several of these (such as a single term of seven years for the SG, rigorous selection criteria, etc.) have been echoed by others such as the Commission on Global Governance. It is a pity that the world community, and the powers that be in the UN, have not taken up the recommendations seriously. At any rate, *A World in Need of Leadership* must be required reading for anybody interested in assessing how things at the top are handled.

A recent addition to the reform debate has been the edited work by Maurice Bertrand and Daniel Warner (1997). Drawing from the proceedings of a meeting held in Geneva in early 1995, the book focuses on the need for a change in the fundamental conceptions behind the original United Nations by launching an entirely new Charter. The proposals prepared by Bertrand for an organisation that could take the place of the existing UN, the Bretton Woods organisations, and the specialised agencies would constitute the response to the changed global situation. This 'Bertrand Proposal' is at the core of the recent argument that since there have been changes in the types of challenges in the world today, and since the existing UN and other international organisations have not been able to do much about it, it is time for more dynamic ideas to emerge on how to prevent future crises and conflicts.

In the same year, Bertrand himself came up with a solo piece on a historical evaluation of what has gone wrong with the UN and how to reform it (Bertrand (1997)). By focusing on economic and social issues, he draws out key conclusions for UN reform, and concludes by saying that what the UN needs now (as do other global organisations for that matter) are radical reforms. This is one of the many pieces that Bertrand has written on the issue of UN reforms over the years.

In 1997 as well when there was so much disappointment (over failed funding proposals) and hope (over the Annan Agenda), Joachim Muller's edited volume (1997) that charted the history of the reform process and also gave an insight into new initiatives, was welcome reading. Muller was in an excellent position to edit that particular volume since five years ago he had also led a similar effort. Muller's intimate knowledge of the UN (he is a staff member of the UN Office in Vienna) has obviously helped him see the reform process from a more personal and micro perspective.

In the same year that Muller came out with the latest edited volume on UN reforms, the proceedings of a 1994 UN reform-related conference in Pontignano, Italy, were published in book form. Edited by Paul Taylor and others (1997), the book highlights seven key areas of UN reforms, the major ones being the legitimacy of UN intervention within state borders, the institutional mechanisms and associated resources necessary for effective UN intervention, the issue of UN finances, UN Secretariat reforms, and Security Council reforms. Many of the papers in the book, however, had already been published elsewhere and so there is not substantive new material here.

Since the end of bipolarity in the UN (starting the late 1980s), and particularly after the 50th anniversary of the UN, much attention has been placed on the issue of reforming the organisation. The general consensus has been that the UN has not been able to effectively fulfil its mandates, and that given the altered global conditions from the time the organisation was formed in 1945 immediately in the aftermath of the Second World War, the organisation needs to undergo substantive changes. This whole issue of reforms has been approached differently by different people. Park (1996) identifies three approaches to the reforms of the UN: conservative, moderate, and radical. The conservative view insists that there is nothing wrong with the way the UN is structured and as such member states must instead focus on revitalising – rather than restructuring – the organisation.[23] The moderate approach goes a bit further than this and argues that there should be efforts to do away with some of the structural shortcomings and mismanagement in the organisation. The Nordic UN Project of 1991 (discussed in Chapter Three) is an example of a moderate approach at strengthening the UN. The radical approach, on the other hand, argues that unless substantive and meaningful structural and functional changes take place in the organisation, the UN will continue to be ineffective in maintaining international peace and security a key component of which is the economic development of the poor countries.

One particular study that needs to be brought up here is a product of the 1992 project initiated by the General Assembly of the International Institute of Peace (IIP) and titled "New Tasks for the United Nations" (see Hufner (1994)). The book itself is an outcome of two workshops organised by the IIP in 1993 and 1994 and focuses on a wide range of reform proposals put forth by academics and practitioners. Three key areas related to the work of the UN are analysed in great detail: the UN and its environment, peacekeeping and peace-making activities, and economic and social issues related to various proposed reform efforts. The latter makes compelling reading.

The ideas expressed by Paul Kennedy and Bruce Russett[24] (1995) also merit some mention here. They posit that it is time for the global community to improve the UN's capacities and grant it greater resources, functions, and coordinating powers. They feel that given the magnitude of the problems currently facing the world, the option of minimising the role of the UN would not be very judicious. Their conclusions, judging from their roles in the Working Group, are not surprising, however.

On the particular issue of resources, however, one key report that was published in 1995 was by the Global Commission to Fund the United Nations. It was contained in a book edited by Harlan Cleveland, Hazel Henderson, and Inge Kaul, and it brought forward many challenging ideas on the question of where the UN should get its extra resources. The various essays in it are all written by serving and former senior level officials of the UN and other countries and is a must reading to get an insight into the new ideas that have been thrown around for some time on this issue. It is not likely that many – or even any – of the proposals (such as the Tobin Tax proposal) will ever see the light of day, but it is a source of many powerful ideas on UN reforms in the area of finance.

Related to finance, but focusing more on mandates, methods, and mismanagement, Jesse Helms, Chairman of the Senate Foreign Relations Committee in the US Congress, and the most public and mainstream critic of the UN, threw a challenge in an article in *Foreign Affairs* in 1996 to the forthcoming Secretary-General to do something about the waste and mismanagement that he felt pervaded the organisation. Helms believes strongly in the supremacy of sovereignty and his main complaint against the UN is that it is superseding the nation state and that many things that should rightly have been in the domain of the countries are willy-nilly being transferred to the UN hence adding to its over-burden and consequent miserable performance. Helms' ideas may appear too drastic but it has to be remembered that as long as the Republicans control the Senate, he will continue to be the chairman of the most influential committee that deals with US foreign policy and thus he is in a position to stymie many proposals for active involvement of the US in the UN. On the other hand, attempting to do to the UN what he has proposed would also appear to be impossible only because the UN has 187 other constituencies to play to and cannot afford to listen to only one, no matter how important that member is.

Probably one of the most comprehensive analysis of the UN as it readies for the new century has come out of the Inaugural Symposium of the UN System in the 21st Century conducted by the UN University (UNU) in Tokyo in November 1995. In 1995, the UNU launched a six-year project exploring the future of the UN. Dubbed the UN21 Project, it brought together noted personalities in academia, UN practice, policy-making, and others to discuss key aspects of the UN of the new century, including state and sovereignty, global citizenship, market forces, and regional arrangements. The UNU's *Envisioning the United Nations in the 21st Century* is compelling reading and is recommended for its diversity of views from world-renowned personalities. Of specific relevance to the subject matter of this particular book is the writing on "Ten Balances for Weighing UN Reform Proposals" by Yale University Professor Bruce Russett. Any research on the UN would thus be incomplete without extensive reference to this document brought out by the UNU.

Mention also needs to be made of the 1988 report of the United Nations Association of the USA (UNA-USA) which had convened an international panel in 1986 and 1987 and critically analysed the UN reform issue. At the time, the world was undergoing changes in the bipolarity that had been evident ever since the end of World War Two and there was considerable excitement about the future role of the UN. Gorbachev had already made his intentions of opening up clear and the report that came out of the UNA-USA reflected much of that optimism. It has to be noted that the UNA-USA is considered to be an influential player in the USA when it comes to advocating the role of the UN and Annan has reached out to this organisation to help him get the UN's messages across to the American public and leaders.

It needs to be mentioned that the vast body of the literature on the subject of UN reforms has come from the West, and much of what others outside the UN think has not been made very public. Saksena's 1993 book on *Reforming the United Nations* tries to fill that void as do the books by the Rajiv Gandhi Memorial Initiative for the Advancement of Human Civilisation (1994) and Rasgotra (1995). The latter is a compilation of papers presented at a seminar on the UN in the 21st Century sponsored by the Rajiv Gandhi Foundation in India and is useful reading for the scholar intent upon hearing the other side of the story.

One of the latest additions to the reform debate on the UN is the 1997 work of two Maltese diplomats, Guido de Marco (the President of the 45th session of the General Assembly) and Michael Bartolo (Ambassador to the UN from Malta) who give interesting and useful insights into the reform debate shaping up in the UN. Calling for the creation of a Second Generation Organisation (compare this to Bertrand's Third Generation International Organisation), the authors focus on the General Assembly (the forte of the authors given their background) and assess ways of revitalising it. They also focus on the Economic and Social Council (ECOSOC) and how it could better coordinate its work with the Bretton Woods institutions (i.e., the World Bank group of organisations). This is indeed an important issue to discuss and Kofi Annan has strived to bring in the World Bank group into the affairs of the UN on a more regular basis.

The authors also present views on redefining the work of the Trusteeship Council (which incidentally was presented to the 1998 General Assembly for consideration) but by all initial accounts, many of the members (particularly the US) are not keen to see the Trusteeship Council reorient its work. They would rather see it disbanded than to take on redefined mandates. Many ideas in the book are worthy of further consideration by the UN, in particular the redefined structure of the relationship between the ECOSOC and the specialised institutions including the World Trade Organisation and the Bretton Woods institutions.

Others that have specifically focused on the issue of UN weaknesses and the consequent need for reforms include: Kasto (1995), Rochester (1993), Stassen (1994), Thakur (1997), Righter (1995), Simons (1994, 1995), and Alger (1996, 1998). Work done in the 1980s provides an effective backdrop not only to the raised hopes of an international environment devoid of superpower rivalry but also eventually to the disappointments of the post-1994 fiascos that began to engulf the UN one after another. As such, they make interesting reading and are useful reference materials on the subject of criticisms of the UN and possible reform measures that could be taken. Studies in this group include: Baehr and Gordenker (1984), Harrod and Schrijver (1988), Ewing (1986), Steele (1987), Meltzer (1978), Nicol and Renninger (1982), and Nerfin (1985).

1.3 DESCRIPTION OF THE UN

The final part of this chapter focuses on introducing the UN as an organisation. In order to fully understand the reform process now underway in the organisation, there is need to talk about its various aspects related to the structures, functions, and other variables that denote the type of activities it is engaged in and the environs within which those activities take place. To situate this discussion better, the UN can be looked at in relation to 12 different variables which are described below.

Origins

The origins of the United Nations are grounded in the experiences of the world community in the failed efforts of the League of Nations and in the horrors of World War Two. The organisation had been conceptualised since the middle of the World War but only took shape toward the very end of the War. In a series of consultations among the major powers then (in places such as Teheran, Yalta, and Potsdam) the victors hammered out the broad outlines of the kind of an international organisation that needed to be created in order that the world may never have to face another world war. By the time the signatories to the declaration of war against the axis powers came for the San Francisco Conference in April 1945, the broad frameworks had been more or less organised and the nitty-gritty details had to be ironed out. But even that would require much patience and diplomatic skills of the host nation – USA – which had all the while taken a lead role in the formulation of the concept.

There is a basis for the various assumptions that were made in San Francisco. Primary among them was that nation states had to subsume national sovereignty to international cooperation if world peace was to be maintained. International security was also assumed to be safeguarded by the actions of the victors acting in unison and in mutual understanding. The experiences of the League of Nations were their salutary reminder that if they did not cooperate, another global war was entirely possible.[25]

The UN was legally formed on 24 October 1945 after the San Francisco Conference ratified the Charter. There had been a lot going for the need to have an international organisation of this sort and the architects this time learnt from their mistakes with the League of Nations and started work on creating the framework of the organisation even before the Second World War had come to an end (the League, for its part, was an integral part of the Versailles Treaty and this was said to have been part of the problem). It was US President Franklin Roosevelt who suggested the name United Nations who, in turn, took it from the Declaration by United Nations signed in Washington, DC, on 1 January 1942.

At the time of formal establishment of the UN, there were high hopes because the Americans were involved in its very genesis. They succeeded in Dumbarton Oaks after taking a very proactive stance. Their purpose in pushing through the UN then has to be seen in these two lights (Bertrand (1997: 33)): (a) guilt at not having taken part in the League, and (b) a sense of national pride that an institution that was conceived by the US could not possibly fail.

Principles

The architects of the UN started off with some fundamental premises and principles as to what the UN should stand for. These were at that time quite clear given the circumstances. The war was about to end and the one thing the world needed the organisation to do was to maintain peace and security in the world. Along these lines then, the organisation was founded on three key principles: peace, security, and equality of all nations. These principles were based on the underlying principles of sovereignty and non-intervention in the affairs of the states except in cases of emergencies.

All these three principles deserve further discussion here. As was mentioned earlier, the issue of sovereignty is key to the operation of the UN. It implies that nation states are still supreme in their affairs and that they have not subjugated their rights to a higher authority. They are merely coming together in a forum to share ideas, air grievances, and see how problems might be solved. This sovereignty issue – so valued in San Francisco – has been misunderstood by many. Critics rail against the fact that the UN is actually superseding the nation states and that it has effectively taken authority away from them.

The principle of peace was a key element of the entire UN-building process. Shaken by the experiences of war germinating without the protection of the League, the victors were convinced that they should set up such an organisation that would ensure that such wars could never be waged again. Their assertion was that only an organisation which had the voluntary support of all the nations and in which the victors had the authority to dictate how international conflicts were to be settled would be able to maintain international peace. This explains why the victors insisted upon the veto power. At that time, it was indeed easy to see that they had the political will, the economic clout, and the military might to sustain such a peace: the same cannot be said of all the victors now.

The final principle of equality of all nations is also important to note here for it goes to the heart of what is wrong with – and weak in – the UN. There is also a paradox here for if one were to look at the structures of the UN it is clear that while the General Assembly is entrusted with the overall parliamentary-type powers (where every state has one vote regardless of the size of the contribution to its budget), the actual powers lie in the Security Council (SC) for it is the SC that selects the Secretary-General, it is the SC that dictates how to approach solving specific conflicts (in fact, even which issues to take up for consideration), and the decisions of the SC are binding on all members (not so of the General Assembly except with issues related to internal procedural matters). Thus, it is evident that while the principle of equality of member states is touted as a key strength of the UN, it appears not to be so in reality.

Characteristics

An analysis of the UN as an organisation clearly reveals that there are three key characteristics that define how the organisation has gone about conducting its business. They are:

Universalism and equality of member states – all countries are entitled to join the UN. This is irrespective of their political system or bend of ideology. This universality gives the UN the unique characteristic of being the only global organisation that exists at the moment. There are at present 188 member countries in the UN. But this alone would not have made it an adequate forum for convening global meetings had it not been for the fact that theoretically at least as per Article 2(1)[26] (and as per Article 18 that gives each state one vote in the General Assembly), there is equality of member states. The system of one-country-one-vote is regardless of the level of contributions or of the size of the country. Hence, Fiji has one vote in the General Assembly as does China (however, see the discussion above on the practical aspect of this equality).

Pre-eminence of the Security Council – the second characteristic of the UN is that it is dominated by the Security Council. Even though there are six – theoretically equal – principal organs in the UN, there is little doubt that the Security Council is the first among equals. This issue has been touched upon earlier. In the Security Council, there are five permanent members (the US, UK, China, France, and Russia) and each has a veto power that it can choose to employ at any time over any substantive issue. There are also ten non-permanent members elected for a period of two years each by rotation. It has to be noted that Security Council resolutions are binding while those of the General Assembly are not.[27]

Broad mandates and breadth of institutional machinery – the final characteristic of the UN is that its mandates are extremely broad and this breadth is reflected in the institutional machinery as well. The UN is also present in almost every country in one form or another. The key mandates of the UN are maintaining peace, international security, and fostering economic and social development. Over time, to these mandates have been added scores of others practically all being justified on the grounds that they impinged on the quality of life. Thus, the UN is involved in issues such as outer space, nutrition, vaccination, refugees, gender development, population activities, and countless others.

One such mandate that was not originally envisaged in the Charter, but that now threatens the viability of the organisation, is that of peacekeeping missions. While the UN was originally only meant to ensure that international security was facilitated and peace ensured, that mandate was gradually extended to mean keeping the peace in strife-torn countries. At first, this function did not really overwhelm the organisation (although several countries did renege on their obligation to pay their share of the expenses), but as the number of such operations grew dramatically,[28] the negative financial implications of such growth began to be clear. As it stands now, there is a considerable lack of resources to fund the existing peacekeeping operations. There are several proposals on the table to remedy the situation, but it is likely that resources to fund these operations will not be increased anytime soon.

It is important to understand these three characteristics[29] of the UN so that the reform proposals and efforts can be seen in the proper context. The founding fathers were quite aware of these characteristics (except maybe of the different permutations of the peacekeeping activities) and it must be assumed that they were optimistic that the UN would be able to carry itself quite well.

Charter

The UN Charter was adopted on 24 May 1945 and signed on 26 June 1945 at San Francisco. It comprises a Preamble and nineteen Chapters divided into 111 articles[30] (see Table 1.1; see also Annex One). Of these nineteen chapters, the ones that have been discussed the most in the reform process have been those related to the Security Council, Pacific Settlement of Disputes, Threats to the Peace and Acts of Aggression, Economic and Social Council, the General Assembly, and the Secretariat. Even among these six areas of focus, most of the reforms have been evident in the Secretariat since that is directly under the control of the Secretary-General and for many changes to be made there, the Secretary-General does not have to seek the permission of the General Assembly, normally a long and drawn-out process and fraught with the vicissitudes of member states' sentiments.

Table 1.1. The UN Charter and its Components

Chapter	Subject Matter	Articles
Chapter 1	Purposes and Principles	1-2
Chapter 2	Membership	3-6
Chapter 3	Organs	7-8
Chapter 4	The General Assembly	9-22
Chapter 5	The Security Council	23-32
Chapter 6	Pacific Settlement of Disputes	33-38
Chapter 7	Action with Respect to Threats to the Peace, Breaches of the Peace, and Acts of Aggression	39-51
Chapter 8	Regional Arrangements	52-54
Chapter 9	International Economic and Social Cooperation	55-60
Chapter 10	The Economic and Social Council	61-72
Chapter 11	Declaration regarding Non-Self-Governing Territories	73-74
Chapter 12	International Trusteeship System	75-85
Chapter 13	The Trusteeship Council	86-91
Chapter 14	The International Court of Justice	92-96
Chapter 15	The Secretariat	97-101
Chapter 16	Miscellaneous Provisions	102-105
Chapter 17	Transitional Security Arrangements	106-107
Chapter 18	Amendments	108-109
Chapter 19	Ratification and Signature	110-111

Source: adapted from the official UN website (http://www.un.org/aboutun/charter/), 1999.

It is not the intention of this study to discuss the nuances of the Charter, but one thing to keep in mind is that it is quite difficult to amend the Charter and has been done so only twice before (both times to increase the level of representation in two principal organs: the ECOSOC, and the Security Council). Substantive changes in the Charter (such as ensuring, for example, that a weighted voting system be instituted in the General Assembly, or that the veto power be withdrawn) would require the application of Article 108. This would mean a vote of two-thirds in the General Assembly (that in itself would pose little problem), but more importantly, the amendments would also have to be ratified in accordance with the constitutional processes by two-thirds of the member states including all permanent members. Hence, unless there is concordance among the permanent members over any reform proposal, it is not practical to call for an amendment to the UN Charter.

Mandates and Functions

The mandates of the UN are clearly stated in the Charter. However, since its creation in 1945, there have been other mandates that have been given to the UN. As is evident in the conceptual progression discussed earlier, these include narcotics, AIDS, environment, etc. It is possible to assume that there will be more added as the world begins to move in directions that were not conceived of at the time of the drawing up of the original Charter.

The mandates also highlight specific areas where the UN is to function. Wilenski summarises these numerous functions of the UN into five key (1993: 438-440):

(1) establishment of a collective security system,

(2) prevention/settlement of regional conflicts,

(3) promotion of economic development,

(4) spread of human rights, democracy, etc., and

(5) dealing with an emergent international agenda that includes, among others, global environment, AIDS, etc.

With respect to the establishment of a collective security system, it was designed that the UN – through the Security Council – would ensure that international security was sustained through cooperation among the great powers. This assumption of the framers of the Charter as well as of the leaders that propelled the idea of a United Nations was found to be not tenable almost from the very beginning of the UN until the very end of the Cold War in the late 1980s. The superpower rivalry that was evident outside the arena of the UN was also eventually reflected within it as well and this constrained the various efforts that the UN had made to enhance collective security.

In relation to the prevention and/or settlement of regional conflicts, it was the hope of the founders of the UN that the body would be used as a forum by the concerned parties to air their grievances and that the collective wisdom of the body would be used to find a solution to the crises. The assumption here was that the UN would be able to contribute to the settlement of regional conflicts before they escalated into an uncontrollable world war.

The third function of promotion of economic development was what the poorer of the 51 original members forced upon the founders of the UN to incorporate into the UN. To give added weight to this function, the ECOSOC was created and designated as a principal organ. In later years, as the number of Third World countries grew in the UN, this function began to grow in importance[31] and today constitutes one of the main activities the UN is involved in. An interesting development now is that the UN has increasingly attempted to show that there is a strong linkage between peace/security and economic development (that without the latter, there will be no peace at all).[32] This linkage has been highlighted to show that the UN's focus on economic development is, after all, for the enhancement of international peace and security and hence resources are not necessarily being wasted when spent on economic and social development activities.

With respect to propagating human rights, democracy, etc., the UN has always taken an active role in this exercise. The Universal Declaration of Human Rights that the UN initiated in 1948 and that has received worldwide acclamation is one of the ways in which the UN has tried to improve human rights in the world. The recent creation of the post of UN High Commissioner for Human Rights (UNHCHR), currently headed by the former Irish Prime Minister, Mary Robinson, is a high-profile body that seeks to ensure that human rights are guaranteed in countries around the world. In the matter of democracy, the UN has helped monitor elections, assisted countries in formulating constitutions, trained government officials and members of the police forces in many countries in the application of basic rights, and assisted community groups and women in participation in the constitutional and development decision-making processes.

Finally, on matters of dealing with an emergent international agenda that includes, among others, global environment, AIDS, etc., the UN has tried to take the lead role in instituting systems and processes in countries around the world to deal with these problems. In that exercise, it has created institutional mechanisms of its own (for example, the UNEP for dealing with issues of environment, UN Programme on HIV/AIDS for AIDS activities, etc.) to help member countries develop programmes and activities in support of these mandates. It is this proliferation of the mandates and functions of the UN that critics have targeted as being symptomatic of an organisation that has become too big, too spread-out, and too involved in what should essentially have been national concerns.

Structure[33]

To help meet the mandates of the organisation, the UN has been structured in a rather logical fashion. However, it does consist of several sub-organisations, and to a lay-person, this whole system of organisations can be quite confusing. At the macro level, what is known as the UN system has two main sub-divisions to it: the United Nations Organisation (UNO)[34] whose mandates have been detailed above, and a set of function-oriented specialised agencies which are autonomous from the UNO but are still in association with it (through specific provision made for in the UN Charter). For both of these parts, however, the structural orientation remains more or less the same: both have at the top a plenary level, followed by the executive body level, then the Secretariat level, and finally the member state level (see Elmandjra (*op cit*: 38-44)). At the most micro level of structures, both sets of organisations retain representation of various countries.[35]

There are two kinds of UN organs: principal and subsidiary. The principal ones are the General Assembly (GA), the Security Council (SC), the Economic and Social Council (ECOSOC), the Trusteeship Council (TC), the International Court of Justice (ICJ), and the Secretariat. With the exception of the ICJ, which is based in The Hague, Netherlands, all the others are located at UN Headquarters in New York (although a part of the Secretariat, such as the Human Rights Centre, is located in Geneva, and the ECOSOC Commission on Human Rights meets in Geneva as well). Surprisingly, while all principal organs are equal in status, the ECOSOC and the TC are under the General Assembly. And given its judicial independence, the ICJ stands outside any hierarchical order.

In the General Assembly, there is an elaborate structure of committees and sub-committees. There are six main committees on: (a) disarmament and international security, (b) economic and financial matters, (c) social, humanitarian, and cultural matters, (d) special political and decolonisation matters, (e) administrative and budgetary matters, and (f) legal matters. There is, in addition, a 28-member General Committee whose job it is to coordinate the proceedings of the General Assembly. Another committee related to procedures is the Credentials Committee which reviews the credentials presented by each national delegation at the beginning by each session of the Assembly.

In addition to these subsidiary bodies, there are also two standing committees that have been in the limelight during the reform debates. The first is the Contributions Committee whose job it is to assess the level of dues of each member state (where much of the debate between the US and the other members is currently raging), and the second is the Advisory Committee on Administrative and Budgetary Questions (ACABQ) which deals with questions of coordination within the UN system in the areas of budget and administration.

Finally, there are three other main subsidiary organs of the General Assembly within the area of administration coordination:[36] the Joint Inspection Unit (JIU, established in 1968), Joint Staff Pension Fund (JSPF, set up in 1949), and the International Civil Service Commission (ICSC, established in 1974). Of these three, the JIU has been at the forefront of initiating reform proposals. The JIU is the UN's only independent system-wide inspection, evaluation and investigation body. It is composed of 11 inspectors nominated by the General Assembly and who serve in their personal capacity. These inspectors have experience in financial and administrative matters and they have very broad powers of investigation in all matters pertaining to the efficiency of services and use of funds. They make recommendations to the General Assembly.

The other two subsidiary organs of the General Assembly are more involved in administrative coordination related to personnel matters. JSPF provides retirement, death, disability and other benefits for staff of the United Nations and other organisations that might join it, of which there now are 20 (the latest – Seabed Authority – joined in 1999). On the other hand, the ICSC makes recommendations to the General Assembly for the regulation and coordination of conditions of service for the UN, the specialised agencies, and all organs which participate in the Common Personnel System of the UN.[37]

The second principal organ of the UN is the Security Council (SC). The SC, by the UN Charter, has primary responsibility for the maintenance of international peace and security. It is organised in such a manner that it is in session continuously, and so a representative of each of its members must be present at all times at

UN Headquarters.[38] While all Security Council meetings are normally held in New York for logistics reasons, there have been instances in the history of the UN where the Security Council meetings have been held elsewhere (notably, in 1972, a session was held in Addis Ababa, Ethiopia, and the following year in Panama City, Panama). The presidency of the Council rotates monthly according to the English alphabetical listing of its member states. In the SC, each member has one vote while decisions on substantive (rather than procedural) matters require nine votes, including the concurring votes of all five permanent members. This latter is known as the veto power of the Great Powers, and is at the centre of all efforts at UN reforms at the present time.

The Security Council is assisted in its work by a Military Staff Committee (MSC) which was formed in 1946 to advise and assist the Council for the application of armed force. The Committee is composed of the Chief of Staff of the permanent members of the Council. It is generally agreed, however, that the MSC has not performed its functions and has been recommended for major reconstitution.[39]

Under the Charter, all members of the UN agree to accept and implement the Security Council's decisions. While other organs of the UN (such as the General Assembly) make recommendations that the member states need not necessarily follow (note, however, the caveat made earlier while discussing the characteristics of the UN), the Council's decisions must be carried out by the member states. Failure to do so is a violation of the UN Charter.

The third principal organ of the UN is the Economic and Social Council (ECOSOC) which draws its basis from the General Assembly. In the ECOSOC, there are four standing committees on: (a) non-governmental organisations (NGOs), (b) programme and coordination, (c) natural resources, and (d) development planning. There are also ten functional commissions (such as on Population and Development, Status of Women, etc.), and five regional commissions (one each for Asia and the Pacific, Africa, Latin America and the Caribbean, West Asia, and Europe). Also under the ECOSOC, there are bodies of governmental experts, ad hoc intergovernmental working groups, and expert bodies composed of members serving in their personal capacity. All in all, there are 29 such bodies whose work the ECOSOC is supposed to coordinate. This excludes coordinating the activities of autonomous agencies such as UNDP, UNICEF, etc. as well as of the 14 specialised agencies of the UN.

The fourth principal organ of the UN is the Trusteeship Council whose job at one time was to administer all trust territories. But with decolonisation almost complete, and many former trust territories now independent (such as Namibia) or having been made self-governing territories (such as Palau in the South Pacific),[40] the Trusteeship Council's work is now complete. Supporters of the UN and the Council want it to be involved now in the management of the Global Commons (see Chapter Two) while critics want it to be disbanded altogether.

The fifth principal organ of the UN is the International Court of Justice (ICJ). Located in The Hague, the ICJ acts as the judiciary wing of the UN. It retains its independence from the main UN organisation although the GA plays a role in the election of its judges. The ICJ has been said to be under-utilised by the member states and its credibility has waxed and waned over the years. The decision of the United States, for instance, not to accept the Court's 1986 decision on the matter of the US mining of the harbours of Nicaragua is said to have weakened the position of the ICJ as a final voice in matters of international adjudication.[41] This refusal is in direct contravention to the provision in Article 94(1) of the UN Charter which stipulates that all UN members agree to comply with ICJ decisions in matters to which they are a party.

The sixth and final principal organ, and probably the one that gets the most ire of the critics, is the UN Secretariat. To run the affairs of the UN, there is provision made in the UN Charter for a Secretariat. The Chief Administrative Officer of the Secretariat is the UN Secretary-General. Under the Secretariat, there are departments and centres as well as commissions, etc. The Departments include: Political Affairs, Peacekeeping Operations, Humanitarian Affairs, Administration and Management, Public Information, and Economic and Social Affairs (formed after the merger of Policy Coordination and Sustainable Development, Economic and Social Information and Policy Analysis, and Development Support and Management Services in 1997).

In addition, a new Office of the High Commissioner for Human Rights was formed in 1997 (by consolidating the former Office of the High Commissioner for Human Rights and the Centre for Human Rights) and two offices assisting the Secretary-General

Executive Office (the Office of Legal Affairs, and the Office for Internal Oversight Services). The UN Secretariat has a three-tier structure: at the HQ level, at the regional level, and at the country mission level. The strength of the Secretariat in the mid-1980s was at a high of over 12,500 Staff members, but given the pressures to downsize, the last two Secretaries-General have been able to bring this number down by over 30 percent (in the 54th General Assembly session (1999), Kofi Annan proposed a staffing table of 8,802 posts for the Secretariat).[42]

One of the key Committees that the Secretariat uses in order for the Secretary-General to do his work is the Administrative Committee on Coordination (ACC). ACC is important because it brings together the executive heads of UN agencies and programmes, and the Secretary-General chairs the meetings. These meetings are important since they are the only formal link at the upstream level where the specialised agencies and the main UN organisation can talk to each other. These meetings take place every two weeks and are used as a forum by the Secretary-General to monitor what is happening in the outer reaches of the UN system. The key criticism that has been levelled against the UN is that its specialised agencies are too important and that reform efforts initiated in the UN do not necessarily apply to the specialised agencies. In that context, the role of the ACC becomes that much more critical.

No discussion of the UN is complete without mentioning the fourteen specialised agencies.[43] These are agencies that were created outside the rubric of the UN system although they are still bound by several coordinating mechanisms initiated in the ECOSOC. Some specialised agencies (such as the ILO, ITU, etc.) pre-date the UN organisation. These agencies have their own budgets, constitutions, and executive committees. They rely quite minimally on the support of the UN organisation although at the country level it is not uncommon to find IFAD or FAO, for instance, actively consulting – and getting support from – UNDP.

Having specialised agencies avoids the emergence of an inflexible organisation too monolithic in structure. The fact that specialised agencies also deal separately with technical questions as opposed to general policy ones is meant to enhance their effectiveness. While the rules of the UN are not immediately binding on other international organisations, nothing in Article 57 precludes the establishment of subsidiary organisations (the Article merely states that specialised agencies will be brought into relationship with the UN) – hence the creation of agencies such as UNCTAD, UNDP, UNEP, UNICEF, UNIDO,[44] etc.

Membership

At the time of the San Francisco Conference at which time the Charter was signed, there were 50 original states (Poland – the 51st member – joined the group prior to 24 October 1945 which is considered to be UN Day). There are currently 188 members in the UN; Kiribati, Nauru, and Tonga, who joined in September 1999, are the latest entrants. Tuvalu – a tiny Pacific island nation – was recommended for admission by the Security Council in February 2000 but the recommendation has yet to be formalised by the General Assembly. Of the 188 members, there are over 100 that have a population up to 10 million people, and almost 60 percent of the membership is categorised as small states.[45]

It is instructive to see the growth in the membership of the UN since the transformations that have occurred in it (discussed further on in this chapter) have been impacted by the arrival of new member states. When the original talks began, there were obviously only a handful of influential states that were a part of the discussions. The US played a lead role throughout and was instrumental in getting together the countries that would eventually be the original members of the UN. At the time of the ratification of the Charter, there were 51 members (see Annex Four). It is of note that of the 51 members, there were only four African and eight Asian states.

Gaining entry into the UN after it was established was not initially as easy as it is now. The fact that there was bipolarity in the organisation meant that the USA or the Soviet Union (USSR) would eventually veto the admission of any new potential member that was seen to be under the ideological persuasion of the other superpower. Many times, groups of countries would become members at the same time having been waived through as a concession based on mutual agreement between the US and the USSR. The numbers in the UN began to swell in the 1960s with the rapid decolonisation that took place then. The consequent increase in the size of the UN by poor Third World countries (who were all theoretically equal and had one vote in the General Assembly just as the superpowers) eventually meant that the agenda of the organisation (and particularly the GA) began to be dominated by those put forth by the poor countries. The Soviet Union, for practical purposes, aligned with these countries and was able to reap political capital out of the strident anti-US rhetoric that began to emanate from the General Assembly and elsewhere. This was, in essence, the start of the disenchantment phase of the Americans with the UN.

With the collapse of the Soviet Union in 1990, and the consequent independence of its constituent republics, the number of members in the UN increased further in the early 1990s. In the meantime, perennially difficult political questions of membership for such countries as South and North Korea, and the two Germanys, were handled on a basis of mutual understanding between the superpowers and they were allowed to join the organisation as well. In this manner, the membership of the UN at the present moment incorporates practically all the countries (Switzerland is a major exception, by choice) and this fact gives the UN its defining universal characteristic.

Finances

There are two issues related to finances that should be of interest to this study: that of dues and assessments, and that of budgets.

Dues Assessment

The primary source of funding for the UN comes from the payment of dues assessed to each member state. The dues are assessed on the principle of ability to pay of each member and of the country's share of world wealth. As such, as of 1999, the top three contributors to the UN were the US (at 25 percent), Japan (at 19.98 percent), and Germany (at 9.80 percent). At the other end of the spectrum, the poorest countries pay a mere 0.001 percent of the budget although this level was initially set at 0.04 percent. When more and more developing countries came in as members, the floor was lowered to 0.02 percent in 1973. This was subsequently reduced to 0.01 percent in 1978. In the 1999 General Assembly session, a proposal was tabled – and accepted by the member states – whereby assessments for 2001-2003 are to have a floor of 0.001 percent meant for the poor countries.

It should be noted that while on an absolute level the US is to pay the most, on a relative scale, there are other countries whose per-capita contributions are much higher than that for the US. For example, the Nordic countries pay much more than the US does per-capita. As a matter of fact, tiny San Marino with a share of the 1999 UN regular budget at $4.20 per citizen pays considerably more per-capita than the US whose corresponding figure is $1.11 per American.[46] The latest assessments for selected countries are presented in Table 1.2.

Table 1.2. New Assessment Scale
(in percent, 1998-2000)

Country	1998	1999	2000
United States	25.00	25.00	25.00
Japan	17.98	19.98	20.57
Germany	9.63	9.80	9.85
France	6.49	6.54	6.54
Italy	5.39	5.43	5.43
United Kingdom	5.07	5.09	5.09
Russian Federation	2.87	1.48	1.07
Canada	2.82	2.75	2.73
Spain	2.57	2.58	2.59
Netherlands	1.62	1.63	1.63

Source: United Nations Press Release GA/9389, 22 December 1997, Annex II, p. 11.

On the issue of being assessed based on the ability to pay, the USA, in particular, has been irked by what it sees as having to shoulder a disproportionate share of the expenses of the organisation.[47] In reality, its displeasure over this issue is not so much at the absolute level of the contribution, but more at the fact that the US does not get political mileage out of its contributions to the UN. It sees the UN as a place where there is considerable anti-US sentiment among the member states and where the will of the US – outside the forum of the Security Council – is not heeded. Critics within the UN, such as the Heritage Foundation, make it a point to assess the utility of the UN to the US by the extent to which there is support for the US within that body. By comparing the voting records of the various countries that are recipients of US foreign assistance, they ascertain whether or not the US is getting any political capital out of the UN. So far, the overwhelming response is "no" which is why there is so much opposition to the funding of the UN in the US Congress. Other member states, for their part, and even traditional supporters of the UN (such as Canada, the European Union, etc.), have been on record as having said that they would prefer the US to pay the arrears that it owes to the UN currently and then the reform process can go on.

The Budget

The financing of the UN can be divided into three categories: the regular budget, the peacekeeping budget and the extra-budgetary programmes for development, the environment, refugees and other assistance financed from voluntary contributions.

The regular budget covers mainly the administrative expenses of the UN (including salaries and allowances, office equipment, etc.) and can be said to constitute the cost of public administration at the UN. It is approved biennially by the General Assembly. Previously it used to be approved by two-thirds majority but, given the insistence of countries such as the US, it has since 1986 been approved by consensus which gives these countries the power to manipulate the budget somewhat. The source for this budget is the assessed contributions[48] by all member states (with the highest for the US at 25 percent and the lowest for many least developing countries at 0.001 percent).

The reference to the budgetary problems in the media are to this budget. The UN regular budget in recent years has seen a gradual decline given the pressures on the Secretariat to downsize and to come up with zero-growth budgets. For the 1994-1995 biennium, the regular budget was $2.7 billion which was reduced to $2.529 billion for 1998-1999. For the 2000-2001 biennium, an amount of $2.536 billion was proposed which the 54th GA session (1999) accepted in December 1999.[49] At the session, the US stressed that the figure should be lowered to $2.533 billion (virtually the same in relative terms as the 1998-1999 budget). Interestingly, the Group of 77 countries expressed alarm that the proposed budget was less than the $2.545 billion suggested by the GA in 1998.

The peacekeeping budget, for its part, was financed originally from the regular budget, but since 1956, this was altered to come out of special accounts. During the early 1960s, when there was some confusion as to whether peacekeeping expenses incurred in this manner were actually expenses of the organisation, the ICJ, in an advising opinion on 20 July 1962, re-confirmed that they were indeed so.[50] During the 46th General Assembly session (1991), the method for calculating the share of a member to the peacekeeping budget was formalised based on a classification of countries into four groups.[51] Given the rise in peacekeeping operations since 1988, clearly this aspect of the UN's budget has complicated the financial picture of the organisation. The problem has also been exacerbated by the fact that the UN had been borrowing from the peacekeeping special accounts whenever there was a shortfall in the regular account and now even this special account is in the red.

The extra-budgetary programmes are financed from voluntary contributions, and as such, have a problem of lack of predictability. With donor fatigue mounting in the nineties, UN agencies have had to come up with hard-selling techniques to generate resources from rich donor nations. It is this sort of problem that has forced agencies such as UNDP to cut programmes by a quarter in the early nineties (for UNDP, as well as for the specialised agencies, the budget comes from voluntary contributions).

Leadership

Article 97 of the Charter gives the Security Council the powers to nominate the Secretary-General although it is formally the General Assembly that appoints the individual. In the Security Council, a veto can be applied in the recruitment process of the Secretary-General (as was evident in the American veto of the re-election bid of Boutros-Ghali in late 1996). The term of office of a Secretary-General is – by convention – five years, to be renewable as many times as possible although – also according to convention – a Secretary-General has tended to serve only two terms.[52]

The leaders of the UN so far have included: Trygve Lie (1946-1952), Dag Hammarskjold (1953-1961), U Thant (1961-1971), Kurt Waldheim (1972-1981), Javier Perez de Cuellar (1982-1991), Boutros Boutros-Ghali (1992-1996), and Kofi Annan (since

1997). (See Annex Three for further information on the tenure of these Secretaries-General).

It is very important to discuss the leadership issue of the UN since that goes to the heart of the reform process (being as it is always led by the Secretary-General either in the formulation stage and/or eventually in the implementation stage). The Secretary-General is the head of the Secretariat and it is his responsibility to act as the Chief Executive Officer of the UN. Much rides on his ability to bridge gulfs, to seek consensus, to lead the Secretariat staff, and, in general, to ensure that the UN is running smoothly.

However, in addition to that, he is also seen as a Chief Political Officer whose job it is to ensure that the UN is able to fulfil its various mandates through the cooperation of all member states. His is a job that places a premium on diplomatic skills, on empathy with the stated positions of the warring parties, and on infinite patience. National sensitivities have to be recognised and he cannot be seen to be playing to any one state or group of states. Keeping the Secretariat running smoothly is hard work alone, having to deal with 188 member states, and an equal number of hugely inflated national egos, is a very difficult task indeed.

Implicit in the detail above of what a Secretary-General has to do in the post is the fact that he should, at all times, strive to be impartial and independent. His credibility is diminished greatly anytime he is seen to be manipulated by any party. In this process, the issue of the independence of the post of Secretary-General has been rekindled with the departure of Boutros-Ghali. Boutros-Ghali was seen as being fiercely independent and because of that he incurred the wrath of the Americans. The superpowers have never liked the Secretaries-General to be independent (Hammarskjold had a problem with the Soviet Union during the latter phase of his tenure) and the US could not stand to work with someone who openly argued that the Secretary-General had to be independent (as did Boutros-Ghali in a revealing article in *Foreign Affairs* (USA) in March/April 1996). Probably the Secretary-General who was considered to be the most unobtrusive was Kurt Waldheim who so ingratiated himself to the superpowers and others that at the end of his second tenure, he was almost elected for an unprecedented third term until the Chinese vetoed his candidature not so much because he had offended them but because they wanted to make political capital out of their perceived support for a Third World candidate.

At any rate, this issue of independence will continue to dog whoever is in that particular post. For his part, since the Americans had pushed for his candidature, Kofi Annan's independence was initially seen to be compromised (the fact that within weeks of being elected Secretary-General he travelled to Washington, DC, did not help matters any although he had gone there for a different purpose and certainly not as one currying favours).

The International Civil Service

The creation of an international civil service is central to the effective running of the UN. Article 100 of the Charter provides for an international civil service, and stipulates that the civil servants of the UN should refrain from taking instructions from member states or others. It also stipulates that member states, for their part, will not seek to influence the civil service of the UN in any way. All Secretaries-General have repeatedly called for this independence of their staff members as they have of their own.

The civil service of the UN has been under a microscope ever since the creation of the organisation. The international civil service (ICS) is a strange creature when one really looks at it beneath the surface. The emphasis is on bringing in people (most of whom will have to leave their countries of domicile), who are of high-calibre, and who are willing to give up their allegiance to their countries for the time that they are working for the UN. All UN employees – upon being recruited – have to agree to the condition that they will not take orders from any other source but the supervisors and leaders of the UN. But since some bureaucrats in the UN are seconded by their governments, there is a danger here that their independence might be compromised.

The other issue that is of import here is that of the method of recruitment of staff into the UN. The rules clearly state that such recruitment should be done based on merit but that it should be tempered with the principle of geographic equality (that is, all the geographic regions are equally represented in the UN staffing based upon pre-approved criteria). As it has turned out, there appears to be more emphasis placed on the geographic distribution criterion than on the merit one (this issue is picked up further in the subsequent chapter).

Inasmuch as the composition of the UN bureaucracy is concerned, it needs to be noted that there is a difference between the staff of the UN Secretariat and those of the specialised agencies. While most agencies are under the UN Common System arrangement (and thus subject to similar personnel rules, regulations, and benefits), some (such as the World Bank group of agencies) are not. Mention should also be made here about the bureaucrats that are sent by the Foreign Ministries of the member states to act as delegates to the UN General Assembly. They too can be considered a part of the UN bureaucracy and often, they attempt to jump over to the Secretariat, usually in high positions. Other human resources of the UN include experts, consultants, and volunteers (both national and international).[53]

Salaries and benefits for the staff are based on a system that is divided into four categories: (a) professional and higher, (b) general service, (c) short-term or temporary staff, and (d) National Professional Officers (although this latter category does not come under the ICS grade, it is applied to all national professionals working at the UN Country Offices). A fifth category could be added for UN Volunteers whose remuneration is strictly termed allowances but who also enjoy several privileges that other UN employees do (such as health care, post-adjustment multipliers, etc.).

Salaries at the UN are set according to what is known as the Noblemaire Principle. According to this Principle, the salaries of professional staff are set by reference to the highest-paying national civil service with which, in terms of size and structure, a suitable comparison can be made. Since its inception, the federal civil service of the US has been taken as the comparator (although there are reports that the civil service of Germany has overtaken the American one).[54] This comparison is expressed as an average ratio over a twelve-month period and is known as the margin. It is felt that the margin has to favour the UN since account has to be taken of the international character of the employment and since the implication is that the staff member is involved in expatriate service. The desirable range of the margin is 110 to 120, with a mid-point of 115 (for 1996, the margin was 114.6; for 1999, the ICSC determined that the margin was 114.1[55] which means that the staff salaries should realistically be increased by 0.9 percentage point to ensure compatibility with the comparator).

An analysis of the UN position classification, salary, and incentive system revolves around the categorisation of posts designated as the professional and higher categories. These categories comprise five professional grades (P-1 to P-5), two Director levels (D-1 and D-2) as well as the levels of Assistant Secretary-General and Under-Secretary-General.[56] Staff members in these categories are recruited internationally and are paid on the basis of salary scales applied worldwide through application of the Noblemaire Principle.[57] The salary comprises of: (1) a base or floor (minimum) salary, and (2) post-adjustment, both expressed in US dollars. The base/floor salary is used to calculate the amounts of post-adjustment/cost-of-living differential and represents the minimum remuneration payable. ICSC reviews annually the level of the base/floor salary scale (in 1999, however, the ICSC decided that no such review would be done until 2001). Post-adjustment is a cost-of-living adjustment meant to preserve equivalent purchasing power for all duty stations.[58]

The salary is divided into net salary either at the single (Net S) or the dependent (Net D) rate. As for salary increments, within-grade increments are awarded – normally year-to-year – on the basis of satisfactory service. While most increments are granted annually, there are certain salary bars that have been identified as a general rule (see Annex Five for more information on this). UN staff members are also eligible for various incentives, allowances and benefits including rental subsidies, education grants, repatriation grants, etc.[59]

The bottom line in relation to the salaries is that the system should be able to attract the best in any country. One item to note here is that critics have charged that the salaries of the UN officials are excessive and that the staff members do not merit such high salaries (see Annex Five for the existing UN salary scale).[60] This issue has been raging for some time now and is not likely to be resolved any time soon given its sensitive nature and also given the rigorous positions taken by the staff unions as well as the ICSC.

Methods of work

In introducing the UN, mention must be made of the methods of work of the organisation for so much of the criticism of the UN is based on its work. At the core of the organisation, the General

Assembly holds one session each year that lasts for about ten to 12 weeks starting in September. This session proves to be the only venue and forum for the leaders of the world to convene in and to make their opinions known about various issues that might be of concern to them then. At the annual session also, resolutions are passed that show what the UN intends to do about a particular issue and, in turn, what it would like the member states to do. These resolutions are not binding on the member states, however. The General Assembly has also used these sessions to ask for many reports from the Secretary-General in support of the work of the UN. As a matter of fact, this request for more reports has tended to irk the Secretariat and the various Secretaries-Generals have on occasions asked the General Assembly to show self-restraint in this respect (Simma (1994: 364)).

Apart from the General Assembly sessions, there are also expert committee meetings and hearings, open-ended working groups (meaning, any member state can decide to join the group), and Security Council meetings (some of which have been held away from New York). The Security Council, unlike the GA, is continuously in session so as to be ready to discuss any issue that might arise all of a sudden. The UN also uses international conferences and meetings to highlight various problems and to generate ideas for their solutions. Important conferences in the immediate past have included on social development (Copenhagen, 1995), on population activities (Cairo, 1994), on the environment (Rio de Janeiro, 1992), on human rights (Vienna, 1993), on settlements (Istanbul, 1996), and on women (Beijing, 1995). While these conferences have been deemed to be very useful by the UN (see United Nations (1997(b)), critics see these as just another way to spend a considerable amount of resources to hear leaders talk with very little done as follow-up.

The UN's method of work also includes a considerable degree of country-level presence to be involved in various fields of activities including development, humanitarian assistance, peacekeeping, election monitoring, and technical assistance. This field level presence is touted as being one of the underlying strengths of the UN since it gives the organisation the ground-level presence to assist member states in various areas. Along with the country-level representation of the UN, it is also present at the regional level throughout the world (note the presence of the Regional

Commissions as well as the Regional Bureaus of such agencies as UNDP). Virtually every country and every region has a UN office of some sort, and Annan's proposals for reforms have also targeted this as one area of improvement.

Finally, the UN's methods of work also include maintaining relationships with entities other than nation-states. These relationships are maintained with four types of observers: (a) non-member states (such as Switzerland), (b) specialised agencies (such as WHO, ILO, etc.), (c) intergovernmental organisations (such as the European Union (EU), League of Arab States, etc.), and (d) national liberation movements (PLO, SWAPO, etc.).

Phases of Transformations

The final variable to consider when detailing the United Nations is that of the various phases of transformation that the organisation has gone through. This brief historical review should enable the reader to get an idea of how the UN has progressed over the years and what trends are likely to be evident now. Within the UN, since its creation, there can be identified four consecutive phases although precise dates may not be able to be pinned on them.[61]

Phase 1: Western Domination

In this phase, the organisation was still in its infancy, and there was a clear majority in the General Assembly for the Western bloc (as a matter of fact, it was due to this majority that the US was able to get the United for Peace resolution on Korea through after the Security Council was deadlocked). The Secretaries-General were also themselves from the Western nations. The end of the phase came during the Suez crisis in the 1960s when even the US voted against the interests of Britain and France.

Phase 2: Expansion, Polarisation, and Disillusionment

The second phase itself can be discerned in three distinct time slots. By 1960, it was evident that there was going to be a dramatic change in the composition of the UN. As a result of decolonisation, Third World nations began to dominate the UN, at least in numbers. At the end of 1960, the total membership level of the UN was 100; in 1970 it was 127, and in 1986, the number had gone up to 159.

As a result of the expansion of the UN with the entry of numerous Third World countries (who came with their own colonial baggage), there was in evidence a focus on the strengthening of the positions taken by Third World countries which ultimately led to a polarisation of the UN. The seeds of such polarisation were sown in the 1970s with passage of the New International Economic Order, the New World Information and Communication Order (which led ultimately to the departure of the US from UNESCO), and the codification of the Law of the Sea. These were all positions that were strongly pushed for by the Third World countries, and there was bound to be a backlash. The "Zionism as a Form of Racism" resolution passed by the General Assembly in 1975,[62] and later the various anti-US sentiments freely expressed in this period, clearly showed that the East-West divide was being replaced by a more potent and divisive North-South divide.

And with each passing year, there was increasing aggravation and polarisation in the UN among the various groups of member states. The US took a lead role in trying to distance itself from the organisation, and unilaterally decided to scale back its contributions to the UN. To make matters worse, the hawks in the US were manoeuvring Reagan to disassociate the country from the UN to the extent possible.

It was in this phase that the Charter was amended twice (both for membership purposes). This phase also saw a shift in the focus of the UN from maintenance of peace towards decolonisation and economic and social development. There were also several instances of Third World militancy and member-state disingenuity that led to the disillusionment in the organisation. These included the Third World's call for a New International Economic Order (NIEO), the passing of a Charter of Economic Rights and Duties of States during the 29th General Assembly (1974), the Soviet invasion of Afghanistan (and its comparatively soft denouncement), and no denouncement of the genocide in Kampuchea. These were all episodes that clearly showed that there was disillusionment with the organisation.

But no manifestation of the disillusionment was greater than the decision by the US to first reconsider, and then to outright refuse, payment of dues to the organisation. By 1986, with the US showing increasing belligerence on this issue, the funding problem had begun to worsen. The Americans felt that they had very little hand in determining the fund disbursements even though they contributed the most. The US threatened to unilaterally cut its contributions from 25 to twenty percent and, in an equally ominous move, both the US and the UK withdrew from UNESCO in 1985.

Phase 3: The Honeymoon

By mid-1987, however, there was in evidence a subtle shift in the way in which the UN did its business. Resolution 598 urging Iran and Iraq to stop their ten-year war was passed unanimously in the Security Council and it heralded the dawn of increased cooperation between the two superpowers. This was obviously a function of the *perestroika* policy initiated by Mikhail Gorbachev in the-then Soviet Union, but it marked a period of honeymoon for the UN. Soviet troops pulled out of Afghanistan during this period, and generally the end of the Cold War meant that the UN could be free of the bipolarity straitjacket.

Around this time, Gorbachev, writing in his country's papers and in other international fora, also began to call for an increased role for the UN in the conduct of international affairs. Since up to that time the problem with the UN had been bipolarity caused as a result of the inflexible positions taken by the Soviet Union, and to some extent by the US, this change of attitude was welcome news to the supporters of the UN. Gorbachev's downfall in the early part of the 1990s and the consequent rise of Boris Yeltsin did nothing to dampen their enthusiasm. The role that Russia (as the natural successor of the Soviet Union in the Security Council) played during the period immediately preceding the Gulf War, and during it, confirmed the belief that henceforth the UN would be a different organisation. The possibilities of better things to come were very heady for anyone observing the UN at that time.

Phase 4: Disillusionment

By 1993, however, the honeymoon had begun to end. Wars were still being fought, development was still elusive, and local politics in the US was squeezing the UN dry. The weather vane for the UN was the public sentiment in the US which – largely a function of the pictures and stories out of Somalia – clearly showed that the general citizenry was getting weary of the UN's faults. In November 1994 when the Republicans won control over the US Congress after a lapse of more than half a century, it became very clear that the US would be taking a very tough line against the UN. The manifestation of all the frustrations against the UN was symbolised by Congressional leaders such as Senator Jesse Helms and Representative Chris Smith, and with increasing forcefulness the US continued to refuse to pay its arrears to the organisation. That crippled the organisation, and with its peacekeeping operations expanding, there was very little the UN could do to leverage its positions. This further exacerbated the situation within the UN and elsewhere, and all this boiled over to include the the-then Secretary-General himself who was in the midst of trying to settle himself for another term as the UN head. The US, eager to pin the blame on someone, settled on Boutros-Ghali and after a year of acrimonious debates, Boutros-Ghali lost out.

When Kofi Annan became the new Secretary-General in January 1997, he tried to calm things down and to turn the tide of sentiment against the organisation. He visited the US Congress immediately after taking over his post to push his case personally, and in the summer of 1997 came up with rather detailed and ambitious reform plans. The US Congress shot them down rather speedily, but the rest of the world has given Annan some time to redeem the organisation.

In that regard, it can be said that since 1997, the organisation could probably be at the tail-end of the disillusionment phase. Annan was able, during his initial period at the helm of the world body, to stabilise the negative image of the UN and build fences. He won some reviews for his handling of various crises and, in general, succeeded in diverting attention away from the UN's purported ills to the more important task of focusing on the positive and on rebuilding the organisation. It is too early to say now whether the disillusionment in the US toward the UN will be ending soon but Annan has gone a long way to contributing to a swing in public perception.

Before moving on to the next chapter that talks of what ails the UN, it is instructive to take stock of what the context of the UN is in these changed times. There have been fundamental changes in the way governments have been involved in national affairs. The role of the governments has tended to decline and the private sector – and to counteract that, the civil society – has begun to take the lead in enhancing development and growth in all regions around the world. This altered context of the role of government has also meant that the role of organisations, such as the UN, is being re-considered. What is paradoxical is that while the demands on the UN are increasing as a result of marginalised societies in countries (and marginalised countries in the family of nations) asking for greater intervention, the resources that would have had to complement those new mandates are dwindling. A much greater level of funding is being channelled through non-governmental sources. In this context, then, much is demanded of the UN yet much is not being given to the UN, and that is the challenge that Kofi Annan has had to deal with in search of his reform efforts. How he manages this paradox while keeping the UN relevant is the all-important question.

Endnotes

[1] There is debate as to which one offers more relevance in studying an organisation of this nature. This study asserts that both are important in the study of the UN. Much of what has been proposed by Kofi Annan makes sense only when looked at from the various rich perspectives offered by Organisation Theory and practice; and yet the very genesis and the internal processes of the organisation can be put into proper perspective only by looking at what the IR school describes. In reality, then, these two approaches can be divorced from each other in the study of the organisation.

[2] As contained in his *Politics among Nations* (1948) and *In Defense of the National Interest* (1951).

[3] As such, the specialised agencies have their intellectual underpinnings in functionalist theory and are based on the liberal internationalist approach towards cooperation. It is this functionalism that gives the specialised agencies the unique characteristic that they have, and it is the purported inexorable move away from functionalism in agencies such as ILO and UNESCO that has tended to alienate countries such as the USA and the UK leading to their withdrawal at various times from these and other agencies (including IAEA). By the 1970s, Third World countries had been able to "politicise" key mandates of these agencies and thus the disenchantment in the West grew. For example, the calls for the New World Information and Communication Order at UNESCO, Health for All at WHO, and World Employment Programme at ILO, were seen by the West as efforts to politicise the work of what are supposed to be purely function-oriented agencies. Passage of the New International Economic Order in the General Assembly of the UN could be

tolerable (although even that was made to wither away after only a couple of years of dominance), but injecting any calls that smacked of politics was not considered right in the specialised agencies.

[4] Article 2(7) of the UN Charter specifically states that the UN shall not intervene in matters which are essentially within the domestic jurisdiction of any state or shall require the members to submit such matters to settlement under the present Charter without the permission of the national government concerned. This constraint of intervention has been the defining feature of the UN's efforts at maintaining international peace and security. And yet it can be said that Article 2(7) itself – when viewed in conjunction with Chapter 7 – does provide for the preponderance of international action over domestic jurisdiction primarily in the form of enforcement action that is available to the world body. The problem is that powerful member states do not always use the UN as a platform for such enforcement.

[5] In a very cogent analysis of the concept of sovereignty as it applies to the work of the UN, Kofi Annan, in an invited article for *The Economist* (18 September 1999) uses the examples of Kosovo, East Timor, and Rwanda, to argue that "the international community reach consensus – not only on the principle that massive and systematic violations of human rights must be checked, wherever they take place, but also on ways of deciding what action is necessary, and when, and by whom" (Annan (1999: 49)). On a related front, his views on sovereignty and its implications on the work of the UN have met some flak from some quarters (including from within the UN itself).

[6] See ICJ Reports (1986), "Military and paramilitary activities in and against Nicaragua (Nicaragua vs. United States of America)," Merits, Judgment, p. 14.

[7] See, for example, Jonsson (1986) for a discussion of this issue.

[8] Kofi Annan in his June 1997 Commencement Address at the Massachusetts Institute of Technology (MIT) compared the UN along the lines of science and engineering. Both, he argued, are constructs of reason and are experimental (i.e., learning by trial and error). It is this focus on experimentalism that is at the core of what he proposes to do for the UN as a way of changing the manner in which the organisation goes about fulfilling its mandates. Towards this end, Annan exhorted his audience to remember that the UN is not an end in itself but just a means to get to the goals of international peace, security, and development. As such, Annan says that the UN must be closely attuned to its environment, quickly correct its mistakes, and constantly generate new ways of doing things. This philosophy has then been encapsulated in his reform proposals made in 1997.

[9] A fitting example of this in relation to the UN would be the borrowing of money by the UN Secretariat from the peacekeeping special accounts budget whenever the regular budget was in the red as has happened very often.

[10] One key element of the rational calculation is the management technique of strategic planning. It is not certain to what extent the UN had ever practised strategic planning prior to Annan's tenure but since he took over in January 1997, he has insisted that strategic planning, backed by analysis from an internal think-tank, the Strategic Planning Unit, be a part of the organisational process at the UN (at least in the Secretariat). In that sense, it can be said that the UN currently practices Organisational Learning.

[11] *When Knowledge is Power: Three Models of Change in International Organisations*. Berkeley, CA: University of California Press, 1990.

[12] By extending this, it is clear that there is a link between this and the notion of rational calculation put forth by Bedeian since the issue of strategic planning (which further rests on the receipt, and application, of new knowledge) appears to be central to both. This linkage appears incongruous, however, since rational calculation is diametrically opposite to experiential learning which in itself appears to be closely tied to Organisational Learning. This is an area that merits further analysis in the context of UN processes and reforms.

[13] One citation will suffice here: Haas argues that in adaptation, the ultimate objective of the organisation is not put to question whereas in OL, the purpose itself is redefined. This substantive rationality (as opposed to technical rationality) of the adaptation mode has been touched upon by various people (most notably Bertrand (1997)).

[14] See also Weiss (1975, 1982) and Pitt and Weiss (1986). The former is a bit out-dated but still very instructive (the author, however, focuses more on the specialised agencies than on the UN itself). The latter is an edited volume that contains some of the most insightful analysis of the UN bureaucracies in the available literature.

[15] It is clear from the expressions of the UN itself that it would like to be taken as a tool, a "vehicle to serve the interests of all and the welfare of the planet" (remarks made by Razali Ismail, former President of the General Assembly, at the 23rd Annual Yale Model United Nations at Yale University, 27 February 1997; see the entire text of his speech in United Nations Press Release GA/9220). Long before Ismail, such notables as Gunnar Myrdal (1955) and Inis Claude (1967) had also specifically delineated the role of the UN as a tool (instrument) for the policies of individual governments. On the other hand, the noted Bertrand (1997: 61) believes that the UN is an arena for conflicting interests of states to be battled out. Whether an arena or a tool, it is generally accepted that what the UN is not is an actor. This should then effectively do away with the misconception in the minds of the critics of the UN that it is a world government with a will of its own and the capacity to enforce that will against those of the member states themselves.

[16] The 1995 compilation was done by Joseph Baratta for the International Organisation Series for Transaction Publishers at Rutgers University, USA. The author has, in meticulous detail, highlighted the annotated work of over 1,350 academic materials on various facets related to the UN, and is a must reading for the interested scholar.

[17] The 1993 version is the second edition, and the first edition in 1988 was reviewed as being "one of the most objective and measured assessments of the UN system near the end of the Cold War" (Baratta (1995: 8)). The books contain discussions on international security, economic development, UN reform, etc.

[18] It is extremely interesting to note though that a mere two years after Haas and Haas concluded the excellence of the UNEP, Annan actually targeted that same organisation for change. It is possible that the external dynamics of UNEP underwent a fundamental upheaval in that period (it could not be the internal dynamics if the organisation had indeed engaged in learning).

[19] A review of the history of the UN, however, shows that in that organisation, reform impetus has been more externally-driven than internally-developed. The context of the Annan Agenda, and the US's intransigence on the matter of reforms, is a case in point.

[20] For scholarly material on the UN vis-à-vis other countries/regions, see, e.g., Gorbachev (1992) and Kolosovsky (1991) on UN/Soviet Policy; Foreign Affairs Committee (1992-93) on UN/British Policy; the rather-dated Cosgrove and Twitchett (1970) on UN/EEC Policy; and Jackson (1983) on UN/Non-aligned Nations. With the exception of these and a few other countries (such as India, see Rajiv Gandhi Memorial Initiative (1994)), there are not too many scholarly materials on the UN's relationship with other nations.

[21] These include: "A UN Success Story: The World's Fattest Pensions." Backgrounder No. 378. Washington, DC, 11 September 1984.

[22] Heritage Foundation, "How the United Nations can be Reformed: The Recommendations of Four Former Ambassadors to the UN*," The Heritage Lectures No. 66*, Washington, DC, 7 August 1986.

[23] Park argues that Boutros-Ghali's 1992 report titled "An Agenda for Peace" represents the conservative approach.

[24] Kennedy and Russett had been Co-Directors of the Secretariat to the Independent Working Group on the Future of the UN since 1993, and are intimately familiar with the issue of reforming the UN.

[25] It is not the intention here to go into great detail on the failures of the League of Nations. But undoubtedly the UN as an organisation cannot be understood without first understanding why the League failed. The demise of the League contributed in many ways to the advent of World War Two. By hindsight, what was missing from the operating ingredients of the League was that nations decided to give supremacy to the issue of national interests over multilateralism. That is one of the key lessons to be drawn regarding the undoing of the League.

[26] Article 2(1) states that the UN is based on the principle of the sovereign equality of all its members.

[27] On this issue, a clarification is necessary. The GA is only expected to make recommendations to member states on external and non-procedural matters but when it comes to internal and procedural matters, the rulings are binding ("the authority of the GA to make legally binding decisions only covers the area relating to internal organisation, that is, to 'housekeeping matters'" (Simma (*op cit*: 237)).

[28] Note that from 1948 to early 2000, there were a total of 53 peacekeeping operations that the UN had been involved in, with 40 of them created since 1988, and a full 30 since 1992.

[29] Gerbet (1981: 47), for instance, also opines that two additional characteristics of the UN are flexibility of procedures, and capacity for change. In hindsight, however, it is clear that the organisation has neither of these two characteristics.

[30] For an excellent analysis of the Charter, see, for example, Conforti (1997), Simma (1994), and Cot and Pellet (1991), the latter material being in French.

[31] The Third World countries were, for instance, successful in 1977 (by Resolution 32/197) to have the UN establish the post of Director-General for Development (reflecting the importance with which they would like the UN to view the problem of underdevelopment). Under pressure from the West, the post was eventually abolished by Boutros-Ghali in 1992.

[32] Schiavone (1997: 246) remarks: "Unlike the Covenant of the League of Nations, the UN Charter reflects the awareness ... of the close relationship existing between the maintenance of world peace and the promotion of international economic and

social stability, including the safeguarding of human rights and fundamental freedoms".

[33] For a detailed description and analysis of UN organs, see, for example, Simma (1994: 195-206).

[34] What is referred to here as the UN is, in essence, the UN organisation. However, whenever the term UN is used, it is usually taken to mean both the UNO and the specialised agencies. If a distinction needs to be made between the two (given that issues related, for instance, to reform are somewhat different in context and content), authors will specifically detail which particular organisation is being referred to. For purposes of this study, the UN is taken to mean both the UNO and the specialised agencies unless specified otherwise.

[35] Note that usually a country will be a member of the UN as also of a specialised agency. On the other hand, not all members of specialised agencies are UN members.

[36] There are bodies in areas other than administration, including the Board of Auditors, International Law Commission, etc.

[37] See Bulkeley (1997) for an excellent analysis of the role of ICSC in the development of a career system at the UN.

[38] As of January 2000, the fifteen members of the Security Council included: (a) the permanent five (P5), including USA, UK, France, Russia, and China; and (b) the temporary ten (T10): Argentina, Bangladesh, Canada, Jamaica, Mali, Malaysia, Namibia, Netherlands, Tunisia, and Ukraine.

[39] See, e.g., Simma (1994: 645-651) for a cogent discussion of the inadequacies of the MSC.

[40] Palau had its trust status terminated in 1994 when it became a self-governing territory in free association with the USA.

[41] The Court's decision is contained in "Military and paramilitary activities in and against Nicaragua (Nicaragua vs. United States of America)", Merits, ICJ Reports 1986), p. 14. Another instance of the refusal by member states to comply with ICJ decisions is the rejection by the Soviet Union and France to pay their share of the UN peacekeeping expenses in the Congo (similarly for the Arabs and peacekeeping activities in the Middle East); the Court's decision is contained in "Certain expenses of the United Nations (Article 17, Paragraph 2 of the Charter)", Advising Opinion, ICJ Reports (1962), p. 151.

[42] United Nations Press Release GA/AB/3322, 27 October 1999.

[43] While the role that specialised agencies play in international economic and social development is an important one, this study does not include them here because they are in many ways outside the rubric of the main UN organisation and as such they are not directly affected by the reform efforts currently underway. The Executive Boards of each specialised agency will have to decide on its own how it should be reformed and the Annan Agenda does not extend to it except only by implication.

[44] UNIDO was first a subsidiary organisation of the UN until 1985 when it became a specialised one.

[45] There has been since 1991 a Forum of Small States in the UN. Membership is by population size alone, and with the latest entrants there are currently over 75 members of the Forum. Singapore initiated the Forum in 1991 (see *The Straits Times* (Singapore), "Collective clout, not size, has helped smaller countries," 2 October 1997).

[46] United Nations, "Setting the Record Straight: Some Facts About the United Nations," DPI 1753/Rev. 17, 1999.

[47] Actually, its 25 percent share is a lot less than the original assessments. The initial proposal was to have the US contribute 49.89 percent of the UN's budget. This was considered to be too high for any country, and also to be tied too heavily to one source, and the level was dropped to 39.89 percent at the time of the establishment of the UN. By 1954, the level had dropped to 33.3 percent and the US unilaterally in 1957 dropped the level further to 30 percent and then to 25 percent in 1973. There have been several calls within the US to lower this further, once again unilaterally, to something below 15 percent, preferably ten percent. A compromise proposal is currently making the rounds informally wherein the USA's share will first drop to 22 percent and then after two years, to 20 percent. There has not been much formal discussion on this proposal because the other member states want to see the US first pay its existing dues and then they could entertain proposals on the issue. In the meantime, though, the US continues to table a draft resolution in the General Assembly proposing that its share of the assessments be reduced to 20 percent starting immediately although the US Ambassador to the UN – Richard Holbrooke – has hinted at a compromise at 22 percent (see his remarks made during the Fifth Committee debate on scale of assessments, United Nations Press Release GA/AB/3314, 18 October 1999).

[48] Briefly, the assessed contributions are based on a six-year average of a country's Gross Domestic Product (GDP) (the length of the period is designed to account for the lean as well as good years). The GDP figure is then adjusted for poor countries with low income but high debts, and also placed within a range to prevent a country from going up or down very rapidly every biennium. There has been considerable debate lately, with draft proposals from the US to change the modality of the assessments. For one, there is disagreement over the number of years to take into consideration (the range has been from a minimum of three – which the US favours – to nine), and also over using GNP rather than GDP to get a more accurate picture of a nation's wealth. For a detailed description of the budgetary process and methods of the UN (including of the UN specialised agencies), see, for example, Beigbeder (1997(a)).

[49] For comparison purposes, this figure can be matched with the budget of the UN in 1946 ($19 million), 1956 ($49 million), 1966 ($122 million), 1976 ($373 million), and 1986 ($428 million).

[50] "Certain expenses of the United Nations (Article 17, Paragraph 2 of the Charter)," Advising Opinion, ICJ Reports (1962), p. 151.

[51] The first group consists of the permanent members of the Security Council, and they pay higher than their regular budget share since the poorer countries pay less than their share. The second group consists of countries (mostly in West Europe) that pay as much as their regular budget share. The third group of countries (the less developed ones) pay 20 percent of their regular budget share; and the fourth group (the least developing countries) pay ten percent of their regular budget share.

[52] The United Nations' first Secretary-General, Trygve Lie, resigned two years into his three-year contract extension, Hammarskjold died while in his second tenure, and the next three SGs served their full two terms. Waldheim would have been Secretary-General for a third term given the lack of any great disenchantment with him and/or his work, but China at the last moment vetoed his candidacy in favour of

someone from the Third World. Boutros-Ghali had to leave after one term given the US's dissatisfaction with him, and it is certain that Annan will also serve only one term to make way for someone from another continent. On the matter of the length of tenure of a SG, the appropriate Articles in the Charter do not make any mention of number of years, and it is only through convention that a five-year time period has been established and followed.

[53] The UN supports the national volunteer scheme (for example, through its TOKTEN programme) as also the international one (through its UN Volunteer and UNISTAR programmes). The use of volunteers (both national and international) is being encouraged by the UN in light of the expenses being incurred by the expensive international staff and the even more expensive international consultants and experts.

[54] In November 1996, the ICSC reported that while the US federal civil service had been used as the comparator since the inception of the UN, the superior conditions of the German civil service in relation to those of the comparator could be considered as a reference point for managing the remuneration margin (see the debate in the Fifth Committee, United Nations Press Release GA/AB/3118, 25 November 1996). It did feel, however, that, on the whole, the conditions for changing the comparator were not in place then. It also decided that in the comparisons of total remuneration between the Swiss and US federal civil services, the former could not be considered as an alternative to the current comparator. The ICSC is set to look at this issue again in 2001.

[55] See United Nations Press Release GA/AB/3324, 28 October 1999.

[56] The designations for each level below that of the Assistant Secretary-General are as follows: D2 – Director, D1 – Principal Officer, P5 – Senior Officer, P4 – First Officer, P3 – Second Officer, P2 – Associate Officer, and P1 – Assistant Officer.

[57] For locally recruited staff – and nationals of the member states – that work in the UN Field Offices, the Flemming Principle for setting salary scales is used under which they are compensated based on best prevailing local conditions.

[58] Thus, it is entirely possible that two officials at the same grade but based in different countries would be drawing different salaries. Beigbeder (1997(b): 145) exemplifies this by pointing out that in 1995, for example, a staff member with a pay grade of P5 (i.e., upper middle/lower senior management) would draw $313,200 in Geneva while only drawing $223,200 in New Delhi, the difference being mainly due to the cost of living. The post-adjustment multiplier then takes into account this difference.

[59] The UN common system of salaries, allowances and benefits can be categorised as under five headings: (a) salaries and duty-related allowances (including post adjustment, rental subsidies and deductions, overtime and night differential, special post allowance, dependency benefits, education grant, disabled dependants, language allowance, etc.), (b) entitlements related to travel, relocation, and mobility of staff members (including travel expenses, assignment grant, hardship allowance, removal and shipment costs, home leave, family-visit travel, transportation of a privately owned automobile), (c) leave (including annual leave, sick leave, maternity leave, special leave, and official holidays), (d) separation payments (including commutation of accrued annual leave, repatriation grant, termination indemnity, and a death grant), and (e) social security (including health and life insurance, compensation for service-incurred death, injury or illness, and pensions). The issue

of salaries and pensions has featured rather prominently in the criticisms levelled against the UN.
[60] One of the best analyses of this issue is provided by Beigbeder (1997(b): 144-161) under the title "Are UN Staff Overpaid or Underpaid?" While he does not specifically answer his own question, he does conclude that the UN should be focusing more upon engaging UN Volunteers.
[61] This analysis here extends what Simma (*op cit*: 12-23) has proposed. He speaks of only five but since the time the book was published, there has tended to be evident a different phase in UN transformation. On the other hand, Bertrand (1997: 37-59) says that the activities of the UN since its formation and until 1985 can be divided into three periods:

(1)   1945-1955: domination by the West,

(2)   1956-1965: tensions and wars connected with decolonisation, and

(3)   1966-1985: marginalisation of the UN and creation of a new majority.

 To this list can be added two more: (1) 1986-1992: cooperation and ascendancy of the UN, and (2) 1993-present: re-marginalisation of the UN.
[62] Franck (1985: 205) considers this resolution to be perhaps the most fateful to be taken by the General Assembly precisely because it marks the exact moment when the US finally decided that the UN was not conducive to US (and Israeli) interests. The withdrawal that was to follow later was stemmed somewhat by the appointment of Andrew Young by President Carter as the US Ambassador to the UN but with the election of a conservative president (Reagan) in 1980, the end of the US enchantment with the UN had finally arrived. In many ways, the US has never since then (with the brief exception of the Gulf War and the immediate post-Cold War period) shown much interest in the UN.

Chapter Two
"Humpty Dumpty had a great fall...": The Marginalisation

Ever since the creation of the UN, there has been considerable focus on the shortcomings of the organisation – both ingrained in the Charter and its assumptions, and in the operational nuances of whatever the body gets involved in. To be sure, there is an impressive list of achievements (in areas, for instance, of decolonisation, child health, etc.) but notwithstanding that, in the past ten years or so, there have been evident several instances (Somalia, Bosnia, Rwanda, to name a few) which have highlighted very clearly to the average person in the street the inadequacies that is the United Nations.

There are some who continue to look at the bright side of things,[1] but there are also several purported weaknesses that have debilitated the organisation. Structurally, it is argued, the UN is not in tune with the new realities of the post-Cold War (and the various facets of the Security Council are put forward to exemplify this); functionally, the UN is attempting to do too much and in too many parts of the world, thus over-stretching itself; and managerially, whatever it is supposed to do, it is not doing too well (with some notable exceptions). There is a myriad of sub-organisations and keeping track of all of them is a nightmare; there exists very little coordination among these UN agencies – a charge made even by present and former UN officials; the UN is asked to do more with less; and to cap it all, it does not have a reliable resource base such that it can readily tap the revenue source. Given these weaknesses and problems, the UN is perceived to be ineffective and inefficient in its work, and hence marginalised in the management of global affairs.

To understand the nature of the problems besetting the organisation, it is essential to look not only at the genesis of the project itself but also the manner in which the organisation has taken up new functions, modalities, and structures since inception. This chapter then looks at the question surrounding the weaknesses of the UN and details the various problems that have been associated with it. The chapter will also review the scathing criticisms levelled against the UN, and discuss the issue of its marginalization. The contents of this chapter form the preface to the subsequent ones that detail the reform efforts.

2.1 CATEGORISATION OF WEAKNESSES

The weaknesses of the UN can be categorised thus:[2]
- (1) assumptions in the Charter and the Charter itself,
- (2) structural proliferation and inadequacies,
- (3) administrative and procedural,
- (4) managerial, including financial,
- (5) inputs from member states, and
- (6) miscellaneous, including public image, etc.

Assumptions in the Charter and the Charter Itself

Any study on the UN has to begin by taking a critical look at the Charter and its implied assumptions on the nature of how nations behave. Given the preponderance of the philosophy of ensuring that all nations are equal, the Charter has actually put in place a system whereby major contributors to the organisation now feel that they have been short-changed for their resources. The Charter also does not really give too many powers to the Secretary-General of the United Nations to do his work. The post is constrained by the whims of the permanent powers in the Security Council.

At the time that the Charter was being debated, the US and other great powers were adamant that they should have the power of veto and that major decisions on international peace and security should emanate from the Security Council. They did acquiesce on matters of giving the General Assembly the power to look into various issues and to be guided by a one-nation-one-vote arrangement. But given that the Security Council continues to be the major player in the UN system, the great powers have a stranglehold on the organisation. In hindsight, it is possible to argue that even though the Security Council is the predominant organ of the UN, and the victors in World War Two continue to hold sway, the US would not have had it any other way. The other nations had to either yield to the Security Council composition the way it was presented, or the US would walk out of any negotiations on creating an international organisation. Despite all this, at the time of the creation of the UN, there was considerable global attention paid to the capacity of the organisation to attempt first to address – and then to solve – the ills of the world.[3]

The Charter is also based on the liberal internationalist philosophy where national sovereignty is important but is expected to be subsumed to the greater global good. This assumption, it is evident now, was clearly off the mark. In the more than half a century since the inception of the UN, it has been very evident that states have not subsumed their national interests in favour of the global good. And yet there is a paradox here: with increasing globalisation and greater interdependence, there should have been more that the UN could have been made to do by the member states who would accede their national sovereignty in many respects. Yet, this has not been so. Bennett (1995(b): 4) describes the paradox as being "the insistence upon state sovereignty, supremacy, and independence in a shrinking, interdependent world". This leads to a situation wherein "each state declares its right to determine its own course of action regardless of the effects upon other states and, at the same time, is increasingly dependent upon the action of the states in vital areas of mutual concern" (*ibid*).

Given the inflated hopes in the UN in the immediate aftermath of the creation of the organisation, there were also exaggerated expectations. This very exaggeration also meant that the UN was given issues to handle for which it clearly did not have the capacity or the willingness to handle. It should be noted that the UN was not meant for intervening in areas where instead of consenting parties there are factional leaders. The UN is also ill-equipped (both in terms of resources and of logistical facilities) to engage in sustained peacekeeping activities. Such resource-demanding activities require the support of all member states but the support has not been forthcoming. Over the course of time, this has tended to debilitate the organisation.

The discrepancy between what was evident in 1945 and now can best be exemplified by the problems besetting the Security Council. There are two main issues that are said to be at the core of the problems with the Council, and by extension, reflective of the whole UN since the Council is such an integral part of the organisation. The first issue has to do with that of representation while the second with the use of the veto power.

Issue of Representation in the Security Council

The current composition of the Security Council is a continuation of the power positions that were in place in 1945 and considering that the global situation has changed much, continuing with the current makeup of the Security Council is but an anachronism. With the exception of the US, the other four permanent members in the Council have lost much of their political might and there have been new powers that have arisen (notably Japan and Germany – both ironically former enemy states of the allied powers). Despite this, the five countries continue to hold sway over global affairs by virtue of their access to the veto power. It is also quite obvious that these countries are not about to relinquish their hold over that power.

Third World countries, and other critics of the current arrangement, cite figures to show that while the number of countries in the global body has increased more than three-fold, the representation balance in the Security Council has remained constant (see Table 2.1). There are various reform proposals that have been made which seek to redress this imbalance but there has been no progress on this front. The subsequent chapters discuss this further.

Table 2.1
Security Council Representation vis-à-vis Total Membership
(various years)

Year	Level of Membership (UN)	Level of Membership (SC)
1946	51	11
1965	118	15
1994	185	15
2000	188	15

Source: various UN documents.

It is clear that the Security Council has not been altered in its representation aspect despite the big increase in the total number of members of the UN as a whole. Many nations that are not permanent members of the Security Council, and that have to wait a long time for their turn as two-year non-permanent members, feel that this is a key weakness of the UN as a whole.

Issue of Veto

The second issue related to the Security Council is that of the use of the veto power. As stated earlier, the founding fathers of the UN decided that five countries (the US, UK, France, Russia, and China) would have access to the veto power and would be able to apply it anytime. If such an arrangement was not going to be accepted by the other countries then there was little doubt that the US, the principal actor in the UN-setting dialogue at that time, was going to withdraw from the organisation. The spectre of not having the US as a part of the global body was enough to ensure that the other countries went ahead with the granting of the veto power to the five countries.

This issue of veto power then is another issue that has been debated widely at present. Various proposals have been put forth but are unlikely to be implemented. It was because of the closed nature of the Security Council with permanent membership guarded very jealously, and the dominance of the Council in UN matters, that it was described as a "snooty old club that guards its sway over the rest of the world ... with an obsession".[4]

Structural Proliferation and Inadequacies

This granting of various functions to the UN – in the mistaken belief that as a global organisation it should shoulder the burden of solving the world's problems – has led to a situation wherein the UN is characterised by what can only be described as structural proliferation. There has indeed been a notable tendency in both the General Assembly and the Economic and Social Council (ECOSOC) to approve the creation of a new structure to look into any problem that arises. Today, more than 150 separate entities report through the ECOSOC to the General Assembly. Of these, more than a half dozen each are dedicated to sectors such as health, environment, forests, food and agriculture, nutrition, etc. It is this characteristic of the UN that has led to critics to complain about the excesses of the organisation and assert that the UN is a "multi-layered monstrosity of some 100 special commissions and agencies, many of which are operated like fiefdoms".[5] The fact that there are currently countless agencies in the UN has also meant that in many instances, there are also overlapping mandates, and consequently lack of coordination.

This problem of lack of coordination has often been cited as a serious weakness of the UN. With so many agencies operating in so many fields, there is bound to be some duplication of work but the charge against the UN is that it is not making a serious effort to coordinate the activities of the various agencies. For example, in 1997 it was reported that the issues of "environment and sustainable development were being dealt with by no less than eleven UN institutions some of which overlapped one another, and some even working against each other".[6] Similar problems of coordination exist, for example, between some of the work of the UNEP and UNDP. Annan himself has highlighted this problem of lack of coordination in the UN,[7] as has the outgoing President of the 53rd General Assembly, Didier Opertti of Uruguay.[8] It is, furthermore, added that "improved coordination of the agencies is an elusive and ill-defined goal" (Wilenski (1993: 463)).

In addition, the ECOSOC and the Second and Third Committees of the General Assembly have the same working methods (i.e., general debates and preparation of resolutions) and focus on the same themes, yet they exist side by side. There are other examples of lack of coordination that have been documented. Bertrand (1997: 80), for instance, cites the examples of lack of communication between FAO and UNESCO in relation to agricultural education, or between IMF and ILO or UNICEF in relation to social impacts of structural adjustment policies. He goes on to say that this lack of any great degree of coordination in the UN system "is not for the lack of proposals for its provision, nor for want of organs set up over the years to provide it... but the continuous reinforcement of the machinery of coordination has resulted in nothing but ever greater complexity without actually achieving any effect at all" (*ibid*).

Part of the problem is that the 14 specialised agencies are assumed to have become too independent and are not known for accepting any effective coordination from the Secretary-General. On the other hand, there is a three-tier structure of the UN under the Secretariat itself that adds to the structural complexity of the organisation: Headquarters level, regional level (through the regional commissions), and country missions. Additionally, agencies such as UNDP and WHO have regional bureaus. This is one of the reasons for the very high overhead costs of the UN.

Just as the specialised commissions have been put under a microscope, the Regional Commissions too have met a similar fate but have not come out very favourably. Even UN-insiders feel that the Regional Commissions are not really doing good work and that they rely instead on the UN Country Offices for quality in their work.[9] Perceived to be a place for lifetime tenure, they have been put under a considerable amount of strain lately. In 1996, at a time when major structural changes were being contemplated at UN Headquarters as a result of the strong pressures for reform being exacted upon the leadership, there were serious questions raised about the very existence of the Regional Commissions. The JIU in October of that year came up with a rather strong report[10] that asked the Secretary-General to look at the role of the Commissions in a fresh light and to evaluate various others aspects of their work.

In direct response to the JIU report, and the general public skepticism about the role of the Regional Commissions, the Commissions went on an offensive and starting November 1996, came out with a twice-a-year <u>Regional Commissions Development Update</u> to give their side of the story and to update the readers on the various reform efforts undergoing in the five Commissions. In the very first such Update, the-then Coordinator of the Regional Commissions and Executive Secretary of ECLAC, Gert Rosenthal, wrote in the editorial that while the Commissions were then on the defensive over the reform issue, they actually had a lot to offer that was good for the UN system.[11] He went on to respond to four arguments that had been put forth to question their role.[12] Refuting each and every one, Rosenthal said that in the 1996 initiatives launched by the Efficiency Board, "the response of the Regional Commissions was as far-reaching as that of any department within the system".[13]

It is doubtful if the Regional Commissions will ever be disbanded and their mandates and functions hived off, but getting the cue just right, their leaders have begun a painful process of downsizing and re-engineering their organisations.

Administrative and Procedural

Secretary-General Annan himself has said that the UN is "too complicated and too slow ... over-administered... and (have) too many rules and too many regulations".[14] The implication is clear that if the UN is to realise its global mission of furthering peace, security, economic development, and human rights, it must manage its resources better. While Annan is honest to admit the extent of administrative complexities, Maurice Bertrand, himself no stranger to the inner sanctum of the UN, takes the procedural aspect one step further. He says that:

> "there is a climate of unreality in which the UN organisation exists. This is a climate which allows people speak with confidence of objectives which are grandiose but obscure, paying but little attention to the fact that they will never be attained; in which the language of daily intercourse is official jargon; which allows the proliferation of ambitious resolutions, the majority of which make but little sense, and the most forceful conclusions of which consist in calling for yet another report from the Secretary-General; in which people give their approval to principles which no one intends to respect and adopt; plans for the medium term so vaguely formulated as to render verification of the implementation impossible, and in which thousands upon thousands of pages of report are written which no one ever reads" (1997: 66).

Little wonder then that the former US Ambassador to the UN, Daniel Moynihan, called the UN "the theatre of the absurd".[15]

Two key weaknesses can be distinguished in the administrative and procedural aspects of the UN: (a) of mismanagement, and (b) of deficiencies in modality of organisational processes. Both are at the core of what the UN-bashers have cited incessantly to denigrate the organisation.

Mismanagement

When it comes to mismanagement within the UN, to its supporters, the issue is simple: in a global organisation employing thousands of people in offices flung worldwide, there are bound to be isolated incidents of mismanagement. To its critics, the issue is more complex and these are not isolated incidents. More importantly, they feel that the UN does not seem to be doing anything to curtail such instances of mismanagement.

Documented evidence of mismanagement – mostly collected by the UN audit agencies themselves – does exist, and there is no telling what goes unreported every year.[16] For example, the third annual report (in 1997) of the UN's own Inspector-General's Office (the Office of Internal Oversight Services, OIOS) showed that contracts were awarded and money disbursed with little regard to the organisation's financial regulations. Contracts for various services (such as air-charter, catering, etc.) seemed to be particularly prone to abuse. In September 1997, a former staff member of UNCTAD was sentenced to jail for 18 months for embezzling at least half a million dollars. Also in 1997, several staff members were under investigation because audits found six million dollars in overpayments for construction costs in nine countries.[17] Karl-Theodor Paschke, the former no-nonsense Head of OIOS, has said: "there used to be a practice of sweeping irregularities under the rug in the past... there was a certain reluctance in the organisation to deal with the complexities of diplomatic immunity and liasing with national courts".[18]

Modality of Organisational Processes

There are various aspects of the modality of organisational processes that have come under searing attacks by critics. The first is that historically the organisation has sought to do things by consensus.[19] While this is praiseworthy in and of itself, in practice; it is a nightmare that clogs the machinery of decision-making. There are 188 countries that are members and each obviously has its own views on how things should be done in the organisation. Probably no other issue brings this out more tellingly than the current debate over how to reform the Security Council.[20] Actually, there is nothing new about it, the debate has been going on for a long time but was formalised only six years ago with the establishment of the Open-Ended Working Group on Security Council Reforms. For the seventh year running now, the Group has been working on coming up with proposals to table for discussion on reforming the Security Council, but all to no avail.[21] The fact that no consensus appears to be emerging, and that there needs to be an incessant search for the lowest common denominator, is a very vexing problem for the UN.

Another modality of organisational processes in the UN is the implicit reliance on doing things according to tradition and convention in order not to bruise national egos. For example, it is accepted that the heads of UNDP and of the World Bank will be Americans, or that the Under Secretary-General for Political Affairs will be a Russian, or that the head of the Department dealing with economic and social affairs will be a Frenchman. While there is nothing wrong with this arrangement in and of itself, and particularly if the individuals so chosen are qualified, it does go to show that hidebound traditional practices such as these constrain the organisation in its change process. It gives strong hints that the organisation does not have the will to change.

Then there is the criticism of red tape in the organisation[22] which in itself is a product of several variables worthy of note. Given that there are several organisations dealing with similar mandates, that most of the offices are located throughout the world and thus have to be constantly in touch with Headquarters since very little decentralisation has been allowed to date, and since accountability requirements necessitate considerable amount of paper work, there is apt to be evidence of a considerable amount of red-tape. This extends to all facets of organisational processes and to programme management. Annan himself details the problem as such: "Management of human resources has come to be characterised by labour-intensive day-to-day staff administration and mechanical compliance with complex rules and cumbersome processes...and not doing enough to maximise the contributions of staff".[23]

This inadequacy in the administrative process is reflected in massive amount of paperwork that is produced by the UN every year. Annan, for example, notes that just between the 1988-89 and the 1994-95 biennium, the volume of words printed (requiring translation into six languages) had increased by 43 million, or 25 percent, and that in the second two-year period 200 million more pages were printed, for a total of nearly 1.6 billion, a 14 percent growth in printing output.[24] In 1997, Under Secretary-General Connor cited that on an average, a UN office sent nearly 20,000 pages of reports annually to Headquarters and rarely got feedback.[25] Also as of 1997, it was reported that the UN produced 1,570 million pages per biennium to support the parliamentary process.[26] In the International Criminal Tribunal for the Former Yugoslavia in The Hague, for example, it was estimated that per month there were one million photocopies produced in the course of work of the Tribunal.[27]

There are several aspects to this. For one, the UN *is* an international bureaucracy and there are many issues the organisation is involved in; this necessarily entails much paperwork and that is unavoidable. But the fact that there are six official languages and that most documents need to be translated into all – if not at least in English and French – means that the amount of paperwork is bound to be high. Headquarters also sends to the Country Offices reams and reams of information that is meant for general consumption but which very few people peruse. It is not uncommon to find a UNDP Country Office, for instance, receive daily an average of at least 150 or so pages of "junk mail" from Headquarters. The reports are read by no more than one percent of the staff members, at best.

The General Assembly and the Security Council, among others, also request that a lot of reports be submitted by the Secretary-General and others in support of the agenda items that are under discussions before, during, and even after every General Assembly session or Security Council debate. This tendency of asking for more reports can be seen as a way of hiding behind mountains of paper work to fudge on the issues. That, and the fact that the reports tend to be verbose,[28] effectively kills any momentum for prompt action.

Turf battles at the UN can also be particularly evident. Bureaucrats in the UN – as elsewhere – do not like to lose organisational clout and visibility, and bureaucratic turf battles are legendary. Only three years ago, the Decolonisation Unit at the Secretariat was transferred from the Department of Political Affairs to the Department of General Assembly and Conference Services as part of a larger attempt to merge and consolidate several UN departments to improve efficiency. Yet, the-then Chairman of the Committee on Decolonisation fought tooth and nail to get it reversed. He felt that his organisation – whose mandate has all but been met – was being downgraded in importance.[29]

The red-tape nature of the organisation also extends into the bureaucratic process whereby decisions take a long time to be made and actions take even longer.[30] Having meetings appears to be a favourite past-time of the leadership in agencies.[31] Practically all staff members will cite instances of long delays in decision-making and inflexibility of application of rules in even the smallest matters, yet at the same time, these same staff members will also add that in isolated instances, the organisation has also been known to be very understanding, flexible, and accommodating. It is this parallel behaviour of staff members in the interpretation and application of rules and regulations that the general public finds so perplexing.

Managerial, Including Financial

The financial problems of the UN are by now well-known to everybody. Since 1986 when for the first time serious cost-cutting measures were implemented (such as in capital expenditures), the organisation has lurched from one financial crisis to another. There are three key problems/weaknesses related to financing in the UN:
  (1) assessment scales and prompt payment,
  (2) enhancement of resource base, and
  (3) cut-backs on operational costs.

The first problem deals with altering the calculations of which country pays how much and ensuring that dues are paid on time. The problem with financing, the way the US sees it, is that at present, there is over-reliance on a few countries for the bulk of the resources. The top three countries contribute over 50 percent of the total regular budget, and a little over 80 percent of core resources is provided by only ten countries. On the other hand, 88 countries pay a mere 0.26 percent of the regular budget.[32] This invariably leads to a situation whereby the organisation is over-reliant on the ability to pay of particular member states.

This is actually not a problem if the political will to make the payment exists. This explains why, on the one hand, the US will not pay its arrears, and on the other, Japan has readily agreed to a higher share if it should be a permanent member of the Security Council. The US, for its part, has concerns with the current assessment system and wants its share of the regular budget dropped to 20 percent and that of the peacekeeping budget to 25 percent (the latter from the current 31 percent). The US also wants the newly-industrialising countries such as South Korea and Singapore to put in more.[33]

Paying late is also a problem. However, even though Article 19 of the Charter (considered by many to be an inadequate deterrent against late payment) says that voting rights in the General Assembly will be withdrawn if dues are not paid for two years, Article 6 does allow a country to be expelled for the same offence upon the recommendation of the Security Council. Hence it is unlikely that the US will vote to throw itself out of the UN. As at end-1999, the UN was owed almost US$3 billion (for both the regular and the peacekeeping budgets) with the US owing over half of that.[34] Others, such as Argentina, Brunei, Mexico, Turkey, etc., have also been guilty of maintaining arrears although nowhere near the level of the US. On the other hand, while less than half the countries (75 out of 185) paid their regular dues on time in 1994 (this figure was only 11 a few years before that), the situation has improved substantially now, with 117 countries out of 188 having paid their dues in full at the end of 1998.[35]

The second issue in relation to that of financing the UN has to do with the important question of finding ways to enhance the resource base of the organisation. With the ever-increasing workload of the UN, it has for a long time now been felt that the UN should seriously seek other sources of funding. International taxes on use of the global commons has been one such proposal (see, for example, Felix (1995) for a discussion of the Tobin Tax proposal on foreign exchange transactions), the other is reverting to the private sector (as Annan has increasingly referred to – he is the first Secretary-General to seek private sector aid for the UN).[36] This private sector option was rekindled after an unexpected $1 billion contribution in 1997 from media-moghul Ted Turner to be disbursed over 10 years.[37] Both proposals, however, are fraught with difficulties and liable to open a Pandora's box of headaches for the UN.

The US has already categorically rejected the first option of some sort of an international tax to augment the coffers. As such, that avenue must remain closed as long as the US makes it known that it is not amenable to it. The second option might solve the organisation's short-term problem but is bound to create situations of conflict of interest. No one knows for sure to what extent individuals or private companies will demand preferential treatment from the UN for their contributions should they make any but the possibility does frighten more than a few people. This corporatisation of the UN may not be a healthy trend for the organisation.[38]

That then effectively leaves the UN with precious few options to solve the financial crisis. Lowering operational costs (see below) will indeed offer some relief but there is obviously a lower limit to it beyond which the organisation cannot go. Prompt payment of dues by member states would certainly be an ideal solution but judging from current trends, that remains a pipe dream. Probably the creation of credit facilities to the UN might offer a way out, and a variant of this proposal has been an ongoing issue of discussion in the General Assembly.

The third relevant issue under the finance aspect of the UN has to do with the need to cut operation costs as a way of maximising the available resources. At present, almost 38 percent of the budget is used to pay for administrative costs – a rather high figure.[39] Bringing it down would free resources for other much-needed purposes. Cutting costs has been a key US demand in all the reform efforts at the UN and the organisation needs to seriously think about this issue. For one, staff costs and other service costs tend to be steep at the UN. It is true that in order to recruit top quality individuals to join the UN, pay packages must be made attractive (see Table 2.2; detailed information is provided in Annex Five) but staff costs are indeed felt to be rather high.[40] In any development project, for example, it is not uncommon to find staff costs exceeding 50 percent – or even 60 percent – of total project costs.

Table 2.2
Salary Scales for UN Professional Staff
(End-1997 and March 1999; in US Dollars)

Professional Level	Gross Pay	
	End 1997	March 1999
P-1 (Assistant Officer)	$35,382	$36,422
P-2 (Associate Officer)	$46,458	$47,805
P-3 (Second Officer)	$57,720	$59,386
P-4 (First Officer)	$70,619	$72,631
P-5 (Senior Officer)	$85,685	$88,099
D-1 (Principal Officer)	$97,119	$99,848
D-2 (Director)	$109,741	$112,824
Assistant Secretary-General	$133,994	$137,683
Under Secretary- General	$147,420	$151,440

Source: for 1997, adapted from United Nations Press Release GA/AB/3193, 17 November 1997; for 1999, from UN General Assembly, A/RES/53/209 (12 February 1999); also note that salary scales for positions P1 to D2 are quoted for Step I of that level.

What should be noted here is that the reference is to the issue of staff costs and not necessarily staff salaries. The former incorporates all costs associated with maintaining a post in the organisation, and salaries are but one part of that. For example, in the mid-1990s, the UN employed more staff on personnel work (a ratio of 1:37) than many other organisations of similar size and complexity (United Nations, 1997(a), paragraph 230). This adds to the staff costs. In general, the average budgetary cost (all staffing costs included) to a UN organisation for a post is about 16 to 20 percent greater than the annual net pay of the staff member (for an example, see Beigbeder (1997(b): 145)).

The rising trend of staff costs is probably best evident in the recruitment of international experts and consultants. For every consultant that is hired for a project, the UN office has to set aside anywhere from US$8,000 to US$10,000 per month for expenses related to the consultant alone. This does not include the person's travel and other expenses (such as health care coverage). More cost-effective mechanisms of using the expertise of outsiders have been identified in the UN but very few managers are using these mechanisms.[41]

The point being made here is that while cutting back posts in the UN will aid in minimising the expenses of the organisation, that alone will not suffice, and may even indeed be missing the point altogether. For it is better to retain the post and minimise the cost of maintaining it than to do away with it altogether but still retain the cost disadvantage of maintaining the system in general. This particular observation, however, seems not to be in circulation in the UN yet even though the US and other critics seem intent on post reduction as well as on enhancement of efficiency in personnel administration.

Personnel Issues

This focus on personnel issues, apart from the financial one, is quite evident in the managerial aspect of the UN's problems. This is a key feature of Annan's own reform proposals, and it is appropriate to look at this problem here in some detail.

The UN's personnel management system has been variously described as "cumbersome and disorganised"[42] or even worse, "atrocious".[43] While several issues are brought out here (that of recruitment, staff development, staff attitude, etc.), the whole system itself is under attack. The UN, it has been charged, has become "excessively politicised and endowed with a bureaucracy at the same time weighty, inefficient and far too costly" (Bertrand (1997: 65)). Yet others have targeted specific parts of the body to criticise (e.g., that the UN Secretariat was "stacked from basement to 38th floor with deadwood").[44]

There are three basic types of bureaucrats in the UN: (a) the national delegates (who are in the committees of the General Assembly, the ECOSOC, etc.), (b) the careerists at the Secretariat, and (c) the careerists in the specialised agencies. But given that the prime focus here is not upon the latter group of agencies, this study will restrict the discussion to the first two types of bureaucrats. In this regard, it is quite obvious that it is the first group of bureaucrats that control the Secretariat since they are in the Fifth Committee and that Committee oversees financial and administrative matters, determines salary scales and conditions of employment, etc. It is also these candidates that push for high-level jobs in the Secretariat and mar the professionalism of the Secretariat (while Bertrand (1997) tends to put the blame on the national delegates for the decline in the calibre of the staff, Bulkeley (1997) tends to put the blame on the Secretariat for allowing this to happen at all).[45]

At present, it appears that there needs to be more infusion of new blood into the UN staff resources, which is why agencies such as UNICEF are actively seeking new candidates from unconventional sources. Note that the average age of the UN professional staff is 49 years, with only 14 percent of staff below 40 years and less than five percent under 35 years (United Nations (1997(c), Table 17) – largely a product of the hiring freeze instituted about a decade ago in the wake of severe US pressure against enhancement of the bureaucracy. This age profile of the UN has its pros and cons but critics have tended to maintain that this means that old-timers who have outdated ideas on how to manage an international organisation and an international bureaucracy predominate in the organisation.

Bringing in younger and more qualified candidates with knowledge of modern management techniques is something the UN has had to think on for a while but its system of recruitment has been described as chaotic (Bulkeley (1997: 279)). Considerable pressure is applied by national delegates on the Secretariat to hire nationals of their countries, qualified outsiders applying for UN positions rarely get considered because there is a long list of internal candidates still to be considered, and the UN has historically tended to apply the criterion of geographic equality rather than that of merit in recruitment.[46]

The UN Charter mandates that recruitment for UN service be done based on merit but tempered with geographic equality.[47] This has, however, over the years evolved into a quota system and the UN has fiercely adhered to this system of recruitment so as not to hurt the sentiments of particular member states. And as with all quota systems, there is a tendency to bring in candidates who are not necessarily the best but who have to be brought in anyway. This discounts the calibre of the staff as a whole.

The preoccupation with geography, coupled with the tradition of inherited posts has diminished the professionalism of the recruitment process. Added to this is the not infrequent problem of finding candidates based solely on word of mouth and of tending towards recruitment primarily of men (in early 1997, less than 20 percent of senior level posts (and 36 percent overall) was filled by women)[48] (United Nations (1997(a), paragraph 230)). All this makes the recruitment process at the UN haphazard indeed.

Going beyond the recruitment issue, that of staff development also looms as a major concern. The fact that Annan has placed considerable attention on this issue shows the level of concern that has been placed on staff development. Senior managers, in the initial years of Annan's tenure, were generally considered to be untrained in human resource management (*ibid*), including performance appraisal and employee counselling. Complicated rules and procedures also constrained advancement and mobility of staff, and still do to a very large extent.

Over the years, it has been evident that the UN has had inadequate human resource planning which has seriously hampered the organisation's ability to plan for its long term staffing needs. It is also only lately that systematic development programmes for managers have been put in place. This lack of a rigorous management development programme is symptomatic of the insufficient investment made in building the organisation's substantive and managerial capacity. For instance, the Management Training Programme that the UNDP used to host every year for promising young Programme Officers has been stopped for over six years now and with the budget cutbacks, there does not appear to be any evidence that it will be reinstated anytime soon.

Related to the above point, it is quite evident that until only very recently, there was no systematic approach to staff development either by way of management training or overall career planning.

There has been an increase in training funds in the current biennial budget, but the amount of money being spent on training has always stayed below one percent (for the 2000-2001 biennium, the level is around 0.6 percent).[49] While the amount has certainly increased over the years (the 1998-1999 amount of US$14.2 million was in itself 30 percent greater than that of the preceding biennium), the level is not considered to be adequate for the training needs of the organisation.[50] What is even more glaring is that managerial training and development has tended to be neglected, and by the UN's own admission, "unlike other organisations, we have not ensured that these staff get the intensive training they need when they assume managerial responsibilities".[51]

There is also clearly a lack of career prospects in the UN. Given that two-thirds of all resignations in recent years has come from junior professional staff assigned to the UN,[52] it is clear that these future managers do not see any career prospects in the organisation. The problem may not be acute for labour supply from the countries of the South (where employment opportunities in the UN are looked upon as choice jobs) but in order to attract potential candidates from the countries of the North, this trend is not likely to be seen as being very encouraging.

In this light, John Washburn, a former American diplomat and an advisor in the Secretary-General's Office from 1988 to 1994 says that until very recently there has been no career development programme and few honest employee assessments at the UN.[53] Only recently (i.e., since 1995) have staff assessments been done with the rigour that a good personnel management system demands.[54] Yet, former Under Secretary-General for Administration and Management, Richard Thornburgh, in his March 1993 testimony to the House Subcommittee (of International Relations) on International Security, International Organisations, and Human Rights said that a good 90 percent or so of the staff members receive positive assessments in a year. Clearly, there is need for a more rigorous application of the staff assessment exercise.

Yet another problem that critics point to related to UN personnel is the generally elitist and haughty attitude of the UN staff members themselves both at Headquarters and in the Field Offices where the stature of even a middle-level manager is much greater than that of a senior manager at Headquarters. The behaviour and attitudes of managers such as UNESCO's Amadou-Mahtar M'Bow or FAO's Eduard Saouma are by now legendary (for documentation, see, for example, Righter (1995),[55] Hancock (1989); see also *The Straits Times* (Singapore), 24 January 1998).[56] These may well be the most celebrated cases, and that too in specialised agencies (which are outside the area of purview of this study) but critics have honed in on this issue in other agencies and the overall UN as well. Righter (*op cit*: 156), for instance, says that "the UN has never had a customer-conscious culture" and, therefore, critics charge that there is little incentive to be approachable.

The general public in a country does not really get an opportunity to see the person inside the UN post but rather the façade that tends to be created around the persona. It is thus no surprise that Tom Masland, writing in *Newsweek*, says that the widespread view in Africa is that "the United Nations is hopelessly ineffective, an organisation peopled by a privileged elite who ride in air-conditioned Land Cruisers over pot-holed African streets".[57]

The perceived arrogance of the institution as a whole could well be a function of bureaucratic negligence or resentment at having its turf trampled upon. It could also be that there are indeed things to hide and the UN then uses the cover of diplomatic immunity to put aside the problem. One noted case at the moment concerns the role of senior officials in the UN on the matter of Rwanda. The UN has been criticised for not taking action on tips received prior to the massacre of 800,000 Tutsis in Rwanda in 1994. A Belgian legislative commission is looking into whether the leadership of the UN peacekeeping force stationed in Rwanda could have done more to act on the tip. Apparently the information was transmitted to higher authorities in the UN. The commission would like to talk to the leadership of the force but Annan has refused to agree to let them testify, citing diplomatic immunity.[58] Interestingly, Annan headed peacekeeping operations at UN Headquarters then. This case is cited here to show that the public perceives that the UN is using the cover of diplomatic immunity too liberally.

On the Secretary-General

There is one more important point to focus on in relation to personnel matters before moving on to other issues – and that deals with the selection of the leader of the UN itself. The Secretary-General, as has been noted before, is a key figure in the organisation, leading as he does not only the Secretariat but also acting as the spokesperson of the whole organisation. This is an important post and it should, in that sense, be a product of an equally rigorous selection procedure. But it is not.

Secretaries-General have been recruited based on processes that can only be characterised as "disorderly" (Urquhart and Childers (1996: 30)), and the process is indeed haphazard, opaque, and disorganised which produces mediocre results.[59] Anyone that followed the drama at UN Headquarters and Washington, DC, in the second half of 1996 would have got a sense of the clandestine nature of this recruitment process. Five key impressions of this process shine out:

(1) its unpredictable and last-minute nature,
(2) the extremely parochial manner in which the permanent members of the Security Council look at this issue,
(3) the extensive horse-trading among the powers,
(4) the lack of opportunity for substantial input from almost all other member states, and
(5) the extreme secrecy of the proceedings.

As a matter of fact, there is no organised search for suitable candidates, no formal interviews, and no systematic and rigorous assessments of the candidates' qualifications. The fact that all seven Secretaries-General have turned out to be above-average (given the conditions in which they were selected) is attributable more to their own impressive efforts on the job than to the merits of the selection process itself.

Inputs from Member States

The issue of support from its members is at the centre of whether or not the UN will/can be reformed. As has been mentioned earlier, the UN is a collection of nations and it will only move as fast they will allow it. For this, there has to be some degree of coagulation around some core principles and values that the UN should take and that should also guide the behaviour of the member states.

The UN is based on the fundamental principle of cooperation among members and on the premise that member states will readily give up some degree of sovereignty for the greater global good. Judging from the experiences thus far, this has not happened. What has happened, however, is that a considerable degree of lip service has been paid to the ideals of the UN but this has not been backed by concrete actions.[60]

There are various manifestations of this input from the member states that would make the UN more viable as an organisation – but all of them can be grouped under the concept of political will. Bertrand (1989: 32) brings out this issue clearly when he says that the trouble with the UN lies in the fact that it is based on certain attitudes of governments that seek to favour national interests over global ones. Member states are not willing to make decisions that would normally not advance national interests but would advance the cause of the world as a whole. As long as countries do not get away from this parochial practice, the UN will continue to flounder for it would go directly against the basic premise on which the organisation was founded (see also Bertrand (1997: 66-67) on this issue, and the closing remarks made by the President of the 51st session of the General Assembly in 1997).[61]

It is not surprising to note that even at the close of the 53rd General Assembly session, the-then Assembly President, Didier Opertti of Uruguay, echoed similar sentiments when he opined that on many key matters, such as Security Council reforms, "there was as yet no genuine universal political will to reform that would facilitate agreement on the main issues".[62] To exemplify further this lack of political will, mention can be made of the decisions in the early 1960s by the Soviet Union and France not to pay their shares of the peacekeeping expenses in the Congo, or that of the Arab states in doing the same for the missions in the Middle East. The same can be said about the refusal of the US to pay up its arrears at present. In the case of the latter, there is clearly evident the interplay of domestic politics which the leaders of the US – both the Democrat President as well as the Republican leadership in Congress – are unable to transcend and lend support to the UN, except in words.

The UN, through no fault of its own, is subject to the vagaries of internal politics in the US. Clearly, the tussle between the Republican majority in Congress and the Democrat President has meant that the UN is relegated to a by-issue in the political manoeuvring that takes place in Washington, DC. For example, at the end of April 1998, the Congress sent a bill to the White House for the President's approval that would have started payment of almost US$1 billion to the UN except that the bill also contained an anti-abortion component that the Republicans in Congress were certain Bill Clinton would veto. And he did, which also killed the funding possibilities to the UN. In this manner, the UN is being made to pay for the domestic politicking that has taken place in Washington, DC. And once again, it has become evident that the US is not capable of exhibiting leadership qualities when it comes to this issue.

This withdrawal of the US from the confines of the UN has led to a perceptible decline in effectiveness of the UN. For its part, the US is under the illusion that by withdrawing from the world body, it will force it to reform drastically. It does have history on its side, however: the ILO, for example, is now considered to be one of the more efficient specialised agencies in the UN system and it had suffered from a withdrawal of American support between 1977 and 1980. Those on the right of the political spectrum in the US, led by the Heritage Foundation, have always argued that the US should withdraw as a way of forcing the UN to change its ways.

But to call a spade a spade, the US is not alone in using the UN for its own purposes. The lack of political will to make the hard choices to reform the UN is evident among the poor countries themselves. As a matter of fact, it can be argued that the genesis of the US's disenchantment with the UN was the very anti-American sentiments expressed by the UN's Third World member states in the 1960s and onwards.[63] The virulent attacks on the US went on for a long time and were coupled with a total lack of concern for how the UN should do its work. As such, the Third World states continued to ram through the General Assembly resolution after resolution that not only attacked the US but also created more and more programmes, and to support them, more and more structures. To fund these programmes and structures, more funding was essential and the primary source of funding was from the coffers of the rich nations. It was no surprise then that the rich nations argued that it was not fair on them to be criticised on the one hand, while at the same time, be asked to give more and more to the UN for programmes that they never had any control over in formulation.

This attitude of the Third World nations to want to increase the programmes and the budget of the UN is still evident even after all the debate about the need to streamline the work and the budget of the UN. In December 1997, for example, even when Annan had already given his proposals for a reduced budget, the Group of 77 countries (with the-then Chairman, Tanzania) warned that the group would submit proposals that could push the budget beyond the proposed amount. A similar move was made by the Group in 1999 over the 2000-2001 budget submission made by the Secretariat. It is this attitude of the vast number of member states in the General Assembly that has led to American disenchantment with the General Assembly, in particular, and the UN, in general.

Miscellaneous

There are other problems and weaknesses that need to be touched upon as a prelude to understanding the reform proposals that have been made thus far in relation to the UN.[64] Several can be highlighted here that appear central to the reform debate.

One of the growing worries of the member states (particularly those of the Third World as well others such as the Nordic countries) is that in the area of economic and social affairs, the UN is being increasingly marginalised. This issue is nowhere more evident than in the relationship between the ECOSOC and the Bretton Woods institutions (BWI).[65] At the end of the War, a system of global institutions was envisaged which had four pillars: the UN, the World Bank, the IMF, and an International Trade Organisation (ITO). The coordination among these was to be done by the ECOSOC. The IMF would monitor the exchange rates and would assist countries with short-term balance-of-payments problems. The World Bank would assist in the reconstruction of Europe (the idea of assisting the Third World came only much later) and would leverage private capital for development. The ITO was to be involved in ensuring the prevalence of free trade in the world (its modern-day version is the World Trade Organisation which stemmed from the General Agreement on Trade and Tariffs, GATT). Formally, the Fund and the Bank are UN agencies although they have considerable latitude in their work and management. They have opted out of, for example, the UN Common System (for personnel management), and their independence is guaranteed although they are required to consider UN decisions and recommendations. They are also to submit a report on their activities to the ECOSOC every year.

In practice, however, they have functioned as if unrelated to the UN. Their reports to the ECOSOC are more formality and follow pro-forma conventions. The Secretary-General was for a long time not even invited to the World Bank/IMF annual meetings

(Griesgraber (1995: 242)).[66] The Bank has turned to its own in-house expertise on issues such as gender and environment rather than rely on the UN's considerably more extensive network of expertise (only sometimes does the World Bank liaise with UNICEF, WHO, etc.). The rich countries prefer to go through the Security Council when it comes to matters of international security and through the BWIs when it comes to the global economy (or even better, the G-8 (Group of Industrialised Countries)). This enables them to get away from the one-nation-one-vote constraint of the UN General Assembly and the ECOSOC. It is this fact that the Third World countries decry since it means that the rich countries are not attaching importance to the UN.

What is then clear is that the UN – a political body – is marginalised when it comes to matters that are economic. In that context, then, the question of international security is being divorced from that of its social and economic context. While this may not have been the intent of the framers of the UN Charter, it is clear that the secondary role that the ECOSOC plays in the management of the global economy has hampered the efficacy of the UN as a whole. Of late, there has been greater awareness of the strong link between the maintenance of peace and security and the development of poor countries, but that realisation has not translated into a more meaningful role for the ECOSOC vis-à-vis the BWIs. Unless that is done, the UN is going to continue to play second fiddle to the IMF and the World Bank.

Another weakness of the UN has to do with the adverse image created in the minds of the public thanks to the behaviour of the representatives and diplomats of the member states of the UN. At the Headquarters level, there is no clearer manifestation of this than the issue of unpaid traffic tickets amassed by various national delegations in New York, and publicised in 1996. Actually, it is not so much the level of fines incurred by them but their attitude to the whole affair that has contributed to the UN being seen as an organisation of officials who are quite arrogant and elitist and misuse the facilities and amenities given them. For example, in New York alone in 1996, diplomats amassed almost 135,000 unpaid traffic tickets, nearly twice the level of 1994.[67] And North Korea, with only five cars, had 2,297 traffic tickets in 1996. As mentioned above, the more serious issue is not that these fines were given in the first place (diplomats after all have immunity from these sorts of things) but that the UN made such a hue and cry over this issue that it only served to give an image to the public that it was a place where such facilities could be abused by people attached to the UN. The cavalier attitude of the diplomats also rankles many members of the public and such incidents (although not necessarily related to traffic citations alone) must certainly abound elsewhere as well.

The UN is also said to be weakened by the fact that it takes on too many things it has no capacity to handle. In actuality, this is not the fault of the Secretariat since it merely takes on what the General Assembly asks it to be involved in. As the UN itself concedes "... in all to many instances, the UN maintains Secretariat units to deal with issues which it simply does not have the capacity to deal with effectively. The result is a dispersion of UN resources and a dilution of its effectiveness that contributed significantly to the unsatisfactory performance of the UN in so many areas and the reduction of confidence in it" (United Nations (1995: 233); see also Touval (1994)). Unless the leadership initiates steps to draw back from every field of activity, and more importantly, unless the member states, through the General Assembly, refrain from targeting new areas for the UN to intervene in, this dilution will continue to worsen. It is only of late that at the field level, organisations such as UNICEF, UNDP, UNHCR, etc., are bringing in NGOs as partners in development activities and to disburse funds through them. Righter (1995: 156) points out that the UN has "never had a customer-conscious culture, and has been reluctant even to bring voluntary organisations and foundations, its closest constituencies, into its internal deliberations". Annan's proposals deal partly with this problem, but the General Assembly has to decide the modality of this association.

The work itself of the UN has come under severe criticism from all sides. This includes criticisms not only for the work in the peace and security arena but also equally damaging in the economic and social arena. With the increasing misfortunes that began to befall the UN in the 1990s (in Somalia, Rwanda, and in Yugoslavia), the goodwill generated at the end of the Cold War and the period of the Gulf War dissipated all of a sudden. The standard accusation against the UN was that it came in late and then did not do enough. In Rwanda, the refrain was heard again after Somalia and Yugoslavia.[68] Interestingly, it was Annan who as the Head of the UN Peacekeeping Operations at that time was accused of not ensuring that the UN responded promptly.[69]

In the areas of economic and social development, Pranay Gupte (editor of *The Earth Times*) has described the technical assistance programmes of the UN as the "poverty party circuit" and the bureaucrats and consultants that do the work as "povertycrats".[70] Gupte further says that 70 cents of every development dollar goes into sustaining international bureaucracies, and he casts some doubt about the genuineness of the efforts of the international aid officials, whose daily expense allowances is many times more than the annual income of the beneficiaries they are purportedly serving. He says that "fashionable concepts such as sustainable development concocted in the boardrooms of the aid industry have become largely irrelevant to the concerns of everyday people in the developing world".[71] These are not the sentiments of one analyst letting off steam; in private, officials of the UN itself accede that they have not yet been able to make a positive impact on poverty reduction in the Third World.

2.2 THE AMERICAN ATTITUDE

A key element of the weakness of the UN has to do with the negative attitude of the US (or more specifically parts of the US Congress) toward it. The fact that the US is the principal component of the UN cannot be in doubt. The Americans have always been at the forefront of this organisation and whether they pay their arrears or not, they are still able to dictate the course for the organisation to take. It is important here then to focus some more on the very important issue of how there has been a fundamental transformation of attitude on the part of the US towards the UN. As is clear from Chapter One, the US had the primary role to play in the creation of the UN and until the late 1960s was generally very supportive of the organisation. With the advent of the Nixon Administration in 1969, and the consequent dominance of Henry Kissinger in the foreign policy planning of the US, support for the UN started its slow march downhill. The events leading up to the 1975 landmark "Zionism as a form of racism" resolution in the General Assembly, and the overt militancy of the Third World against the US in the organisation, effectively turned off the American public and the legislators.

Critics in the US generally feel that the UN is over-staffed (hence their insistence on reductions in posts; Senator Helms, for one, would like to see a 50 percent reduction). The critics also feel that the staff members of the organisation do mostly useless paper-pushing, and that they are too bureaucratic. Furthermore, the critics feel that the UN officials are too hung-up on internationalism[72] at the expense of national sovereignty, and finally that they are too reliant on the US for resources, and yet, ironically, are virulently anti-American.

The American stand, as stated by former Ambassador Bill Richardson in October 1997 during the General Assembly's Fifth Committee (Administrative and Budgetary) meeting, is that the United Nations must not be dependent on a single member state for its financial underpinning. The Americans like to point out that in 1946 the Committee on Contributions chose to limit the maximum contribution of any one member state based on the principle that the equality of member states might be jeopardised if one of them were to dominate the organisation's finances. Recognising this danger of dependency, the General Assembly had established a ceiling on assessments. US would merely like to alter that ceiling now.

The Americans propose that the following four principles be considered in any debate on assessments:

(1) that no nation must be asked to pay so much that the UN is effectively overly dependent on a single member state – a situation that has been going on for the last five decades,

(2) that maintenance of the present status quo of the US's share of 25 percent for the regular budget and over 30 percent for the peacekeeping budget is not an option and that the current scale of assessments be altered,

(3) that any changes in political boundaries and subsequent corresponding changes in a nation's economic position should be immediately reflected in that member state's scale of assessment,[73] and

(4) that the methodological criteria for determining scales must be transparent, and an acceptable minimum rate of assessment should be required of all members.

The Americans also believe that the peacekeeping scale of assessments should also follow these principles and must be considered in the current debate. The US two years ago tabled a draft scale of assessments seeking a 20 percent ceiling rate. Surprisingly, even its traditional supporters, such as Canada, and others such as Mexico, China, etc., spoke out against the move. Only the Netherlands, speaking on behalf of the European Union, called for a consensus on this issue. Unfortunately for the organisation, this issue does not seem to be anywhere near to settlement.

For all the negativity of these charges, it is arguable that the Americans may be right on all these counts. On the matter of paper-pushing, for example, even the UN says rather bluntly: "...much of the Secretariat's work involving perhaps half, or even more, of its staff members is devoted to areas and issues that are now accorded marginal priority by member states or can be done better by others either inside or outside the UN. It is likely that a very large proportion of the UN Secretariat, probably well over half, is now engaged in activities that would fall into these categories" (United Nations (1995: 230)). And on the issue of bureaucratisation of the UN, Annan himself, while presenting his Track II reform proposals, conceded that the UN was characterised by "obsolete issuances, over-regulation, too many layers of rules, and poor access to them".[74]

Since the mid-1970s, then, and with the exception of the Andrew Young tenure at the UN during the Carter years (1977-81) and a brief interlude at the end of the Cold War, the American leadership has not really looked to the UN as a forum where its global interests could be furthered. It can be argued that this is a function of two variables:

(1) the rise of the conservative leadership in the White House first (Richard Nixon, Gerald Ford, Ronald Reagan, and then George Bush) and in the Congress next (1994 and onwards with the likes of Newt Gingrich and Jesse Helms) that did not necessarily take a very endearing attitude toward the UN (which was fuelled from below by the incessant scathing reports from organisations such as the Heritage Foundation), and

(2) the existence of an internal hubris at the UN which prevented it from doing two things: one, genuinely reforming what was said to be going wrong, and two, not being able (or willing?) to convey to the world more effectively what it was doing right.[75] This latter issue has been picked up by Annan very strongly in the current reform movement, and deserves further mention here.

The epitome of the American antipathy towards the UN is shown in the bill introduced in 1998 by Representative Joe Scarborough (Republican from Florida) calling for the US to withdraw from the UN. Termed the United Nations Withdrawal Act, it would require the US to withdraw from the UN by the year 2000, while retaining membership in the few independent agencies that the Americans still have faith in. This bill is but the latest move taken by Congress to delimit the parameters of its relationship with the UN (the others included the 1985 Kassebaum-Solomon amendment, and the Omnibus Appropriations bill of the 104th Congress).[76]

The Americans also feel that the UN is always eager to want to tax the citizens of the world to generate more funds to waste in more programmes. This they have always opposed (as is reflective of their own opposition to similar proposals domestically as well). In issues such as the role of the UN in international taxation and policing matters, the US has registered severe opposition. One fear of the US is that there will be a force composed of foreign soldiers stationed all over the world to do the bidding of the UN. While this may be a far-fetched notion to others outside the US, the average American politician takes a more credulous view of this. Annan has had to allay the fears of many Americans on this issue.

Finally, the American attitude towards the UN is also shaped by the fact that it considers its scale of assessments excessive. This is true not only for the regular budget (at 25 percent)[77] but also the peacekeeping budget (at over 30 percent). Once again, some understanding must be expressed of the US stand. Take, for example, the UN peacekeeping budget. Prior to 1990 when there was not too much activity on this front, the budgets meant for this purpose were small. Even in 1990, the UN's peacekeeping budget was a mere US$700 million. But given the various interventions of the UN since then, by early 1997, this had ballooned to US$3.5 billion. The US, for its part, is being assessed 31.7 percent of this budget while countries such as Russia, UK, France, etc. have at the most 8.5 percent (this figure is applicable to Russia, France is assessed 7.6 percent and the UK 6.3 percent). And yet, it is the latter three countries that have had more at stake in the Bosnian situation, for instance. By and large, these countries have more direct interest in the various UN expeditions than the US has. The die-hard critics of the UN in the US would like nothing better than the Congress to not only reassert its authority over the US armed forces and prohibit the President from authorising any American soldiers for UN peacekeeping purposes but also for the Congress to decline any new funding possibilities for future peacekeeping purposes.

For all the anger of the other countries against the US, the latter knows that without its active participation, nothing much will get done at the UN. Boutros-Ghali himself, who should know a thing or two about American wrath, said in an interview with Arnaud de Borchgrave of *The Washington Times* on 11 November 1996 that without the US, the UN was finished ("the UN cannot survive without the support, the assistance and the attention of the US"). He also went on to add that the relationship between the UN and the US "is one of the most important jobs of the Secretary-General".[78] And the US knows that it is the most important member of the UN.

2.3 PUBLIC RELATIONS OF THE U.N.

To revert to the issue being discussed before about the state of public relations of the UN, it can be said that before Annan came along in 1997, the public relations programme of the UN (if there was ever one) was in shambles. The organisation was being ridiculed by the press and by other leaders throughout the world. It did not help that the world situation, and particularly, the intervention points that had been targeted by the UN (in particular, Somalia, Bosnia, Rwanda) did not lend a supporting hand to let the world know that the UN was indeed on target and was serious about doing something about the world's ills. There were several clear manifestations of this public relations damage: the traffic tickets and parking-space fiasco in the summer of 1996, the purported ostentatious lifestyle of UN bureaucrats particularly in the Third World, the never-ending high-profile conferences that only seemed to result not in action but in resolutions and in more follow-up meetings, etc.[79]

For an organisation that is so much in the limelight, it is fair to say that it has not done a very good job of packaging itself well and selling it to an increasingly sceptical public. Some individual UN agencies (such as UNICEF) have succeeded phenomenally in tapping the goodwill of the public but others (such as the Secretariat) have not – and have thus allowed themselves to be cast as inefficient, wasteful, and arrogant. Maybe they are, maybe they are not – the point to remember is that the UN needs to do a better job of selling itself to the common public. Ambassador Richard Butler of Australia, himself a veteran of several UN reform groups, said that the UN's public relations were "appalling".[80]

It is pertinent to mention here that while support for the UN among the general public in member states may be sustained, it is rather weak among governments of these states. Part of the blame is to be taken by the UN itself, in that until very recently it never made much effort to create an image in these countries, leaving this job to the national governments instead. And yet, in very few nations does the UN have a constituency powerful and/or dedicated enough to push for the causes of the UN and to lobby for claims to the national budget for UN activities. The situation in the USA exemplifies this paradox. There, public support is rather high (a clear decrease, however, was evident during the Reagan presidency)[81] and while there are a few groups pushing for payment of dues, there is no lobby group powerful enough to take on the legislators that have stopped funding for the UN.[82]

For his part, Annan himself stated at his first press conference upon being elected Secretary-General that he would work toward demystifying the UN and not make it so bureaucratic and distant from the average person. After presenting his Track I reform proposals, he formed a Task Force on the Reorientation of United Nations Public Information Activities with the objective of putting the United Nations – and the Secretariat, in particular – back on the public map. His proposal was to transform the Department of Public Information into the Office of Communications and Media Services so as to "strengthen the capacity to provide relevant and timely communications services to governments, media, and civil society".[83]

To date, however, three years into Annan's tenure, it is fair to say that the UN has done a much better job at projecting an image of an organisation that is serious about reform and that is taking a tougher stance on internal mismanagement issues (the public exposure of the findings of the OIOS is proof of that). To what extent they will be able to bring about a change of heart in the US congressional leadership remains to be seen.

It is fair to say that the weaknesses and problems of the UN have been documented much more extensively than its strengths and promises. There is a good reason for that – the organisation does suffer from serious weaknesses, some are of its own doing, and others are not. Implicit in the discussions above is clearly the notion that the UN is an organisation that was created by the countries of the world coming together to work for a common cause: international peace and security. The Charter of the UN is so structured that it does not give the organisation any more powers than what the member states themselves are not comfortable with. There is little danger that the UN will turn out to be a supranational body dictating to other countries and, by and large, usurping national sovereignty. No matter how much the critics of the UN wish to make that the defining issue, it simply is not true.

It is true, however, that the organisation suffers from many of the problems that other large bureaucracies do: turf battles, lack of coordination, institutionalised inefficiencies, staffing inadequacies, lack of quality control, and most of all, subject to external control (for resources). Unlike other organisations, however, the UN cannot do much about the unwillingness of member states to provide the resources. It has no authority to do so other than moral persuasion.

All these weaknesses and problems of the UN highlighted here have been the focus of several reform efforts since the UN was established. In order to better understand the most recent one, it is necessary first to extricate all the others that preceded it for much of what Annan wants to do has already been brought up before. It is this subject matter then that the next chapter turns to.

Endnotes

[1] Note, for example, the remark made in Asiaweek's lead article (February 28, 1992): "Against all odds, it has become a far more effective institution than many would have predicted at its birth" (p. 19).

[2] Simons (1995) takes a different angle on this issue. He classifies the problems of the UN as under that of power, of management, and of representation. While the classifications here differ from those of Simons', the elements within them are surprisingly similar. On the other hand, the noted Maurice Bertrand maintains that a diagnosis of the UN's problems shows that they are contained in the following (1993: 428): (a) lack of political will among member states, (b) lack of effective management, and (c) lack of structural coherence in the area of programme and budget. This study's arguments on the nature of the problems plaguing the UN go beyond these.

[3] This set of problems (ranging anywhere from the environment to overpopulation to economic vicissitudes, etc.) is what is known as the Global *Problematique* (Haas and Haas (1995), Ruggie (1979-80), Addo, et al (1985)). Much later, the term Global Commons was introduced by, among others, the Commission on Global Governance (1995(a) and 1995(b)) to denote the set of assets that the various countries have at

their disposal (such as the seas, forest cover, etc.). This idea of using the Global Commons to solve the Global *Problematique* was squarely contained within the scope of activities of the UN whether or not the organisation had the capacity to do so.

[4] *The Straits Times* (Singapore), "American Gambit," (editorial), 23 July 1997.

[5] *The Straits Times* (Singapore), "Halt the UN gravy train," (editorial), 6 February 1996.

[6] *The Straits Times* (Singapore), "Modest results but it was a useful exercise," 8 July 1997.

[7] There is an apparent gap between the discourse and the practice of system-wide cooperation and coordination that needs to be filled to attain the objective of a reformed United Nations. These sentiments were expressed by the UN Secretary-General in response to a 1998 policy issue paper and internal document prepared by the former ECLAC Executive Secretary, Gert Rosenthal, on the matter of system-wide reform in the UN. See also United Nations (1995: 242) for comments on the UN's record on proper coordination of various activities. Finally, note also the level of duplication in, and consequent lack of coordination among, the ECOSOC, UNCTAD, UNIDO, and the five regional economic commissions. All of their work, it is argued, could be subsumed under one agency/council.

[8] United Nations Press Release GA/9590, 13 September 1999. The Press Release has this to say about the reactions of the President on this issue: "More than once, he was surprised and even perplexed in noting that despite sporadic contacts of representatives, the bodies with major responsibility – the General Assembly and the Security Council – had acted without coordination and transparency."

[9] The five Regional Commissions were meant to bring development closer to the countries themselves. In large part, their functions were to provide authoritative analyses of the economic and social problems of the regions in which they were operational. But while their utility may have been evident in the past, now that member states in the regions and organisations such as the World Bank, the regional banks such as Asian Development Bank, and even other UN agencies such as FAO in the agricultural sector, have amassed considerable expertise in the same areas, the *raison d'etre* of these Regional Commissions has been increasingly questioned by many (including those within the UN system, as well as those outside, such as the Commission on Global Governance).

[10] See the October 1996 report by JIU (A/51/636-JIU/REP/96/3) on Coordination of Policy and Programming Frameworks for More Effective Development Cooperation.

[11] "Relevance of the United Nations Regional Commissions," *Regional Commission Development Update*, November 1996.

[12] The arguments were: (a) that the UN should concentrate on global cooperation leaving the field of regional cooperation to other intergovernmental organisations, (b) that the regional commissions have no clear mission within the UN system, (c) that the additional layer that the regional commissions entail within the Secretariat's structure contributes to overlapping and duplication, and (d) that their efficiency and effectiveness leaves much to be desired (*ibid*).

[13] *Ibid.*

[14] Remarks made at a series of meetings at the end of October 1998 of member states and UN staff during which he presented his report on management reform (see United Nations Focus Series – "Staff become focus of United Nations

modernisation: New management culture key to revitalisation", DPI/2018, November 1998).

[15] Cited in *The Sunday Times* (Singapore), "Are UN issues being driven by US policies?" 4 January 1998.

[16] Some of the most damaging documented evidence has always come from the Heritage Foundation and from the American Sovereignty Project, both in the US. See also *The Straits Times* (Singapore), "UN officials 'involved in illicit spending scam'," 3 November 1997.

[17] *The New York Times*, "UN agency reports $6 million cost over-runs," 8 March 1997.

[18] *The Straits Times* (Singapore), "UN's top sleuth probes three cases of major internal fraud," 4 October 1997.

[19] Even the budget process in the General Assembly which used to be characterised by a decision-making process that was based on a two-thirds majority vote was amended in 1986 to include a vote by consensus.

[20] There are many elements to Security Council reform (e.g., working methods, use of the veto, etc.) but the one that has the members at each other's throats is that of membership in the proposed expanded Council. Italy vigorously opposes Germany's inclusion as the third European country in the permanent membership of the Council; Pakistan and Argentina have openly opposed the proposed and much-discussed about inclusion of India and Brazil respectively; the US, for its part, wants to limit the expansion of the Council to at most 20 or 21 total members, Britain and Germany want 24 (as did the widely-respected former President of the General Assembly, Razali Ismail), and the Third World well over 26. Another former General Assembly President, Hennady Udovenko of Ukraine, is on record as having said that the issue of Security Council reform is "probably one of the most difficult issues the United Nations has tackled throughout its history" (see *The Straits Times* (Singapore), "No accord on expansion of UN Security Council," 26 August 1998). Going by the experiences so far in this regard, it is doubtful if any meaningful – and satisfactory – outcome will ever result.

[21] This is what Razali Ismail had to say about the way the UN did its work: "In the UN, we are past masters in delaying tactics. It's like you put something out and they add killer amendments. In the end, what you have is not a resolution anymore, but a Christmas tree with the baubles, the lights and little bears hanging there" (*The Sunday Times* (Singapore), "Malaysian lion wants UN to have bite," 20 April 1997). In the same story, Ismail said: "The UN must take stock, agonise and come up with clear solutions. We haven't done too well on that." Finally, "some countries ...don't want any decisions taken (on reforms). Discussion, counter-discussion. Analysis, paralysis. And then they don't move."

[22] The UN itself describes this problem thus: "Too often, the delivery of mandated programmes is hampered by excessive bureaucratic procedures and rules, and with responsibility for management of resources in the hands of administrators who have no accountability for programme delivery" (United Nations (1997(a), paragraph 236)).

[23] *Op cit*, paragraph 229.

[24] See "Letter dated 17 March 1997 from the Secretary-General addressed to the President of the General Assembly" (Document A/51/829). In his press conference that day, the Secretary-General told reporters: "I think most of you are also

concerned with the volume of paper you have to go through. I once jokingly said that I sometimes worry that this building will sink under the weight of the paper it generates. So I am happy to be able to do something about that" (United Nations Press Release SG/SM/6183).

[25] See "Letter of Transmittal from Under Secretary-General Joseph E. Connor to Secretary-General Kofi Annan," 22 April 1997, Table 7, in United Nations (1997(c)).

[26] *Op cit*, Table 12.

[27] A reporter posed a question related to this issue to Annan at a press conference at the UN Headquarters on 17 March 1997 (see United Nations Press Release SG/SM/6183). Annan did not dispute the figure.

[28] The degree of verbosity in the UN and its reports is near-legendary. Bertrand (1997: 76-77) has cited several examples of such language, and the UN leadership and management would do well to review that.

[29] Thalif Deen, "United Nations: Reforms Undermining Decolonisation?" 19 May 1997, Inter Press Service, Global Information Network.

[30] Over a quarter century ago, Robert Jackson in his famous Capacity Study on the UN Development System wrote that "the machine has become unmanageable....it is becoming slower and more unwieldy, like some prehistoric monster" (as cited by Sir John Weston, UK Permanent Representative to the UN, on 10 April 1997, at the British-American Chamber of Commerce, 'The Future of the United Nations: A British View'). What Jackson opined back then is still very apt.

[31] In their defence though, and to be fair, it is obvious that there is a lot that these agencies need to do and the best manner in which coordination can take place is to meet very regularly. For a discussion on this issue related to the General Assembly, see Reisman (1997).

[32] See "Status of contributions as at 30 June 1999," Annex II, UN Secretariat (ST/ADM/SER.B/543), 2 July 1999. It is also felt – although not vocalised – that countries that are holders of the veto power in the UN are not contributing in proportion to their status. France and UK, for instance, only pitch in 6.5 and 5.0 percent respectively while China is even lower at less than one percent (it used to pay more but was successful in 1980 in getting the UN to reduce its level to that of a developing country's). China has also recently argued against ideas circulating in the UN to make permanent members of the Security Council pay above a minimum amount (ostensibly as a price to pay for their membership to the exclusive club; see United Nations Press Release GA/AB/3314, 8 October 1999).

[33] See *The Straits Times* (Singapore), "Richer Asian nations 'should give more to UN'," 20 February 1997.

[34] There is disagreement over just how large the actual size of US's arrears is. The Clinton Administration, based on information provided by the State Department, says it is about $1.02 billion; the Senate Foreign Relations Committee pegs it at $625 million; the UN Reforms Act in the US Congress says it is $819 million; while the UN attests that the amount is closer to $1.36 billion.

[35] See DPI/1815/Rev. 16, United Nations, June 1999.

[36] See *The Straits Times* (Singapore), "Annan seeks private funding for UN," 14 August 1997.

[37] Ted Turner then hired a former Democratic Senator, Tim Wirth, to head the foundation that was to oversee release of the funds (see *Newsweek*, 1 December

1997, p. 33). The Foundation set out to achieve four goals: (a) help Annan in his reform efforts, (b) support "good UN programmes" such as children's health, environment, etc., (c) raise money for these UN programmes from the private sector, and (d) make a pitch to the American public about the good work of the UN.

[38] The trend towards corporatisation has also been criticised by staff unions who feel that there is too much emphasis in the UN on cuts and serving as a corporate entity and less on operating as a good global employer (see the remarks made by Mehri Madarshahi, President of the Coordinating Committee for International Staff Unions and Associations of the United Nations System (United Nations Press Release GA/AB/3325, 29 October 1999)).

[39] In 1997, Annan himself mentioned that this level was 38 percent (see United Nations Press Release SG/SM/6183, 17 March 1997). It is very conceivable that in the years since, the level has diminished somewhat although the UN itself has not yet analysed this.

[40] The UN, for its part, argues that it is losing out to other employers (multilateral organisations as well as the private sector) in recruiting the very best people because of non-competitive salaries and benefits (see, for example, United Nations Press Release GA/AB/3325, 29 October 1999). UN professional salaries are said to be significantly lower – as much as 50 percent – than those at such organisations as the European Union (EU) and the World Bank. UN professional salaries are also reportedly, on average, 30 per cent lower than those for comparable work in the US private sector. The UN thus argues that it is getting harder to attract – and retain – staff (particularly at the higher grades) from countries with high pay levels.

[41] The UN Volunteer Programme is one such mechanism and yet few UN agencies have utilised this source (from the author's own experiences in Africa, it was very difficult to convince the senior managers of UN agencies to make more use of the Programme even in light of the funding crisis; see also Beigbeder (1997(b): 159-161)). Another mechanism is to encourage nationals to return as experts for a while to work at a lesser cost than an international expert. While TOKTEN is a useful exercise, it is not used extensively because it has bureaucratic processes embedded in it. Other national experts could be brought in at a negotiated level well below the pro-forma amount specified. Some far-sighted UN senior managers have practised this with considerable success.

[42] Remarks made by Karl-Theodor Paschke, former Under Secretary-General for Internal Oversight Services ("UN report: Waste and abuse but no money for reform" (http://www.nando.net/newsroom/ntn/world/102695/world635_11.html), 26 October 1995).

[43] *The Straits Times* (Singapore), "Halt the UN gravy train," (editorial), 6 February 1996.

[44] See *The Economist*, 12 June 1993, p. 23.

[45] Bulkeley says that "... the Secretariat has permitted creeping nationalisation in the UN personnel system" (1997: 268). He provides a very critical analysis of this issue and the piece deserves extensive reading by the interested scholar. See also Ameri (1996) for a discussion of both sides of the issue.

[46] This is how the Iraqi representative to the UN described these problems in 1986: "With regard to recruitment, we beat about the bush; we talk about examinations, and we talk about member states putting pressure on the Secretary-General. Let us face it, in eight out of ten cases – and that might be a conservative estimate – we find

jobs for people; we do not recruit the best people for the job. We are all guilty of that, every delegation is guilty" (Muller (1992: 145-146)). For a historical perspective on this issue, see, for example, Ameri (1996: 67-90).

[47] The appropriate Article (101(3)) reads: "The paramount consideration in the employment of the staff and in the determination of the conditions of service shall be the necessity of securing the highest standards of efficiency, competence, and integrity. Due regard shall be paid to the importance of recruiting the staff on as wide a geographical basis as possible". It is argued by UN supporters that there is need for geographic balance among the staff because the staff of the Secretariat must necessarily reflect the full membership of the UN (since the UN itself is a universal organisation), and so that it will be sensitive to a wide diversity of political, social and cultural systems. However, as of June-end 1999, 24 of the 185 member states were not represented at all in the Secretariat (and thirteen more were under-represented; see United Nations Press Release GA/AB/3345, 19 November 1999). Regarding employment of consultants and experts, in 1998, five countries (Canada, Chile, France, UK, and US) accounted for one-third of all UN consultants, and six countries (Chile, Ethiopia, France, Lebanon, UK, and US) for more than half of individual contractors (*ibid*). Relatedly, the General Assembly has incessantly called for more adequate representation of developing countries in the Secretariat, in particular at the senior levels.

[48] At the end of 1996, women filled 35 percent of the core professional posts, up from 22 percent in 1981. This still had not reached the desired level of 50 percent, however, by the end of 1999, and has tended to hover around 37-40 percent. The UN does report, however, that during the period mid-1995 to mid-1999, "the number of female staff members at the D-1 grade and above went up from 57 to 92 – an increase of 61.4 per cent" (United Nations Press Release GA/AB/3345, 19 November 1999).

[49] About US$15.64 million is being requested for the next biennium. For 1998-1999, the amount was US$14.20 million (see United Nations Press Release GA/AB/3340, 10 November 1999). Yet, the ACABQ has not yet accepted the request for increase until the Secretariat addresses the weaknesses identified in the evaluation of training carried out in early 1999 (such as, for example, the problems being faced regarding the decentralisation of training programmes to individual departments). The Secretariat is to report on this during the next budget session and only on the basis of those findings will the ACABQ agree to the increase in the appropriation for training.

[50] Compare this figure with two percent and above for other UN funds and programmes, and up to five percent (or even more) for organisations in the private sector and some public sector bureaucracies around the world (such as that of Singapore).

[51] Remark made by Assistant Secretary-General Rafiah Salim, Head of the newly-reconfigured Office of Human Resource Management (OHRM) (see United Nations Document DPI/2018, November 1998).

[52] See United Nations Document A/53/414, reported in DPI/2018, November 1998.

[53] *The New York Times*, "Amid tumult, UN turns 50," 22 October 1995.

[54] The performance appraisal system introduced in 1995 is based on a "management by objectives" (MBO) approach where there is emphasis placed on establishing work plans and objectives that are mutually agreed-upon by the employee and his/her

supervisor and included as a formal part of the Performance Appraisal Review (PAR). The employee gets to describe his/her own interpretations (supported by critical incidents) of how he/she did on the job which provides a zero-degree process of performance evaluation. This self-evaluation is key in the PAR.

[55] Former UNESCO Director-General Amadou Mahtar M'Bow is reported to have said at one meeting in 1985: "I permit nobody to criticise anything whatsoever" (cited in Righter (1995: 60)). It was Righter who described M'Bow, UNESCO's Director-General for 13 years, as the "most obviously disastrous and corrupt of the UN Chief Executives" (p. 60).

[56] *The Straits Times* (Singapore), "So what if my deputy lied about his degrees?" 24 January 1998.

[57] Tom Masland, "The United Nations: Hardly a hero's welcome," *Newsweek*, 18 May 1998, p. 50G.

[58] See Alan Zarembo, "Toward a True History," *Newsweek*, 17 November 1997, p. 2.

[59] *The Straits Times* (Singapore), "Close down the UN and build it again," 15 August 1996 (reprinted from *The International Herald Tribune*).

[60] Note, for example, that at the time when Ronald Reagan was vigorously opposing the UN, he addressed the General Assembly in 1986 and proudly proclaimed: "And members have my word for it: my country, which has always given the United Nations generous support, will continue to play a leading role in the effort to achieve its noble purposes" (cited in Muller (1992: 56)).

[61] A former President of the General Assembly, Razali Ismail, put this problem very lucidly: "... basically, the nature of negotiating in the UN is predicated entirely on stating first the national position ... if only we can get all the ambassadors to think beyond national positions, and look at multilateralism and allow it to grow, to take root, we could have had a much better result..." (United Nations Press Release GA/9291, 15 September 1997).

[62] See United Nations Press Release GA/9590, 13 September 1999.

[63] For a cogent analysis of this, see Brian Urquhart, "Looking for Sheriff", *The New York Review of Books*, 16 July 1998. The well-noted Urquhart says that it was the rhetorical activism of the Third World's adolescent years that was a major factor in the US's disillusionment with the UN. More often than not, encouraged by the-then Soviet Union, Third World advocacy of many agenda items that were anti-Western (such as the NIEO, the "Zionism equals racism" General Assembly resolution, etc.) generated hostility in Washington, DC, which directly destroyed any bipartisan support in the US Congress for the UN. This ultimately played directly into the hands of conservatives such as the Heritage Foundation.

[64] For further description of problems in the areas of management and made by the UN's own OIOS, see "UN report: waste and abuse but no money for reform," 26 October 1995 (www.nando.net/newsroom/ntn/world/102695/world635_11.html). For criticisms from outside the UN, see, for example, Morris (http://www.unwatch.org/, May 1996), and van Atta (*Reader's Digest*, December 1995: 47-52). Pranay Gupte, editor of *The Earth Times*, focusing primarily on the work of the UNHCR and UNHCHR, brings out the main thesis of the critics of the UN: "UNHCR and the Human Rights Commission can complain all they want about their financial distress and political plight. But it's vision and management skills that they're lacking" ("No help for the weary," *Newsweek*, 17 August 1998, p. 2).

[65] The Bretton Woods institutions include the World Bank group and International Monetary Fund. The World Bank group, in turn, includes the World Bank itself, the International Development Association, the International Finance Corporation, and the Multilateral Investment Guarantee Agency. It is common, however, to hear mention made of primarily two of these agencies: the IMF and the World Bank.

[66] The first time a UN official attended a closed meeting of the Bretton Woods Development Committee (BWDC) was in April 1999 when the UN Under-Secretary-General for Economic and Social Affairs, Nitin Desai, travelled to Washington, DC, to discuss the decision by BWDC to refer its deliberations on social policy to the UN's review of the 1995 World Summit for Social Development, scheduled to take place in the UN General Assembly in June 2000. Conversely, the first time ever an official of the IMF attended a meeting of the ECOSOC was on 28 October 1999 when its Managing Director came to a joint meeting of the ECOSOC and the Executive Directors of the IMF. Of late, though, there has been an increasing trend of personal meetings among senior officials of both the entities.

[67] See Clyde Haberman, "In NY, illegal parking by UN diplomats is the mother of all crimes," *The Straits Times* (Singapore), 4 April 1997 (reprinted from *The New York Times*).

[68] For further analysis of these issues, see, for example, Simons (1994: 192-201 and 206-221) and Simons (1995: 105-109).

[69] The case was further aggrandised when as Secretary-General, Annan refused to let two previous UN senior officials testify to the commission investigating the Rwanda crisis. This has haunted him ever since, and during his 1997 trip to Rwanda meant as a fence-mending mission, he was rebuffed by the political leadership and rebuked publicly by the Foreign Minister. In response, Annan has said publicly that he could not act upon the information that had been forwarded to him without intervention from the powers-that-be (who had been informed) and that blame for the massacres cannot be pinned on him. In a press conference in December 1999, Annan had this to say about the Rwandan fiasco: "it was painful and tragic that we could not have done more to avoid (Rwanda) ... but we did the best we could with the assets we had under those circumstances..." (United Nations Press Release SG/SM/7259, 14 December 1999).

[70] *Newsweek,* "The poverty party circuit," 22 December 1997, p. 2.

[71] *Ibid.*

[72] Helms put it very powerfully when he said (1996: 4): "UN reform is about much more than saving money. It is about preventing unelected bureaucrats from acquiring ever-greater powers at the expense of elected national leaders. It is about restoring the legitimacy of the nation state." And therein lies the crux of the problem inasmuch as the UN and national sovereignty is concerned (see Chapter One).

[73] This could then apply to Germany (for an increase) or to Russia (for a decrease).

[74] United Nations (1997(a), paragraph 238).

[75] For a lucid analysis of the UN and its image problem see, for example, Menon (1995: 175-193).

[76] This bill included a provision that withholds payments of US arrears unless the UN meets two of three specific reforms: (a) the UN budget must be less than the $2.6 billion 1996-97 budget, (b) the UN Secretariat staff must be reduced by ten percent, and (c) the UN must make net budget cuts of $100 million. All three conditions have been met by the UN since then.

[77] On the matter of the regular budget, the US might have a valid point. The 95 poorest countries do not contribute much (as a whole, less than one percent of the cost of the UN). When the next 60 countries are considered – which include all the members of ASEAN (Association of Southeast Asian Nations) and OPEC (Organisation of Petroleum Exporting Countries) – they contribute altogether only about twelve percent of UN costs. Clearly, there is a mismatch between what the countries have as wealth and how much they are assessed.

[78] *The Washington Times*, "The Change in the Administration's Position is a Mystery," 11 November 1996.

[79] This is what the former President of the General Assembly, Mr. Razali Ismail, had to say about the issue of UN and its penchant for conferences: "All major conferences have spawned spin-offs, as is the case with Rio, leading to a hectic global conference circuit on the follow-up, avidly followed by diplomats, non-government organisations, academia and United Nations staff alike, some like conference junkies, generating masses of information, rhetoric and jobs for consultants, calling more meetings with questionable results. We are all overloaded with facts, findings and figures, but can we not move from continuous strategising and consensus-building into a fully operational and action oriented-phrase, please?" (see United Nations Press Release GA/9221, 4 March 1997).

[80] Cited in *The Straits Times* (Singapore), "Annan floats 10-point plan for tighter UN ship," 19 March 1997. For a discussion of the image issue of the UN, see also Menon (1995).

[81] Beigbeder (1987: 17) reveals that in 1950, opinion polls showed that 58 percent of Americans thought the UN was doing a good job, as opposed to 36 percent that did not. By 1983, the corresponding figures had become 35 percent for a good job and 42 percent for not a good one. However, by 1995, the positive numbers had gone up (to 54 percent), by 1996, the UN's favourable rating had gone up to 67 percent, and in 1998 rested at an all-time high of 72 percent (the 1998 poll was conducted by the UNA-USA).

[82] Two groups that have to be cited for their active work in this area are: (a) the Emergency Coalition for US Financial Support of the United Nations whose coalition includes members such as former President Jimmy Carter, and former Secretaries of State James Baker and George Shultz, and (b) the United Nations Association of the USA (UNA-USA) which has played an active role in disseminating information to the public but has never aggressively gone about courting legislators. This was why in 1997 when Annan addressed the UNA-USA, he specifically asked the organisation to take on a more vigorous stand in helping convince Congress that the UN had to be funded.

[83] United Nations Press Release SG/SM/6183, 17 March 1997.

Chapter Three
"All the king's horses...": The Earlier Reforms

Having looked at the problems besetting the UN, the study now reviews the proposals and efforts that have been made to date to reform the organisation. Reform efforts at the United Nations are not new. Even the first General Assembly session in 1946 had proposals for restructuring and streamlining the organisation. And every Secretary-General has had to contend with this issue to some degree or other.[1] However, it is only in recent years (as a matter of fact, since 1986 when the severity of the issue of financial constraints first publicly burst into the scene) that the issue of UN reforms has so occupied the minds of the UN leadership as well as its detractors and supporters.

This chapter takes a look at the various reform efforts that have been made but puts particular focus on proposals made up to 1996-end when Boutros-Ghali's tenure came to an end. This discussion will then help put the Annan Agenda in proper perspective and will give an insight into what is new that he has proposed and is, therefore, worthy of trying out.

There are two different interpretations of the term reform.[2] On the one hand, it means improving the existing processes, structures, functions, etc., and in that sense, implies a continuous process (for this, the JIU probably plays the most important hand from within the UN although increasingly outsiders such as the Heritage Foundation continue to publicise the deficiencies of the UN). On the other hand, reform is a broad concept that includes an alteration, if necessary, in the very premise and institutional structure of the UN itself. This latter interpretation of reform is a by-product of the changed international context in which member states are currently operating. One such change occurred in the 1960s when many previously colonised countries became independent and sought to enter the UN. When they did so, they began to impinge on the manner in which the UN worked as an organisation. Another such monumental shift in international relations was evident in the 1990s. With increasing globalisation and the end of the Cold War, the nature of the relations between and among states has begun to alter dramatically, and it is now widely believed that the UN as an organisation should change as well.

Bertrand (1993: 423) has categorised reform attempts at the UN as falling into two distinct periods: the first which lasted until the mid-1960s where the initiatives came from the Secretary-General primarily (note such committees as Lie's Group of Three Experts in 1954, Hammarskjold's Group of Eight Experts in 1960 to help restructure the Secretariat, etc.); and the second which began after Hammarskjold's death when the member states began to take the initiatives. UN reforms also tend to fall into two camps: preserving the status quo by administrative fiat, or transforming the UN into a genuine world government capable of maintaining the rule of law globally.

Given the multitude of areas that the UN is involved in, there is a plethora of literature on UN reforms, in general, as well as related to specific UN structures and functions, in particular. A closer look at the literature reveals that the sources of these ideas can be broadly classified as being contained in those generated from within the UN (for example, from the General Assembly, JIU, the ECOSOC, Secretary-General, Security Council, etc.) and outside the UN (for example, from countries (such as the Nordic UN Project, from UK, USA, Canada, etc.), and from individuals and agencies). What appears below is not meant to be an exhaustive list of all the major proposals made on UN reforms but more symptomatic of the kind of work that has been generated in this regard. To provide a more coherent framework of discussing these proposals, this study includes them in the context of the approximate time period in the tenure of the individual Secretary-General at the helm of the UN then.

3.1 THE INITIAL YEARS

Even before Trygve Lie took over as new Secretary-General, and certainly during and after that fact, there emerged in the UN a bipolarity that effectively began to cripple the organisation. In that context, and the fact that newer countries had not gained admittance into the UN meant that the status quo that had existed since 1945 permeated the UN throughout the first decade. There was also increasing realisation that the Charter had not provided all the answers as to the structures and processes of how the UN was to do its work and the General Assembly itself took the lead role in coming up with ideas on how to reform the organisation. The first major effort at UN reform in the 1940s and 1950s could be considered the 1957 Commission to Study the Organisation of Peace ("Strengthening the United Nations"). By that time, it was quite obvious that the bipolarity that existed in the UN would not be a passing phenomenon and the leadership of the UN needed to find ways around it to enhance the role of the organisation or else it would forever be relegated in importance.

A bolder effort was initiated by Dag Hammarskjold in 1960 when he formed the Group of Eight Experts to define the Secretariat's structure. The Group, among other things, recommended that the number of Under Secretaries-General for Special Political Affairs be increased from two to five (in keeping with the role the UN was playing in global political affairs at that time) and that set criteria for the implementation of geographical distribution be accepted. The creation of the Group was an important move since it was becoming increasingly clear that the Secretary-General and his top staff would have to play a more meaningful role if the UN was not to be totally paralysed by the stalemate that had engulfed the organisation. Other administrative regroupings followed and Hammarskjold – by sheer dint of his personality – seemed to be taking the organisation toward a more meaningful role. Unfortunately, he died in a plane crash during a mission to the Congo, and it appeared that along with him went the opportunities to have the UN carve out a niche for itself with the Secretariat playing a key role.

His successor, U Thant, realised soon after solidifying his position that there existed great potential for the Secretariat, in general, and for the Secretary-General, in particular, to take the lead role in re-shaping the UN. True, there was a fair degree of politicking going on even within the Secretariat, particularly in the staffing function of UN administration, but there was still room for a dynamic Secretary-General to make a difference. This much was quite evident from Hammarskjold's experience as Secretary-General, and U Thant intended to make sure that he did not fall behind in doing his best for the organisation. As such, he took some steps along the lines of restructuring the UN. During his ten-year tenure, the General Assembly acted on his proposal to form a committee of experts to consider ways of increasing UN efficiency and effectiveness, and various special committees charged with recommending reforms have been established since.

U Thant's tenure is best characterised by an upsurge in the number of members of the UN that came from the poor Third World. This meant that the previous sentiments that reigned in the UN were no longer the only operative ones. All of a sudden, the immense economic and social problems that were at the core of these countries began to dominate the UN debates. One such forum where these concerns were naturally aired was the ECOSOC which underwent severe pressures to change accordingly. It ultimately did (in the increase in its membership) but, more to the point, this increase in the membership of the Third World countries in the UN also meant that new agencies were created to account for the concerns of these countries. Hence, agencies such as UNDP (in 1965) and UNIDO (in 1966) were created which tended to reduce the prominence of the ECOSOC.

The mid-1960s is an important period in the UN. For some time then, countries such as France and the Soviet Union had refused to pay their share of peacekeeping expenses in the Congo.[3] This led to somewhat of a crisis in the UN (which at that time faced a $100 million deficit created by the peacekeeping operations in the Congo and in the Middle East), and this is said to be the genesis in many ways of the present-day financial crisis of the UN. In that context, U Thant had gone along with the General Assembly's proposal to form in 1965 an ad hoc committee of experts to examine the finances of the UN and the specialised agencies (also called the Committee of Fourteen). A year later, the Committee submitted its proposed measures (52 recommendations in all) to deal with the non-payment issue. The countries still refused to pay, however. Luckily for the organisation, it was able to tide over that particular problem (by floating bonds) but it was to come back to haunt the UN in later years. At the time that this happened, it was the US that chastised the member states for not paying their due share to the organisation. In what is known as the Goldberg Reservation, the US delegate to the UN then stated that if some countries could insist on making an exception on financial responsibilities to certain activities, then the US reserved the same right to do so in the future.[4]

On the management side, member states realised that unless there was a strong and independent body to inspect the activities and processes of the organisation, efficiency might suffer irrevocably. As such, in 1966, the Joint Inspection Unit (JIU) was established (at first, on an experimental basis and made permanent in 1978).[5] The

JIU is composed of 11 inspectors who are officials of the UN but are not its staff members. The office is located in Geneva and it is supposed to be given considerable latitude to investigate the activities of the UN. It has turned out, however, that the JIU may not be as independent as hoped for.[6] At any rate, the JIU has since then played a rather key role in identifying areas where the organisation could be made more efficient. With capable people like Maurice Bertrand involved in it for a long time, it has made considerable progress in areas related to recruitment of personnel, adoption of medium-term plans and programme budgets, of monitoring and evaluation of programmes, etc. The problem has been that not much has been done by the agencies concerned to follow up on the JIU reports. The JIU has the key functions of investigating all matters that relate to the efficiency of the organisation, and pursuant to that, of proposing reforms in any area that it considers relevant to the enhancement of efficiency. Concerned agencies are then to work on the reports and inform the General Assembly of how they proceeded to deal with the issues.

In 1968, U Thant had felt it necessary to reorganise the Secretariat to make it more attuned to the task of taking a lead role in the management of the rising number of programmes that were being sanctioned by the General Assembly. The Committee on the Reorganisation of the Secretariat (also known as the Committee of Seven) was a direct product of this realisation. In its report, the Committee focused on several themes: grading up top-level posts, establishing a new post of an Under Secretary-General for Administration and Management (a post that exists to this day and that plays a key role in the internal management of the UN Secretariat), reducing the number of conferences and meetings (a point taken up by other Secretaries-General that followed U Thant, with the probable exception of Boutros-Ghali who clearly stated that he was for emphasising such conferences), and instituting a long-term plan for recruitment and equitable geographical distribution of staff posts.

It was also during U Thant's tenure that the much talked about Jackson Report[7] was prepared (in 1969). The Report has been described as the most serious proposal of reform of the UN economic development system until the proposals of Maurice Bertrand or those of Erskine Childers and Brian Urquhart (Baratta (1995: 347)). The Report called for a comprehensive overhaul of all facets of activities of the key UN agencies related to economic development, and the creation of a UN Staff College to train career personnel.[8] The Report was promptly opposed by the specialised agencies who felt that it called for too much power to be given to the ECOSOC and its subsidiary organs. Designed primarily to focus on issues of development, the Report sought to make UNDP the central coordinating body for technical cooperation, and a source for channelling voluntary funds to specialised agencies. While not all of Jackson's proposals saw the light of day, UNDP has continued to play a dominant role in the area of technical assistance. Its role, however, has tended to diminish as its resource base has shrunk faster than that of the specialised agencies.

3.2 THE 1970s AND 1980s

When Kurt Waldheim took over the helm of the UN in January 1972, the Cold War was still raging and there was just as much evidence of bipolarity as before. By the end of his tenure, this would change (albeit only marginally) and there would be some signs of a softening up of the rivalry. But in the initial stages of his tenure, the situation in terms of superpower cooperation was still rather bleak. The 1975 Soyuz-Salyut joint mission in space and the Helsinki accords would denote somewhat of a thaw in US-USSR relations, but that was still a good three to four years down the road.

The financial situation of the UN continued to bother the leadership, and the General Assembly in 1972 agreed to form a special committee to assess it (the so-called Committee of Fifteen). Its reports did not much change the financial situation of the UN although the magnitude of the problem was hardly as severe as it is now. In 1974, the General Assembly finally approved a number of recommendations made in the 1971 JIU report on personnel problems related to the professional category and higher. These recommendations dealt with defining a staff structure for the Secretariat, and putting in place a new promotion scheme, a training programme, and various other management-related measures. Two years later, however, the JIU had been vexed over the delay in getting a timetable in place for implementing all the reform proposals.

A distinct trend by that time was the rising strindency of calls by the poor Third World countries for various changes not only in the UN but also in the wider global arena as well. In the mid-1970s, there was a call for the creation of a New International Economic Order (NIEO), and there was also a distinct alignment evident in the General Assembly of poor countries voting against the US and on a more pro-Soviet Union line. This, coupled with the 1975 General Assembly declaration of the "Zionism as a form of racism" resolution did nothing to endear the organisation to the West, particularly the US. The-then US Ambassador to the UN, Daniel Patrick Moynihan, was so enraged with the organisation that his book on his experiences in that body is titled *On Dangerous Ground.*[9] The true disenchantment that the US eventually felt toward the UN has its genesis in these troubled early and mid-1970s. By the time Jimmy Carter became President in 1977, and he brought in the mild-mannered Andrew Young to be his UN Ambassador, the US, it could be said, was beginning to tune out the UN for all practical purposes.

Notwithstanding that, and the repeated US opposition to various proposals brought in by the Third World countries, in 1975 a group of 25 experts (known as the Group of Experts on the Structure of the UN System) delivered a report titled "A New UN Structure for Global Economic Cooperation" which recommended, among other things, institutionalisation of consultative procedures to achieve consensus on controversial issues, and a revitalisation of the ECOSOC. This report, for its part, eventually led in 1977 to the report of the Ad Hoc Committee on the Restructuring of the Economic and Social Sectors of the UN system (also known as the Committee of the Whole or the Dadzie Committee). The report dealt primarily with ways to improve the activities of the ECOSOC. As a result of the Ad Hoc Committee report, the post of a Director-General for Development and International Economic Cooperation was established and the person filling the post then not only chaired the ECOSOC sessions but also took the lead role in ensuring international cooperation on matters of development. This was strongly demanded by the Third World states, and for its own political ends, was supported by the Soviet Union (the post was eventually abolished by Boutros-Ghali in 1992).

Back in 1974 and 1975, the UN had also undergone some reviews on the personnel side of operations, and in 1975 the International Civil Service Commission (ICSC) was established although discussions for such a body had been going on for a very long time. The ICSC has since then been weakened considerably by staff disenchantment (for example, for not instituting measures to enhance staff welfare). To outsiders, however, the ICSC stands as a monolithic agency that repeatedly thwarts efforts at curtailing staff benefits as part of any reform effort. These and other issues as well as efforts at institutional reform in the UN in the 1970s are lucidly described and analysed by Meltzer (1978).

Waldheim, for his part, was acutely aware that the organisational processes were getting more and more bureaucratic and made some effort to stem the tide. For instance, he consistently argued for savings through fewer meetings, and a reduction in the flood of documents in the organisation. He also called for fiscal restraint but the General Assembly kept on voting new programmes and more budgets and, in many ways, that contributed measurably to the financial woes evident in the late 1980s and 1990s. However, given the global context in which he was serving as Secretary-General, he was always under pressure to appoint people recommended by influential member states and consequently during his tenure the number of high-level jobs in the UN increased by 25 percent. Waldheim also used these appointments as a way of currying favours from the member states.[10]

Toward the end of Waldheim's tenure, in 1980, the General Assembly established a rather high-sounding Committee of Governmental Experts to Evaluate the Present Structure of the Secretariat in the Administrative, Finance, and Personnel Areas. Its 17 members were appointed by the Secretary-General. The Committee, however, after noting some of the positive steps that had been taken to enhance the administrative and managerial aspects of the Secretariat made no specific recommendations.

By the time Javier Perez de Cuellar took over from Waldheim in January 1982, Ronald Reagan had already been elected President of the US. Reagan came to the White Office with a very clear conservative agenda one of whose components was a rather critical look at the role played by international organisations. Independent of what was happening at the UN in terms of reforms, the Reagan team had more or less decided to go slow on supporting the organisation for it did not see much utility of supporting an organisation that came across so clearly as being virulently anti-US. His nomination of Jeanne Kirkpatrick as the Ambassador to the UN did not send any comforting signals to the leadership of the UN nor to the Third World countries who continued to look to the UN as a ready source of help for their economic and social woes.

The dominant focus of the organisation (at least in the General Assembly) continued to be on economic and social development[11] while the Secretariat worried more about how best to position itself in the work of the organisation. Starting in 1981 and continuing throughout Cuellar's tenure, reform proposals related to coordination problems of the various agencies of the UN abounded. For this, the International Civil Service Commission (ICSC) and the Joint Staff Pension Board (JSPB) were asked to develop particular activities in that field. But once again, it was the ECOSOC that dominated the headlines in terms of reform efforts in the area of structures. Given the increasingly important issue of economic development in the world at that time, it was but natural that the ECOSOC be at the core of the reform efforts. Starting from the 1981 UNITAR Policy and Efficacy Studies series, and ending with the disappointing performance of the Special Commission of the ECOSOC in 1987, Cuellar's tenure was taken up by much soul-searching on the role of the ECOSOC.

To propel the reform process further within the Secretariat, and largely to stem the rising tide of criticism from the conservative bulldogs in the US, Cuellar in 1983 established a high-level advisory group on administrative reform with the mandate to study areas where changes could be made. This was followed a year later with the Office of Personnel Services (now known as the Office of Human Resource Management (OHRM)) setting up a task force to develop a systematic approach to career development in the UN pursuant to the recommendations of the ICSC and the JIU. As a result of the recommendations of the groups, Cuellar was happy to introduce several changes in the Secretariat, including instituting a staff incentive programme, upgrading the automated processing systems in the personnel and financial areas, and streamlining procedures to control official travel. Such administrative reform efforts were clearly made with an eye to the rising criticism that was being heard from the US, in particular the Heritage Foundation.

By 1984, the Heritage Foundation had set its sights on the UN and would not let go until its barrage of severe criticism (most of which continues to this day) forced Reagan to stand up and take real notice about what was said to be happening at the UN. In 1984, Burton Yale Pines at the Heritage Foundation edited a book titled *A*

World Without the United Nations in which he hammered home the point that the UN was a wasteful place, and that US tax dollars were financing all the waste. The Heritage Foundation fired several strong salvos[12] during the Reagan years and was successful in getting the US, at a maximum, to withdraw from some UN organisations (such as UNESCO, ILO, etc.) and at a minimum, to coalesce US demands for a lower scale of assessments and lower levels of support to the UN main body. The Foundation has not stopped its attacks on the UN, however. Even after the departure of Reagan as President in 1988, it was busy publishing critical studies of the organisation. In 1988 itself, as a matter of fact, the Heritage Foundation publicised the highly-critical *The United Nations: Its Problems and What to Do About Them* (Heritage Foundation (1988)).

The Foundation had support for its positions not only within the Executive branch of the US government but in Congress as well. The legislators, in turn, frustrated over not having a greater say in assigning programme priorities and formulating budgets at the UN, unilaterally gave conditions to the UN for continued US support. In 1985, Senators Nancy Kassebaum (Republican from the State of Kansas) and Gerald Solomon (Republican from the State of New York) hammered through an Amendment[13] in the US Senate on the State Department authorisation bill which can be considered to be the apex at that time of the resentment being felt in the US against the UN.

UN member states obviously criticised the Kassebaum-Solomon Amendment for unilaterally attempting to institute a system that mimicked that of the Bretton Woods institutions, and in that process seek to wrest control of the UN and take away from the equality characteristic of the UN. They argued that member states were under legal obligation to pay what they were assessed and which had been formally and legally agreed upon. They called the US thinking on this issue the *à la carte* approach to funding – paying for what they liked and refusing others. But the US refused to budge on this, and the enactment of the Kassebaum-Solomon Amendment, combined with a shortfall in appropriations over several years in the mid-1980s, brought the UN to the brink of insolvency. But the US had not exactly set a precedent here by attaching conditions to the payment of its assessments; that dubious honour goes to the Soviets and the French for refusing to pay their share of assessments for the UN peace missions to the Congo in the early 1960s, and to several

Arab countries for doing the same in relation to the missions in the Middle East.

The incessant attacks of the Heritage Foundation, and the sympathetic ear that the Foundation found in the conservative Presidents, had manifested in an anti-UN rhetoric that only served to marginalise the organisation in the US. As such, by the mid-1980s, the organisation was in limbo: not only had bipolarity eroded any semblance of impact of the UN, but the largest contributor to its budget was also undergoing a serious review of its own continued association with the body (as a matter of fact, the fact that the US actually withdrew from UNESCO and ILO only aggravated the situation). In this environment, Cuellar had to steer the international organisation towards having more relevance and clout.

Related to the decision of the US to show less support to the UN, in 1985 Olof Palme, as Prime Minister of Sweden, presented a proposal to the General Assembly that secured significant support among the members. It was to place a ceiling on the contribution of any member state, with consequential adjustments in the assessments of other member countries with a capacity to pay. The proposal made a lot of sense since that way neither the US could complain of being asked to share a larger portion of the burden nor could the UN be made hostage to the internal politics of a powerful member state. Related proposals on this issue have come from Cuellar himself who had proposed a level of 20 or 15 percent as a ceiling, and from Aga Khan and Maurice Strong at ten percent.[14] The middle-income states would then share a considerably larger portion of the UN burden. But while all these proposals had the tacit approval of the US, other member states (particularly the middle-income and other high-income countries) refused to endorse them since that would mean that they would end up having to pay much more than their present levels.

Spurred by the apparent venom of the Kassebaum-Solomon Amendment and its implications for the future of UN operations, Japan proposed – and the General Assembly accepted in December 1985 – the creation of the Group of High-Level Intergovernmental Experts to Review the Efficiency of the Administrative and Financial Functioning of the UN. This body of experts, better known as the Group of Eighteen, was formed largely as a result of the concerns of major donor nations about the credibility gap of the ECOSOC. The Group, for its part, complained about the complexity of organisational structures, the number of conferences, the oversized secretariats (in particular, the proliferation of Under Secretary-General and Assistant Secretary-General posts), and the unfavourable structure of organs and subsidiary organs. However, the Group failed to reach consensus on a reform plan for the planning and budgeting mechanisms although it recommended other administration-related measures[15] designed to streamline the organisation and also to continue to show to its critics that the UN was serious about implementing reforms.

By hindsight, the Group of Eighteen was a very serious reform effort during the Cuellar years. The fact that Japan, a strong supporter of the UN both financially and otherwise, had recommended the Committee lent it a considerable degree of legitimacy and import.[16] The Group of Eighteen worked for five years focusing on several areas of reform. Its work ended in 1990 when the General Assembly considered and approved the final assessment and implementation of the reform efforts (for a detailed look at the work of the Group, including the contributions of the various UN representatives to the debate, see Muller (1992)).

It needs to be mentioned at this juncture that the initial impetus for the current round of budgetary reform came in the early 1980s when Western industrialised countries were becoming increasingly resistant to what they perceived as out-of-control budgets at the UN. In their view, a new Third World majority in the UN General Assembly, where each state has one vote, had been setting the program priorities and advancing the budgets to go with them.

Parallel to the resentment against the UN in the US, within the UN itself a few supporters began to come forward with far-sighted ideas on how best to steer the UN so that countries such as the US would begin to see more relevance in it. In 1985, the opening salvo came from a very experienced UN-hand, Maurice Bertrand, whose *Some Reflections on Reform of the United Nations* (as a report of the JIU) generated considerable attention. Bertrand is probably one of only a handful of people that have gained worldwide respect as a knowledgeable scholar, practitioner, and supporter of the UN. Among some of his suggestions made in that report were to make the UN a more economic body (for this, he wanted to restructure the parts that dealt with the economic functions of the UN and transfer them to regional levels); and to create an Economic Security Council to replace the ECOSOC and UNCTAD. He also proposed that much of the UN work be farmed out to regional associations (a theme later picked up with gusto by Boutros-Ghali). His proposals generated attention but the lack of political will among member states in the UN prevented the proposals from being anything more than excellent academic arguments. Many of his arguments have since been re-hashed into other proposals but the bulk of what Bertrand proposed in the mid-1980s has tended to lose its momentum now although he has had occasions to pound on similar themes in the years since. Of note is his 1989 book *The Third Generation World Organisation* which is considered to be a path-breaker in this area.

In the same year (i.e., 1985), a second set of proposals came from Marc Nerfin who focused more on the issue of representation of the people in the UN (through a three-tier Assembly structure: one for governments (as now), one for businesses (such as MNCs), and one for civil society). But he did not go much into the details of the relationships in this tripartite arrangement. The Commission on Global Governance later on picked up on some of these themes of popular representation. It has been a popular refrain of academics now to call for a Parliamentary Assembly as a corollary to the presently-constituted General Assembly. It is an idealistic proposition and not likely to be put into practice even though it is appealing on paper. The UN was created to be a meeting place of states and not of individuals.

By the UN's 40th anniversary, it was increasingly clear that the organisation needed prompt attention to structural reform. There were too many bodies operating in the economic and social fields because the General Assembly and the ECOSOC had a penchant for creating subsidiary bodies at whim. Stemming from the findings of the Group of Eighteen, the General Assembly in 1987 established the Special Commission of the ECOSOC on the In-depth Study of the UN Intergovernmental Structure and Functioning in the Economic and Social Fields. This Commission did analyse quite thoroughly the issues that were plaguing the ECOSOC then and also sought to upgrade the importance of the ECOSOC's activities as a coordinating organ. But in the end, the state representatives in the Commission failed to agree on recommendations as well as a common report.

At the heart of the disagreement to plague the Special Commission's work, and an issue that is prevalent to this day, is the debate on just how to go about giving the ECOSOC the major role that it apparently deserves to coordinate activities in economic and social affairs. The poorer countries have all along felt that the ECOSOC does not have as much power as the Security Council, and they would like the ECOSOC to have more teeth. In particular, the Group of 77 has called for an increase in the membership of the ECOSOC while the developed countries have opposed this and, in turn, have wanted to streamline the intergovernmental bodies associated with the ECOSOC.

Before that, however, even by mid-1980s, it had been quite obvious that the organisation had not been able to meet the expectations of the member states (neither of the poor Third World countries in terms of economic and social development, nor of the rich countries of the North in terms of international peace and security and internal UN reforms). The financial situation of the UN had also been quite untenable and there was a widespread feeling that something needed to be done to get the organisation on an even keel.

1986 is considered to be a watershed year in the history of the UN since for the first time the Secretary-General and the General Assembly decided to apply cost-reduction measures across the board (i.e., in capital expenditures, staff resources, as well as programme activities). The member states slowly began to accept the fact that the financial crisis was finally on them, and visibly stung by the enormity of the Kassebaum-Solomon Amendment, they realised that a very fundamental assessment of how the UN was to be reformed was essential. Cuellar's report to the General Assembly that year brought out in stark terms the fact that the UN was confronted by financial problems of such magnitude that they were bound to have profound implications for the viability of the organisation. He felt that management improvement and reinstating regard for obligations as stated in the UN Charter were the only means of reversing the situation.

Realising that it needed to get its act together if the organisation was to be successful in meeting its mandates, and pressed by the fact that the Americans were withholding their dues, the 41st General Assembly in 1986 passed a reform package that, among other things, called upon member states to reach consensus at each step of the budget process. This was a significant victory for the US for gaining consensus meant taking into consideration its views as well. This gave some room for the US to exercise more effective leverage over UN functions because unless a budget agreement was reached, the USA could make the process come to a halt until such a consensus was indeed achieved. The US, for its part, expressed satisfaction at this arrangement although it would have still preferred outright the weighted voting system. Incidentally, this reform effort enabled Reagan in September 1988 to call for the payment of arrears accumulated under the Kassebaum-Solomon withholdings. By the early 1990s, most UN specialised agencies had also adopted consensus-based budgeting procedures.

The same General Assembly reform package – possibly the most comprehensive offered to that point by the UN itself and based entirely on the Group of Eighteen recommendations – made over 70 proposals which included a call for cutbacks in staff, for reducing the top-heavy structure of the Secretariat, for reducing the number of UN meetings, and for better coordination of the work of numerous Secretariat departments dealing with social and economic affairs. By 1987, some semblance of the financial reality became evident at the UN when under pressure from its largest contributors, the General Assembly approved the first zero-real growth programme budget permitting adjustments for inflation but prohibiting new programme expenses without reductions to offset them.

Also in 1987, John Renninger put forth various suggestions on improving the UN system.[17] His ideas are rather relevant to the discussion at hand and are thus brought up here. In his article, he put primary emphasis on two key aspects of UN work: the ECOSOC and the international civil service. Interestingly, some of his ideas on the ECOSOC (such as having it focus more on specific key issues only) have been taken up by Annan in his current reform proposals. Likewise, his proposals on the international civil service and efforts to revamp it have reached sympathetic ears a full decade later. Renninger, for instance, had called for reviewing the competence of every UN staff member every five years and for the establishment of a Staff Training Centre to enhance the KSAs (knowledge, skills, and abilities) of the staff members. As will be evident later on, Annan's proposals on staffing issues are surprisingly close to these.

In 1987, the United Nations Association of the USA (UNA-USA) formulated major ideas on new directions the UN could be taking and its work is considered to be key in the organisation's reform process (see, e.g., UNA-USA (1987)). The study not only dug up old themes but also ventured into new territories in relation to UN reforms and has been used as a benchmark to assess the current reform proposals put forth by Annan.

In 1990, Urquhart and Childers came up with their well-thought out *A World in Need of Leadership*[18] which recommended two key things: (a) improving the quality and image of the UN bureaucracy, and (b) focusing on the financing of the UN system. Brian Urquhart and Erskine Childers, two old hands of the UN, have done much work on the issue of UN reforms, and their 1990 study was complemented by several others (many under the aegis of the Dag Hammarskjold Library in Sweden). Annan, for his part, has picked up these same themes as well in his own reform efforts.

Also in the early 1990s, the US focused attention on the need for a better-managed UN and advanced initiatives to establish an auditing unit at the UN to root out alleged bureaucratic waste and abuse. Following extensive negotiations with other member states, the Office of Internal Oversight Services was established in 1994. A gradual decline in the UN's personnel levels has also taken place, although critics disagree on the magnitude of reductions. Finally, calls by various countries to better consolidate the Secretariat's work in social and economic development are now being acted upon.

After the 1990 and 1991 General Assembly sessions, there were also some structural changes that were implemented to streamline the organisation's functions. These included in 1990 the amalgamation of the three pre-existing drug bodies into the UN Drugs Control Programme (UNDCP), and following the 1991 General Assembly session, the establishment of the Department of Humanitarian Affairs to coordinate all activities related to humanitarian assistance.

Finally, mention needs to be made here of the Nordic UN Project related to UN reforms. The project was started in 1989 when four Nordic countries (Denmark, Finland, Norway, and Sweden) got together to assess how to make the UN more effective. The Project Report[19] came out only in 1991 and in it the Nordic countries focused primarily on the economic and social fields and argued for reforming the management structure as well as the system in place for financing development operations. Similar to Bertrand's proposal on an Economic Security Council, it called for a central level body (the International Development Council) to coordinate the economic functions of the UN. It also proposed a three-tier funding alternative to the current dues and assessment structure which was to include voluntary contributions, assessed contributions, and negotiated pledges (i.e., the commitment from countries to fund the organisation but one based on negotiations as to the exact level). It is of interest that Annan has directly picked up this theme, but the proposal has been critiqued thus far and is not likely to go further unless the US relents on the funding mechanism.

The Nordic Report probably went the furthest in terms of generating widespread interest in having the UN reformed. Given that the Nordic countries were behind the proposal (and given that they are some of the staunchest supporters of the UN), there was less animosity towards their proposals from all quarters. It also obviously helped that their report also took to task the donor countries for the state of UN affairs and more or less refrained from pointing fingers at the UN's bureaucracy and staff incompetence for the organisation's ills.

In that regard, then, when the Nordic countries presented their report to the Secretary-General in May 1991, and then to the General Assembly in October 1992, there was widespread optimism. In the end, however, in June 1993, Boutros-Ghali informed the ECOSOC that negotiations on various components of the Nordic Project had failed to yield anything. This clearly showed that the UN as a body was not able to come up with any meaningful consensus on any matter of substance.[20]

It was during the tail end of Cuellar's tenure as Secretary-General of the UN that there appeared a major fault-line in the organisation with the winds of change emanating from the-then Soviet Union. Gorbachev's open-door and reform policies of *perestroika* and *glasnost*, for example, had enabled the Soviet Union to be more flexible and understanding of the West's position on many issues. The demise of communism in the erstwhile Soviet Union, and the consequent end of bipolarity in the UN, brought about monumental shifts in the thinking of how international institutions such as the UN were to be reformatted to absorb the altered global political economy. To be precise, other inter-governmental organisations (primarily the North Atlantic Treaty Organisation, NATO) went through the same exercise.

3.3 BOUTROS-GHALI'S TENURE

It was during Boutros-Ghali's tenure that the UN underwent frequent spasms of introspection. The public debate on the UN and its role in maintaining international peace, security, and development waxed and waned from the heady initial days of post-Cold War cooperation to the bitter departure of a Secretary-General who was considered by many to be the most respected UN leader since Hammarskjold. While the US argued that it was Boutros-Ghali that had come to symbolise the major stumbling block that was hindering genuine UN reforms, he did indeed make a strong effort to renew the UN and some of his proposals (such as linkages with regional multilateral organisations for maintenance of regional security) merit further focus. During Boutros-Ghali's tenure, there was also considerable external focus on the UN, primarily related to financing, and discussions on reforming the organisation were done in the context of – and largely driven by – the financial problems being faced by the organisation.

At the time that the Nordic Project report came out, there was much optimism in the UN. It was riding a high of successes and unprecedented cooperation among the members (as evidenced by the solidarity shown in the Gulf War). When Boutros-Ghali took over in January 1992, he was asked by the Security Council to give his ideas on matters of peace and security and the UN's role in it. This turned out to be the much-talked about *Agenda for Peace* report which laid down clearly what the new Secretary-General thought should be the focus of the UN. Taking advantage of the opportunity of the high level of cooperation among member states, the Secretary-General used the *Agenda for Peace* report to call for many changes in the manner in which the Security Council did its job in the area of international peace and security. These were not fundamental structural changes but did manage to raise some eyebrows when the document was released in 1992.

Within a year or so of taking over as Secretary-General, and clearly in need for some quick action to demonstrate to his supporters and detractors alike that he was intent upon revitalising the UN, Boutros-Ghali took into further consideration the proposals made by his predecessor to remedy the financial situation of the UN. Of the three that were made, the only one Boutros-Ghali could implement was that concerning creation of a $50 million

Humanitarian Revolving Fund to be used in emergencies. The other two (charging interest on overdue assessments as well as authorisation to the Secretary-General to borrow commercially, and establishment of a UN Peace Endowment Fund) did not muster enough support.

He also responded promptly to the call of the member states to initiate various administrative reforms and undertook some changes in the UN Secretariat, the organ over which the Secretary-General exercises direct control. One of his initiatives resulted in better coordination of the preventive diplomacy, peacekeeping, humanitarian, and human rights aspects of the Secretariat's work. Boutros-Ghali's reorganisation plan merged a plethora of units into six departments, and to monitor the peacekeeping operations around the world, he subsequently established an around-the-clock communications centre at New York Headquarters. He also suppressed about 14 Assistant Secretaries-General and Under Secretaries-General posts in the Secretariat, and was able to cut the number of deputies reporting directly to him to eight from 30. This was designed to show that he was serious about downsizing the organisation. In all this, he was credited with taking a "bolder step in the consolidation and streamlining of Secretariat activities than had ever been taken before" (Wilenski (1993: 452)).

In 1992, and timed fully to take advantage the mood of cooperation evident among the powers of the UN, the UNDP, through its *Human Development Report* (HDR), came up with some very drastic proposals for changes in the UN. In the area of financial and economic reforms, it called for the creation of a central World Bank in charge of a common currency, a merger of GATT (which since 1995 is the World Trade Organisation) and UNCTAD into an International Trade Organisation, and an imposition of several taxes (such as a world income tax and a tax on the environment). Not too many people paid much attention to these proposals not only because they were too bold but primarily because the focus seemed to be on getting more revenues to the UN's coffers rather than altering the management style of the organisation (something the donor countries had been insisting upon).[21]

One such key donor – Japan – fully aware of its rising status not only in the UN but also around the world, had begun to show greater interest on the issue of reforms since it figured to be a key player in any major changes in the UN. Though the following report did not originate in the Government, the Japan Economic Research Council published in April 1992 a report prepared by independent consultants titled *To Think about a Grand Design of the World: In Search of a Better Human Survival* (see Uchida (1999: 81)). The report made some very revolutionary suggestions such as dismantling the ECOSOC and the Trusteeship Council. Obviously, the proposals did not go very far but it might be relevant for all members to note that given Japan's rising contributions to the UN (and paid in time too), what it says might be worth giving a fair hearing.

1992 was also the year that Boutros-Ghali's *Agenda for Peace* report was released with considerable fanfare. When it was released, it generated considerable debate on just how the UN was to go forward from that point (largely to take the existing sense of cooperation among the great powers to its maximum). The *Agenda for Peace* report focused on the specific issues of improving preventive diplomacy, and areas related to peacekeeping.[22] It was becoming increasingly clear that the UN would have to be more involved in the peace and security aspect of its mandate, and since there were many such operations that were being recommended, a blueprint had to be in place that would guide action on this issue.

While the *Agenda for Peace* report did not call for any structural changes, it did focus on strengthening the existing organs (e.g., encouraging greater consensus in the Security Council), and it called for greater UN cooperation with regional agencies. Boutros-Ghali felt that this not only could lighten the burden of the Security Council but could also contribute to a greater sense of participation among member states in international affairs.[23] It is important to note that Boutros-Ghali also identified the key role of the international civil servant in any effective functioning of the organisation.

The *Agenda for Peace* report is significant for putting on the table the issues related to financing of the organisation. Given that he still had considerable sympathy in the UN, in general, and the Security Council, in particular, Boutros-Ghali had the luxury of propounding his ideas on many issues that were relevant to the UN, and financing was obviously key. In the *Agenda for Peace* report, he reiterated what Cuellar had tried to hammer in during his ten-year tenure to no avail. These proposals deserve mention here because some of them are controversial and some are very sound.

The first proposal was a set of ideas on how to deal with the cash flow problem in the organisation. Ideas included charging interest in the overdue amounts of assessed contributions, and authorising the Secretary-General to borrow commercially (both clearly over-reaching the powers of the Secretary-General). Other ideas included increasing the Working Capital Fund of the UN to a level of a quarter of a billion dollars, and establishing a temporary peacekeeping reserve fund. All these ideas were based on the premise that the Secretary-General needed flexibility and quick access to resources to undertake all the functions that were entrusted to the organisation.

Another proposal was to create a Peace Endowment Fund (PEF) with an initial target of a billion dollars. In and of itself, that proposal would not have created a stir. It was just that Boutros-Ghali stated that the funding for the PEF would. come not only from voluntary and assessed contributions from member states but also from contributions from the private sector. The goals of the Fund were noble indeed but the method of funds collection did appear as unorthodox. The fact that the UN would accept contributions from individuals would open up a Pandora's Box of concerns and the member states were not willing to consider that option.

Other ideas in matters of financing (such as some form of international tax, for instance, on arms trade, futures trading, use of airspace, etc.) were also broached but the discussion on this has been muted for a long time predominantly because the United States is very opposed to such resource-generating sources. What is clear from the *Agenda for Peace* report is that the tenure of Boutros-Ghali was overshadowed by his constant need to request funding for the increased activities of the UN. A quick reading of the report reveals that Boutros-Ghali then sought to put some form of mild pressure on the delinquent nations by stating that steps to generate public awareness and support for assuring financial security would be heightened.

The release of the *Agenda for Peace* report generated considerable interest at that time (although the Security Council only agreed to take it into consideration rather than seriously discuss the implementation of the proposals contained in it).[24] Boutros-Ghali must have been perturbed for he had prepared the report on the suggestion of the Security Council, and yet only France among the permanent five members voiced strong support for his proposals.[25]

There were several rejoinders though to the *Agenda for Peace* report, and once such complement was put forth by the-then Australian Minister of Foreign Affairs, Gareth Evans. In his *Cooperating for Peace* report (1993), Evans put forward numerous ideas which while appealing did not really catch the fancy of the powers in the UN. He had, for instance, called for the establishment of a system of four Deputy Secretaries-General with each one responsible for a different area of UN operations (peace and security, economic and social development, humanitarian affairs, and administration and management) so that the Secretary-General himself would be free to be more involved in preventive diplomacy activities. Evans focused also on the need for the UN to beef up its preventive diplomacy and dispute resolution functions with the establishment of a Peace and Security Resources Centre. His idea on using regional organisations was echoed by Boutros-Ghali numerous times and is even now a favourite topic of UN officials.

With the release of the 1992 report on *Agenda for Peace*, there was indeed pressure – although not overt – on Boutros-Ghali to come up with something similar in the area of development. Partly in response to that, and partly to stem the rapidly deteriorating funding situation – and loss of confidence in the UN – Boutros-Ghali in 1993 invited member states to submit their opinions on the restructuring of the Security Council and did receive nearly 100 replies from individual states as well as regional groups. These suggestions formed part of his feedback process for reform ideas and he also drew from the ECOSOC and the Group of Experts convened by the President of the 1993 General Assembly Session to come up with his *Agenda for Development* report in 1994.

The report clearly drew a link between peace and security and development (and in that process, neatly brought together the two reports). The document was lucid on many counts and equally evasive on others.[26] In the main, it focused on giving voice to the people themselves in the decision-making processes related to development. Most of the proposals contained in the *Agenda for Development* report called for greater policy coherence and coordination among the various agencies and organs involved in the economic and social fields. Part of this coherence was to be generated by relying on the UNDP and its system of Resident Coordinators in the Field Offices (this is incidentally one of the cores of the Annan reform agenda as well). Boutros-Ghali's preoccupation with involving the ECOSOC was evident in this report as well and he proposed to revitalise it.

Despite Boutros-Ghali's best efforts, by 1992-end – a mere 12 months into his tenure – it appeared that his honeymoon with the US had effectively ended. *The Washington Post* that year (20-23 September 1992) published a four-part series written by members of *The Washington Post* Foreign News Service titled *The UN Empire* that was very hard-hitting and that may nor may not have contained all the truths about how things got done in the global organisation. But the reports had the effect of coalescing public opinion against the UN, and the euphoria of great power cooperation and camaraderie in the UN evident just before and during the Gulf War was effectively over.

In the meantime, there was considerable attention drawn to the report filed by Dick Thornburgh in 1993 on the issue of UN management reform. Thornburgh had been hoisted upon the UN by the US (in turn as demanded by the US Congress) in the capacity of Under Secretary-General for Administration and Management. Thornburgh's report was scathing and was so controversial that it has never been officially released by the UN.[27] In the report, Thornburgh seems to have taken a magnifying glass and identified sources of waste and inefficiency. This was coupled with documentation of non-functional procedures, bureaus, etc. of the UN. He also asserted that the UN totally lacked any effective means to deal with fraud, waste, and abuse by staff members. Thornburgh had to leave the UN for reasons of internal politics and, according to UN critics, the work that he started there has not been taken up with such critical gusto since then.

1993 was also the year when an independent advisory group co-chaired by Shijuro Ogata of Japan and the well-respected American Paul Volcker, under the aegis of the Ford Foundation, presented a number of constructive recommendations for a more effective financing of the United Nations. Ogata and Volcker addressed the flaws of the existing assessment system and called for, among other things, that dues be paid quarterly with provisions being made for interest to be charged on unpaid amounts, that the size of the Working Capital Fund (WCF) be increased to $400 million, and that three-year averages of GDP be used to calculate dues (at present, it is six years). With the exception of the proposals of the Working

Capital Fund and the calculation ratios, the others are not even on the discussion table seven years after they were made.

One group that did voice strong support for the Ogata-Volcker proposal on the WCF was the United States Commission on Improving the Effectiveness of the United Nations that published a report in September 1993 and that made some very far-reaching proposals for reforms. Among others, it supported creating a rapid reaction force, reactivating the Military Staff Committee in the Security Council, and enlarging the Council in terms of membership. However, with the Republican onslaught on Capitol Hill a year later, the Commission's Report was quickly overtaken by events.

Also starting in 1993, the General Assembly set up the following five working groups to seek agreement on reforms:

(1) Working Group on the Questions of Equitable Representation on and Increase in the Membership of the Security Council and Other Matters Related to the Security Council – Created in 1993, this Group has been examining proposals for increases in permanent and non-permanent seats in the Security Council, the regional rotation of permanent seats, and the use of the veto. Its work is politically charged and even as of 2000, it had not been able to agree upon any substantive measure on Security Council reform.

(2) Working Group on *Agenda for Development* – Created in 1994, this ad-hoc open-ended working group was able to come up with some consensus on how the UN should proceed with work on the *Agenda for Development* report presented by Boutros-Ghali in 1994. Its work was hampered somewhat by the lack of enthusiasm showed by many donor nations.

(3) Working Group on *Agenda for Peace* – As follow-up to the proposals made by Boutros-Ghali in his 1992 *Agenda for Peace* report, this open-ended working group has worked on reviewing suggestions for strengthening the UN's peacekeeping capacities and has submitted resolutions to the General Assembly to improve preventive diplomacy and early-warning capabilities. Many other subgroups on specific aspects of such issues as post-conflict peace-building, and the use of sanctions, are still working on a consensus on how the UN should proceed on this issue.

(4) Working Group on the Financial Situation of the UN – This open-ended working group was established in 1994 to address the long-standing financial crisis caused by non-payment of dues by member states. Given the insistence of the US on the lowering of its

scale of assessments, and given the lack of consensus on this issue among the Group members, discussions are still ongoing although there is little hope that anything constructive will come through anytime soon unless one or all parties climb down from their stated positions. The work of this group is at the core of the non-payment of dues by the US, and hence the financial problems of the UN.

(5) Working Group on Strengthening of the UN – The final open-ended working group began meeting in 1995 to review the various studies and proposals on how to strengthen the UN. It has been able to reach consensus on many potentially non-sensitive issues (such as strengthening the work of the General Assembly and its main committees, improving performance appraisals of staff members, etc.), and some of these recommendations are already being implemented by the Secretary-General.

It is unfortunate that the 1994 *Agenda for Development* report never got as much attention as Boutros-Ghali would have liked it (even though a working group on it was formed). By the time the report was released, there was much focus on matters of peace and security around the world, and development hardly featured as a major concern in the minds of the donor agencies. Boutros-Ghali himself confided in interviews toward the end of his tenure that he felt that the major cause of lack of focus on development post-1994 was the donor-fatigue among the rich countries. These countries were themselves trying to get out of the economic downturns, and foreign aid – with the exception for a few Nordic countries – was hardly at the top of the foreign policy agenda of any donor.

At about the same time, there was also much ire at the Secretary-General himself from the US for wanting to be too independent.[28] While the Charter may call for independence, and while that may or may not have been the intentions of its framers, the fact that there was indeed a Secretary-General who sought to retain his independence rankled many in the West, particularly in the US. As it turned out, what little goodwill Boutros-Ghali had with the Americans lasted only as long as the 50th anniversary celebrations in October 1995 and all attention after that seemed to focus on the Secretary-General himself rather than on the real issues facing the UN.

As such, by late 1995, there was already talk of a backlash against the Secretary-General. Failed peacekeeping efforts in Somalia, Rwanda, and Bosnia did not help matters any, and the goodwill generated by the Secretary-General's own promising reform efforts initiated when he first took over (wherein he made some fundamental structural changes and also cut back some senior posts) did not help in his standing as the leader of the UN. As such, all of 1996 was actually wasted because of the focus on the personality of the Secretary-General rather than the substance of his reform efforts or the key problems facing the world at that time.

In the summer of 1994, after years of negotiations by the US, the Europeans, and other member states, and drawing mainly from the Thornburgh report, the General Assembly approved the establishment of an Office of Internal Oversight Services (OIOS; informally, the Office of Inspector-General) silencing for that time criticisms about the alleged lack of oversight of UN programmes. The General Assembly also appointed Karl-Theodor Paschke, a German diplomat, to head the office.[29] OIOS's responsibilities and areas of coverage extend to the offices of the Secretariat, the five regional economic commissions, peacekeeping operations, humanitarian operations, and, to a degree, UNICEF and UNDP, although unfortunately not the specialised agencies (and in this limitation the OIOS is critiqued by UN-watchers as not focusing on organisations that also seriously need to be reformed).[30]

After taking over the OIOS in November 1994 for a period of five years, Paschke was able to dig out some waste and inefficiency, and efficiency drives have been considered to be an integral part of the management culture of the UN now. But it has also been constrained in this process by funding limitations, lack of independence, and the obfuscative actions of various member states.[31]

While Boutros-Ghali in 1994-95 was going through his own crisis of legitimacy and acceptance by the member states and the US, reform proposals from various quarters were still pouring in. These were largely due to the wave of interest generated by the 50th anniversary celebrations of the UN and it appeared an appropriate time to discuss the UN and where it should go henceforth. Timed with the release of the *Agenda for Development* report, Childers and Urquhart[32] released in 1994 their new and updated ideas on how to renew the UN system. Some proposals were bold and looked utopian (such as creation of a UN Parliamentary Assembly in which people's representatives could be democratically elected) and some whose time had not yet come (such as the creation of a UN Staff College,[33] or concentrating all development assistance into one UN System Office in a country). It is interesting to see how closely Annan's proposals in these areas mirror Childers and Urquhart's. The fact that these two people, along with Bertrand, have had some of the most long-lasting impact on the issue of UN reforms is indisputable.

Also of note in 1994, in July a conference was convened at the University of Siena in Pontignano, Italy, to take stock and evaluate the recent debates and literature on UN reforms. Some of the most well-known individuals in the field of research on the UN were present at the conference. Their presentations were included in an edited volume by Paul Taylor, Sam Daws, and Ute Adamczick-Gerteis.[34]

If one were to analyse the various reform proposals that were made in the period 1992 to 1994 (i.e., immediately preceding the 50th anniversary of the UN), it becomes evident that there are four common threads running through them: (a) that the UN's peacekeeping operations and philosophy need critical analysis, (b) that there is need for continued restructuring of the UN organs, primarily the Secretariat and the Security Council, (c) that funding mechanisms need to be re-evaluated with urgency, and (d) that management and administrative changes need to support the cause of fundamentally altering the manner by which the organisation operates and cannot be merely cosmetic changes.

During the 50th anniversary celebrations of the UN in 1995, and coinciding with it, there were several studies and analyses done on the issue of a restructured and revamped UN. A few that can be mentioned here include a series of conferences organised by the Stanley Foundation starting in 1994 but continuing even up to the present,[35] the Commission on Global Governance (CGG)'s *Our Global Neighbourhood* in 1995, the South Centre's report in 1995, the Independent Working Group's 1995 report, and the United Nations University's in November 1995. The Stanley Foundation, in its various conferences, has called for some fundamental reorganisations (such as a representative parliament akin to a Parliamentary Assembly, examining other means of financing and generating revenues for the UN, etc.) as well as short-term moves designed to make the organisation more effective (such as enhanced coordination with the World Bank group of organisations, enabling greater NGO input into the UN process, etc.). It has also focused upon the issue of personnel reforms and Security Council[36] operations in relation to the proposed International Criminal Court.

For its part, the CGG focused on the specific issue of governance and built around it three concepts that the UN should take into consideration: security, UN structures (the General Assembly and others), and financing. For all the attention it received, the CGG actually came up with many proposals that were clearly utopian and even with the end of the Cold War at that time, it was not conceivable that the US would realistically consider these proposals. For example, the CGG proposed:

> (1) that the UN Charter be amended to ensure that the international community could intervene when international security was threatened, and further, to enable such an intervention, to set up a UN Volunteer Force,
>
> (2) that the ECOSOC be dissolved to be replaced by an Economic Security Council,
>
> (3) that the Trusteeship Council be given a new mandate over the Global Commons, and
>
> (4) that there be imposition of some sort of global taxes to steady the UN's financial base.

The CGG's proposals on revamping the Security Council by expanding the membership and abolishing the veto provision are being echoed to this day. The few realistic proposals of the CGG were, however, heeded very much by the two Secretaries-General since then, and Annan, in particular, has worked diligently in the areas of reform proposed by the CGG related to improvements in management and introduction of relevant practices and methods developed in the business world.

One particular reform proposal that the CGG made related to the selection process of the Secretary-General. This theme has been taken up by various reformers outside the UN and is relevant to the study here given the identification of this particular problem in Chapter Two. The CGG's main proposals centred on the following:

> (1) the veto would not apply to the nomination of the Secretary-General, but candidates from the five permanent members could be considered (to date, they have been excluded),
>
> (2) the appointment of the Secretary-General should be for a single term of seven years,

(3) governments should systematically and seriously consider the qualifications required – and suitability – of the Secretary-General, and

(4) the Security Council should organise a worldwide search for the best qualified candidates.

The CGG went on to argue that the procedure for selecting the heads of UN programmes, funds, and specialised agencies should also similarly be improved to secure the best possible candidates.

For its part, the South Centre,[37] dedicated to fighting for the causes of the Third World countries in the UN, in 1995 came out with very forceful recommendations that have largely been used as a basis for all Third World demands on UN reforms since then. A close look at its proposals shows that while some of them resemble what had earlier been brought out by such organisations as the CGG (for example, in calls for identifying new sources of revenues for the UN), many others are equally utopian and strictly based on the interests of the Third World countries (such as transferring the leadership in international economic issues to the UN by uniting all economic agencies including the Bretton Woods ones).

The South Centre, however, did approach the issue of UN reforms from a very logical perspective. Its starting point was that the Charter had to be the basis of all reform efforts for there could be no other relevant guide; besides, the Charter is indeed the base on which the UN rests. With that fundamental principle in mind, the basic reference points for reforms of the UN were then contained in:

(1) democracy (Preamble and Article 2(1)),[38]

(2) accountability (Articles 2(2)),[39] and

(3) respect for diversity and pluralism (Preamble and Article 1(3))[40] (South Centre (1995: 27-31)).

All reform efforts then should take into consideration these three elements. For all its lofty pronouncements and utopian ideals, the South Centre does provide a very powerful and useful framework for approaching the issue of UN reforms.

On the other hand, the report brought out by the Independent Working Group on the Future of the United Nations in the summer of 1995 (titled: "The United Nations in its Second-Half Century") appears a bit more realistic (for example, calling for the limit of the veto power to peacekeeping and enforcement issues, establishing a working group to examine the alternative sources of financing, expanding the Security Council to a maximum of 23 countries, etc.).

The Working Group also focused on the creation of three councils in areas related to security, economic affairs, and social issues (in essence, asking for the hiving off of the social functions from the ECOSOC) which were then to be coordinated by the Secretariat.

Finally, in November 1995, the UN University (UNU) in Tokyo held a symposium to discuss the role of the global organisation in the 21st century. The symposium actually was part of the overall five-year project of the UNU to assess critically five core research areas related to the UN: state and sovereignty, global citizenship, market forces, regional arrangements, and international organisations. Its inaugural symposium (which was contained in the UN21 Project Annual Report of 1995) brought out the views of many scholars and practitioners of the UN on the subject of reforms. One whose views are widely respected was Olara Otunnu (former Foreign Minister of Uganda and Director of the New York-based International Peace Academy). In a rather lengthy piece, Otunnu talked of possible divisions of labour among the UN and other organisations on the matter of maintaining international peace and security, and also talked of the international community keeping an eye open for the Grey Zones in such situations.[41]

In late 1995, Boutros-Ghali, under his own initiative, created an Efficiency Board (replaced with a Management Reform Group by Annan) that he hoped would encourage UN managers to focus on methods of cutting back costs while at the same time increasing the efficiency of the organisation. To augment the Board's work, Under Secretary-General for Administration and Management, Joseph Connor, who replaced Thornburgh, directed efforts to establish standards of management accountability and overhaul the Secretariat's personnel, procurement, and planning systems. Since then, rigorous performance evaluations have been adopted (discussed in Chapter Two).

Some of the things the Efficiency Board was able to do in its initial years of operations included reducing the length and number of documents produced, reducing travel expenses, out-sourcing more routine services in the organisation, and using information technology more effectively to cut back on information dissemination costs. When Annan in 1997 asked Connor to report back on the efficiency measures in support of his Track I proposals, the latter was able to cite some pretty impressive numbers although Connor himself maintained that much remained to be done.

By 1995, then, Boutros-Ghali was able to boast that since taking office, he had abolished nearly a third of the higher-ranking positions. But the General Assembly then created several new departments – an Under Secretary for Humanitarian Affairs, a High Commissioner for Human Rights, and an Inspector-General – adding more jobs. By 1996, Boutros-Ghali had been rather pre-occupied with the lack of impact of the reform process, and constrained by the difficult stance taken by the US, he began to lose a lot of the steam of his own reform proposals. He felt that his various efforts at reform had not been entertained seriously by powerful member states (even though he was constantly being exhorted to do more). For example, his 1995 proposal to the Group of Eight (G-8) countries to allow the UN to issue bonds (as a way of generating additional revenues) was not adopted. These and other setbacks had largely disillusioned Boutros-Ghali by 1996, and even though he continued to maintain that he had accomplished much,[42] as well as retain a deep interest in being re-elected to the Secretary-General post, he was well aware that the US, in particular, was not in his corner.

In the meantime, the General Assembly voted the first negative-nominal growth budget in UN history, establishing a budget ceiling and allowing no room for expansion. Concurrently, the Clinton Administration submitted a detailed reform plan to the General Assembly which brought to the fore several of the suggestions made by Helms (see below) but falling short of entirely toeing the Republicans' line. The Administration's proposals also highlighted three other issues:

(1) a serious review of the scale of assessments,
(2) the creation of a new post of Deputy-Secretary-General to handle administrative responsibilities and some routine matters so that the Secretary-General can spend more time with the broader tasks of the organisation as well as provide more sustained intellectual leadership to the UN, and
(3) extension of the OIOS's mandate to the entire UN system including the specialised agencies. The first suggestion has been hopelessly bogged down in pointless debate; the second has been approved, and the third is not even being considered as the General Assembly has little control over the specialised agencies.

Where the US's own role during Boutros-Ghali's tenure was concerned, it is instructive here to review what Senator Jesse Helms, probably the UN's fiercest critic in mainstream US national politics, has said about what needs to be done at the UN. Writing in *Foreign Affairs* (the same source where some months earlier Boutros-Ghali had put forward his own case for UN reforms), Helms said that these were the reform efforts that needed to be instituted in the UN (Helms (1996)):

(1) stop the encroachment of the UN in matters of national sovereignty (meaning, at a minimum, reduce the number and scope of UN mandates),

(2) reduce bureaucracy by half (including terminating unnecessary committees and conferences),

(3) limit all UN missions,

(4) radically overhaul the UN budgetary process (by instituting a bidding process for contributions), and

(5) overhaul the peacekeeping functions of the UN and have it limited to monitoring truces, policing cease-fires and serving as buffer between parties rather than the gamut of peace-related activities that Boutros-Ghali had called for (such as peace-enforcing, etc.).

Since Helms continues to dominate the main Congressional committee that approves funding for the activities of the US State Department (under which UN affairs appear) his benchmarks for reform – while apparently not practical – are certainly a fact of life for the UN. He made this painfully clear once again when he was afforded the rare opportunity for a US Senator to address a closed-door meeting of the Security Council in January 2000.

Going into the final year of his tenure, Boutros-Ghali was still hard on the path of putting the UN into a reform mode. The financing crisis took all of his time, and later on in the year, his own re-election diverted most of his attention. Constrained by the difficult stance taken by the US, Boutros-Ghali began to lose much of the momentum of his own reform proposals. He was also hopelessly bogged down in trying to get the member states (primarily the US) to pay their dues to the UN. In February 1996, he actually threatened to shut down the UN if no funding was incoming.[43] But he doggedly worked on new proposals to set the UN on the right path. In March, as a way of streamlining the Secretariat's work and to cut red-tape, he proposed organisation-wide expert clusters to focus on specific activities within the Secretariat. The proposal did not get anywhere and was bogged down in his re-election bid.

Boutros-Ghali may have been hampered by all the external turbulence regarding funding and reforms, but there were others within the Secretariat and elsewhere in the UN that were still brainstorming on how best to restructure the UN and give it new directions so that the US – among other member states – would finally realise that the UN was indeed serious about reforming itself. One such bold proposal in 1996 (as a matter of fact, considered one of the boldest yet at the Secretariat)[44] was made by the-then UNDP Administrator, James Gustave Speth, in which he called for a massive regrouping of the UN Secretariat and further proposed to even alter the very basis of UNDP by having it focus more as an umbrella structure of the proposed UN Alliance for People. This Alliance would bring together all the UN's operational activities, both development and humanitarian. Annan's proposed UN Development Group (UNDG) picks up in large part from this proposal although there are important differences. At any rate, Speth's proposal did not go the rounds long enough to be debated in detail given the rising spectre of a change in leadership in the UN.

Independent of the US initiative in 1996, the Nordic Countries again made an effort at highlighting some key areas that they felt needed urgent attention in the reform of the UN. They focused on four key areas:

(1) activities at the country level (wherein they called for integration of UN activities, a suggestion which Annan later completely took to heart),

(2) activities at the Headquarters level (wherein integration among the various actors and agencies was called for as was a suggestion for greater integration with the Bretton Woods institutions),

(3) governance of the UN system by member states (wherein the role of the ECOSOC was to be thoroughly reviewed and streamlined), and

(4) financial reform and predictable funding (wherein, among others, all three sources of funding – voluntary, negotiated, and assessed – were encouraged to be considered).

In relation to the fourth proposal, it is obvious that Annan has also taken it to heart completely. It is a measure of the respect and influence that the Nordic countries have in the UN that their proposals have always tended to be taken very seriously by the leadership of the UN.

Until his last few days in office, Boutros-Ghali was adamant that the US was playing hardball politics and out to get him since it needed a scapegoat for the continuing ills of the UN. Part of the problem was that he had, more knowingly than unknowingly given his streak of independence, criticised the US quite strongly about its lack of commitment to the UN as evidenced by the fact that the Americans had not paid their dues. He felt that this was being dishonest, and particularly vexing was the argument of the Americans that they were withholding payment because the UN was ineffective and yet it was this same withholding that largely contributed to the ineffectiveness.

He also felt – rightly, as it turned out – that he was a victim of US domestic politics with the Democrat President in battle with the Republican Congress. He was not alone in that line of thinking and all the member states of the UN for quite some time into his re-election bid stood by him. But the US had clearly enunciated a position and was not about to back down. Asking for a return of the post of the Secretary-General to play a more administrative role – rather than a political one – the US was in search of someone who was more a bureaucrat than a politician. In a UN Day speech at Columbia University on 24 October 1996, the-then US Ambassador to the UN, Madeleine Albright, said, among other things, that the ideal Secretary-General should be a good administrator and not aspire to be a world leader or a prominent diplomat like Boutros-Ghali. In that regard, the stage had been set for Kofi Annan.

Endnotes

[1] In a rather deriding manner, Smouts (1999: 29) opines that every five or six years the fever (of reforms) strikes the UN, including talk of reorganising the Secretariat, changing the procedures of the General Assembly, revitalising the ECOSOC, etc.

[2] One of the most noted personalities in the field of UN reforms, Maurice Bertrand, however, points out three usages of this term (1993: 420):
    (1)   dealing with the structure of the Secretariat,
    (2)   redefining programmatic priorities, and
    (3)   reorganising the machinery.
In the third usage, he argues for a distinction to be made between reforms that are possible with and without amending the Charter. In a different context, it has become evident that UN reforms for the rich countries of the North have, by and large, tended to mean an increase in efficiency in the operations of the organisation whereas for the poor countries of the South, the term has strong implications for a reorientation of the priorities – and the commensurate reallocation of resources – to concerns of economic development. These countries of the South would also like to see reforms implemented in strengthening the roles of such organs of the UN as the General Assembly (GA), the Economic and Social Council (ECOSOC), etc. See also Muller (1992: 1) for a review of the meaning and implications of the term 'reform' in relation to the UN.

[3] In Chapter One, under the heading "Structure" (p. 40), the case and the ICJ's ruling on it has already been discussed.

[4] The US seems now to be applying the Goldberg Reservation in its dealing with the UN, although in its blanket refusal to pay arrears to the UN, it exceeds the Goldberg Reservation since the latter only applied to exceptions of certain activities.

[5] The creation of the JIU was recommended by an ad hoc committee pushed for – ironically – by the Soviet Union and France and charged with looking at issues of finances. The JIU was modelled after the US General Accounting Office and France's *Inspection des Finances*. Over the years, the JIU has received strong support from sources such as the USA and the European Union.

[6] The JIU's effectiveness suffered because the member states did not whole-heartedly support it (they would, for instance, nominate under-qualified candidates to fill vacancies) and, not surprisingly, there was also a considerable degree of suspicion within the UN itself.

[7] The main author of the Report was Sir Robert Jackson. It was formally titled: "A Study of the Capacity of the United Nations Development System".

[8] Almost three decades later, the UN did establish such a College in Turin, Italy, in 1997.

[9] Daniel Patrick Moynihan with Suzanne Weaver (1978).

[10] This partly explains why he was initially recommended for an unprecedented third term as Secretary-General in December 1981. The move was thwarted by a veto from China which wanted a Third World individual as Secretary-General.

[11] See Davidson and Renninger (1982) who have provided a cogent analysis on the restructuring of the economic and social systems of the UN.

[12] For example, in just five years from 1982 to 1987, it had published 70 scathing reports on the state of the UN. It has continued its attacks on the UN even to this day. One of its latest attacks is contained in the 1997 "Reforming and Working with the United Nations" by Schaefer and Sheehy.

[13] This Amendment adopted by the US Senate in August of that year was intended to force a unilateral reduction in the share of US contribution (to 20 percent) to the UN unless a system of weighted voting (similar to that evident in the Bretton Woods institutions) was introduced in the General Assembly where the US felt that it was

perennially being out-voted in budgetary matters over which it had to put up the bulk of the funding but had very little say in how it was being spent. The Kassebaum-Solomon Amendment (which was incorporated into the PL 99-93 bill for 1986-87) was also but one of the many relevant pieces of legislation that were pushed through the US Congress that year that had significant impact on the financial viability of the UN.

[14] See Sahruddin Aga Khan and Maurice Strong, "United Nations: Reform might help its work," *International Herald Tribune*, 9 October 1985.

[15] These measures included reducing the number of conferences and meetings, reducing the regular budget posts by 15 percent within three years, reducing by 20 percent all official travel, reducing annual leave from six weeks to four weeks, etc. Practical as these proposals were, not all of them were implemented to any satisfactory degree (which has added to the refrain of the critics today that the UN is quick to come up with proposals but never implements any of them). Cuellar, however, did institute a rule of 20 percent reduction in official travel, as well as strict controls on levels of documentation. Staff benefits Cuellar did not even touch; the ICSC would have thwarted it at any cost.

[16] Smouts (1999) argues, however, that the Group's work was the first of three missed opportunities in recent years to reform the UN. She says that the organisation reverted to doing something that it has been adept at: "change just enough to uphold the status quo" and also to "stall for time" (p. 32).

[17] Renninger (1987(a) and 1987(b)).

[18] The authors in 1996 came out with a revised second edition of the book which was widely received for its vision related to how the Secretary-General should be elected.

[19] The report was titled *The United Nations in Development: Reform Issues in the Economic and Social Fields – A Nordic Perspective, Final Report*.

[20] Smouts (1999: 32) cites this as the second missed opportunity for genuine UN reforms in recent times.

[21] UNDP was bold enough to come up with further proposals on UN reforms and restructuring two years later in its 1994 edition of the *Human Development Report*. Some of the proposals were familiar (for example, the creation of an Economic Security Council) while others were not (for example, establishment of a world police authorised to bring States before the ICJ). It is understandable that in view of who its readership is, UNDP is apt to come up with such proposals, but realistically, it is inconceivable that the donors would pay much attention to such ideas being generated from within the UN itself. In that particular regard, UNDP should have known much better. It is precisely such ideas as a world police that send shivers down the spines of the Americans and they are not apt to look favourably at proposals that are this drastic.

[22] The origin of this report was the first-ever meeting of the Security Council at the level of heads of state and government in January 1992. At that meeting, the Security Council had requested the new Secretary-General to put forth his ideas in the area of peace and security.

[23] Boutros-Ghali returned to this theme of regional cooperation toward the end of his tenure although at that time it was designed more to reduce the costs of the UN.

[24] It must be the penchant for this sort of marginalisation that leads Smouts (1999: 35) to conclude that the *Agenda for Peace* report was the third missed opportunity for long-lasting UN reforms.

[25] See, for example, Uchida (1999: 66-68) for a discussion of the reactions in the Security Council to the *Agenda for Peace* report; Appendices 4.1 (pp. 88-93) and 4.2 (pp. 94-105) are also very useful reading materials.

[26] Smouts (1999: 35) calls it a "disappointing piece".

[27] To publicise his report, Thornburgh testified in March 1993 before the US House Subcommittee (of International Relations) on International Security, International Organisations, and Human Rights. The testimony served to gel negative sentiments on the UN in a very direct manner.

[28] Boutros-Ghali's penchant for wanting to be independent ran deep. While his actions had all along shown that he was not particularly beholden to any one country or group (although his conservative critics in the US will dispute this), Boutros-Ghali specifically vocalised this need for independence in an article he wrote in the influential *Foreign Affairs* in its March-April 1996 issue. *Foreign Affairs* is the leading establishment foreign policy journal in the US and is the one sure forum that Boutros-Ghali knew would give prominence to his viewpoints. The article was titled "Global Leadership after the Cold War" where toward the end of the article, he says: "If one word above all is to characterise the role of the Secretary-General, it is independence. The holder of this office must never be seen as acting out of fear of, or in an attempt to curry favour with, one state or group of states. . . He must be prepared to resist pressure, criticism, and opposition in defending the Charter's call for all member states to respect the exclusively international character of the responsibilities of the Secretary-General and the staff and not to seek to influence them in the discharge of their responsibilities" (1996: 98).

[29] Paschke's term of office ended in mid-November 1999 and in February 2000, Annan announced his replacement. Dileep Nair, a Harvard-educated banker from Singapore, was selected as the second head of OIOS after a gruelling ten-month search. Nair had previously been associated with the UN's Efficiency Board and so is not new to issues of management at the UN.

[30] The specialised agencies, for their part, insist that they are also quite serious about reforms and point to various steps being taken among them to do things more efficiently. At UNIDO, for instance, since 1995, there has been an attempt at what is called a bottom-up participation to reform. In it, the Staff Council and the staff of UNIDO's Quality Assurance Unit have initiated a series of group discussions to draw staff considerations into the reform process. This focus on the Total Quality Management (TQM) component of management processes is evident in other UN agencies as well.

[31] In mid-1995, the US Congress expressed concerns that the OIOS was not being given access to all the information, and also that there were no whistle-blowing safeguards in place. Consequently, Congress directed that 20 percent of the US contribution to the UN regular budget be withheld each year pending certification by the President that the OIOS was accomplishing what it was intended to accomplish, based on criteria set forth in the founding resolution. This was a major blow to the credibility of the UN and of Boutros-Ghali as well. This time around, however, it is the developing countries in the UN that have criticised the work of the OIOS. One case in particular concerns the assertions made by the OIOS in its fifth annual report (covering activities from July 1998 to June 1999). The report states that the staff-management relationship is characterised by antagonism rather than a spirit of cooperation, and that there is an overly critical attitude of many member states

towards the UN bureaucracy resulting in numerous examples of micromanagement by the legislative organs. In a Fifth Committee debate in late 1999, developing countries accused the OIOS of being very "pessimistic" and of not "scrupulously" implementing Assembly decisions (see United Nations Press Release GA/AB/3325, 29 October 1999).

[32] Childers and Urquhart both have been giants in the study and practice of the UN. Urquhart has been described as "the UN official who, after Dag Hammarskjold, did the most to develop the concept and practice of peacekeeping" (Baratta (1995: 3)). Their joint work, primarily through the Dag Hammarskjold Foundation in Uppsala, Sweden, is mandatory reading for any serious scholar of the UN.

[33] In early 1997, the newest UN organisation, the UN Staff College, was opened in Turin, Italy.

[34] *Documents on Reform of the United Nations*. Aldershot, UK: Dartmouth, 1997.

[35] These conferences were of two streams: the first was the "UN of the Next Decade" series, and the second was the "UN Issues Conference" series.

[36] See, for example, Stanley Foundation (1996, 1997(a), 1997(b), 1998).

[37] The South Centre came into being in July 1995 and traces its origins to the work of the South Commission which itself was created in 1987 resulting from the Non-aligned Summit meeting in Harare, Zimbabwe. The Centre (as does the Commission) works on enhancing cooperation among Third World countries (also known as South-South cooperation). The Centre is an intergovernmental body with 46 governments as members, and is located in Geneva.

[38] In the Preamble, the appropriate section reads: "...to reaffirm faith (in) the equal rights of men and women and of nations large and small..." And in Article 2(1), the appropriate section reads: "the organisation and its members ... shall act in accordance with ... the principle of the sovereign equality of all its members". The democratic value is obvious in these assertions.

[39] The appropriate section reads: "All members, in order to ensure to all of them the rights and benefits resulting from membership, shall fulfil in good faith the obligations assumed by them in accordance with the present Charter" (referring, for example, to the non-payment of dues by the US). The accountability value is manifested in the fact that member states – in return for the rights and benefits – must fulfil their obligations. In that sense, they need to be answerable to themselves that they have deserved to be members.

[40] The appropriate section in the Preamble reads: "to practice tolerance and live together in peace with one another as good neighbours". The appropriate section in Article 1(3), on the other hand, reads: "Respect for human rights and for fundamental freedoms for all without distinction as to race, sex, language, or religion".

[41] The Grey Zone is "the space between traditional peacekeeping ... and all-out war fighting. Situations encountered in the grey zone often require responses that are neither traditional peacekeeping nor full-blown enforcement action, but something in between" (Otunnu (1995: 8)).

[42] Boutros-Ghali's handiwork in the five years that he was Secretary-General included: departments and offices cut from 20 to 12, high-level posts in the Secretariat 40 percent less than in 1986, staff reduction of 20 percent since 1986, and a zero-growth budget as mandated by the General Assembly. In a speech on UN Staff Day on 13 September 1996, Boutros-Ghali said that he had also introduced a

mandatory programme of people management training (in which over 90 percent of D-1 and D-2 staff at all duty stations took part).
[43] See *The Straits Times* (Singapore), "I may have to shut down UN soon, says Boutros-Ghali," 23 February 1996.
[44] See *International Document Review*, 7, 28 (22 to 26 July1996). (Author's note: The IDR is the weekly newsletter on the United Nations published in New York).

Chapter Four
"And all the king's men ...": The Latest Attempts

In December 1996 when it became clear that Kofi Annan would succeed Boutros-Ghali as the seventh Secretary-General of the UN, there was some anticipation that finally things would be moving in the right direction again. There were several reasons for this. First and foremost, Annan was seen, rightly or wrongly, to be a US-candidate since Boutros-Ghali had been opposed only by the Americans and hence it was assumed that anybody replacing him would but be supported by the US. Given that it was the US that was the most belligerent and demanding when it came to matters of funding, reforms, etc., Annan's ascendancy to the Secretary-General post was seen as a comforting sign.

Second, Annan was a UN bureaucrat through and through unlike his predecessors who were also diplomats and government functionaries. In the context of the demand being made for the primacy of management of the UN, it was deemed that someone with considerable administrative and bureaucratic experience would be highly appropriate for the Secretary-General post. Annan fitted that bill perfectly.[1] Also of considerable relevance was the fact that Annan's experience at the senior echelons of the UN was in two key areas – financial/management and peacekeeping. Both these areas have dominated the headlines in the context of UN reforms.

Third, given the bitterness which had hung over the UN Headquarters office since mid-1996, it was seen essential to have someone who could literally bring a healing touch, someone more conciliatory, less aggressive, and, above all, someone that could be seen as mending fences. While it can be argued that anyone filling Boutros-Ghali's shoes in January 1997 would have, of necessity, been someone with humility, the choice of Kofi Annan, in particular, appears by far the most appropriate.

Much then was riding on Annan as he took over from Boutros-Ghali. There was much expected of him and the world was watching to see how he would proceed to placate the US while at the same time not shirk from being seen to be supportive of the demands of the other 184 countries who too were members of the UN. He had many constituencies then to consider – the staff of the UN, the specialised agencies, the governments of member states, and particularly that of the US, and even more specifically the hard-liners in the US Congress for that was where the eventual nod for release of much-needed funding would come from. He also must have realised that the onus was on him to revitalise the UN and make it more meaningful by exhorting the member states to somehow shed their disagreements over – and apathy of – the body. In all this, then, Annan must have realised in January 1997 that the entire future of the UN rested on him and him alone.

It is necessary to go into this background because the conditions in which Annan took over as Secretary-General were rather unique. He might or might not have aspired for that post (although under assumptions of normal course of events, it would have been clear that Boutros-Ghali would serve two terms and then the post would go to a non-African hence effectively denying Annan the opportunity) but now that he was indeed the Secretary-General, the demands on his leadership and managerial skills were tremendous. Within that context, then, came what can be called the Annan Agenda for UN reforms.

This chapter looks at three things specifically: (a) the reform efforts made by others parallel to that contained in the Annan Agenda; (b) the Annan Agenda itself which forms the bulk of the chapter, and (c) a few key areas for reform that appear to be common in all the efforts made thus far. However, in order to present a more holistic picture of the Annan Agenda, all three issues are contained under one main discussion point.

4.1 THE FIRST STAGE

In order to get started on this important assignment ahead of him, Annan in January 1997 approached this task very logically. First, he assembled a team at the UN Secretariat whose job was to review all the proposals and ideas that had already been made to date. Not only was there no need to re-invent the wheel, so to say, there was also a good deal to be said for putting his own forthcoming proposals in proper perspective. Second, he reasoned – not wrongly – that he needed to get the Americans (particularly the Republicans in Congress) on board his own thinking and get their pledge of support at best or a pledge of serious review of any proposal at a minimum. Third, he recognised that the entire reform process was very complex and that while there were areas where his influence and control might do the work, there were others where he could only be a moral force, and nothing else. Fourth, he had to ensure that the content and assumptions of his proposals were well-understood and accepted by the member states and others, and for that he and his senior staff had to lobby hard and go on a selling mission after the proposals were presented. Finally, he also realised that he needed to take prompt action and that these actions had to be revolutionary or else there was a real danger that the impetus that he had going into the job would be lost for good. As such, any reform proposal he put forth had to have been well-thought out, logical, results-oriented, practical, and image-enhancing.

In assembling a team around him that he could trust, and more importantly, that the world could take as proof of his seriousness of purpose, he appointed Maurice Strong as Executive Coordinator for UN Reform in January 1997. The right-wing of the US political establishment was not very pleased with that appointment but accepted the choice meekly anyway. Annan then also nominated Joseph Connor, Under Secretary-General for Administration and Management in the UN Secretariat, to help augment Strong's work. This too was considered prudent by UN-watchers. Connor, former Chairman of Price Waterhouse, was known for insisting on quality management in organisational processes and on introducing private sector business practices in public organisations. In the UN's context, then, this was a very appropriate decision on the part of the new Secretary-General. Annan also put in place in a short period of time a core team of do-ers in various agencies and Field Offices whose job was to provide inputs to the reform process being initiated in New York. At the time of the presentation of his proposals, Annan went on record to thank his team for putting in a considerable amount of work.

The next task for Annan was to ensure that he reached out to the particular constituency that would play a central role in whether or not his reform proposals would succeed – the Republican legislators in the US Congress. In the latter part of January, then, Annan set out for Washington, DC, and was prepared to use some of the political capital he already had amassed as a result of being seen in a different light than Boutros-Ghali. Annan also, unlike his predecessor, had a greater understanding of the American psyche having studied there and having spent some part of his life in New

York. He was thus more able to tune into what the nuances of American politics were and how to react to them.

His visit then to the White House, the Congress, and other public places where he could speak out (such as the National Press Club) was designed to give the critics of the UN a personal glimpse of the man who would be leading it for the next five years and who was going to come up with valid proposals for reform. The White House was suitably impressed and Vice President Al Gore said all the right things in his meetings with Annan. President Clinton himself spoke of the need to get US funding on track and to ensure that the US continued to support the work of the UN and its own role in it.

In Congress, Annan met with the legislators whom he knew would go through his proposals with a magnifying glass to ensure that it met their demands. The meeting itself went rather well and, the jokes and light banter aside, it gave the two sides an opportunity to size each other up. Senator Jesse Helms was as usual forthright about the conditions in which the UN would be getting US money[2] and Annan reiterated that he would ensure that the reform process was underway soon. He also maintained that the US had an obligation to pay its dues and that the organisation was suffering as a result of it. Legislators, such as Representative Cliff Stearns (Republican of Oklahoma) responded that they were pleased that the new Secretary-General recognised the necessity of streamlining the bureaucracy within the UN. There appeared to be a sense, and an implicit conclusion, that with reforms would come the funding. For Annan himself, it had become increasingly clear that in order for US funding to be renewed, his forthcoming proposals would have to address the key concerns that legislators such as Helms and Stearns were vocalising in public.[3]

Later on in his visit to the American capital, in various public forums, Annan mentioned that the UN was being held hostage as a result of the non-payment of dues by members. He reminded his audiences that the US had freely accepted to pay a quarter of the UN regular budget[4] and that while changes in the scale of assessments, etc., could certainly be discussed as part of any reform proposal, the US had to ensure that payment of arrears were also made. At the end of his visit, it was quite clear that Annan had got some political mileage out of it and that he did not appear cowed by the legislators or others. Speaking at a press conference later, when asked if he was paying too much attention to the Americans, he replied that he would "devote the same amount of time to any member state that pays 25 per cent of the budget and owes $1.3 billion".[5]

Once back from Washington, DC, and immersed into defining the reforms that he would like to put forth for the UN, it became clear that he would have to do things in two rounds. Keenly aware of the fact that while as Secretary-General he heads the entire UN system of organisations, his own direct influence and control are only over the Secretariat, Annan then decided to come up with a two-track approach to initiating reforms within the organisation. The first one would be centred around the activities and structure of the Secretariat (and that would be formulated immediately) while the second one would be other issues related to the UN as a whole but on which the member states – through the General Assembly – would have to act upon. The first set of proposals was contained in what eventually became known as Track I proposals (announced in March 1997), and the second in Track II (announced in July the same year). The Track I and Track II proposals – collectively termed the Annan Agenda here – are analysed in detail further on in the chapter.

Once the proposals were announced, Annan and his team had to then also ensure that they received as much publicity as possible and that the member states and other constituencies not only understood them but also accepted them. Much correspondence took place between the Secretariat and the other parts of the UN system (such as the specialised agencies) that explained what was being proposed, why it was being proposed, and how that would impact the other agencies as well. For instance, to publicise the Resident Coordinator system in Field Offices, and to get the support of other agencies with field-based activities, UNDP (the Administrator of which is the designated convenor of the Economic and Social Affairs Executive Committee) wrote to the World Health Organisation (WHO) to request it to study the relevant proposals and to respond as to how WHO could more effectively participate in the activities of the United Nations Development Group.

Such communications also went out from UN Headquarters to various Field Offices to apprise lower-level staff of the reform proposals and how they would affect the operations and procedures at the field level. Resident Coordinators were urged to share the communications with all staff members and, in turn, to provide feedback to New York should there be any. It was not only written communications that were used to convey the proposals to the Field Offices. Videotapes were also prepared and disseminated, and staff members were urged to view them to understand the prevalent thinking on what the UN was doing and how the change process in the organisation was going to affect them. Probably for the first time in the history of the UN was there so much effort being made to ensure that all staff members understood the meaning of the reform process as well as its contents. More importantly, it was designed to ensure that there was ground support for the reforms being initiated within the organisation.

This support was also cultivated by Annan himself whenever he visited the various UN agencies as well as other governments. He exhorted UN staff members wherever he met them to understand that the UN was going through a tough time and that an irrevocable process of change was upon them. It was natural for staff members to feel apprehensive about the changes being envisioned and it was up to the leadership to allay their fears. Similar sentiments were being expressed by member states that were not privy to the internal dynamics of how the reform proposals were being generated. Third World countries wanted to know what the reforms would mean for assistance from the UN for development work, and how proposed cutbacks in the organisation were going to affect development assistance. On the other hand, the richer nations wanted to know to what extent the cutbacks were actually going to enhance the efficiency of the organisation and how deep the cuts were going to go. It was left up to Annan and his senior team members to respond to all these concerns that came up not only at the time of the presentation of the proposals but also during the ensuing General Assembly debates every year since 1997.

4.2 THE ANNAN AGENDA

Even before his trip to Washington, DC, Annan had already crystallised in his mind how the reform proposals would be conceptualised and structured. There was further input into this from the European Union (EU) which in late January 1997 came up with several proposals for reform of the UN system in the economic and social areas.[6] The EU has been seen to be rather supportive of the efforts of the Third World countries in economic development and so its proposals acted as a powerful precursor to Annan's own first in

March then in July of that year. With an apparent dig at the US, the EU's proposals stated that reform of the UN in these fields was not about cost-cutting (a refrain heard from practically all poor countries at the UN) but rather about strengthening the UN and reasserting the pivotal importance of its roles in these areas. Some of the suggestions put forth by the EU were ultimately taken up by Annan and have since been operationalised (such as ensuring that UN interventions in the development field be country-based, and that UNDP continue to be used as a vehicle for the Resident Coordination missions in Field Offices).

The starting point for Annan's own two-track reform proposals were the very criticisms that had been hurled at the organisation: that it was inefficient, dysfunctional, and slow. In totality, then, Annan wished his reform proposals to be seen as something that would make the UN leaner, more focused, more flexible, more responsive to changing global needs, and organised around its core competencies vis-à-vis other international organisations. In this entire range of goals of the revamped UN are hidden different euphemisms that need to be brought out more clearly.

When Annan talks of making the UN leaner, the clear reference is to downsizing. This had been an ongoing effort ever since Boutros-Ghali started cutting posts in 1992. The thing to note here though is that the downsizing is only in reference to the Secretariat over which the Secretary-General has control; and even here he needs the permission of the General Assembly to effectuate sweeping cutbacks. The Third World countries have maintained that wanton abolition of posts is not likely to solve the real problems of the UN while countries such as the US have said that the cuts have not tended to go far enough. Actually, with the reduction in Secretariat staff from over 12,500 members in the mid-1980s to about 8,700 by the end of the 1990s, the cutbacks have been severe indeed and have been on track with the benchmark set by the US earlier on during Boutros-Ghali's tenure. At any rate, Annan's wish to make the UN leaner refers directly to reducing the Secretariat size (he has no control over other organs or agencies) although in 1999 he did present plans for slightly increasing the size of the Secretariat staff.

The phrase "more responsive to changing global needs" implies that Annan would like to see the UN develop a capacity to handle the myriad situations that crop up around the world and that necessitate the UN's attention. One prime example of this is the aftermath of the economic crisis that hit the Southeast Asian region in 1998. While the UN is clearly not able to handle crises that are purely economic in character (for which the IMF, and to some extent the World Bank, are suitable), it should certainly be in a better position to enter into the picture once the social and political ramifications of the crisis become manifest. The fact that the UN has not really been prominent in these areas even now demonstrates just how far it needs to go to develop this capacity.

Finally, the phrases "organised around its core competencies" and "more focused" are euphemisms for the desire to reduce, to the extent possible, the areas of UN intervention and involvement. This is one of the key criticisms of the UN and Annan's intent is to ensure that the UN only focuses on areas where it is strong (e.g., in areas of governance, refugee assistance, etc. – areas where clearly there is considerable comparative advantage to the UN given its interaction with – and access to – governments). It is not Annan's intent to seek to alter in any way the mandates which the Charter has assigned to the UN, but he would very much like to see the organisation be involved in a lot fewer activities and leave the rest to organisations that clearly have a comparative advantage over the UN.

The paradox here, however, is for all to see. While Annan would like the UN to develop capacity to deal with new problems, he would also, on the other hand, like the organisation to stay focused on core competencies. Despite this apparent conflict here, Annan specified the objective of his reform proposals as being the following: "to narrow the gap between aspiration and accomplishment" with the overall goal being "to ensure greater unity of purpose, coherence of efforts and agility in responding to the pressing needs of the international community" (United Nations (1997(a), paragraph 6). Riding a high in his first six months in office, Annan at the commencement address in June 1997 at his alma mater, Massachusetts Institute of Technology (MIT), said that his proposals for UN reform would be the most thoroughgoing institutional reform ever attempted at the UN and that it would compare favourably with any such reform yet undertaken by any public sector organisation, anywhere.[7] These remarks were made three months after his Track I proposals and one month before the all-important Track II ones.

In its totality, the Annan Agenda can be categorised under three broad classifications (structural, functional, and managerial/procedural):

(1) <u>related to the structures</u>: as evidenced in the decrease in 1,000 Secretariat posts,[8] creation of a Senior Management Group and a Strategic Planning Unit, and setting up a post for a Deputy Secretary-General,

(2) <u>related to functions</u>: as evidenced by the call for a reorientation of the General Assembly's work in various areas, and the need for greater coordination of UN activities at the field level (including with NGOs), and

(3) <u>related to managerial/procedural matters</u>: as evidenced by his focus on sunset provisions on new programmes, shifting from an input accounting system of budgeting to one of results-based accountability, providing electronic access to as many UN offices and publications as possible, preparing a Code of Conduct for all UN staff members to abide by, and focusing on the human resources development aspect of the organisation, including career planning, gender balance, etc.[9]

As has been mentioned earlier, there is yet another way of looking at the Annan Agenda: that of type of measure envisaged. There were three such measures:

(1) those the Secretary-General himself could undertake on his own initiative,

(2) complementary measures that the member states could take the lead role on (such as approving structural and functional changes of intergovernmental bodies), and

(3) long-term measures for which sustained discussions and debates would have to be initiated seriously.

Clearly, Annan had in mind that these reform proposals would serve as a basis for further and ongoing reforms within the organisation, which is why he termed this a process and not an event (United Nations (1997(a), paragraph 25).

4.3 TRACK I PROPOSALS

The genesis of the Track I proposals was in a series of administrative moves Annan made immediately after becoming Secretary-General. The key ones were the following:

(1) The appointment of Maurice Strong as the Executive Coordinator for UN Reform. This was done in January 1997 and was widely hailed although a murmur of dissent could be heard from the Far Right in the US.

(2) The establishment of a Policy Coordination Group (PCG) in January 1997 which included in it Heads of Departments and Offices of the Secretariat (including Heads of UNDP, UNICEF, and UNFPA).

(3) The establishment of four Executive Committees (EXCOM) in the following sectors:[10] peace and security, humanitarian affairs, economic and social affairs, and development operations. A fifth area – human rights – was considered to be cross-cutting and would be included in all EXCOMs. Each EXCOM had its own designated convenor. While the main functions of the PCG and EXCOMs were policy and managerial in nature, they would be used rather extensively in matters of reform as well.

(4) The establishment of a Steering Committee on UN Reforms chaired by the Executive Coordinator of UN Reforms.[11] The membership of the Steering Committee included several senior UN officials, and it was to play a central role in monitoring and coordinating the reform process within the Secretariat.

(5) Finally, a Management Reform Group (MRG)[12] within the Department of Administration and Management was to be established whose job was to focus on furthering management reform measures across the UN Secretariat. The MRG would be complemented by reform groups to be established in each Department, Fund and Programme.

On 17 March 1997, Annan announced his first set of reform proposals which were targeted only at the Secretariat. Calling it a quiet revolution, he meant the proposals to make the UN leaner and more effective. The broad goals of the Track I reform proposals were listed as being four:[13]

(1) accelerate and expand managerial reform,

(2) reduce the non-programme costs of the organisation,

(3) modernise and enhance services and information provided to member states, and

(4) increase the accountability and responsibility of programme managers.

These were to be achieved through significantly simplifying and rationalising organisational structures, and working closely with member states and with such UN organs as the General Assembly. For each of these goals, there was a specific challenge that was attached to it to guide the reform process:

(1) for the first goal, the challenge was to accelerate and integrate managerial reform into the work of the UN,

(2) for the second, the challenge was to streamline administration,

(3) for the third, the challenge was to modernise and enhance services for member states to support the parliamentary process and programmes while reducing the quantity of hard-copy documentation, and

(4) for the fourth goal, the challenge was to align responsibility and accountability for results, and provide better, more cost-effective, support services to programmes and managers.

Driving these goals were specific ingredients of the Track I proposals which contained the following measures:[14]

(1) Reduction in the 1998-99 budget by $123 million to bring it to a level benchmarked by the US. The savings were to come from a series of efficiency measures that had been started under Boutros-Ghali's Efficiency Board and that were complemented by the work of the OIOS.

(2) Reduction in staffing levels by 1,000 posts. This is also something that was benchmarked by the US. It is important to note here though that it was actually Boutros-Ghali who had taken steps to make the posts vacant but he was not successful in abolishing them given opposition from the General Assembly. Thus, he could not really take credit for that particular move.

(3) Reduction in administrative costs from the-then existent level of 38 percent of the organisation's resources to a more acceptable level of 25 percent. Annan also called for a 25 percent reduction in documentation at the Secretariat, and specified that the savings resulting from these reductions would be channelled for development activities in the developing world.[15] This was done to

allay the fears of many countries of the South that rampant cost-cutting would needlessly jeopardise several programmes that they felt were of benefit to them.

(4) Improvement in UN integration at the country level so that the UN could speak with one voice. In formulating this proposal, Annan did two things: (a) he clearly accepted the proposals made by the Nordic countries and the EU to enhance the UN's capacity to respond to country-level situations in the economic and social areas, and (b) he addressed the concerns of critics who charged that the UN is fragmented in the Country Offices and much duplicative work is evident therein. Such integration was to be strengthened through the Resident Coordinator (RC) system whereby the RC would take the lead role in the country to help develop common programmes. This was to lead to greater coherence in planning, programming, and implementation of UN support activities in any given country.

(5) Consolidation of economic and social departments in such a manner that the existing three departments involved in the area of economic and social activities (Department for Policy Coordination and Sustainable Development, the Department for Economic and Social Information and Policy Analysis, and the Department for Development Support and Management Services) were to be amalgamated into a single Department of Economic and Social Affairs. The resultant savings from such a consolidation were proposed to be channelled back into the various economic and social programmes.

(6) Streamlining of technical support currently provided by the Department of General Assembly Affairs and Conference Services in such a manner that the services provided by the Secretariat to inter-governmental bodies (such as the General Assembly) would lead to greater coherence, quality, and efficiency of services.

(7) Reorientation of the Department of Public Information evidenced by a proposed transformation of this Department to a new Office of Communications and Media Services. This move was designed to strengthen that body's capacity to provide timely communication

services to member states and others. This move was also part of a larger effort to aggressively market the UN's strengths and achievements.

(8) Consolidation of administrative, financial, personnel, procurement, and other services so as to provide them more efficiently. The idea of a common service was aggressively pushed here and focus was also placed on supporting the principle of devolving responsibility to the most effective managerial level.

(9) Finally, development of a UN Code of Conduct, upon insistence of the US. The Code had been drafted at the time of presentation of these proposals and included three elements: (a) a commitment to excellence through specified expectations for conduct and performance, (b) a framework for accountability for performance, and (c) a requirement for financial disclosures by senior officials. This last measure had been championed unsuccessfully by the Clinton Administration when Boutros-Ghali was Secretary-General.

At the time that these proposals were announced, there was general acceptance but not much commotion as expected (except among the UN staff who were concerned about how these proposals would affect their careers, work conditions, terms of service, etc.). The reasons for the lack of commotion were several:

(1) the proposals only concerned management changes that were to be localised to the Secretariat, and that is but one – albeit key – component of the overall UN system,

(2) the greater problem of reform was always felt to be outside the realm of the Secretariat and in the other organs of the UN (such as the General Assembly, Security Council, etc.), and

(3) the even greater concern that UN critics have had about the UN system is the independence of the specialised agencies and need for reforms inherent in them as well (since the Track I proposals were contained only within the Secretariat, the world still awaited the proposals to be made four months hence).

After the proposals were made, Annan went about implementing many of the proposals for which he did not need any permission from the General Assembly. In support of this, he also asked Strong to report on the various efforts being made to implement the proposals. Strong's detailed response[16] five weeks later operationalised all the proposals and gave a point-by-point account of what the organisation had done thus far and what the targets and time frames were for the future.

In order to put into perspective the Track II proposals to come, it is essential to take a more detailed look at the ones presented in March (see Table 4.1 for a summary).

Table 4.1. Summary of Track I Proposals on Managerial Reforms

Challenge	Specific Goal	*Raison d'etre*	Selective Reform Milestones
1. Accelerate and integrate managerial reform into the work of the UN	Institutionalise reform into the work of the UN; gain efficiencies on a continuous basis; spread Best Practices	Organisations not following efficiency and effectiveness measures are not likely to succeed in the long run	Efficiency projects fully integrated into the budget process by 2000-2001; one-third reduction of non-programme costs
2. Streamline administration within the Secretariat	Reduce non-programme costs from 38 percent of organisational budget to no more than 25 percent	Less costs on administration means more funds for social progs; simpler processes also facilitate better services	By 2001, reduce cost of administering travel requests from $66 to $44; reduce costs of adm processes by 1/3; increase budget going to programmes from 65% to 75%
3. Enhance services for member states	Help connect all missions electronically; expand access to UN information	Clients deserve efficient services; technology offers opportunities to raise efficiencies	By 1998-end: connect all missions in New York, Geneva, Vienna; reduce hard copies of documentation (25%)[17]
4. Focus on responsibility as well as accountability for results	Greater accountability of managers for results; focus on mandates such as geographical equality, focus on common services, etc.	Decentralisation in managerial process leads to a more efficient organisation and also to better results	By 1999, there should be Secretariat-wide improvement in various benchmark indicators such as percentage of female professional staff, geographical equality, quantifiable measures of outputs identified and used, etc.

Source: adapted from "Letter of Transmittal from Under Secretary-General Joseph E. Connor to Secretary-General Kofi Annan," 22 April 1997 in United Nations (1997(c)).

Annan's report also provided the inputs he needed to give form to his Track II proposals. Major portions of the forthcoming proposals were falling into place and through a process of discussions and feedback from various sources (including the Field Offices, Regional Commissions, subsidiary organs, etc.), the Track II proposals began to take shape. Several of the proposed moves brought about howls of protest from concerned agencies and they only served to remind Annan that the entire reform process was going to be a very rocky one indeed. His internal constituencies were already drawing battle lines and designating "sacred cows" from among the premium programmes and themes, and meddling with any one of them was going to be costly. Annan knew this and diplomatically, and in his characteristic conciliatory manner, tried to defuse the crises as they appeared.

The results were announced four months after his Track I proposals and remarkably swiftly considering the nature of the organisation, the task, and the conditions in – and pressures under – which he and his team had to work. It is also evident from a reading of the proposals that his team made every effort to cover as many areas as possible. This was seen to be both positive and negative. Supporters pointed to the fact that the new leader was taking a macro perspective and was looking at the entirety of issues facing the UN. Opponents decried the fact that in bringing in so many issues, the efforts would be diluted and that it would have been preferable to have focused on the most pressing issues first.

4.4 TRACK II PROPOSALS

On 14 July 1997, Annan then unveiled the much-awaited Track II reform proposals. Much was expected of him and his proposals were eagerly debated immediately upon release As mentioned earlier, this set of proposals had been designed to take the reform process beyond the Secretariat level and engulf various other organs and issues. The proposals were detailed and extensive and they included various efforts already underway in Track I but presented together so as to give a holistic picture of the entire reform process.

At the time of presentation of his second set of proposals, Annan gave a detailed background view of where the UN had come from and what the future challenges were. He contextualised the proposals in light of the various successes the organisation had been credited with (such as decolonisation, human rights, etc.) and also was remarkably honest about its weaknesses. The fact that the Secretary-General himself had openly talked about the magnitude of the problems at the UN was seen as a sign that the organisation, under a new leader, was ready and willing to face up to its problems.

These priority areas were identified in Track II:

(1) a new leadership and management structure, including streamlining the organisation (Secretariat) proposals for which had been tabled under Track I, and focusing on the management culture accompanied by efficiency measures (which largely drew from Connor's 22 April 1997 report); also included was a focus on human resource management and on enhancing the KSAs (knowledge, skills, and abilities) of staff members,

(2) the funding crisis and ways to address it,

(3) prioritisation of sustainable development and service to the UN's inter-governmental bodies,

(4) peacekeeping operations and ways to improve them, and on a related matter, post-conflict peace-building,

(5) the fight against crime, drugs, and terrorism,

(6) human rights and ways to extend them,

(7) disarmament (dealing with reduction of armaments and weapons of mass destruction),

(8) humanitarian needs (and enhancing response time), and

(9) public information (and redesign of the communications strategy) as well as proposals on refocusing on the work of the General Assembly, on the Charter, etc.

The specific means by which the key priority areas were to be operationalised, and the consequent steps that were to be taken, are summarised in Table 4.2.

The key proposals within the Track II reform efforts included the following: creation of various posts and groups, changed management culture, overhaul of human resources, creation of a development dividend, enhancement of peacekeeping and post-conflict peace-building, extending human rights, enhanced response to humanitarian needs, and reorientation of the UN's public information campaign.

Table 4.2. Summary of the Annan Agenda Reform Proposals

Purpose	Means	Specific Proposals
1. Strengthen capacity of the SG to provide leadership and ensure organisational accountability	Establish a new leadership and management structure	(1) Create post of Deputy Secretary-General (2) Establish SMG and SPU (3) Decentralise decision-making and consolidate UN field presence (4) Strengthen the four Executive Committees set up in January 1997
	Enhance Secretariat	Establish Eco and Social Affairs sectoral group
2. Address the funding crisis	Ensure solvency until a long-term solution is found	Create a Revolving Credit Fund of up to US $1 billion financed from voluntary contributions
	Focus on efficiency measures	(1) Eliminate at least 1,000 posts (2) Reduce admin costs by one-third (3) Effect more savings in personnel, etc.
3. Streamline the UN	Consolidate org structures	(1) Integrate twelve Secretariat units into five (2) Consolidate five inter-gov bodies into two
4. Enhance staff capacity	Overhaul existing HR policies and practices	(1) Ensure staff have skills to do jobs right (2) Ensure that all staff enjoy requisite conditions for effective service
5. Promote sustained and sustainable development	Consolidate structures dealing with development	Create a UN Development Group that will bring together various UN funds and programmes with development operations
	Ensure funding and make it more predictable	(1) Shift resources from admin to dev (2) Find new means of mobilising new finances (3) Encourage burden-sharing and negotiated multi-year voluntary pledges
	Focus on environment	(1) Strengthen, in particular, UNEP in Nairobi (2) Strengthen env aspect of other UN activities
6. Enhance international peace and security	Improve ability to deploy peacekeepers	Enhance the rapid reaction capacity of the UN
	Strengthen capacity for peace-building	Designate Department of Political Affairs as a focal point
	Bolster efforts to combat crime, etc.	Consolidate programmes and activities under an Office for Drug Control and Crime Prevention
	Push for disarmament	Establish a Dept for Disarmament and Arms Regulation to address reduction of armaments
7. Propagate human rights	Org restructuring and programme integration	(1) Reorganise the human rights secretariat (2) Integrate human rights into all principal UN activities and programmes
8. Respond to humanitarian needs	Realign orgl processes and work methods	Replace the Department of Humanitarian Affairs with a new Emergency Relief Coordination Office and have it focus on complex emergencies

Source: adapted from United Nations (1997(a)).

Creation of Various Posts and Groups

Deputy Secretary-General

As envisaged by Annan, the Deputy Secretary-General was to undertake responsibilities at the request of the Secretary-General and was to perform a particular role in ensuring the success of activities and programmes that were cross-cutting in nature and that thus intrinsically brought all Secretariat units in the domain of the Deputy Secretary-General's coverage. As also envisaged by Annan, his deputy would also head the Office of Development Financing (ODF) in a bid to generate more funding for development operations. This was – and continues to be – an important field of activity as the financial crisis currently engulfing the organisation is expected to get worse unless some innovative approaches can be figured out and sold to the member states. It was the US that had ardently pushed for the creation of this post so as to give the Secretary-General more time to be involved in engaging the various crises around the world.

Senior Management Group

The membership of the Senior Management Group (SMG) at the Secretariat included the convenors of the four EXCOMs as well as several senior managers selected by Annan himself. The primary purpose of the SMG was to assist Annan in leading the process of change and instituting sound management in the organisation. This inner circle of managers was also expected to be a brain trust for coming up with solutions to the organisation's problems related not only to internal management but also to other areas of activity of the United Nations. The SMG was to be in regular touch with other managers in various other parts of the world and brainstorm ideas.

Executive Committees

As soon as Annan took over as Secretary-General, he reorganised the work of the Secretariat around the five areas that comprise the core missions of the UN. These missions include: peace and security, economic and social affairs, development cooperation, humanitarian affairs, and human rights. All the UN departments, programmes, and funds were then grouped into these five missions and subsequently

Executive Committees (EXCOMs) were established in all five areas with the exception of human rights which was considered to be cross-cutting and, therefore, participating in each of the other four. The purpose of setting up EXCOMs was to reduce duplication of effort across the core groups and also to facilitate complementarity and coherence of actions. The heads of the UN entities were expected to consult with one another on work programmes as well as other matters of concern (such as in administration). Finally, the hope was that by having the EXCOMs interact with each other, there would be greater likelihood of facilitating joint planning and strategic decision-making in the United Nations.

UNDG and the Resident Coordination System

Keeping in mind the increasing focus on development, and given the existence of numerous agencies and programmes in the specific field of development cooperation, the Secretary-General decided to form a United Nations Development Group (UNDG). The UNDG comprised the major UN development programmes and funds as well as departments and relevant agencies. This agglomeration was at the Headquarters level but was to be mirrored in the field as well (i.e., regional and country levels). Also, under the UN Development Assistance Framework (UNDAF), the country-level assistance provided by each UN programme and fund was to be integrated with each other. The primary purpose of the UNDG was to facilitate joint policy formulation and decision-making thus leading to cooperation among these various entities involved in development operations. Associated with the UNDG would be the participation in some form – not finalised yet – of the World Bank.

The UNDG was meant to be a key result of Annan's plan to consolidate all activities within a country under a Resident Coordinator system. The idea was to speak with one voice to the government. The Resident Coordinator system was something that Boutros-Ghali had used as a way of enhancing the cohesiveness of the UN's efforts at the field level and the designation of a Resident Coordinator was to aid in the creation of a one-UN approach to helping a country. This approach was contained in Annan's Track II proposals in the form, among other things, of a UN House. The UN House referred to all UN entities with missions at the country level operating in common premises and under one flag.

Strategic Planning Unit

Given the increasing complexities of the work at the UN these days, Annan felt that he would be best in a position to lead the organisation effectively if he had access to relevant information and if he was able to make use of it. In that regard, he set up the Strategic Planning Unit (SPU) in the Secretariat to help him in his planning functions. In its support of the work of the Secretary-General, as well as of the SMG, the SPU was to identify emerging global issues and trends, analyse their implications for the UN, and subsequently devise policy recommendations for the Secretary-General and SMG to review. The SPU formed a key component of Annan's desire to engage in strategic planning at the UN.

Revolving Credit Fund

As a way of dealing with the funding crisis, Annan proposed to set up a Revolving Credit Fund (RCF) of up to $1 billion (to be financed from various sources but for now only voluntary contributions were identified). Annan also specified that this Fund was merely a stopgap measure pending permanent resolution of the funding problem at the UN. The Fund was to give the Secretary-General more leverage in meeting financial targets while the organisation was awaiting payment of dues by member states. The Fund would then be reimbursed for every dollar taken out during the period the dues payment was not effectuated.

    While the RCF was designed to assist in solving the financial crisis, Annan also proposed measures for burden-sharing and enhancing predictability in funding through multi-year negotiated and voluntary pledges in addition to the present system of assessments of dues. This was a bold step taken by Annan, and as will be detailed in the subsequent chapter, one that has not gone down very well with donors.

Changed Management Culture

It is in this proposal that Annan recognised that not much was likely to alter at the UN if the culture of doing things did not change. This implied, furthermore, that the staff members needed to be made aware of new practices of operations and the need to institutionalise them. The core of this proposal was contained in the Connor letter of 22 April 1997 to Annan and was considered to be one of the key proposals related to internal management that Annan would have to continuously keep an eye on. For the time being, the changed management culture included:

    (1) elimination of 1,000 posts,

    (2) reduction of administrative expenses by one-third, and

    (3) generation of additional savings in terms of personnel and costs.

Overhaul of Human Resources

Keeping in mind the above-mentioned desirability (of a management culture that institutionalises change), Annan put considerable focus on the human resources of the organisation. He called for more investment in staff, simpler procedures, and more authority for managers. All of this was designed to ensure that the UN had the right people with the right skills in the right job at the right time. The Annan team insisted that the changes would also enable the UN to provide its staff members with more opportunities for challenging and satisfying careers. The team had let it be known that the changes were going to be carried out via a human resources strategy that was fully integrated into the overall organisational strategy.

    The proposed reform efforts related to staff development were based in large part on the findings of a task force of human resource management experts charged with recommending an overhaul of the personnel system of the UN Secretariat. In presenting these ideas to the 1998 General Assembly, Annan had specifically stated that the UN would be searching for the best practices in the areas of management. And in the area of human resource planning, the Annan Agenda has been quite vigorous given the realisation that without capable staff, the Organisation would not be able to meet its mandates. In particular, the UN was set to address the need for a more effective system for forecasting staffing requirements. As part of the Annan reform agenda, the Office of Human Resource Management (OHRM) was to develop a human resources forecasting and modelling system that would upon completion integrate human resources planning with financial planning.

Creation of a Development Dividend

At the time that Annan was formulating his proposals, there was much anguish expressed by the poor countries of the South that the cutbacks at the UN would jeopardise development activities and programmes needlessly. Their popular refrain was that reforms did not necessarily mean merely cutting costs. To allay their fears, Annan proposed a development dividend to be financed by the range of savings that were to result from the new efficiencies gained. This amount was expected to be in the $100-$200 million range and was to be used for high-impact development projects to be implemented in various poor countries.

Enhancement of Peacekeeping and Post-Conflict Peace-Building

Like Boutros-Ghali before him, Annan too had been caught up in the drive to ensure that the UN was ready in cases of intervention in global crises. The UN's peacekeeping missions had come under considerable flak (given the failures of Rwanda, Somalia, etc.) and Annan wished to ensure that the organisation had the capacity to react quickly to similar crises. In presenting his Track II proposals, he exhorted the member states to agree on arrangements and provide the means that would enable the UN to mount and deploy peacekeeping operations rapidly. But the whole idea of peacekeeping missions was – and continues to be – so fraught with problems of formation, composition, funding, and location of command that many key member states have tended to give it a cool reception.

The UN has also now taken up the issue of peacekeeping one step further and institutionalised the concept of post-conflict peace-building. It has argued that peace-building is not only a logical progression of activities from peacekeeping but that it also effectively helps preclude future crises which would warrant peacekeeping missions. The US, for its part, is convinced that peace-building is merely another cover for an expansion of the organisation's activities.

Extending Human Rights

One of the successes of the UN is said to be the propagation of human rights around the world. The Universal Declaration of Human

Rights – formulated in 1948 with the active participation of the UN – is held as a symbol of what the UN can do when it receives the support of its member states. To give impetus to the UN mandate of propagating human rights, the General Assembly in 1993 had created the post of High Commissioner for Human Rights. There was also separately created a Centre for Human Rights located in the Secretariat and it appeared at times that there was not adequate coordination between them in their work programmes even though the Centre was formally under the overall supervision of the High Commissioner for Human Rights. Annan thus proposed that the Centre now be formally a part of the High Commission. The High Commission, for its part, was to be involved in three key activities:

(1) information, analysis and policy development,
(2) support to human rights bodies and organs, and
(3) actions for the promotion and protection of human rights.

Enhanced Response to Humanitarian Needs

The nature of humanitarian assistance provided by the UN has undergone subtle changes over the years. No longer is it only the act of saving lives in situations of post-large scale conflicts. Humanitarian assistance now covers actions such as early warning, prevention, provision of emergency assistance, advocacy of humanitarian and human rights principles, protection and monitoring, etc. This requires that the UN be adequately prepared to provide the assistance when called upon. That, in turn, requires that the funding be available and that there be in place a system whereby prompt action is possible. This means, for example, that there must be effective mechanisms of coordination and cooperation within the UN system and that division of roles and responsibilities among the various entities are very clearly specified.

Since this was generally assumed to be lacking, Annan proposed that the General Assembly designate an Emergency Relief Coordinator (ERC) as the UN Humanitarian Assistance Coordinator (the office was to be located at UN Headquarters). As a result of this creation, it was recommended that the existing Department of Humanitarian Affairs be discontinued. Furthermore, several of the functions of the ERC related to coordination of natural disaster mitigation activities were to be transferred to UNDP. Annan further recommended that a humanitarian affairs segment be established at the ECOSOC so that the connection between development and humanitarian assistance would be more evident.

Reorientation of the UN's Public Information Campaign

Realising the importance of an effective communications strategy to further the reform process, after his Track I announcement, Annan had created a Task Force on the Reorientation of UN Public Information Activities. The report of the Task Force was presented prior to the formulation of the Track II proposals and Annan specified that Maurice Strong, the Executive Coordinator for UN Reform, would look into the proposals to highlight areas for him to consider. There were a few conclusions that emerged from the Task Force report that were significant:

(1) that the UN had not been able to translate the broad support that it had had into anything significant in terms of positive public relations,

(2) that the UN could do more to diminish the general perception of the public that it was a distant global bureaucracy with little relevance to the ordinary citizens, and

(3) that no new mandates in the area of communications should be accepted unless there was a corresponding provision made for funding such mandates.

A key element of the public information reorientation was proposed to be an Electronic UN. According to the proposals, the UN was to provide electronic access to all permanent missions in New York and elsewhere, to non-governmental organisations, and to the public in all countries. This access was to be to all UN publications, documents, and other pieces of information. Towards this end, the UN Web Site was already being developed and all missions and the public as well would be able to access it. The website was also to be presented in the various official and working languages of the UN. While this was seen as one of the services that the Secretariat had to provide to the member states and others, there was also a realisation that this offered a unique opportunity for the United Nations to present its own case more forcefully and in a more positive light.

In addition to these key proposals, Annan also touched on practically all areas of UN operations, and made several other interesting proposals.[18] A few of these need to be mentioned here for they go to the heart of the debate about what is perceived to be wrong with the organisation.

On the General Assembly

Pointing out that the General Assembly and the Secretary-General needed to work together and have a close and complementary relationship, Annan proposed that the member states consider reforming the manner in which the General Assembly conducted its business. There were several components to this:

(1) having focused legislative debates whereby the principal features of UN conferences were to be incorporated into the programmes of the General Assembly and the ECOSOC,

(2) focusing the work of the Main Committees in the General Assembly thematically and addressing each area in detail at each General Assembly session, and

(3) streamlining the Agenda of the General Assembly since over the years many items have remained on the agenda and time is wasted rehashing the same issues.

On Programmes and Programming Methods

Annan also made a giant leap into revitalising the organisation by proposing that the General Assembly consider instituting a sunset provision to new programmes. This meant putting in place at the start of a programme a clause that said that after a certain number of years (say, five), the programme would automatically die out unless the General Assembly made a specific decision to continue with it. This imposition of a time limit on any new programmes would do away with a key concern of the critics that the work of the UN keeps on expanding and that old programmes do not fade out at all even though they may have met their mandates.

Another element here is the proposed provision of a results-based system of budgeting. The focus here was to be on shifting the basis of budgeting from one of input-based (such as personnel, equipment, etc.) to output-based (such as extent of project/programmes objectives fulfilled, etc.). The idea was for the General Assembly to specify what the specific programmatic outputs were to be and the Secretariat would be held responsible for the attainment of these outputs. The Secretary-General, as the head of the Secretariat, would exercise greater responsibility for determining the precise mix of inputs to generate the desired outputs.

On the Trusteeship Council

The sunset provision mentioned above was said to refer primarily to the Trusteeship Council (TC). The TC's mandate has now been completed, having dealt with the last of the colonised territories (Palau in 1994 to be a self-administering territory). Yet the bureaucrats in the UN have continued to retain the TC and several critics have pointed out the irony in this (although to its credit, the Council in 1994 did amend its rules of procedures to meet as and where the occasion may arise rather than on a regular basis). In presenting his Track II proposals, Annan said that it appeared to him that member states wanted to continue retaining the TC, in which case, he suggested that it be given a new mandate altogether.

This picks up on a theme that had been dealt with in some detail by the Commission on Global Governance and others who had proposed that the TC be asked to look after the Global Commons as well as be involved in administering countries where internal chaos reigns and governance is very weak (countries such as Somalia, for example). Once again, this has evoked mixed reactions from various segments of the member states. The poorer countries of the South have generally welcomed the idea saying that it would ensure that the UN would be assisting the very needy people of these countries. On the other hand, the countries of the North have, by and large, said that this is merely a way to continue with a structure whose mandate has been fulfilled and which should, therefore, be disbanded with the savings in costs to be channelled elsewhere.

Focus on the Charter

In the Track II proposals, Annan also made a bold move by suggesting that the Charter of the UN needed some looking into. His call for a ministerial-level commission to examine the need for fundamental change through a review of the Charter was not likely to receive a very sympathetic ear but it did show that Annan was quite willing to make his reform proposals revolutionary. For his part, however, Annan recommended the Charter revision because he felt that there was too much encroachment from the General Assembly into his own work and he needed the revision of the Charter so that he could have a freer hand in running the organisation. Annan felt that while at times the General Assembly had constrained the Secretary-General (for example, in matters of staffing the Secretariat),[19] at other times, there had not been enough guidance on how to proceed with programme implementation.

Reaching out to Civil Society

The fact that non-governmental organisations (NGOs) have been able to contribute substantially to the attainment of the UN's own mandates is beyond doubt. The NGOs have played an increasingly active role in various spheres of activities (including public health, economic and social affairs, support to disadvantaged groups such as refugees and women and children, etc.) in the developing world as well as in the recently-independent countries of Central Asia. Various UN agencies (such as UNHCR, WFP, UNICEF, etc.) have already developed comprehensive systems of programmatic linkages with NGOs and it is quite obvious that the latter's role in development operations will only increase in the future. In that context, then, Annan proposed that all UN agencies make more effort to draw in the NGOs through increased consultation and participation in the programme development processes.

The UN System

Mindful of the fact that the specialised agencies of the UN system also continue to come in for a considerable amount of criticism, and that there is said to be very little coordination between the UN itself and its various agencies, one of the things Annan proposed to do was to strengthen the role of the Administrative Committee on Coordination (ACC). Since he himself chairs the ACC, he could use it in such a way as to better facilitate coordination with the specialised agencies. However, Annan is also aware that the Charter of the United Nations gives him very little scope for manipulating the specialised agencies (i.e., he can only make recommendations for their coordination). It is thus that he asked for a ministerial-level commission to review the Charter, as well as the various legal instruments from which the specialised agencies derive their mandates, and point out ways of enhancing further cooperation between the UN and its specialised agencies.

International Criminal Court

Finally, in his proposals, Annan specifically cited the fact that there was a considerable need for an International Criminal Court to bring to justice perpetrators of crimes against humanity, and that he lent his support to the establishment of such a court. Efforts at coming up with an ICC have been going on for a very long time now. A year after he made his proposals, a diplomatic conference was held in Rome to discuss the various issues related to the creation of an ICC. While a Preparatory Commission is working towards its establishment, given the strong opposition of the US, the issue is not likely to get very far.

It needs to be mentioned here that the long-term measures that Annan included in his Track II proposals mirrored the concerns that others before him have raised numerous times. In 1993, for example, Bertrand had already identified some trends in UN reforms concerning the main organs of the organisation for which the Charter itself would have to be amended:[20] (a) economic and social reform (dealing specifically with the restructuring of the ECOSOC), and (b) reform of the Security Council. At least in relation to the first component here, Annan's ideas were not new. Bertrand's own 1985 *Some Reflections on Reform in the United Nations* had called for a restructured ECOSOC as had the UNA-USA. Others that have harped on a similar theme include the Nordic UN Project in 1991 and even UNDP's *Human Development Report* in 1992 (see the previous chapter for a discussion of this).

While presenting his reform proposals to the General Assembly in his Annual Report for 1997, Annan brought to the fore three key issues that he felt needed to be urgently addressed by the world as a whole in relation to the UN:

(1) to create appropriate structures in the Secretariat to help the Secretary-General in leading the organisation towards meetings its mandates,

(2) to delineate between the Secretariat and the other constituent parts of the UN (more specifically the General Assembly) the various functions that are mandated by the Charter, and

(3) to accord high priority to the issue of staff resources in any new reform agenda.

In presenting his two-track reform proposals, Annan asserted that reform was not an event but a process.[21] This appears to be a direct response to the US's call for sweeping changes to precede the release of any new funds. While Annan started the reform process from the very moment he took over as Secretary-General, as his Track II proposals showed, there was much that still remained to be tackled. There were many intractable problems at the UN (such as personnel costs, reforming the Security Council to make it more democratic and representative, etc.)[22] that had not yet been highlighted, and much work needed to be done yet to revitalise the organisation.

Having looked at the components of the Annan Agenda, the next chapter will then assess not only the reactions to it, but will also detail how the reform efforts have progressed since they were presented in the summer of 1997. That analysis will then enable a broad holistic view of the range of reform efforts that have been made at the UN and will also help in assessment of the potentialities of any of them being successfully implemented.

Endnotes

[1] Over a period of 30 years, Annan moved up through the ranks at the UN with a reputation for intelligence, fairness and effectiveness in difficult posts such as personnel, finance, and budgetary matters, and finally peacekeeping operations. He is said to be quiet and courteous, and anybody who has seen him in action, will agree that his style is very mellow. As for his career at the UN, it is said to be impressive, to say the least, being credited with streamlining various processes in his former job in peacekeeping, a Department that was said to be the best-managed (in most areas, the only effectively organised) unit in the entire UN. Annan is also largely

acknowledged as being one of the half dozen (others say one or two) best managers in the UN Secretariat.

[2] Just for beginners, Congress wanted Annan to look into three key issues:
(1) establishment of a code of conduct for UN staff,
(2) a salary freeze, and
(3) procurement reform.

It has to be noted that Annan has so far delivered on two of the three demands. The Code of Conduct continues to be debated in the General Assembly, and the Inspector-General's Office is looking into matters of procurement control and has made some inroads into the murky waters of that process. The salary freeze, however, is another matter. The ICSC would have to be brought to the table on a more extensive level and it is not sure that the UN staff, demoralised as they are over cutbacks in posts, etc., will necessarily not fight any salary freeze proposal. So far, Annan's proposals have not included this last component.

[3] Prior to Annan's visit, Congressman Stearns had introduced House Resolution 21 that would force the UN to adopt certain reforms or suffer the loss of American financial support. This Resolution referred to the fact that the UN had evaded the Kassebaum-Solomon provisions to the Foreign Relations Authorisation Act for 1986-1987 which required the US to reduce its 25 percent share of the general UN budget to 20 percent unless a weighted system of voting on budget matters was adopted by the organisation. What the resolution failed to mention was that Reagan had already certified to Congress that by insisting on a consensus modality of making decisions on budgetary matters, the US had, in essence, been given some form of control over the budgetary process.

[4] Speaking at the National Press Club during his trip, Annan was quite forthright when he chastised the US for not agreeing to pay its share of the dues. Saying that the US freely agreed to the current rate of assessment, Annan urged the US to live up to its word (United Nations Press Release SG/SM/6149, 24 January 1997).

[5] Transcript of a press conference by Secretary-General Kofi Annan at United Nations Headquarters on 13 February 1997 (United Nations Press Release SG/SM/6156).

[6] See European Union (1997).

[7] See United Nations Press Release SG/SM/6247, 6 June 1997.

[8] Annan had proposed that these posts be eliminated altogether after earlier showing some signs that he might just want to leave them vacant to be filled later if the need arose.

[9] In his reform proposals, Annan paid particular attention to staff resource development. He described it as its most vital, and sometimes neglected, resource. In a 1998 report to the General Assembly on human resources management reform (United Nations Document A/53/414), he outlined a vision for a new management culture of empowerment, responsibility and accountability. The overall objective was to align human resources with global mission.

[10] Annan's decision to reconfigure the Secretariat's work programme follows closely the proposal put forward in the General Assembly by the US in 1996, and meant for the UN as a whole to focus efforts and resources on four core functions:
(1) maintaining peace and security,
(2) ensuring rapid and effective response to humanitarian emergencies,

(3) establishing, and monitoring observance of, international legal and technical norms, and

(4) promoting sustainable development.

[11] The membership of the Steering Committee included: Maurice Strong as the Chair; and the UNDP Administrator, Heads of the Departments of Administration and Management, of Political Affairs, for Policy Coordination and Sustainable Development, and of Humanitarian Affairs, as well as the Legal Counsel, the High Commissioner for Refugees, and the Executive Secretary of ECLAC, as members.

[12] The MRG replaced the Efficiency Board and its working group created by Boutros-Ghali.

[13] "Letter of Transmittal from Under Secretary-General Joseph E. Connor to Secretary-General Kofi Annan," 22 April 1997, in United Nations (1997(c)).

[14] The measures are detailed in a Background Note prepared by the UN on 17 March 1997 and titled "Secretary-General details bold two-track reform plan," (http://www.un.org/reform/sginit/bgnote.htm).

[15] This was actually based on a recommendation made by the Group of Industrialised Countries (G-8) meeting of 1996 in Lyons, France.

[16] "Letter of Transmittal from Under Secretary-General Joseph E. Connor to Secretary-General Kofi Annan," 22 April 1997, in United Nations (1997(c)).

[17] Annan's proposals were to effectuate a 25 percent reduction in paperwork in 1997 and to lower the current page limit for Security Council documents from 24 to sixteen and for General Assembly documents from 32 to 24.

[18] For a detailed listing of the proposals made as well as the strategies to be employed to implement them, see United Nations (1997(a)).

[19] Annan has looked at history in this regard. Bertrand (1993: 425) says that reform efforts in the UN have at times been resisted from the Secretariat (particularly those that came from the General Assembly since the Secretariat felt that its turf was being trampled upon). This is what Cuellar meant when he argued: "it would be a refreshing change if the General Assembly and individual member states were to exercise more forbearance and give the Secretary-General the flexibility he needs to ensure the smooth and efficient functioning of the Secretariat" (1993: 138).

[20] Bertrand (1993: 430-431) lists three but they can be effectively grouped into two: (1) reforming the ECOSOC, and (2) reforming the Security Council. The latter includes not only reform of membership (i.e., the need to increase the participation of more developing countries as well as the need to phase out the veto power) but also enhancing the Council's effectiveness by putting at its disposal a military force (Boutros-Ghali's *Agenda for Peace* report made special mention of this).

[21] The phrase is actually Boutros-Ghali's who first mentioned it at a dinner given by the-then Foreign Minister of Germany, Klaus Kinkel, at Lubeck, Germany, on 17 October 1996.

[22] Annan is curiously silent on the matter of Security Council reform. It is true that at the time he was working on his own reform proposals, the Open-Ended Working Group on Security Council Reforms was also hard at work and its Chairman, the former President of the General Assembly, Razali Ismail, had, in fact, presented a set of detailed proposals on this very issue. It is possible that Annan did not want to pre-empt whatever proposals Ismail may have been working on.

Chapter Five
"Could not put Humpty Dumpty together again"(?): The Results

While presenting his two-track reform proposals, Annan said that they were the most comprehensive in the history of the UN. There is no disputing that, but will they work? Having reviewed all the major proposals that have been presented thus far, and having also looked at what this Secretary-General has had to offer, the next logical thing to do is to assess the possibilities of reforming the UN at all. At a minimum, there is need to assess the reactions to the Annan Agenda and then to see what has happened to it since he offered it over two and a half years ago.

This chapter does two key things: the first is to review the reactions to the proposals to get a sense of the possibilities of their being accepted by the member states and being successfully implemented. The second is to assess the do-ability of the proposals themselves. Keeping in mind the discussions of the intellectual underpinnings of the organisation, there is need to contextualise the proposals and see if they were merely utopian or whether there was really any operational feasibility in them. (This particular aspect of the analysis will form part of the last chapter as well).

5.1 REACTIONS TO THE ANNAN AGENDA

Reactions to Annan's proposals were as varied as they were instructive of the global situation facing the UN. On the positive side, the Executive Director for Policy Studies of the UNA-USA gushed his praises for the proposals[1] while on the negative side, Senator Jesse Helms and other US legislators called the proposals clearly "very underwhelming".[2] In many respects, the proposals met with the predictable hostile and sceptical response (with some saying that it had not gone far enough, and others that it had excessively done so). But a bare four months into the announcement of the proposals, it was reported that Annan's reform proposals were "grinding to a halt due to a maze of objections".[3]

There was indeed considerable hype at the time that Annan not only took over office but also the six months succeeding that when his proposals were being finalised. Different camps had different ideas on what should be done and what to expect. For the staunchest critics such as Jesse Helms, there either had to be a complete overhaul of the bureaucracy with massive cuts or the US would pull out. For those in developing countries, there was a sense that the developed countries (particularly the USA), having scuttled Boutros-Ghali, were also now intent on minimising the importance of the reforms.

Reactions to the Annan proposals came in from various sources. The Group of 77 countries, in particular, was adamant that the reforms of the organisation should have been geared more towards strengthening its development functions. The Group did not feel that the reform efforts should be motivated by the aim of downsizing the UN[4] – a belief that runs very counter to what the developed countries believe in. The Group was also very opposed to the proposed weighted system of decision-making in the organisation. Finally, the Group of 77 countries wanted the General Assembly to take the lead role in staffing decisions in the Secretariat and called for an equitable representation in the staffing of the Secretariat. All these proposals have run into heavy criticisms from the developed countries and it is difficult to see how compromises can be hammered out.

The Group of 77 has also for some time now continually harked on the same themes in reform proposals with no hint of compromise at all. It has rejected calls, for example, for a ceiling or a floor for the members to pay their dues. It asserts that any new adjustments to the dues assessments of member states should not lead to an increase in the dues of individual countries that existed prior to the adjustments. Its sister organisation, the Non-aligned Group, has also asked that no selective expansion of the Security Council be made that would deny the Third World countries an opportunity to be represented on a permanent basis in the Council. The Group has once again asked for the elimination of the veto power in the Security Council. The Organisation for African Unity (OAU), for its part, strongly stated that Annan's reform proposals would not be supported if it meant sacrificing economic projects for the sake of efficiency. All these show clearly that given the nature of the proposals being made, there will never be any dramatic reform of the United Nations.

For their part, US lawmakers who were hoping for a radical plan from the Secretary-General they had so strongly pushed for were rather bitterly disappointed. Annan's plan failed to pacify the Americans in two key respects: (1) a promise to reassess the American share of the UN budget, and (2) crediting funds that the US had paid toward peacekeeping operations against the $870 million Washington owed then in back membership fees. Loud and disapproving noises came from the US Congress, but Annan, emboldened by the rather warm support for his proposals from other quarters such as the Nordic countries and the newly-industrialising industrial economies, said that he was not going to be fazed by such criticisms especially since his proposals had not been thoroughly reviewed by the critics. He is reported to have been offended by the rather brusque manner in which proposals were rejected outright.[5]

For US President Bill Clinton, however, the proposals were sound enough that he used them as a lure for Congress to agree to start paying arrears to the UN. He was positive about the reform proposals when first announced and a full year and half later, he was on record as saying: "I will be bold enough to say that the UN has gone through more reform in the past few months than we have in many decades."[6] This was strong praise indeed for the stewardship exhibited by Annan in the matter of reforming the UN, but it still did not get Congress to cough up the money.

On the other hand, the Carlsson Group of Sixteen Heads of State or Government, represented then by the Czech Republic President, Vaclev Havel, welcomed the proposals and urged the UN reforms to be bold but not unacceptably radical.[7] All in all, reactions from around the world were predictable only to the extent that Third World countries wanted less cuts in development spending and programmes regardless of what was proposed to be restructured in the UN, and the donor nations, by and large, wanted to see the organisation more streamlined. For Annan himself, this was the most dramatic and radical set of proposals he could come up with and he intended to push his own Agenda to sell these reform proposals.

5.2 ANALYSIS OF THE PROPOSALS

Independent of the reactions that the Annan Agenda received in its initial months, there is need to analyse critically the merits and demerits of some of its more salient points. The analysis that ensues draws considerably from the 30 months or so of experiences that the UN has had in the implementation of some of the proposals, and the debate of others.

Before looking at the possibility of reforming the UN, it is necessary to lay down guidelines and a framework within which the reform efforts should be discussed. Bruce Russett (1995) provides one of the most extensive frameworks in this regard, and this study makes use of it here. At the core, the reform process is through and through a political process and can thus only be see in that light. Russett's framework includes viewing the reform proposals within the context of judging them by ten standards (or what he calls "balances"). The balances are contained in several dichotomies[8] (such as between perspectives of state and non-state actors, between effectiveness and justice, etc.). However, of the ten, this study argues that for analysis purposes, there is need to assess the reform proposals on the balance between practicality and vision (or, to put it in consonance with the discussion in Chapter One, between reality and idealism).

It is clear from the proposals that Annan has shown signs of a bureaucrat that has had to contain his proposals for reforms within realistic boundaries although in a few instances there is evidence that he has played to the crowds in the South and has detailed ideas that clearly will not see the light of day. He has also not made any attempt to tackle the more thorny issues of reforms of the Security Council, the ECOSOC, or more importantly, the specialised agencies. As a matter of fact, the Annan Agenda is so silent on the specialised agencies that critics have pooh-poohed the proposals and considered it dead-on-arrival. By focusing on the universe of the Secretariat and some universal functions of the UN, it could be argued that Annan has sought to take the easy way out on these matters of reforms. But strictly on matters related to the Secretariat, there can be no question that Annan has given considerable attention to the resolution of long-seated problems.

Following Annan's own line of logic, the three areas in which he seems to have put in considerable emphasis (i.e., leadership and management, structural streamlining, and increased managerial efficiency) are the areas where the Secretariat needs the most emphasis. As was mentioned in the earlier chapter, Annan has been able to effectuate a rather radical administrative rationalisation by replacing the dozens of departments, units, and agencies that nominally report directly to him with a leadership structure organised around five main sectors.

In the area of structural streamlining, he presented his ideas in more concrete form to the General Assembly for the 1998 session discussions, and included those on delegation of authority to managers, and a more coordinated response at the country level through the Office of the Resident Coordinator (and contained in the notion of UN Houses). While 11 countries started experimentation with the UN House, by the middle of 1999, this figure had gone up to 36 countries, and 20 more were planned for the rest of the year. Finally, in the area of increased managerial efficiency, Annan has been able to generate savings through enhanced efficiencies and these savings have gone into a Development Account for the poor countries. However, the amount at the moment is expected to be less than $30 million, far short of the $100 million expected earlier.

Given the nature of his position as Secretary-General (part Administrator and part political leader), Annan had in his proposals specified some measures for actions (in keeping with the authority given him) and recommended others for discussion by the General Assembly in its 1997 and 1998 sessions. By 1999, the proposals were supposed to have been debated, agreed upon, and re-formalised, if necessary. More specifically, an analysis of Annan's actions and recommendations reveals the following key points.

Related to Management of the Secretariat

The Senior Management Group (SMG) that Annan proposed, and which he has now constituted, acts as his Cabinet and consists of all senior UN administrators in the Secretariat. This, coupled with his weekly teleconferencing meeting (initiated in September 1997) with other senior officials in UN offices around the world, is at the core of where and how the UN should react to changes.[9] In addition to the SMG, and also to complement it, Annan has also now put into action a Strategic Planning Unit (SPU). This information and research unit reporting directly to him is designed to input to the SMG pertinent information related to the UN's activities and to act as his think-tank.

On the matter of the post of Deputy Secretary-General (DSG), Annan had recommended that one be created and staffed at the earliest possible time. The DSG post had been pushed vigorously by the USA which felt that the Secretary-General was spending too much time on the nitty-gritty of UN activities instead of rightfully focusing attention on the big business of global affairs. The developing countries, for their part, had wanted a similar post too but it was to be focused on development.[10] After all, they had earlier forced the creation of the Director-General for Social and Economic Development, a post that was abolished by Boutros-Ghali in 1992. On this issue, as in others, Annan caved into the Americans' demand, and he recommended the creation of a DSG post and the 1997 General Assembly session approved it. By March 1998, he was able to staff the position. To it, he brought a very capable individual, the Assistant Foreign Minister of Canada, Louise Frechette.[11] Having brought her in, Annan also gave her the rather important task of coordinating all reform-related implementation activities.

Related to Various UN Organs and Other Structures

Annan also recommended steps that could be taken to revitalise the actions of the various UN organs. Once again, he could only recommend actions here since they were not technically under his jurisdiction. However, in so doing, he has not necessarily covered much new ground. For example, his recommendation that the General Assembly sessions be focused differently is nothing new. The Americans have been clamouring for a re-evaluation of the modalities of the Assembly for a long time. In particular, they are not too comfortable with the plethora of conferences and 'talk-fests' that the General Assembly has sanctioned over the past seven or eight years (mention could be made of conferences on population (Cairo), cities (Istanbul), women (Beijing), environment (Rio), etc.).

Another proposal made in relation to the General Assembly is to set aside specific high-priority themes for discussions and also radically revamp its agenda for currently a lot of time is spent on just speech-making by delegates of the various countries that attend the once-a-year session. The practicality of his suggestions is very evident, but it is increasingly difficult to see the member states agreeing to any such radical departure from the norm. To them, this is the only time they can stand on equal terms in front of the other leaders and voice their opinions. Curtailing them of their time on the world stage is not something that is likely to go easy with them. At the moment, these proposals have been put forth by Annan but they have not been taken up for serious consideration.

Annan also touches upon the possible tinkering that could be done with the ECOSOC which is moribund in many ways. Ever since it was expanded to its current size (effected in 1973), many feel that it has been unwieldy. A few (e.g., Commission on Global Governance, Maurice Bertrand, etc.) have gone so far as to recommend the elimination of the ECOSOC altogether and replace it by an Economic Security Council modelled along the lines of the presently-constituted Security Council. The ECOSOC also has weak control over the specialised agencies and there is frustration in the West over the inability of the ECOSOC to rein in these agencies that seem to have a life of their own, affiliated with the UN in generic ways but completely outside the domain of its influence.

Annan senses this frustration but also realises that developing countries will never tolerate any tinkering with the ECOSOC. After all, in the area of social and economic development, this is the supreme UN body. As such, Annan has merely called for more flexibility in the Council's meeting schedule. He also alludes to the necessity of bringing in technical experts rather than diplomats to discuss matters of economic development, but that is not likely to be agreed upon by the developing countries. In this regard, there is not much change that is likely to come about.

Annan also brings to the fore some of the problems that are contained in the subsidiary bodies of the General Assembly. In Chapter One, mention has been made about the role that subsidiary bodies play in the overall UN activities. Given the plethora of these committees and commissions, there was every reason for Annan to recommend folding a number of committees and commissions into larger intergovernmental panels (e.g., the energy and natural resources panels into the Commission on Sustainable Development (CSD)). On the other hand, Annan has recommended that the Advisory Board on Sustainable Development be abolished since the CSD performs similar functions. Once again, Annan is only recommending that these changes take place; as to whether that would indeed materialise is hard to tell at this stage. The General Assembly has not taken up these detailed issues yet although it is obvious that it must have seen these realities for itself as well.

Then there are the five Regional Commissions of the UN. While Annan touches upon them as well in his report, whether by design or not, he does not delve into the problems that these bodies are facing. It appears, however, that many of these Commissions are now in the throes of being irrelevant. Much of the work they do has been taken over by, for example, regional banks (such as the Asian Development Bank and the African Development Bank) and even by national governments whose capacity to do research has improved considerably since these Commissions were formed. In that light, there are many (even within the UN and certainly in the West), that would like to see these bodies abolished. Sensing that mood, Annan does call for the ECOSOC to review their competencies and see how they could be realigned with global bodies such as the banks mentioned above. Immediately after Annan's accession as the head of the UN, and while rumours of potential cutbacks were swilling, several of these Regional Commissions went on the offensive, and argued for a continuation of their existence.

Actually what has transpired is that while the member states have independently gone ahead with having the Regional Commissions go through a reform process (as a result of General Assembly resolution 50/227 which mandated the ECOSOC to undertake a review of the Commissions), Annan himself further asked for their review.[12] There is some confusion as to which should take precedence. Many (such as the Chairman of the Second Committee of the 52nd UN General Assembly session in 1997) do not see an overlap though and tend to give preference to the General Assembly and the ECOSOC measures. For their part, some of the reform efforts that the Commissions have initiated or have been involved in recently include ECE's reform moves on performance indicators.[13] A similar effort has been underway in ECLAC which in 1997 was selected to participate in a "management pilot scheme"[14] designed to introduce a new approach to management within the UN system. Other recent reforms include those in areas of priority-setting, improved management, budgeting exercise, and coordination with other organisations.

There is another issue that has worried the Regional Commissions. Both the Nordic and EU proposals have suggested that there should be a concentration of operational activities in the programmes, and that the conceptual-analytical work should be left to the Secretariat (of which, the Commissions form a part). The Commissions, worried that implementation of these suggestions might lead to a weakening of their own mandates, have fought back and have argued that the two cannot be separated.[15] Annan himself has not come out clearly on this one, leaving it instead to the member states to determine this. The Regional Commissions and their supporters say that the normative work and the operational work have gone hand in hand and have been mutually reinforcing. They further say that this is not what the member states want. On the other hand, supporters of the bifurcation, such as the Vice-President of the 1997 session of the ECOSOC, argue that operational activities are better carried out by the Funds and Programmes which have the advantage of maintaining country-level presence.

The long and short of this issue with the Regional Commissions is that given that their abolition – or even a substantive downward revision of their mandates – would require considerable debate, it is not likely that any General Assembly session will take up this issue anytime soon with any great degree of seriousness of purpose. There might be some perfunctory changes that will be made in the mandates, and the operational methodology, but not much change is likely in the next one to two years when it comes to Regional Commissions.

The other UN structure that Annan focuses on in his two-track reform proposals (although it is contained in a minor way in his second one) is the International Civil Service Commission (ICSC). The ICSC is key in the formation of the international civil service given its mandate over the standards and conditions of service (including compensation scales) throughout the UN system. Annan does not delve too much into the inner workings of the ICSC and how it could be revitalised. There is a common perception among the senior Secretariat officials that the ICSC is technically incompetent, and that, therefore, something needs to be done urgently about reforming the ICSC. Even UN staff members are unhappy with the manner in which this body has gone about representing their interests.

Yet, at the same time, there is a clear feeling among UN officials and outsiders that the ICSC is a rather powerful entity and that it will not allow anybody or any office to push it around when it comes to staff salaries and benefits. This is probably the reason why no manager and executive of the UN has dared to tackle the matter of staff salaries and benefits in any but the most perfunctory manner. Whether or not the current salaries and benefits of UN officials and staff members are adequate is immaterial at this juncture. What is important is that the ICSC is a powerful agency and no Secretary-General has dared to tinker with it radically. Annan has been true to this form here. He has simply called on the General Assembly to review its mandate, its membership, and its mode of operations. The General Assembly, also true to form, has only every now and then cursorily scrutinised the Noblemaire Principle[16] as well as the Flemming Principle.[17] One such review was done in the 1999 General Assembly but both the principles were recommended to be left intact.

The final structures that Annan touches upon in his reform proposals are the United Nations Environment Programme (UNEP) and Centre for Human Settlements (Habitat), both located in Nairobi, Kenya. Driven largely by the Rio Summit, and the pressures applied on him by developing countries, as well as some developed ones, Annan is acutely aware of the environmental impact of all the global activities that have been evident thus far (including the disastrous El Nino system of 1997) and has thus set out plans to develop new measures to restructure and strengthen the UNEP and Habitat. Since no particular or detailed proposal has been made further to this stated plan, it is clear that for now Annan and his team are not quite clear themselves about what particular course of action to take and are thus content to merely express this action and take it up for serious consideration later.

Related to Various UN functions

Peacekeeping and Peace-Building

An area that has particularly taken up the time of the last two Secretaries-General at the UN is peacekeeping (and the various complementary activities related to it). It is no secret that peacekeeping as a UN activity has seen tremendous rise in the last decade. From 1948 to early 2000, there have been a total of 53 peacekeeping operations but a full 30 of them have taken place since 1992. It is also this area that has given the UN most headaches about funding, etc. In that context, Annan seems to be the ideal person to focus on these two areas since his previous work experience at the UN was as the Under Secretary-General of Peacekeeping Operations. It is a job he knows well, and for which he was given much credit. In this particular area then, his recommendations for a rapid reaction capacity (where information-sharing and a model status-of-forces agreement are key ingredients) are worthy of further consideration. These have not been taken up for serious consideration yet, however, but there does not appear much resistance to it from the major UN members except the US. As a matter of general policy, the US has always looked at the rapid reaction component of any peacekeeping mission at the UN with some degree of anxiety, not only because of concerns over funding (for which the bulk would have to come from the US) but also because of the images it seems to conjure in the edgy legislators and the general public about an organisation that is getting so powerful that it could one day have its own standby forces.

On the issue of dealing with "gratis" military officers, Annan is likely to face considerable opposition. Annan's proposal is bold in that he wishes to see the end of the UN dependence on personnel seconded from member states. This not only means that the UN has to be dependent upon the member states but also that their frequent transfer, etc., leaves a vacuum in UN operations. More importantly, for countries such as the USA that have historically opposed such a UN personnel base, this smacks of a UN army, and it is doubtful if the US will agree to the development of a military personnel base at the UN. On the face of it then, this proposal is also dead-on-arrival.

In the area of post-conflict peace-building (something that transcends the usual peacekeeping operations), Annan's proposals are rather sound. Annan would have the Department of Political Affairs (DPA) act as the focal point for such post-conflict peace-building activities. In the past, there have been some organisational turf battles related to this area with such heavyweights as UNHCR, UNHCHR, UNDP, and even the World Bank, entering into the fray. Annan's team would have to tread lightly on this issue if organisational egos are not to be bruised. The DPA would have to be very sensitive to individual organisational prerogatives in order to get this job done. Having said that, there is no doubt that peace-building is an area that rightly needs to be emphasised in UN affairs.

Disarmament

It appears that Annan's focus on disarmament has tended to go against the grain of what his predecessor had attempted to do at the UN. This set of proposals needs to be put in historical perspective here. When Boutros-Ghali in 1992 had restructured the UN, he had "downgraded" the disarmament functions of the UN in light of the historic agreements that had been reached between the US and the Soviet Union (at first) and then Russia. There appeared at that time very little need for a full-fledged department for disarmament. Since then, however, events around the world have shown that it is not only nuclear weapons that the USA and Russia possess that are the source of potential worries. Increasingly around the world, there is arms conflagration, seepage of nuclear weapons technology from the former Soviet republics, land mines continue to be a problem in formerly civil-war strifed countries, and terrorists have been known to have had access to increasingly sophisticated weapons.

In light of all this, Annan has proposed to reinstate to full Department level its disarmament functions taking it away from the Department of Political Affairs where it had been housed since 1992. However, since Annan does not call for appropriate human resources in the form of technical experts to support the work of the Department, it is difficult to see how this Department might actually go about doing its job in an effective manner.

Further on the issue of disarmament, Annan has also called for a review by the General Assembly of the work of the Disarmament Commission as well as the General Assembly's First Committee. There appears to be considerable overlap of functions in these forums and a review is certainly mandated. The only problem is that just as the Secretary-General chafes at the General Assembly's imposition of views related to the Secretariat,[18] the General Assembly itself could have second thoughts about reviewing its own commissions.

Crime and Drugs

The next set of proposals related to UN's functions is that on crime and drugs. With increasing frequency, there has tended to be a link between the two (particularly in South America) and Annan hopes to get the UN to be involved in stemming the tide. There has already been in existence a UN Drug Control Programme operating out of Vienna, and Annan's proposal adds the tasks of crime control to it. The new organisation – called the Office for Drug Control and Crime Prevention – is headed by Senator Pino Arlacchi, the noted anti-Mafia campaigner from Italy. Annan's proposal to also enhance capabilities to deal with international terrorism will need to be studied carefully but has as yet not amounted to much. Money-laundering will also continue to be a focus as it was during the UNDCP days.

Development

It is in the area of development that Annan's proposals have been most closely scrutinised. The developing countries have for a long time now (even before the designation of the First Development Decade in the 1960s) insisted that the UN as an international organisation should be putting primary focus on development. It is fortuitous for them that increasingly these days there is a growing realisation that international peace and security and development are closely linked and so the UN has been putting development high on the agenda. In that regard, Annan has repeatedly said that he will attempt to minimise the negative impact on development of the cost-cutting that has taken place at the UN. If anything, he has recommended that savings generated from the efficiency projects be transferred to a specially-created Development Account.[19]

On the structural side of the development agenda, the Secretary-General has proposed the creation of a UN Development Group (UNDG). This group brings together three semi-autonomous development-related funds – UNICEF, UNFPA, and UNDP – with their respective heads constituting an Executive Committee.[20] The Committee is to be chaired by the UNDP Administrator and he will also represent the three programme funds of the Development Group in the Secretary-General's "Cabinet".[21] The UNDG is to act within the parameters of the UN Development Assistance Framework (UNDAF) in each country of UN presence. On this specific issue of the UNDAF and, more particularly, the UNDG, there has been a considerable amount of scepticism expressed by the various potential pàrticipants as well as others outside the rubric of direct General Assembly/ECOSOC coverage (such as the specialised agencies).

While on paper, this grouping of the three agencies is good, in practice, ever since the idea was mooted, there has been considerable resistance to this primarily from UNICEF and UNFPA as well as from others. As it has developed since Annan made his proposal, it came to pass that UNDP – the convenor of the Executive Committee on development operations, and therefore, the lead agency in the UNDG – actively lobbied for the inclusion of other specialised agencies in the UNDG. One such to-be inclusion was WHO that in July 1997 was asked by UNDP to consider being a part of the UNDG.[22] On the other hand, UNFPA and UNICEF quite clearly expressed their deep reservations about the UNDG.[23] UNICEF went so far as to approach US legislators to lobby Annan on its behalf.[24] It took all of Annan's diplomatic skills to quell the concerns of the particular legislator and of the UNICEF Head, Carol Bellamy, as well.

Internal documents at the UN show that UNICEF opposed vigorously its inclusion citing that its mandate, and more importantly, its comparative advantage in delivery, would be compromised by this inclusion. Actually, what is also key here is that UNICEF has always considered itself to be far superior to UNDP in management of its affairs and did not want to see its role usurped by a less-effective and less-efficient agency. To a large extent, even the UNFPA feels that it does a much better job at meeting its mandates and it too expressed misgivings about this move. UNDP, for its part, would have nothing to lose from its association with UNICEF and UNFPA, or anybody else that cares to join the UNDG for its bureaucratic turf would increase in that case. Also, at the policy and more upstream level, its primacy of role in development would be solidified by its chairing the Executive Committee. And at the operational and more downstream level, its role would continue to be enhanced since the Resident Coordinator, the person designated to lead the UNDG at the country level, has virtually always tended to be selected by UNDP and the Resident Coordinator also serves as the UNDP Resident Representative.

The UNDG has, however, come to be and is operational although there appears to be an uneasy alliance among its constituent parts. The eleven countries[25] in which the UNDAF/UNDG were to be pilot-tested completed their one-year experiment sometime in April of 1998. After detailed evaluations were made of how they fared and what specific operational and programmatic problems arose – and how they were solved – 20 more countries began this exercise in June 1999. It is expected that all countries to which it is applicable will have started the exercise by 2002.

Another issue that needs to be brought out here forcefully is the relationship between the ECOSOC and the Bretton Woods institutions (BWIs) on matters of fostering development. The Annan

Agenda is quite silent on this issue only saying that there will be emphasis laid on linkages with the World Bank. As has been mentioned in earlier chapters, the BWIs have taken the lead role in the area of fostering economic development in less-developed countries, and given that these countries are at a distinct disadvantage in the weighted-voting-system of the BWIs, they feel that their interests are not really given premium. And with the ECOSOC realistically not being able to play more than a perfunctory role in global economic affairs, the idea of UN reforms in the area of development is moot unless the equation of relationships between the UN and the BWIs is reconfigured. This has, however, not been very evident so far since the BWIs – while technically a part of the United Nations – are even further outside the realm of UN influence than the specialised agencies (see the next chapter for further discussion of this issue).

In merely calling for greater cooperation between the ECOSOC and the BWIs but not actually concretising particular efforts, the Annan Agenda has not really contributed much to the development function of UN reforms. Annan did say that he had had consultations with the World Bank on various matters related to reforms in the development arena, but the proposals do not show many manifestations of that liaison. Since the proposals were made, the UN and the BWIs have had several meetings but talks are still at a preparatory stage in terms of how they can coalesce better their efforts at enhancing development. In early 1999, the ECOSOC made linkages with the BWIs one of its seven key tasks for the years ahead (United Nations Press Release ECOSOC/5812, 3 February 1999).

On the whole issue of reform in the UN, and the consequent cutbacks in many areas of operation, the developing countries have made it known that they would not support the reform efforts if these efforts were to adversely affect the development assistance that they had come to expect of the UN. In that regard then, Annan had actually proposed to set up a Development Account from the administrative savings that would result from the efficiency drives in the Secretariat. This dividend for development was expected to reach $100 million by the beginning of the millennium but judging from recent trends, this might be too optimistic (as of September 1998, the savings from administrative reforms were stated to have yielded only about $13 million for the Development Account; the figure did not increase in 1999 since Annan's plan of action for the use of

Development Account funds capped the expenditures for 16 projects at $13.19 million for 2000-2001).[26] The 1998 General Assembly discussed the issue of the Development Account at length and approved it in 1999. However, there are a few concerns that member states have raised regarding the composition and the specific uses of the money.[27]

Humanitarian Relief

It is in the area of humanitarian relief that Annan has made one of the more fundamental changes in the reform proposals. Humanitarian relief continues to be a key UN activity considering the spate of crisis situations around the world. Annan proposes to disband the Department of Humanitarian Affairs (DHA) and hive off its functions to various other agencies. The DHA, which was created only during Boutros-Ghali's tenure, was supposed to coordinate the work of the UN and NGOs providing humanitarian relief, but in reality, it was a very difficult job to coordinate all this work partly because the DHA was not a bureaucratic heavyweight itself and partly because it was all a political game after all. It also suffered from a lack of technical capacity.

In order to enhance this coordination, Annan proposed an Under Secretary-General level Emergency Relief Coordinator but the operational aspects of the humanitarian relief work at the field level will be channelled through organisations such as the UNDP. It is interesting to note that the job of coordinating all this was going to be given to the UNHCR (for long, the premium agency in the UN working on relief to refugees). But it was felt that a narrow-focus agency such as UNHCR would not fit the bill exactly when it came to something that was more macro in nature than the mere functional characteristic of what UNHCR is used to dealing with.

Annan, however, needs to go beyond designating a Coordinator (he further proposed to rename this post the UN Humanitarian Assistance Coordinator). Considering that the person will not have access to much by way of resources (for example, staff members of its own), the post might need some more beefing up in the future. The Coordinator will still have to take on the heavyweights in the system such as UNHCR, WFP, UNICEF, and UNDP. The ERC will also be working with a representative of a NGO providing humanitarian relief. Finally, Annan's proposal that the ECOSOC take on some humanitarian-related issues in its agenda appears sound on paper but given the ineffectiveness of the ECOSOC, it might turn out to be a wasted one. The structural changes have been implemented. It will take some time before results of the reshuffling are known.

Human Rights

In the area of human rights, some of the actions that have resulted from Annan's reform proposals clearly show that he has made some right moves in this area. Previously, during Boutros-Ghali's tenure, the Centre for Human Rights was not in coordinated work with the Office of the High Commissioner even though formally the Centre was a part of the High Commission. By consolidating the Centre with the High Commissioner's Office, Annan has streamlined the agency considerably. To be the head of the revamped Office of the High Commissioner, he also selected the highly-respected former Irish President, Mary Robinson.

Annan has also proposed to give the Office of the Human Rights High Commissioner more resources. Considering that at present various programmes related to human rights are scattered among various UN agencies (for example, protection of children's rights in UNICEF, promotion of democratic governance in UNDP, etc.), Annan's proposal will make it possible to bring together these functions in one office. But this is likely to take a very long time. Organisations in the UN – as everywhere else – do not like to give up mandates since that is how more resources come in, and Annan will have to do a considerable amount of arm-twisting to get UNICEF, for example, to hive off its children's rights mandate to the Office of the High Commissioner for Human Rights. In the meantime, Annan hopes to beef up the New York office of the High Commissioner since the complaint is that the main office in Geneva is too far out of the political loop. Furthermore, given the numerous reporting mechanisms, working groups, treaty monitoring committees, etc., that are involved in human rights coordination, Annan has left it to the High Commissioner to assess and recommend actions to streamline and rationalise the appropriate machinery to bring about more consistency in the work of the Office.

Annan's proposals had also included mention of the International Criminal Court (ICC) and his support of the creation of one. In July 1998 in Rome, the treaty conference did meet and a Statute of the Court was passed. To date, however, less than 100 countries have signed the Statute and it is still a long way before the required 60 countries ratify the Statute prior to it coming into force.[28] The USA, for one, is adamantly opposed to such a Court citing the fact that individual liberties will be trampled upon. The USA's position has been critiqued by various people,[29] but its opposition to the ICC stands.

Related to Various Management and Administration Issues

Delegation and In-Country Management

Annan has for a long time now realised that the UN will not be reformed to any considerable extent if its operational activities at the country level are not coordinated and streamlined. There are just too many agencies with their own mandates (quite a few of which are duplicative) that are doing their own things in the countries of operation and the resultant uncoordinated work that has evolved has not really added to the development cause. To get rid of that, Annan proposed that programmes of assistance in each country be formulated and presented under a single UN development assistance framework (UNDAF). This is indeed a major step for rationalising UN development assistance in the field. The UNDAF is now operational in 31 countries (11 during the trial period and 20 in 1999) where the UNDG is also functioning although field-level managers have complained of being chafed under all the reporting and paper-work that needs to be done now that the new system is in place.

Just as with the UNDG at the policy level, here too, UNICEF, UNDP, and UNFPA are to be integrated into one overall programme although they will be separately identified. This would make it easy for the country to coordinate all the work and also to get the maximum out of UN intervention. But as has been noted earlier, there is considerable scepticism at the ground level that these three agencies will be able to work together to achieve a common goal. The modes of operations, as well as their mandates, are vastly different and everyone appears to be chafing under this added – and so far alien – integration.

As also mentioned above, UNICEF and UNFPA are not necessarily happy that the UN Resident Coordinator (almost always seen as a UNDP person) in each developing country is in charge of the local offices of all the UN agencies (including any UN information centres). It is good that all these agencies are being brought together into one single building (named "UN House", already evident in countries such as Lebanon, Lesotho, Malaysia, South Africa, as well as in over 50 countries), but there is opposition from within the UN to have a UN House in every country just because it would be nice to have one. In many countries, it is felt that existing different offices have served the purposes quite well and that in many instances it might even be too expensive to build a UN House.[30] But in countries around the world, Resident Coordinators are being accredited to Governments as the UN representative. As with all things new, it will take some time for this arrangement to set in and for everybody to be comfortable with it, but there is little doubt that once operational, it will streamline considerably the work of the UN in the countries.[31]

In countries where UN peacekeeping operations are underway, Annan hopes to do away with the scores of different modes of operations and reporting mechanisms and chains of command by having a single Special Representative whose job it would be to bring together all agencies that are engaged in various relief efforts (such as for refugees, food aid, election monitoring, human rights education, police training, etc.). This unitary source of coordinated efforts would then be able to give some direction to the UN's efforts in the country. Such Special Representatives have been operational now, and in Tajikistan, for instance, they have been able to bring together various disparate UN agencies to work together to deal with the civil war that has engulfed the Central Asian country.

To better manage the development functions of the various UN agencies, Annan had also originally thought of calling for integrating the governing boards of such agencies as UNDP, UNICEF, UNFPA, etc. But after a concerted effort by the latter two agencies, he relented. Instead, he now has called for a mere meeting of member states who would consider holding meetings of existing executive boards. These meetings could be held either jointly or back-to-back so that member states will be able to get a better idea of how these three agencies are doing their work. UNICEF and UNFPA have reluctantly gone ahead with this proposal even though it means that they will have to schedule these meetings not independently but in conjunction with UNDP.

Probably one of the stronger of Annan's proposals in the realm of management is that which deals with delegation of authority to senior officials, in the first instance, and then from there to line managers eventually. This is quite different from how Boutros-Ghali and the other Secretaries-General before him had gone about doing their jobs. As a matter of fact, observers have given Annan very little credit for proposing such a delegation of authority. At the time of formulation of this recommendation, it was felt that Annan would not really be able to go ahead with this exercise partly because while all Secretaries-General paid lip service to this delegation, no one had actually been able to implement it. But the 1998 General Assembly took up discussion of this very proposal, and Annan has now begun to slowly come up with details on how he plans to go about delegating more authority.[32]

In that regard, Annan has presented an outline of the existing framework for the delegation of authority, responsibility, and accountability. The starting point is obviously the General Assembly which establishes the basic regulations for managing financial and human resources. The Secretary-General then implements them and reconfigures rules for specific resource management purposes. He then delegates to the Controller authority for the administration of financial resources. Similarly, authority for the management of staff is delegated to the Assistant Secretary-General for Human Resources. Under the pilot project in the reform stage, Annan's proposals show that further authority is to be given to programme and line managers in several areas of human resource management.

The Secretary-General has already given more powers to the Resident Coordinators in their programming and administrative work (for example, in the area of management, Resident Coordinators are now able to independently decide on the manner of implementation of quality control exercises in their offices). Annan should be given considerable credit for this. Obviously, much more needs to be done, and UN officials in the field continue to look forward to getting directives from Headquarters for even minor actions but with a change in the organisational culture as practised in New York, Geneva, Vienna, and elsewhere, it is hoped that this will permeate the entire UN network of offices around the world.

Delegation of managerial authority is a critical task and one that Annan – a former bureaucrat himself – knows is a very crucial element in his reform efforts. Annan himself wants to ensure that there is a fundamental shift towards the increased delegation of authority to heads of departments and their managers and thence further on downward. In order to assist him in this delegation exercise, parallel to the deliberations going on at the General Assembly currently, Annan has also helped foster a communications culture within the Secretariat. He is seen to be building on the weekly cabinet meetings that he instituted when he first took office by bringing issues out into the open and by also talking to staff members more often.

Delegation of authority had been somewhat evident even during the dying days of Boutros-Ghali's tenure. Resident Coordinators at the field level, for example, had already got increasing authority to approve specific projects whose initial outlays exceeded one million dollars. Annan has tried to build on that. But he realises that in a monolithic organisation such as the UN, it is not possible to delegate all at once which is why his annual reports to the General Assembly continually emphasise that delegation would be implemented on an incremental basis, as guidelines, monitoring and accountability mechanisms are developed and put in place and managers are trained to take on their added responsibilities. This training component is important as there needs to be a culture developed among staff members to take the added responsibility and authority and to be accountable for it. For staff members long accustomed to doing things the way they have always been doing (or being told to do things a certain way from higher up), increased delegation of authority comes with some rather stringent controls on monitoring and accountability (this is a theme that has been continually brought up in relevant Committee deliberations at the UN).

The stated goal of this aspect of the reform process currently underway is to let the managers manage without much hindrance from the top. This may necessitate some redundancies in staff posts, but that is unavoidable. The tendency of the UN has been to ensure that staff members that become redundant are somehow or other fitted into other projects somewhere around the world. Since it is quite possible to locate one such project anywhere in the world, the staff member merely ends up changing duty stations but not being made redundant altogether. This streamlining and delegating that is currently being cautiously implemented will hopefully alter that scenario. Managers in this new exercise will now have greater control over the hiring of staff members as well as over planning and allocation of financial resources. They will be expected to take greater responsibility for developing their staff members and monitoring and evaluating their performance.

One of the things the UN agencies are beginning to do in the area of improving management in their organisations is share experiences on "best practices" of management. Joseph Connor detailed this considerably in his 22 April 1997 report to the Secretary-General, and since then many more instances of documentation – and dissemination – of "best practices" have been reported. UNDP at the moment, for instance, has a report on the "best practices" in the Resident Coordinator System (based on the experiences of nine countries – Bolivia, Costa Rica, Lao PDR, Malawi, Mali, Morocco, Pakistan, Vietnam, and Uzbekistan). A UNDP workshop held in Turin in April 1997 brought out these "best practices" in various areas such as administrative management, country strategy notes, etc. This is a useful and very relevant exercise considering that Annan wishes to give more authority and responsibility to the Resident Coordinator at the country level.

Staff Development and Human Resources

Of considerable emphasis that Annan has put in are efforts to enhance the staff and human resources aspect of the UN. Since the issue of staff development is something that takes a long time to impact, only time will tell if Annan's efforts are serious enough to generate the kind of change that he wants to bring about. Other Secretaries-General before him have also attempted to tinker with this particular resource and apparently did not get very far. Annan, in particular, knows that while he has to trim overhead costs (meaning expenses on personnel and other operations), he also has to continue to deliver the outputs and that too with a stripped-down resource base. It is thus that he devotes considerable attention to the issue of managerial reform.

He may also have very little choice in having to consider very seriously human resource issues. There are some structural considerations that he must have taken account of when he took over.

For example, the average age of a UN staff member is now 49 years, and fewer than five percent are under 35 years[33] (this unique situation is due to the hiring restriction imposed in the mid-1980s given the stringent US opposition to UN bureaucratic expansion and lack of cost control). What this means is that nearly 11 percent of the Secretariat staff is due to retire in the next five years but, more critically, almost half the professional staff is due to retire in the coming eight to ten years. This is a dire situation for any Chief Executive Officer of a company to contemplate.

It was thus that Annan asked for a fundamental review of the staffing and human resources aspect of the UN when he took over in January 1997. The able Under Secretary-General, Joseph Connor, led the exercise and by 1998-end, there had been an extensive assessment done of the human resources of the UN.[34] While various review exercises related to human resources continued to be conducted in 1999, these have led to a comprehensive reappraisal of the recruitment and placement policies. Included in the review were issues of career development, and geographical and gender representation.[35] In April 1999, the General Assembly also asked Annan to engage in some very serious re-thinking on HRM issues (United Nations Press Release GA/9551, 7 April 1999) including:

(1) investigating the existence of racial discrimination in personnel matters,

(2) reporting on the reasons for the growing number of resignations of Secretariat staff, and

(3) developing on a priority basis a policy on maintaining a strong international civil service (Annan is to submit the report in the next session of the General Assembly).

The Office of Human Resource Management (OHRM), for its part, was busy in 1998 and 1999 in assessing the core competencies of UN employees to take inventory of their knowledge, skills, and abilities (KSAs) as well as behaviours. This is being done so as to ensure that the management overhaul that Annan has initiated will dovetail with his wider-ranging programme to revitalise the UN. This exercise will enable the UN to pinpoint specific areas of strength within the organisation as well as do multi-skilling, if necessary. It is also expected to yield critical information in identifying candidates for managerial positions. Publication of the human resource framework resulting from the review and assessments is slated for mid-2000.

In general, Annan's overall goal in personnel management reform is to encourage enhanced performance, complete with rewarding or punishing superior or inferior performance, and ensure accountability. The latter is being goaded through his delegation proposals. But this is probably the first time in the UN that staff members are being judged by their performance. Actually, this might be overstating it for in many instances, it appears that non-merit factors are still the key determinants in being recruited and in being moved up. In a related matter, when Connor presented his lengthy report to Annan in April 1997 related to this reform proposal, he had detailed about 600 efficiency projects that were to lead not only to efficiencies, and thus savings, but also, just as important, to a change in the deep-rooted bureaucratic culture in the minds of the UN staff members. To what extent Annan's reform proposals will be able to bring about the desired changes is something that will be evident only later on. For now, the jury seems to favour the judgment that "little progress appears to have been achieved so far" (United Nations Press Release GA/AB/3340, 10 November 1999). Examples cited include the "excessively cumbersome, time consuming and very costly" procedures to effect transfer of staff between units of the Secretariat, to reclassify posts, and to manage vacancies (*ibid*).

There are two other issues that need to be brought out in relation to this issue of personnel management. The first is that Annan has been under pressure to bring down the size of the Secretariat bureaucracy considerably. While people such as Senator Jesse Helms have wanted to have the staff size halved, Annan has done away with over 1,000 posts over the stiff protests of the developing countries. It is thus that from a high of about 12,500 staff members in the mid-1980s, the size of the Secretariat staff hovers around the 8,700 mark now.[36] This reduction in staff size has not necessarily impacted negatively the work of the UN, although Annan has been largely able to bring down the size by having new contracts given only on a short-term basis.

The second important issue in relation to staff size is that in the UN, for every 37 employees there is one personnel officer (37:1).[37] This ratio compares very unfavourably when viewed in light of the 130:1 or so ratio that is evident in many national governments. Annan himself has alluded to this situation when describing the problems facing the UN. It is this that gives the work of the UN the bureaucratic culture that is so prevalent in the minds of the world citizenry and that Annan needs to work hard to get rid of.

One of the key tasks that result from staff cutbacks is that of training for staff members that continue to be retained in the organisation. Towards this end, at the time of the announcement of the Track II proposals, Annan proposed a one-time allocation of about $15 million for a training and re-deployment programme to assist staff that would have been affected by the reform measures. Since taking over the reins of the UN, Annan has also repeatedly asked for – and received – increased funds for staff training (for the programme budget for 2000-2001, resources for training and staff development activities increased by 30 percent for the biennium 1998-1999).[38] While the UN still spends a paltry amount of staff costs on training (0.75 percent),[39] there has been evident a general trend in increases in funding for staff development at the UN, and there is optimism among UN staff members that some good will come out of this.

This fact, coupled with the one that since 1996, over 95 per cent of all UN senior level managers and the majority of middle-level professionals with managerial responsibilities have participated in a People Management Programme as a part of an integrated series of training programmes for staff at all levels,[40] has given training a greater degree of acceptability among the staff and managers. A series of Career Support Programmes has also been launched, including career-planning workshops and lectures. The continuation of such programmes is not expected to meet much opposition in the General Assembly although some member states have questioned the need for such considerably higher levels of training funds. There is also a general feeling in some quarters that at a time when resources are acutely deficient, staff development will turn out to be something that Annan will have to continue justifying to an increasingly sceptical public.

In relation to senior appointments, Annan's proposal is to rely on independent advisors to guide him. At the moment, there are apparently very few rigorous measures in place in the recruitment of senior staff members and much of it is dependent on opaque procedures and inside negotiations (including political considerations). It would appear that even for senior appointments (certainly of positions at the D-2 level and above) there would have to be more rigorous – and transparent – modalities of recruitment. Annan has not, however, focused too much on this.[41]

Annan has also recommended that incentives be identified to encourage mobility across functions, departments, duty stations, and organisations of the UN system. In what is seen as a critical move, lateral movement is to be encouraged, and job rotations within and between departments will give staff the opportunity to take on new responsibilities and learn new skills. Towards the goal of recruiting and retaining qualified staff, Annan has now put in place mechanisms whereby particular attention is being given to junior professional staff as they start their careers. Since two-thirds of resignations in recent years have come from this group, their departure reflects their perception of the lack of career prospects in the UN.

Given that approximately 70 to 80 percent of the Secretariat's budget is spent on its core staff,[42] it has become increasingly clear that enhancement of the UN's efficiency and effectiveness is to a very large extent tied to how its personnel are managed. In this context, Annan's proposals are timely. But to what extent he will be successful is difficult to ascertain at this point. While the staff members themselves have been quite vocal of the need for reforms, it is no secret that any further cutbacks in either posts or benefits will be vigorously opposed by them. Such staff development will also require a heavy dose of unprecedented organisation-wide collaboration between the UN staff and management. Whether or not such collaboration will result is difficult to say at this point in time. Historically, it has not been evident, but Annan has much going for him even at the mid-point of his tenure and may be able to get the various parties to agree to a common agenda.

Where the Secretary-General's policies on staff movement are concerned, there can be no doubt that he is on the right track on this. His decision to facilitate a more systematic approach to mission assignments (through managed rotation) is designed to give more staff the opportunity for development by taking on new responsibilities. Public bureaucracies around the world have for long been practising job rotation and it is a very good way to tap the multi-skilling abilities of staff members. Annan's recommendations on lateral movements, job exchanges, secondments, etc., are very do-able and also very worthy. Since they fall within the domain of his own powers in the Secretariat, it should not pose a serious problem in implementation. Securing the resources would be a different story, however.

In the matter of staff behaviour, Annan has proposed a Code of Conduct (CC) for all UN staff to uphold. Among other things in the CC will be conflict-of-interest provisions, and guidelines for appropriate behaviour in programme and budget management. The CC is still being debated in the General Assembly and some disagreements have surfaced over how it should be codified. The Secretary-General wants to implement the Code through revisions to Article 1 of the Staff Rules while the ICSC wants to divorce the two. This issue has yet to be resolved satisfactorily.

Such CCs exist in all major civil services in the world and are used to guide the behaviour of the staff members. Given the spate of negative publicity of corruption and malfeasance in various agencies of the UN, this is an important piece of document to come out of Annan's reform proposals. It will be interesting to see if it will be diluted in content in the process of being accepted. Independent of the CC debate though, the General Assembly in September 1998 decided that all UN staff members at the Assistant Secretary-General level and above would be required to file financial disclosure statements in respect of themselves and their dependent children (United Nations Press Release GA/9431, 8 September 1998).

All in all though, it is felt that while numerous reform efforts have been attempted before to streamline HRM at the UN, "little progress appears to have been achieved so far" (United Nations Press Release GA/AB/3340, 10 November 1999). For example, procedures to effect transfer of staff between units of the Secretariat, to reclassify posts, and to manage vacancies are excessively cumbersome, time consuming and very costly (*ibid*). Obviously, the UN still has a long way to go before HRM practices can be deemed to have contributed to organisational success.

General Management Issues

Annan also makes it a point to target internal Secretariat managerial issues. On a general level, he calls for more management reviews from departments putting considerable focus on the regular budget process. In terms of this latter aspect of Secretariat work, Annan has asked the General Assembly to review the existing arrangements for budget-making and take it further by focusing on results-based budgeting. Annan has placed high hopes in the swift acceptance by the General Assembly of his proposal that the UN shift to this results-based budgeting and programming mode. Perhaps more than any other measure, this would probably give the UN the flexibility needed to manage resources better while at the same time enhancing both transparency and the Secretariat's accountability to member states. At the time that he proposed this measure, he had not completely formulated his ideas on this matter. Even in the 1999 General Assembly when the issue was still being debated, member states were continually asking for clarifications. The accountability for results that Annan hopes to implement are symptomatic of the type of organisation and process that he would like to see in the UN but there is much that still needs discussion and debate.

One of the more important aspects of this accountability issue is that of timelines. This is better known as a sunset provision and has been in place in several agencies in many governments around the world, particularly in the US. The sunset provisions would mean that for any new mandates there would be set time limits for Assembly review – and possible termination of programmes – thus directly counteracting the trend of institutional inertia said to be so prevalent in the UN. The General Assembly, given that it is considering something of this nature for the first time since its creation, is asking the Secretary-General for further clarifications on the specifics of his proposal. At the end of 1999, this process of clarification was still ongoing. As a matter of fact, a review of the deliberations in the Fifth Committee over the Development Account shows that member states (particularly from the developing world) are quite against the idea of using sunset provisions in projects germinating from the Development Account (see United Nations Press Release GA/AB/3352, 13 December 1999).

In the spirit of putting the UN up as a single entity, Annan had also proposed to consolidate all agency common services so that UN agencies could more efficiently do their work. This extended into areas such as procurement, telecommunications, personnel and medical services, payroll services, etc. Annan also proposed that selective outsourcing be considered although it was obvious that he was restricting these ideas to the Secretariat alone. All these are very sound proposals and Annan should not have any problems from the General Assembly on these issues. On the operational level, many of these proposals are already ongoing at the field level. Many UNDP Field Offices, for example, have out-sourced their transport services to private companies thus effectuating a fair amount of savings. UN offices have also contracted out security services and general housekeeping activities such as gardening to outside firms. All these have not only resulted in savings but have also brought about a more efficient manner in which the work has been done. It has, furthermore, freed up the time of the administrators to do more relevant and important work.

Part of the drive to effectuate savings in the UN, and also to project a more professional image and do things more efficiently, has to do with utilising the technology that exists. Towards this end, Annan's proposals to create a Virtual UN have gone along very sympathetically with outsiders. The UN's presence on the Internet has been considerably widened and access to treaties and conference reports are now possible in the Internet thus reducing costs and access time for customers. This is a phenomenal change in the manner in which the organisation has gone about doing its job particularly since it is accused of wasting too much paper. Field Offices have also now started using the available technology very judiciously and costs for communications have begun to go down considerably. Almost all UN Field Offices now have homepages that have been developed and information dissemination has tended to take up very little time. It is safe to say that these changes would have probably taken place even if Annan had not put so much emphasis on them, but by accepting the utility of this medium, Annan has made it easier for individual agencies to use the technology to its maximum. Annan has also asked for adequate infrastructure and investment to support staff members and services to member states which he is likely to get from the General Assembly. In his own work at the Secretariat, Annan has begun to use technology effectively wherein once a week he teleconferences with his senior staff members from around the world.

In the area of coordination and UN system management, Annan would like to consult more often with the Administrative Committee on Coordination (ACC) which includes the heads of the independent specialised organisations. The ACC is the only direct mode that the Secretary-General has to effectuate coordination with the specialised agencies at the policy and upstream levels and given the criticisms that have been made about duplication of work in the

UN, its importance cannot be over-stated. Annan would like to introduce 'issue management methods' among the agencies and wants to form networks such that one agency would take the lead on a cross-sectoral issue while the rest that are active in that particular area would contribute to the overall planning as well as undertake the implementation of their side of the issue. He is not likely to get much opposition on this matter from either the specialised agencies or the General Assembly. As long as he sticks to the use of the ACC for this purpose, and does not create another bureaucratic layer in the middle, it is very possible that the ACC's own work will be streamlined in due course of time. To help him in this process, he has appointed an Assistant Secretary-General for Policy Coordination and Inter-Agency Affairs which highlights the vigour with which cooperation across the entire UN system is being pursued.

On the issue of reducing administrative expenditures, there is anecdotal evidence that the UN has as of 1998-end been able to bring the level down from 38 percent to the projected 25 percent but this is not independently verified. The biennial budget of the UN for 2000-2001 is $2.536 billion which is a zero-growth budget. The staff size as of 1999-end was about 8,700 in the Secretariat from a figure of little more than 10,500 when Annan took over. The bulk of the cuts, however, have been brought about by simply not filling vacant posts,[43] and there has been a greater tendency to give only short-term contracts to young professionals ranging anywhere from three months to a year (this particular aspect has been difficult to be reconciled with Annan's own stated emphasis on career development within the UN (see discussions in the previous chapter)). One of the down-sides of the reforms as have been practised in the UN since Annan's arrival has been the general difficulties arising because of the cutbacks made throughout the organisation. The general feeling among the staff members seems to be that of frustration at the lack of resources to undertake their work.

Annan's proposals related to UN research institutes are also significant in light of his use of the Strategic Planning Unit and its functions as a think-tank to help him and his cabinet in their work. Annan realises that the various specialised research institutes of the UN are largely under-utilised (the UN University in Tokyo is certainly a case in point), and wishes to have them more involved in providing updated and useful information for planning purposes. Those institutes whose outputs are not up to the mark will have to be reviewed for continuation, but on the whole Annan would like to see that the research institutes are contributing more to the inputs of the planning process. Having said that, the General Assembly does not appear to be taking this set of issues on a priority basis and so the impetus for having the research institutes more involved in quality work will have to be initiated by ideas from the Secretariat for the time being. Towards that end, Annan has proposed to initiate measures to coordinate their activities and to demand greater relevance in their outputs.

Related to Funding and Finances

If there is one issue that will inevitably bring all the reform proposals to nought, it is the issue of financing and funding. From the time Cuellar brought this to the attention of the world community in the mid-1980s, funding has been a core issue in UN reforms. The issues relevant to funding have already been discussed in earlier chapters, and so there is no need to revisit them here. Suffice it to mention that unless the UN can do something about ensuring a steady source of revenues from the dues and assessments of member states, there is very little it can do by way of reforms. This is the fundamental catch that Annan has to deal with. As a matter of fact, his first trip days after taking over as the Secretary-General was to the US capital where he tried to put his case forward in a series of face-to-face meetings with the American legislators and the President. This only goes to show the importance of this issue.

Many proposals have been made about how the UN could generate extra resources to meet its expenses. These ideas are sound on paper, but they fail the reality check since the US has repeatedly signalled its intent that it will never seriously entertain any proposals on revenue generation that go beyond Charter-permitted system of dues and assessments. At least the specialised agencies that rely on voluntary contributions do not face such a serious problem since they are able to cultivate their donors and benefactors based on functional and technical mandates that have over the years been able to retain sympathetic donors in the West. The UN, as a whole, and particularly the Secretariat, does not have that luxury and no amount of detailed proposals on how to increase the funding sources will get it out of its problems.

In that light, Annan's proposals in the area of funding and financing take on a paradoxical twist: on the one hand, it is such an important issue that he has to shape the reform proposals around it, and on the other hand, he has so little control over it that he is helpless in doing anything about it. With that caveat in mind then, an attempt can be made to assess the proposals that Annan has come up with in matters of funding and resources. At least in the area of development assistance, he obviously has pushed for the need for restoring resources for development as quickly as possible. These core resources for development are critical if the UN's work is to continue in such important areas as AIDS, humanitarian relief, etc. He also wishes to see some degree of predictability in the resource flow (which is to be instituted by a system of multi-year advanced pledges without necessarily holding the donors to them rigidly). Annan's calls for an increase in overseas development assistance based upon global targets are merely rehashing what has been said earlier and not necessarily paid heed to by the donors. Some argue that Annan is making a pitch for this only to placate the developing countries who are worried that reforms and cost-cutting at the UN only translate into lesser resources for development purposes.

There are basically three sources of development funding that the UN can take advantage of: voluntary (which is what is evident with the specialised agencies at the moment), negotiated (which is evident in some agencies at present, such as IFAD), and private (which has been manifest in the $1 billion contribution made by Ted Turner in 1996, and which has been debated rather hotly since then). Annan feels that dependence on voluntary contributions is unpredictable since each year the UN has to go begging in pledge drives to attain the requisite level of funding. This also makes funding for development programmes unpredictable. But it is doubtful if the donors will want to change this particular system at this moment. No donor has expressed much enthusiasm for delving into this issue. Negotiated pledges (where a fixed amount for a certain number of years is received from the donor) might be better, but once again it is doubtful if the donors would like to sit down to negotiate funding for the UN's work when they are not sure to what extent the reform proposals will make the organisation more efficient. Finally, private contributions are certainly accepted by the UN, but there has been concern raised that this would then introduce an element of conflict of interest which is not desirable. Hence,

Annan is in a bind here, and his proposals on predictability of funding, etc., are not likely to see much light of day. For sure, the General Assembly will go along and accept the proposals for it is dominated by Third World countries but judging by reactions from key Western countries to this set of proposals, it is doubtful if much will come of it.

Apparently, the issue is of such concern that Annan had proposed that a large part of the job specification of the new Deputy Secretary-General be to study ways of generating resources for the organisation. The Deputy Secretary-General would be supported by a new Office for Development Financing. Frechette is currently deeply involved in the implementation of the reform proposals that are within the jurisdiction and authority of the Secretary-General and so has not had too much time to focus on development financing. But judging by how things are going at the moment, it is difficult to see how she might be able to make a difference on this score unless the West, in general, and the USA, in particular, relents.

On the specific issue of multi-year voluntary contributions, the US delegate to the UN has already said that the USA cannot oblige because its budgetary cycle does not permit it. This has already thrown cold water on to the proposal and it is not likely to go very far in the current General Assembly session. The General Assembly is expected to agree to the proposal but since its resolutions are not binding on member states, nothing much is expected out of this particular proposal.

Almost as if sensing this, Annan then has also proposed that a credit fund be instituted such that the Secretary-General can manage the financial crisis as and when it arises (such as at the present). He puts forth his case very strongly that member states must be ready to institute a Revolving Credit Fund to enable the Secretary-General to leverage the financing process at the UN. Reactions from the member states during the debates at the 1998 and 1999 General Assembly sessions imply that he will have a rather difficult time getting his wish.

Annan does, however, challenge countries to put forward ideas to induce delinquent member states to pay and restore the UN's financial solvency. Yet his own proposal seems fairly tame – it includes no toughening up of the application of Article 19, for example, and no interest charges on delinquencies – and it is unlikely to affect the political dynamics of member state defaults. What he does propose to do is to ask delinquent member states who are three months past due in their payments to certify as to when they actually intend to pay, and then take their certification as security to borrow from the Revolving Credit Fund to be repaid as each delinquent state pays its arrears. The plan's success rests on the faith that delinquent governments will meet their dues, that is, if they even care to respond to the Secretary-General's request for a certification. The plan also depends on the willingness of member states to provide the initial $1 billion to capitalise the Fund; large delinquents are unlikely to be cooperative in making payments to the Fund. Based on current trends in the General Assembly debates, none of the preconditions for the proposal are likely to materialise.

In one particular area, both Boutros-Ghali and Annan deserve praise. Over the course of the last five to six years, they have been able to whittle down the size of the regular budget through several means. Neither has got much credit for doing this although they have succeeded in showing that the UN can indeed come up with budgetary cuts. Over the years, the regular budget of the UN has gone down from about $2.7 billion in 1994-1995 to a little more than $2.53 billion in 2000-2001. That is rather impressive work considering the constraints under which the UN Secretariat works and credit needs to be given where due.

Miscellaneous

There are four other proposals of the Annan Agenda that deserve analysis here:

Related to civil society: In his report, Annan underscores the importance of "civil society" both within nations and globally. Civil society is taken to mean institutions in the private sector as well as those outside the realm of government and encapsulated in the term non-governmental organisations (NGOs). As part of his reform proposals, Annan requires all Secretariat units to designate a contact point for NGOs, and speaks of creating a UN enterprise liaison service for dialogue with the business community. The reasons are not hard to find. It is through NGOs that many UN agencies do the bulk of their field level work and have come to rely on them to such an extent that the increase in marginal utility of bringing these organisations into the programming sphere of the UN agencies is but a foregone conclusion. It would be inconceivable, for instance, that

UNHCR would be able to provide any service to any refugee without the direct involvement of NGOs such as Action Aid, *Medicins Sans Frontiers*, Water Aid, etc.

By the same token, reaching out to the business community is geared to generate more resources for the organisation by tapping into a historically unconventional source for the UN. Forced by deep financial problems, Annan – more than any other Secretary-General – has signalled an intention to turn to the private sector to augment his resource base. He has actually done this through two means: (a) the first – a direct one – by encouraging the private sector to contribute to the causes of the organisation, and (b) more suggestively, by encouraging the business community to lobby for funding for the UN with national governments over whom many businesses – certainly in the West – exercise considerable influence. This aspect of Annan's work has met with some criticism at the General Assembly, however, with several members voicing displeasure at the UN having to rely on private sector funding. For Annan, it is a no-win situation, and he appears to be at his wit's end to find a lasting solution to the funding crisis facing the UN.

A new concept of trusteeship: In his proposals, Annan has embraced an idea that has been a particular favourite of his chief reform adviser, Maurice Strong, and endorsed by a number of commissions studying global governance: conversion of the virtually defunct Trusteeship Council into a forum which would not only ensure collective trusteeship for the integrity of the global environment and common areas (such as the oceans, atmosphere, etc.) but also governance in countries characterised by internal chaos. The proposal arouses scepticism even among advocates of action on behalf of the global environment and international governance as the notion of common areas and national sovereignty can still inspire fierce ideological resistance in some quarters.

To change the mandate of the Trusteeship Council (and a Charter change would have to be enforced given the wide variance in mandates between what the Trusteeship Council has at the present and what has been suggested for it) would be a long and drawn-out affair (see below) and it seems that Annan's proposal related to the Trusteeship Council is also dead-on-arrival. The general feeling among observers of the UN is that Annan had to give in to demands of the developing countries in this regard over the opposition of the

West, but there is likely to be a considerable amount of fireworks when this issue does make it to the General Assembly floor.

Revisions of the Charter: This issue of Charter revision appears a few times in the implications of Annan's various proposals. The case of the Trusteeship Council is one, that of the specialised agencies is another. Given the highly decentralised nature of the UN family of agencies, Annan has emphasised the importance of a greater degree of concerted will and coordinated action throughout the system. He knows that the system has fundamental weaknesses that member states need to correct, and as such calls on them to create a Special Commission, at the ministerial level, to study and, if necessary, propose changes to the Charter of the UN as well as the legal instruments of the specialised agencies from which their mandates are derived. This is to be done so as to enable various actions to be more feasible (such as having the Trusteeship Council manage the global commons as well). However, given that Charter revisions are such tedious affairs with support needed from national parliaments as well, and also given the West's opposition to the re-orientation of the role of the Trusteeship Council, it is highly unlikely that the Charter will be revised anytime soon.[44]

Millennium Assembly: In his report, Annan hopes that the ideas he has advanced can form part of a set of discussion points at a Millennium summit-level meeting of the General Assembly in September 2000. At such a session, Heads of States and Governments would be able to propound on their own vision for the new millennium and agree on a process for fundamental review of the role of the UN. As a matter of fact, this was what many had hoped would come out of the General Assembly summit at the UN's 50th anniversary in 1995 but the funding crisis so permeated the setting that the proposal never took off. Annan's suggestion that NGOs hold a companion "People's Millennium Assembly" earlier in the year has drawn a fair amount of interest despite the lack of a focused agenda but there is wariness about yet another talk-fest.

5.3 A FURTHER ANALYSIS AND REPORT CARD

There are yet other issues implicit in the Annan Agenda that merit analysis here. For example, it is very interesting to note that much of what Annan has proposed in his two-track reform proposal is not new. Take the case of time limits: the sunset provisions that Annan now wants to push through had already been broached by the JIU back in 1979 in its "The Setting of Priorities and Identification of Obsolete Activities in the United Nations" report. And Annan's focus on country-level programmatic coordination is also something that Boutros-Ghali himself had touched upon in 1992 in his *Agenda for Peace* report when he talked of a unified UN presence at the country level. A similar theme was picked up by the Commission on Global Governance in its 1995 *Our Global Neighbourhood* report.

Much to Annan's credit, following the presentation of his reform package to the General Assembly in July 1997, he took every opportunity to explain his plan to member states and to major groups, including the European Union, the Group of 77, and the Non-aligned Movement, all of which had expressed reservations on different points. His designation of Maurice Strong as Executive Coordinator for UN Reform also meant that Strong would chair a Steering Committee of senior officials that would monitor and coordinate the reform process in the Secretariat. Furthermore, he also designated Under Secretary-General Joseph Connor as the Chair of the new Management Reform Group within the Department of Administration and Management. Its efforts have been complemented by corresponding groups in many of the UN Funds and Programmes.

Other points of general interest and agreement that have been reached since the Annan package was presented include:

(1) a decision that the General Assembly should avoid micro-managing the Secretariat,

(2) a decision that there should be a new Secretariat leadership and management structure,

(3) stronger links should be explored between the General Assembly and civil society, particularly NGOs, and

(4) a policy on a uniform four-year term of office, renewable once, for the heads of programmes, funds and other bodies of the ECOSOC and the General Assembly should be initiated.

Proposals on core resources for development, and a new concept of trusteeship,[45] had been shelved for the 1999 General Assembly but that session was not able to come up with anything definitive either. A decision on establishing a high-level commission to review the relationships between the UN and its autonomous specialised agencies is also still pending; and rather importantly, the

General Assembly has yet to decide on whether the ECOSOC should initiate a review of the functions of the five Regional Commissions to evaluate prospects for further rationalisation and consolidation of their work.

To a General Assembly session on 27 April 1998, Annan reported that the measures that fell within his prerogative had been "largely implemented" (United Nations Press Release GA/9403). For example, the work of the Secretariat in its main thematic areas was now being guided by Executive Committees, and the Senior Management Group had proven its worth quickly as the first systematic forum where the leaders of all UN departments, programmes and funds came together to develop policies and ensure managerial clarity. The Strategic Planning Unit, the first in-house think-tank, had also been made operational and it was being used extensively as part of the planning processes at the Secretariat. He also reported that an Electronic UN had become a reality.

For other things, he reported progress but did not specify how and only spoke of achievements in generalities.[46] For example, he said that the UN's work in two major areas – disarmament and humanitarian assistance – had been "given new focus and impetus" but did not give specifics as to how that had happened. The UNDG has now been operational and the organisation is on target to have about 50 UN Houses that Annan had promised last year (36 were in place by mid-1999 and 20 more were planned for the remainder of the year). Annan also said that "significant progress" had been achieved in devising the United Nations Development Assistance Frameworks (UNDAF). In the matters of budget and staff numbers, Annan merely reported that reforms had brought about reductions without giving any details.

Annan has been credited with mobilising the General Assembly behind his ambitious programme and not letting it lose momentum in what was dubbed the Reform Assembly. He has been singled out for possessing demonstrated skill in building consensus among contending parties on sensitive political issues, and his ability to articulate a clear political and administrative vision is said to have led to an increase in confidence in the UN.

Annan has also been involved in global diplomacy which at face value does not seem related to UN reforms but the link is clearly there. By taking the limelight in being involved in intractable problems, Annan has sought once again to show to the world that the

Secretary-General does have considerable latitude to influence the course of world history. And with carefully choreographed moves, he has been able to send the message to everyone that he is serious about doing something about the negative image of the UN. By winning the hearts and minds of the world citizenry, he hopes to effectuate a more favourable world opinion of the UN. In that regard, he could be said to have succeeded to a large extent (as evidenced by his receipt of the Seoul Peace Award in 1998). In specific, Annan in 1997 undertook initiatives to revive the peace process in a number of intractable conflicts, including Western Sahara, Cyprus, Tajikistan, Afghanistan, and Angola. Annan was also instrumental in getting the military in Nigeria to rethink its role in politics and in the ultimate release plans of opposition leader Abiola. And in November 1997, he helped defuse the dangerous stalemate with Iraq over weapons inspections, and recommended the renewal of the oil-for-food programme in that country to offset the humanitarian crisis caused by sanctions. In December 1998, he flew to Libya to see if he could use his good offices to help extradite the two suspects in the Lockerbie terrorist attack.

Annan has also appointed highly accomplished international figures in key UN positions, and delegated substantial responsibility to them. These people include: Louise Frechette (Deputy Secretary-General), Mary Robinson (Head of the UN High Commissioner for Human Rights), Jayantha Dhanapala (Under Secretary-General as Head of the newly-created Department of Disarmament Affairs), Olara Otunnu (Head of the International Peace Academy), and Rafiah Salim (Assistant Secretary-General to head the UN Office of Human Resources Management). With these and other female appointments, the UN has never had so many women in senior positions within the organisation.

Toward the end of 1999, Annan summarised the performance of his reform efforts to the Fifth Committee (Administrative and Budgetary) thus:

> "... it is fair to say that we have made good and determined progress. Coordination among our far-flung entities has improved. Cabinet-style management is now the norm. Budget and staff have been subjected to new and rigorous discipline. We have a Deputy Secretary-General, a Development Group, and a system of Development Assistance Frameworks that we did not have before and which are leaving positive, lasting imprints on our

Organisation... (but) the transformation of our United Nations has yet to attack what I see as an overly burdensome and overly intrusive approach to administration; it has yet to give us the necessary flexibility with which to respond to new and urgent challenges; and it has yet to put us on firm financial footing... (we) are over-administrated; there are too many rules and too many steps. Too many things that should be simple are needlessly complex. Too many things that should happen quickly occur with painful sluggishness." (United Nations Press Releases SG/SM/7160, GA/AB/3311, 5 October 1999)

In May 1999, in an interview with Dale Curtis of the UN Wire, the Deputy Secretary-General highlighted four key areas where she claimed reform efforts had paid up:

(1)   a downsizing of the organisation by 25 percent from the mid-1980s,

(2)   a rationalisation of the UN Secretariat into what she called "logical units",

(3)   procedural changes in the manner in which business is conducted (including the cabinet meetings, implementation of UNDAF, etc.), and

(4)   improvement in management practices (particularly HRM).[47]

The Deputy Secretary-General also made mention of two other developments that she felt were significant: (1) an increasing acceptance of results-based budgeting by the organisation (although more still needs to be done on this), and (2) enhanced linkages with the BWIs (see Chapter Six for further discussion of this issue).

As far as Annan's performance is concerned, a year after he had taken over office, this was said of him: "Secretary-General Kofi Annan has brought a new climate to the management of the UN and a fresh spirit of international cooperation towards the Organisation among Member States."[48] Despite this, however, even top UN officials concede that the reform efforts have been slow,[49] and Annan himself has pointed out areas where much more work needs to be done in the years to come.[50]

Endnotes

[1] Jeffrey Laurenti of the UNA-USA likened the Annan Agenda to the Reinventing Government proposals of the 1993 Gore Commission in the USA. As a matter of fact, he said that the Annan Agenda went beyond the Reinventing Government movement. "Not only does the Annan plan cover streamlining of the UN Secretariat that as the UN's chief administrative officer he can put into effect directly, it proposes reforms to the UN's political bodies to realign agencies and to restructure member states' own oversight of UN activities. Within the constraints of political reality, the Annan programme achieves major consolidation and streamlining of UN administration and bodies and enhances accountability by rationalising reporting lines" ("Renewing the United Nations: A Critical Assessment of the Secretary-General's 'Track Two' Reform Programme", UNA-USA (http://www.unausa.org/programs/track2.htm), July 1997).

[2] *The Straits Times* (Singapore), "UN Chief's reform plans fail to impress US critics," 18 July 1997.

[3] *The Straits Times* (Singapore), "UN reforms grinding to a halt due to maze of objections," 27 October 1997.

[4] It is not lost upon the developing countries that two of the agencies most under pressure for restructuring (UNEP and UNCHS (Habitat)) are both situated in a developing country (Kenya). There is maybe not much in this but Annan did specifically cite UNEP as an organisation where some reform efforts were to be looked at.

[5] Annan maintained that the proposals had to be seen in their totality rather than in individual pieces and was not very pleased that the American lawmakers did not seem to have made the effort to go through the whole set of proposals but looked at it selectively to see if their own suggestions had been taken into consideration. Note his reaction: "I don't know if those on Capitol Hill realise the effect on the other 184 members. But these unilateral demands do not impress, they do not intimidate. In fact, they offend" (*The Straits Times* (Singapore), "UN Chief's reform plans fail to impress US critics," 18 July 1997).

[6] *The Straits Times* (Singapore), "US now holding UN at ransom with abortion issue," 21 October 1998.

[7] Interestingly, these comments of Havel's were made in May; in July, at a press conference at UN Headquarters, upon being asked to respond to initial reactions to his Track II proposals, Annan said he thought that his proposals were "bold but not suicidal" (see the transcripts of his press conference on 16 July 1997, United Nations Press Release SG/SM/6285).

[8] The ten balances are contained in the following dichotomies: between perspectives of state and non-state actors, between the preservation and the erosion of sovereignty, between practicality and vision, between particularity and universality, between civil/political rights and economic rights, between enforcement and neutrality, between effectiveness and justice, between specificity and malleability of the Charter (for malleability, Russett uses the term "plasticity"), and between coordination and diversity and the balance of interests.

[9] Laurenti (*op cit*) suggests that this particular restructuring initiative is similar to a recommendation of UNA-USA's own UN Management and Decision-making

Project in 1987 which called for the Secretary-General to create and chair a small Management Committee in order to establish a coherent administrative structure of manageable proportions. This gathering of senior officials has given the Secretary-General an opportunity to listen in on what the others have to feedback to him and what he, in turn, has to say to them about how to proceed with the work of the UN. The new Deputy Secretary-General, for one, has been clearly impressed with this arrangement.

[10] As a way of placating the developing countries, Annan also specified that the Deputy Secretary-General would be actively involved in generating more money for development operations.

[11] While there were many candidates for the post (including Mary Robinson, who is currently the UN High Commissioner for Human Rights), it was generally assumed that Annan's first choice was Sadako Ogata, the current High Commissioner for Refugees. Annan had also made it abundantly clear in the weeks preceding the creation of the post that he would be bringing in a woman to the Deputy Secretary-General post. While pushing for this post, Annan said that the incumbent would be appointed for not more than his own term of office and with a salary at the mid-point between his own and that of the Administrator of UNDP (see United Nations Press Release GA/AB/3201, 8 December 1997).

[12] Annan's decision to have the Regional Commissions reviewed originates from a October 1996 report by the JIU (A/51/636-JIU/REP/96/3) which requests the Secretary-General to consider ways of enhancing the coordination of UN development activities including ways of enhancing the role of the regional commissions and of promoting the national ownership of regional programmes.

[13] The ECE Workshop on Performance Indicators was held in France in June 1998 with the objective to develop a methodology for measuring performance. A few selected indicators were developed for assessing output delivery, quality, and results. Their application, however, has not been yet been rigorously evaluated.

[14] The Management Pilot Scheme is based on the proposition to establish clearer and enhanced accountability in exchange for greater delegation of authority and flexibility within existing rules. Under the Pilot programme, ECLAC will enhance its performance as a provider of economic analysis and advice in the ECLAC region while obtaining the most value for money from the resources provided to the Commission.

[15] In a particularly hard-hitting editorial in the Second Issue of the Regional Commission Newsletter (July 1997), the-then Coordinator of the Regional Commissions came out very strongly against such a move towards bifurcating the two tasks. He felt that the Regional Commissions were very capable of doing both and besides, he argued, one could not really demarcate clearly which activity was operational and which one normative since there was such an overlap between the two. At any rate, it was stated that even Programmes such as UNDP are also now being involved in both activities, so why not the Regional Commissions? Once again, this strong reaction shows that the Regional Commissions have increasingly been on the defensive ever since the present reform movement started at the UN. So far though they have been able to hold their own and have used their own internal reform movements as justification for keeping their mandates – and their mechanisms – valid.

[16] According to this Principle, the salary levels of professional and higher-level staff are established by reference to the highest paid national civil service which since the formation of the UN has happened to be the United States federal civil service.
[17] Accordingly, conditions of service of the General Service and other locally recruited staff are compensated based on best prevailing local conditions.
[18] Actually, there seems to be no love lost between the Secretariat (representing the "civil servants" of the UN) and the various committees (staffed by delegates from member countries). In November 1996, for example, in a matter concerning the Efficiency Board, the delegate from Mexico is quoted as saying that repeated questions from member states were going unanswered by the Secretariat, and that she was concerned about such a trend in the dialogue with the Secretariat. "It is easier to get water out of stone than to get direct answers from the Secretariat," she said (United Nations Press Release GA/AB/3111, 8 November 1996). Judging by the tone of recent UN press releases and the narration of the views expressed therein by representatives of various member states, it is clear that this suspicion of the Secretariat by committee members has continued unabated. On the other hand, the Secretariat itself has put the committees on notice on wanting to be "unencumbered" in its work (see Annan's very candid remarks to the Fifth Committee in October 1999, United Nations Press Releases SG/SM/7160 and GA/AB/3311, 5 October 1999).
[19] Apparently, not all the savings are going to go specifically to the Development Account. Annan would like to use part of the savings to create a substantive Secretariat staff for the ECOSOC. It is not clear how much of the resultant savings will be used for this purpose, but critics of the UN bureaucracy will not be very happy with this proposal. As if to warn Annan on this, the ACABQ in December 1999 specifically said that it trusts that "implementation and supervision of activities financed under the Account will not lead to the establishment of a structure within the Department of Economic and Social Affairs" (United Nations Press Release GA/AB/3352, 13 December 1999).
[20] The UNDG is composed of these three funds as well as other related UN bodies and programmes that are not specialised agencies but fall within the direct rubric of the ECOSOC (such as the World Food Programme).
[21] It would appear that the UN could bring in more agencies to be a part of this Development Group. The problem though is that the others are specialised agencies and the Secretary-General has very little authority over them to have them included in this grouping. He does, however, call for close associations between the UNDG and the specialised agencies.
[22] In a letter dated 21 July 1997 to the Director-General of WHO, Dr. Hiroshi Nakajima, the-then Administrator of UNDP, James Gustave Speth, "invited" WHO to encourage its representatives in programme countries to support and contribute to the UNDAF and to also participate in its formulation as members of the Country Team (i.e., requesting WHO to join the UNDG at the country level). WHO's own internal review of the proposals was hardly as positive as Speth would have liked (in many areas, WHO felt that it would be more effective by staying outside the rubric of the UNDG). It could be argued, however, that WHO as a specialised agency is not technically covered by the Annan proposal and, therefore, could be excused for opting out.

[23] In a letter dated 16 June 1997 addressed to the Executive Coordinator for UN Reform, Maurice Strong, the UNFPA Executive Director, Nafis Sadik, stated that there were many comparative advantages that the Fund had already developed over the years and it was wary of being a part of an association that might compromise that comparative advantage. Besides, it is no secret that UNFPA has never really enjoyed being under the nominal leadership of the UNDP Resident Representative at the field level, and Sadik's letter states that "in many Field Offices, the standard of service that the Fund receives through this (the Common Services) arrangement has **not** been acceptable" (the emphasis is the Director's own). For many of the same reasons, UNICEF also expressed serious doubts about this proposed association. Once again, it is no secret that UNICEF considers itself a better-managed organisation with a clearer mandate and stronger management principles in place in its Field Offices. In many countries, UNICEF has chafed under the administrative guidance of the UNDP. In Uganda, for example, UNICEF had maintained its own security radio network for its staff members refusing to amalgamate with UNDP's own even though the latter had for a long time run a similar service and appeared to have much wider coverage.

[24] The Executive Director of UNICEF, Carol Bellamy, wrote first to Congressman Sonny Callahan, Chairman of the Foreign Appropriations Subcommittee, in early June 1997 expressing her deep reservations about the proposed inclusion of UNICEF in the UNDG. Congressman Callahan's intervention with Annan through a letter dated 12 June 1997 resulted in a very clearly worded letter of explanation from the latter to Congressman Callahan (the letter reads in part: "there are not and never have been any proposals that would in any way dismantle UNICEF, or, for that matter, UNFPA" and further on down: "I wish to assure you in the strongest possible terms that no recommendation will be made to the General Assembly which in any shape or form would jeopardise the existence of UNICEF..."). However, on the same day that Annan wrote to Congressman Callahan, Bellamy – upon viewing the draft proposals for the reform of development operations – fired off a strongly-worded letter to Annan expressing her "deep concern" with the proposals. They came as an "unpleasant surprise", she said, and regretted that "the process remained one lacking serious consultation on substance". It should be noted that UNICEF's stated opposition to the UNDG is not against it *per se* but in the inclusion of UNICEF in it. For a very cogent and forceful argument against the inclusion of UNICEF in the UNDG, see also Kul Gautam, "Reforming the UN Funds and Programmes for Development," UNICEF internal document, 20 April 1997.

[25] The countries were: in Africa, Ghana, Senegal, Malawi, Madagascar, Mali, Morocco, and Mozambique; in Asia, Philippines and Vietnam; in Europe, Romania; and in Central and South America, Guatemala.

[26] Even this figure of $13.19 million appears to be an estimate since the Fifth Committee in December 1999 asserted that the Secretariat in its second performance report on the DA did not give any indication of the savings realised by efficiency measures (United Nations Press Release GFA/AB/3352, 13 December 1999).

[27] The criteria set by the General Assembly for DA projects include:
  (1) projects have to be on capacity building with demonstrative effects,
  (2) they have to promote inter-regional cooperation, and
  (3) use must be made of human resources available in developing countries.

[28] Annan's 1999 Annual Report on the work of the organisation specified that 84 states had signed the Rome Statute on the International Criminal Court and that only four had ratified it (far short of the 60 required to bring the Statute into force) (United Nations (1999: 91)).

[29] See, for example, the remarks made by Lloyd Axworthy (Minister of Foreign Affairs, Canada) at a Conference on UN Reform at Harvard University on 25 April 1998 (http://www.dfait-maeci.gc.ca/english/news/statements/98_state/98_030e.htm), Department of Foreign Affairs and International Trade, Ottawa.

[30] In May 1997, the UNDP Administrator reporting to the Secretary-General gave numerous reasons why common services do not exist in several countries ("Letter to the Secretary-General from the UNDP Administrator on the subject of UN reforms related to UNDAF," 31 May 1997):

    (1)   physical space constraints within existing common premises,
    (2)   absence of buildings of adequate size,
    (3)   long-term lease commitments,
    (4)   limited duration of presence by an agency, and
    (5)   the provision, in some cases, and to some organisations, of rent-free space.

[31] It has already been evident that since the Annan reform package was presented, at the country level, more and more Resident Coordinators chair meetings of the various UN programmes and agencies, many of which had become accustomed to an autonomy that constrained inter-agency cooperation and coordination in the past. These types of innovations in information-sharing led Annan to say in his 1998 Annual Report on the Work of the Organisation that the institutional change and innovation that had been undertaken had made the UN a more responsive, more efficient and more accountable organisation than that of only a few short years ago.

[32] Annan's delegation plans have focused on three priority areas: classification, administration of benefits, and recruitment (United Nations Press Release GA/AB/3259, 9 November 1998). The Integrated Management Information System allows for new methods of monitoring delegations and entitlements. Annan has also toyed with the idea of establishing a management review panel to review non-compliance with delegations.

[33] These figures haven been cited during relevant discussions on human resource management in the Fifth Committee deliberations in 1998 and 1999. In 1998, it was reported that while 58 percent of the staff is over 45 years, only three percent is under 30 years, and that the average age for staff is 45.5 years (see United Nations Press Release GA/AB/3259, 9 November 1998). A year later, it was reported that the average age for staff at the UN was 49 years (see United Nations Press Release GA/AB/3345, 19 November 1999).

[34] This assessment centred around five areas of human resources that were deemed key at the UN:

    (1)   staff administration,
    (2)   planning,
    (3)   performance management,
    (4)   career support, and
    (5)   conditions of service.

The process of assessing human resources was also done with the active involvement of the staff members themselves. In June 1998, for example, the Global Staff Management Consultative Committee met in Bangkok, and prior to that several

times in New York, to discuss future directions in human resource management. This process of including the staff members in the planning stage speaks of Annan's style of inclusive management.
[35] On all three issues, it appears that much more needs to be done. On the matter of career development, OIOS in October 1999 came out very strongly for further reform saying that this was still necessary (United Nations Press Release GA/AB/3325, 29 October 1999). On geographic representation, Annan had set a specific goal of having someone from every member state represented in the UN staff by 1999 since some poor or tiny member states (such as Nepal or Vanuatu) have no one in the Secretariat. Critics fail to be impressed by such measures saying it is not clear how such a step would necessarily enhance the effectiveness of the Secretariat. The only utility would be the mere factor of representation. At any rate, geographical representation is still incomplete. In the matter of gender representation, consider this: the two most senior grades at the Secretariat (i.e., Under Secretary-General and Assistant Secretary-General) have only 12 percent female representation (United Nations Press Release GA/AB/3259, 9 November 1998). Furthermore, female staff account for only 36 percent of Professional category staff while they constitute almost 57 percent of the lower-end General Service staff echelons (*ibid*). This is still far below the 50 percent that was set for the upper echelons as a target to be attained by the millennium.
[36] Annan has now proposed a staffing table at the Secretariat that seeks to set the number of staff at 8,802 employees (United Nations Press Release GA/AB/3322, 27 October 1999).
[37] United Nations (1997(a), paragraph 230).
[38] United Nations Press Release GA/AB/3340, 10 November 1999.
[39] United Nations Press Release GA/AB/3251, 28 October 1998.
[40] *Ibid.*
[41] As a matter of fact, the general feeling within the UN is that there appears to be continuation of politicisation of management posts (meaning merit alone has not always been practised even after the Annan Agenda was announced). In the final analysis, when short-listed candidates are forwarded for consideration by senior management, political considerations and other non-merit variables have continued to tend to dominate the selection process.
[42] See the views expressed in United Nations Press Release GA/AB/3213, 10 March 1998.
[43] These posts were made vacant by Boutros-Ghali but his own proposal to cut them (as Annan has now proposed) was rejected by the General Assembly. This time around, with the urgency of reform greater, the Assembly did not stop the cuts.
[44] For an incisive analysis of how UN reforms could continue without Charter revisions, see Louis B. Sohn, Editorial Comment, *American Journal of International Law*, October 1997 (http://www.globalpolicy.org/security/reform/sohn.htm).
[45] The proposal is to reconstitute the Trusteeship Council (TC) to exercise collective trusteeship for the Global Commons. However, speaking at the 27 April 1998 General Assembly meeting, the-then US Ambassador to the UN, Bill Richardson, flatly rejected the proposal to have the TC reorient its work to the administration of the Global Commons saying that there were already institutional mechanisms in place designed to account for that. This is symptomatic of the US's desire to see as few institutions as possible are created/used in the implementation of UN activities.

[46] Speaking at the meeting, Annan said that the UN was being transformed, not as an end in itself, but as a means to carry out its mission of peace, development, and human rights. He further added that transformation was not undertaken to please any particular constituency, but to be better able to meet the needs of the world's people and of member states. Finally, he added that the process was not a luxury or a gimmick, and it was not an imposition (see United Nations Press Release GA/9403, 27 April 1998).

[47] See UN Wire, 5 May 1999 (http://www.unfoundation.org/unwire/archives/).

[48] See "Secretary-General sets course for long-awaited UN revitalisation," (United Nations, DPI/1957, January 1998).

[49] See the remarks made by the outgoing President of the 53rd General Assembly session, Didier Opertti, in United Nations Press Release GA/9590, 13 September 1999.

[50] "Secretary-General stresses need for unity of purpose, coherent effort, and greater agility, in address to Fifth Committee," United Nations Press Releases SG/SM/7160 and GA/AB/3311, 5 October 1999.

Chapter Six
Postscript: The Possibilities

Probably the most telling depiction of the state and outlook of the UN was given by the cartoonist Rogers in the *Pittsburgh Post-Gazette* (USA) (and reprinted in *Newsweek*, 24 November 1997) where under the heading "Political Birds of the World", Saddam Hussein was depicted as a cuckoo, Bill Clinton as a lame duck, and the UN as an ostrich with its head burrowed under the ground. It may have been an unfair depiction of the organisation but it clearly drove home the point that the general impression of the UN is an organisation that is oblivious to all that is happening around it. How then does it go about changing that perception? What strengths does it draw upon?

The larger question is: how will the organisation deal with some key issues (such as funding, and reform of the Security Council) that have emerged ever since the UN underwent the throes of reform pains? There is also the overarching problem of the unwillingness of powerful member states to exhibit political will to alter the status quo in the organisation. This has effectively meant that the UN will not be in a position to do anything constructive as long as that attitude persists. Will the organisation then be able to put together a realistic reform package – one accepted by all in its minimum components – so that it may play a greater role in international governance? This chapter argues that given the nature of the UN as an international organisation, and the political milieu in which it operates, there is no other option for the UN but to muddle through. As an international organisation that is not able to control its environment, there is very little that the organisation can do which would enable it to play a dynamic role.

The chapter revisits the key issues related to UN reforms and conducts an analysis to assess the possibilities and constraints of reforming it by looking at some key driving and restraining forces. It then homes in on three key issues that will define the nature and domain of the organisation in the years to come. Finally, by reverting to the analytical framework presented in Chapter One, it puts forth several key concluding points which encapsulate all the discussion items that have been brought out in this study.

6.1 FORCEFIELD ANALYSIS

To understand the interaction of forces that facilitate as well as constrain the reform process in the United Nations, it is useful to employ an analytical technique known as Forcefield Analysis.[1] This method of analysis puts into perspective the strengths and weaknesses of the organisation that impinge on its desired state. In the case of the UN, the Forcefield Diagram can be structured as shown in Figure 6.1 (the variance in the width of the arrows is to denote the strength of impact of the various forces – the wider the arrow, the greater the perceived impact).

Figure 6.1. Forcefield Analysis of UN Reforms[2]

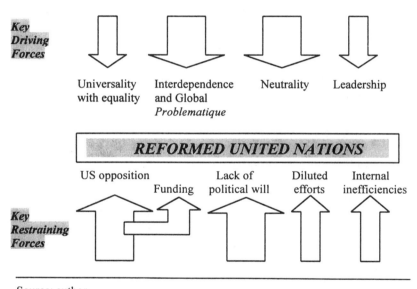

Source: author.

The following analysis can be drawn from the Diagram:

Key Driving Forces

As is evident in Figure 6.1, there are several driving forces that should collectively have a positive impact on the overall objective of a reformed UN. Several of these forces have already been highlighted before. Universality with equality is a powerful driving force because it gives the UN a monopoly on being a forum wherein all the nations of the world are free to join (with only an extreme few as exceptions) and where all the problems faced by the world as a whole can be discussed. The strength is derived from two sources: (a) the convening of nations on an equal basis, and (b) the joint interactions from which feasible solutions can be ascertained and implemented. This universality with equality characteristic of the UN is clearly a major driving force for the UN.[3]

Universality is an important concern because the world is increasingly becoming interdependent in all spheres. For example, forces of political and economic instability (but more the latter) in one country in one region are very likely to be transmitted rather rapidly to other countries in other regions as well. This was evident in the financial crisis of 1998 in East Asia where, like dominoes, Thailand first, then South Korea, followed by Malaysia, then Indonesia all fell (some harder than others). This increasing tendency of interdependence necessitates the existence of a forum that can effectively deal with the multitude of problems across countries, and just as importantly, across governments (contained in what has previously been described as the Global *Problematique*). Obviously, the UN is the only international organisation that has the capability – and the mandate – to talk to governments, and this is a key strength of the organisation.

However, it is not only this capacity to talk to governments that is a force for the UN. It is also perceived to be neutral by all parties which assists tremendously in bringing them together. Neutrality vis-à-vis the UN means that it does not represent any particular national or commercial interest in its interventions. This is particularly useful in situations of conflict where trust in the mediating party is key. Even when there is no overt conflict situation, the UN's presence can have a stabilising effect. The successful interventions of the UN in neutral election monitoring, for example, in Uganda, Cambodia, and South Africa is a very illuminating example of this. The comparative advantage that the UN has in this area is indeed a very powerful driving force for the UN.

There are other driving forces that clearly impinge on the need for a global body such as the UN, and for it to be made efficient and effective so that it can meet the needs of the world. One that has to be mentioned here is that of leadership. While it is true that the selection process of the Secretary-General leaves much to be desired (see earlier chapters for a discussion on this issue), there is little doubt that all the Secretaries-General so far have been very able people in their own right especially given the constraining environment in which they have had to operate. Even for all the wrath that Boutros-Ghali incurred from the US, he certainly did a lot for the UN (including cutting the size of the organisation so as to seek to enhance internal efficiencies and undertaking more reforms of the Secretariat than probably all of his predecessors combined).[4]

Kofi Annan, for his part, has already exhibited strong leadership tendencies to put the UN on a more stable footing image-wise. He has intervened in key trouble spots around the world and has used the UN as a bully pulpit to drive home the message of the need to work together. His managerial style has helped him considerably in this, and while it can be said that anybody else succeeding Boutros-Ghali in the charged atmosphere of late 1996 would probably have come up with a rather similar reform agenda, it is arguable if he/she could have exhibited the intensity and drive that Annan has done. He is considered to be a very effective leader, and his inside experience in the UN for over three decades, as well as his smooth and non-combative style, is considered to be a big plus for the reform efforts.[5]

Having said that, the issue of independence of the Secretary-General features prominently in the analysis. It is obvious now that Boutros-Ghali had to vacate the post not because he was not competent but because he exhibited strong tendencies of independence which the US could not stomach. Neither was the US necessarily enamoured with Boutros-Ghali in the first place with France being the country that had pushed hard for his candidacy. But the question now is: can the Secretary-General realistically be independent? What are the implications for the UN of a Secretary-General that decides to take a more independent stand than, for instance, what the Security Council might hope he/she take? If the argument is posited that the Security Council is no longer truly representative of the general membership of the UN, then to what extent should the wishes of the individual members in the Security Council be taken into consideration by the Secretary-General?

It is instructive in this regard to assess the activities of Annan in the area of international mediation. When he made efforts at playing a key role in mediating in Iraq (on the matter of weapons inspection), the effort backfired on him. It also became quite clear that his visit to Iraq was carefully choreographed in Washington, DC, rather than in New York (under the aegis of the Security Council). More importantly, later in November 1998 when Annan was able to convince Iraq yet once again about cooperating with the UN, it was reported that since the planned air strikes were only hours away, Annan had meddled in the whole affair.[6] Obviously, the criticism is not valid but the point is that the Secretary-General is constrained in numerous ways by the global powers and that is the reality of the work of the UN.

Key Restraining Forces

There are also several weaknesses of the UN that severely constrain the possibilities of reforming the organisation. While most of them have been highlighted in the course of this study, there is need to point out a few key observations here in that regard.

The fact that the US has for quite some time now not only shown a rather high level of disinterest in the UN but also on occasions stridently opposed it is indeed unfortunate and has served as a major restraining force for the reform process at the UN. This is an ironic situation indeed for it is the contention of the US that unless the UN reforms itself, it will not release the funds it owes the body. The UN, on the other hand, contends that it is precisely the lack of funds that is stopping the organisation from getting along with its mandates and initiating the reform process. At any rate, this US disinterest and/or opposition is likely to last for some more years yet. Unfortunately for the UN, US domestic politics has impinged on release of funds, but while that is regrettable, it is not something that is not comprehensible.

The US opposition then manifests itself in the subsidiary weakness of funding. This study argues that funding is a subsidiary weakness because it is only a function of the American opposition and not anything else that has caused the UN to have a low level of resources for its work. If all the member states were to pay their dues on time, there would be no funding crisis. In that regard, addressing the weakness inherent in the US position towards the UN will also consequently largely address the funding weakness at the same time.

The issue of the US opposition to the UN is manifest in the larger problem of a lack of political will among member states to truly contribute to the work of the organisation (by 'will' what is meant is the ability of member states to make some sacrifices in terms of national sovereignty so that the world as a whole would be better off). This issue has been detailed in Chapter Two. Unless urgent steps are taken to address this problem, the organisation will continue to muddle through. This study argues that, realistically, such steps are quite improbable to be taken. This has been the general trend insofar as UN reform is concerned.[7]

The US legislators, for example, will continue to refuse to release funds to the UN, or even if they change their position, they will attach the funds to bills that clearly will not be approved by President Clinton. The President, for his part, has never gone out of his way to lobby hard for the release of funds to the UN. His prowess at arm-twisting is legendary and he has done it for various policies he himself has championed but it is evident that he has not included the UN's work in that selective list of high priority agenda items. That clearly is lack of a political will since he refuses to have a showdown with the Republicans on this issue.

In other fronts, Italy, for example, has never ceased to virulently oppose the inclusion of Japan and Germany as permanent members of the Security Council. Likewise, the permanent members themselves, primarily the US, have never worked wholeheartedly towards giving weight to the work of the ECOSOC, preferring instead to channel their energy and efforts in this area through the Bretton Woods institutions.

This is the reality of the world today and is not likely to change anytime soon. The proponents of UN reforms can either take this into account and come up with realistic proposals for action or they can outline clearly utopian views of what the UN should be doing, and get nowhere. A more appropriate question for them to ask should be: what can the UN do given the constraining parameters of this external environment? Reisman (1997: 7) similarly says that the fundamental issue in reform of the UN, in most general terms, is not "what's good for the UN?" but how the UN "can be shaped so that it contributes maximally to the fundamental goals of the world constitutive process; the maintenance of minimum order; and the achievement of an optimum public order in which human dignity can flourish".[8]

The lack of a political will to work towards reforming the UN is also evident in the fact that the UN is made to do a lot and the member states – particularly the Third World countries – have blithely heaped one mandate after another on the UN thus necessitating more and more organisational structures to sustain the work. Furthermore, they have opposed the abolition of several of these structures even when the need is clearly there. Continuation of the Trusteeship Council is a case in point as is the plethora of committees and commissions that do similar work. These countries – by not exhibiting the political will to cut UN programmes – have diluted the efforts of the organisation that, in turn, has severely constrained the reform efforts. There have been instances, for example, of the Group of 77 countries demanding an increase in the budget of the UN even when the Secretary-General had clearly specified that the funding crisis would not make such increases possible. The Group has also vociferously opposed the work of the OIOS apparently because the Office has been very proactive in weeding out inefficiencies in the organisation and thus seeming to threaten the careers of many UN staff members.[9]

To be fair though, it is not only the Third World countries that have contributed to the dilution of efforts of the UN. One need only consider the increase in peacekeeping missions around the world in the late 1980s and early 1990s to realise that the Security Council – the domain of the world's great powers – has also dramatically increased the extent of work of the organisation. The increased workload itself might not have posed as considerable a burden on the UN except that there was no commensurate increase in resources for the extra work. In refusing to support the UN in its peacekeeping missions by making resources available, the Security Council is no less guilty of contributing heavily to the downfall of the UN.

The final restraining force impinging on reforming the UN is the existence of internal inefficiencies within the organisation and the lack of organisational intent for a long time to do anything about it. The latter sentiment is an important one which also must figure prominently in any analysis of the reform process at the UN.

The UN is an international organisation with offices flung around the world and composed of staff members that come from different countries and backgrounds and, therefore, with varied managerial styles. The UN is also constrained heavily by what its member states wish it to be involved in, and as such, the fact that there are bound to be internal inefficiencies in how the organisation goes about doing its job should come as no surprise. These inefficiencies have been detailed in Chapter Two but what needs to be considered here is the fact that for a long time there appeared to be a singular inability (or willingness) to do anything about minimising these inefficiencies.

It is not that reform efforts have not been attempted in the history of the UN. As a matter of fact, before the Annan Agenda came onto the scene, probably the most serious attempt that the UN made was the Group of Eighteen reform efforts in the mid-1980s whose comprehensive coverage of various issues necessitated a five-year programme of action. The question, however, that needs to be asked is why was not the UN able to reform itself then? And if it could not do so before, then why is it believed that this time around it will succeed? The answer may lie in the assertion made by many that the UN never really had set its heart to reform itself. Maybe the member states were too cavalier about the whole process and the exigencies of the global situation were not very serious then. Maybe there was very little impetus to reform in the first place. At any rate, viewed in this light, the stated position of the US makes considerable sense – that unless the UN reforms itself, the arrears that the US owes will not be released. And since the funding crisis is the most serious to hit the UN to date, maybe this will be the required impetus for the organisation to be serious about changing its ways.

The problem, however, remains. The organisational intent to reform itself is not very evident apart from the lip service that all member states provide. Even a casual review of the debates taking place over the Annan Agenda reveals that the member states – while gung-ho about the proposals – are still hesitant to break any new ground. This point then brings the debate back full circle to that of a lack of political will.

When one looks at the Forcefield Diagram, it is clear where the points of entry of any reform efforts should be. These efforts should not only seek to address the weaknesses but also bolster the strengths. It is clear from Figure 6.1 that tinkering with the Secretariat (and thus in some way, seeking to minimise internal inefficiencies alone) addresses only one part of the problem. Yet, the core of the Annan Agenda focuses on the Secretariat. This is through no fault of the Secretary-General, however, since he does not really control much in the UN besides the Secretariat.

What the Forcefield Diagram then reveals is that all the member states must be involved in coming together to address the problems that affect the UN.[10] This further means that the member states (through the General Assembly) should feature prominently in any reform effort. Yet the Assembly has historically appeared to take a very casual and parochial view of reform efforts. Member states have not been able to bury their differences and bloc politics have tampered with the impartiality of any reform proposals. Unless all member states take these issues seriously, no amount of input from the Secretary-General is going to change the status quo to any degree. Annan can only do so much.[11]

6.2 THE DEFINING ITEMS

It is pertinent to talk at this juncture about the three key issues that will define the parameters of how the UN will look like at the turn of the new millennium. These include: reforms related to the General Assembly, to the Security Council, and the scope of increased linkages with the Bretton Woods institutions and NGOs. The General Assembly is important in the context of the UN because it is the plenary body in the UN and is the only truly representative world body. The Security Council is important for the Charter has given it the authority to be the central figure in the maintenance of peace and security and its five permanent members have the veto power. The Bretton Woods institutions are important since they have tended to dominate the economic arena including development ideology and thought. Finally, the NGOs are important since they have practically taken away the initiative from the states and have forced the UN to feature them prominently in any development activity.

Related to the General Assembly

On the matter of the reforms in the General Assembly, there are three key ideas that have been presented:
   (1) give more voice to NGOs,
   (2) create an assembly as a lower house of the UN, and
   (3) reform the current General Assembly with changes in its procedures, mandates, etc.
   On giving more voice to NGOs, Annan has set the ball rolling by instituting closer contacts with them in development

operations but this is limited only to UN agencies and does not bring the General Assembly into the picture. As a matter of fact, NGOs have never really been given their due weight in the upstream portion of policy planning and international governance although paradoxically at the downstream programme and operational levels they are extremely active. Hence, it is indeed unfortunate that their input in the General Assembly is very limited. The Assembly, however, has not seriously taken up this issue since it is currently more preoccupied with other pressing issues of reform.

Apart from the proposals contained in the Annan Agenda, and the other reform proposals of the other Secretaries-General, there is also talk of the need for a People's Assembly to complement the General Assembly. This widely canvassed suggestion is to establish an assembly of the people as a deliberative body to complement the General Assembly, which is representative of governments. What is generally proposed is the initial setting up of an assembly of parliamentarians, consisting of representatives elected by existing national legislatures from among their members, and the subsequent establishment of a world assembly through direct election by the people.

It has also been suggested that the assembly of parliamentarians could function as a constituent assembly for the development of a directly elected assembly of people. The Commission on Global Governance (CGG), for one, encourages further debate about this proposal. In its opinion, care needs to be taken to ensure that the assembly of parliamentarians is the starting point of a journey and does not become the terminal station. To the CGG, what a People's Assembly will provide alongside the General Assembly is an opportunity for global dialogue among parliamentarians. But it needs to be noted that such organisations as the Inter-Parliamentary Union and Parliamentarians for Global Action already serve that purpose well, and they are among the organisations whose closer association in the processes of governance is desirable.

The final element related to reforms in the General Assembly has to do with the internal aspect of its operations. There appears much that is weak here. The General Assembly sessions, normally only two to three months in duration in a year, are filled with speech-making and other superficial activities. Agenda items remain the same year after year and very few genuinely innovative ideas come through. Invariably, the General Assembly still tends to ask the Secretary-General to submit more reports and explanations and not much productive discussion tends to take place. Annan and others have highlighted this theme of energising the discussion process at the General Assembly but it should be noted that only member states themselves can effectively alter the rules of the game. Annan as Secretary-General has absolutely no control over the General Assembly. While his proposals for the reformulation of the processes of the General Assembly are sound, to date, the latter has made no effort at reconsidering how it conducts its business; nor is much change expected in the near future.

Related to the Security Council

Probably the one major issue that will highlight whether or not the UN can be reformed is that of changes in the Security Council.[12] Given the centrality of the Council in the UN, its reforms act as a barometer of how serious and committed the member states are about reforming the whole organisation.[13] And any reforms of the Security Council will then signify a maturing on the part of the member states to defer to the UN.

The only successful reforms to date of the Security Council have been in relation to the increase in membership in 1963-1965. Other than that, there has been a dead-end on this issue. India's proposal in 1979 to increase the non-permanent members from ten to 14 got nowhere; Italy's idea to replace France and the UK with Japan and the European Community is clearly unacceptable to France and the UK, for obvious reasons; Brazil's 1989 proposal to create an additional category of membership (that of permanent but not with the veto power) has not been accepted universally; and the Third World's demand for the gradual withdrawal of the veto power is a dead-on-arrival proposal.

In more trivial matters, however, the Security Council has indeed begun to open up. In January 2000, the Council outlined new procedures to increase the transparency of its work by allowing non-Council members to participate in public meetings, giving briefings to non-members and the press, etc. But clearly these are rather inconsequential when compared against the two major issues highlighted above.

In what is likely to be heard many more times, the following was the gist of the messages sent out in 1997 by the-then Japanese Foreign Minister (Keizo Obuchi) and his Italian counterpart (Lamberto Dini) on the issue of Security Council reforms: Japan argues that its assessment is almost as great as the assessments of the other (non-US) four permanent members put together and as such feels that any further increases without commensurate changes in the Security Council would be unwarrantable. Italy, on the other hand, feels that this is tantamount to blackmailing the UN as it ties financial contributions to gaining a permanent seat. It is no secret that Italy feels itself left out as the only major former enemy state that will not be included in any reformed Security Council since both Japan and Germany are being touted as shoo-ins. Not wanting to be left behind, Italy has numerous times torpedoed proposals to include Japan and Germany as permanent Security Council members with or without the veto (see, for example, United Nations Press Release GA/9372, 4 December 1997).

On the other hand, Reisman (1997: 12) argues that even if Japan and Germany were brought into the Security Council, its effectiveness would not necessarily increase since their internal constitutional dispensation does not enable them to participate in any meaningful manner in the maintenance of international peace and security. He also says that even if India or Brazil were to be included as permanent members, that would neither increase the effectiveness (for these countries are hardly the powers that the other permanent members are) nor would it increase the legitimacy of the Security Council since neither would necessarily present a Third World perspective. The same can be said of other countries from the Third World that have laid claim to be ideal representatives of the South (these countries include Argentina and Egypt).

Discussions on Security Council reform since the Open-Ended Working Group was convened have yielded two clear, if somewhat contradictory, conclusions: (a) there is little doubt that the majority of member states consider the current composition and working methods of the Security Council unsatisfactory, and (b) it is also equally clear that despite this widely-held view, there are few prospects for any progress. The key difficulties arise not the least from the many contradictions and ambiguities in the positions that the current permanent members have taken on Security Council reform.[14]

The argument of the Third World countries and others about the need for the Security Council of 2000 to reflect the times of today (just as the post-World War II Security Council was reflective of 1945) is a bit disingenuous. For, if the purpose of Security Council reform is to more accurately reflect the post-Cold War world, then, logically, there should now be only one permanent member. Only the United States now disposes of the political, military, and economic clout on a global scale needed to maintain international peace and security. But this is obviously politically unacceptable to the other four permanent members who would not, under any circumstance, yield the veto power. Therein lies a fundamental problem with the Security Council.

It is also quite clear that the Security Council is not necessarily the preferred forum for the only remaining superpower when it comes to settling international disputes. While in the 1950s, the Security Council was sidelined – in favour of the General Assembly – over the Korean War, in the period until the late 1980s, bipolarity and the Cold War tendencies effectively made the Security Council irrelevant given the stalemates caused between the US and the Soviet Union. These days, the Security Council is used by the US if it is convenient (such as during the Gulf War) and ignored altogether if not (such as for the attacks on Iraq). In those conditions, it is pertinent to ask what utility the Security Council serves at all if the US wants to formulate actions related to international peace and security on a unilateral – or at best bilateral – basis.

The study has already referred to the two issues of Security Council reform that are key: (a) the veto power, and (2) equality of representation. It is instructive here to assess the options behind these two issues so as to delimit the scope of genuine reforms in that organ. Table 6.1 details the various options that have been discussed to date regarding the issue of the veto power and its usage. As is clear from the Table, given the conditions in which the Council works, and the dynamics of the relationships among member states on this particular issue, the least likely scenario at the UN is that of an elimination of the veto power (which is what several blocs of nations, such as the Group of 77 and the Organisation for African Unity have demanded).

Table 6.1. Reform Options in Relation to the Veto Power in the Security Council

Option	Acceptance Likelihood	Explanation
Eliminate veto power altogether	Zero	Based on their stated, and unstated, positions, it is not possible that the Perm-5 in the Security Council will ever give up their veto powers.
Extend veto powers to new permanent members of the Council	Near zero	While countries such as Italy have opposed expansion in the number of permanent members in the Council, and while the US has dithered on whether or not to give the veto power to the potential new entrants, it is not realistic to talk of an expansion in the membership of the Council with the veto power being extended to the new members. There appears to be very little support on expanding the number of countries with veto power.
Veto power to be used selectively by all permanent members (a related proposal is the "double veto" – for a decision to be vetoed by two powers before the veto can be applied)	Near zero	Independent of whether or not there will be new permanent members – with or without the veto power – there have been proposals put forth to encourage the current Perm-5 to selectively use their vetoes. It is tempting to think that to appease the majority, the Council powers might just agree to this only as a very last resort to maintaining the existing balance. In reality, the Perm-5 have categorically stated that any attempt to restrict or' curtail their veto powers would not be conducive to the reform process.[15]
Retain the status quo	Very high	For all the debate that has been raging on this issue, the most likely scenario is that the existing situation will continue to hold for the foreseeable future. Since any reform effort will have to be reached by consensus, it is not likely that the Perm-5 will agree to dilute their veto powers in the Security Council.

Source: author.

The most likely scenario, on the other hand, is a continuation of the status quo which also obviously means that the rancour that exists at the UN will continue for quite some more time. The one explanation for this retention of the status quo is that the member states are not willing to exercise their political will to make sacrifices and compromises in their stated positions. This is particularly true of the permanent members of the Council who have in no uncertain terms made it known that they are not willing to negotiate on the issue of the veto power.

The second issue in relation to reforms in the Security Council is that of equality of representation. As has been stated earlier, one of the other contentions of the member states is that there be an increase in the membership of the Security Council to better reflect the changed geo-political conditions of the new millennium. This change in representation is to be in relation to both the permanent seats as well as the temporary ones. While much attention has been placed on who the new permanent members ought to be, there is an equal amount of confusion on how the non-permanent seats are to be apportioned. Every country wishes to be in the Security Council, and there is a backlog of expectant entrants into the field.[16]

The fact that the membership needs to be increased has been broached for quite some time now; it is just that there does not seem to be agreement on two grounds:

(1) that of which countries get to represent which regions in the permanent seats in the Council,[17] and

(2) whether or not these new entrants should get the veto power.

In late 1999, an option was discussed in the General Assembly termed the "two-stage approach" wherein the General Assembly would first decide to enlarge the permanent category by a set number of seats and only in the second stage would the names of the selected countries be known. This was designed to help build on minimum notions of agreements on Security Council reforms. But even this proposal was not accepted as a useful methodology for enhancing Security Council reforms (see United Nations Press Release GA/9692, 20 December 1999).

The analysis of the various options in relation to the issue of representation is provided in Table 6.2.

Table 6.2. Reform Options in Relation to the Expansion in
Membership in the Security Council

Option	Acceptance Likelihood	Explanation
Add new permanent members regardless of the number and composition and regardless of the granting or the non-granting of the veto power	Average	Stated thus, the probabilities are about half that the SC will eventually increase in size. By how much, and whether or not they will be granted veto powers (either *in toto* or selectively) is what the present debate is all about. This study argues that eventually the member states will realise that whatever their specific opposition to the inclusion of particular countries and blocs, an expanded Council is better than the current status quo. To appease the US, the total number of such new members (both in the permanent and non-permanent category) will have to be kept to a maximum of five or six.
Add non-permanent members to the Council	Above average	Unlike the debate on the matter of the permanent members, on this issue, there appears to be more or less a consensus that there should definitely be an increase. The US favours three to four, others more. It is entirely possible that eventually they will be able to reach a mutually satisfactory arrangement.
Retain the status quo	Very high	Just as with the veto issue, there is a very high likelihood that the status quo (of five permanent, and ten non-permanent, members) will be retained for the foreseeable future. For over six years now, an Open-Ended Working Group has been attempting to come up with a consensus just on what to table for discussion, let alone actually debate the issue, in the Assembly. Both Japan and Germany are eager to settle the question as early as possible, while countries such as Italy want to spend more time discussing the issues.[18]

Source: author.

As is clear from Table 6.2, however, it is still quite likely that for the foreseeable future, the status quo will be retained in the Security Council since there is so much opposition to any one particular option. It is precisely in this respect that this study maintains that the UN will only be able to muddle through in its operations.

Related to the BWIs and NGOs

Independent of the focus on the General Assembly and the Security Council, there is the matter of interactions between the UN and the Bretton Woods institutions (BWIs) such that enhancing these linkages would go a long way towards helping the UN locate its proper niche in global affairs, primarily in the development arena. This study has highlighted earlier how the UN (particularly the ECOSOC and its various subsidiary bodies engaged in the development arena) has lost ground to the BWIs in matters of enhancing development.[19] In that context, it is pertinent here to assess the possibilities of strengthening the UN. Should the reform process within the UN move in tandem with an enhancement of the UN-BWI linkages then it is safe to assert that the UN will have reversed the marginalisation process for good.

The starting point of discussion here invariably has to be the twin phenomena of globalisation and market liberalisation (itself a by-product of political liberalisation that has been evident around the world in the last two decades or so). Popularised by the conservative leaderships of Margaret Thatcher in the UK and Ronald Reagan in the US, market liberalisation has revolutionised the manner in which states have gone about the business of providing services to citizens. Increasingly, states are playing a more facilitative than directive role in the economy, and as more and more countries begin to navigate the uncharted waters of this liberalisation and transition to market economies, they have increasingly felt the need to rely upon the support of institutions such as the BWIs.

On the other hand, states have also found themselves having to deal with an increasing presence of non-governmental organisations (NGOs) who, in many instances, have found modalities and mechanisms that are more efficient and effective in enhancing development in the communities. By their very nature, these NGOs have at a minimum restrained the domain of state policies, and have often gone beyond that and actively – and successfully – opposed them. In this context, there is an onus on actors such as the UN to not only consider a macro view and develop linkages with the BWIs but also take a micro view and actively engage the NGOs in the development process. How the UN manages to do that – and whether it is possible to do so – will determine the level of success of the organisation.

This need for duality of linkages can be charted as shown in Figure 6.2. In the Figure, it is clear that for the UN to play a meaningful role in the development arena, there is need not only to enhance linkages with the BWIs at the upstream level but also with the NGOs at the downstream level.

Figure 6.2. Scope and Level of Interaction of the UN

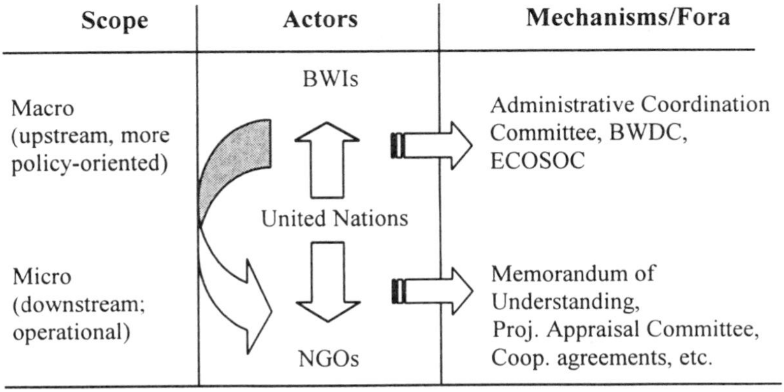

Scope	Actors	Mechanisms/Fora
Macro (upstream, more policy-oriented)	BWIs ↑ United Nations	Administrative Coordination Committee, BWDC, ECOSOC
Micro (downstream; operational)	↓ NGOs	Memorandum of Understanding, Proj. Appraisal Committee, Coop. agreements, etc.

Source: author.

At no point was this duality of linkages more evident than during the economic crisis that hit the East Asian region in 1997 and 1998. There were several issues that surfaced as a result of the crisis but two that are relevant for purposes of this study are: (a) the domination of the management of the crisis by the BWIs (particularly the IMF, but also at a later stage, the World Bank), and (b) the need for policy-makers to develop linkages with NGOs so as to enable them to better have access to – and help – the marginalised populations. Ironically, it was the realisation of this second issue during and after the crisis that propelled the BWIs to begin considering to a greater degree the role of social planning in the management of troubled economies. This has then provided a very good opening for enhanced linkages between the UN and the BWIs.

The organisational rivalry and policy differences between the UN and the BWIs were quite common in the 1980s when the Structural Adjustment Programme (SAP) was roundly criticised by the UN as being too harsh and uncompromising towards the poor.[20] Even now, it is argued that at the policy level, UNFPA and UNICEF as well as the other operational agencies have major differences with the IMF and the World Bank about their role in promoting development (see, for example, Willetts (1996: 285)). Similar criticisms surfaced during the Asian economic crisis as well and while social protection programmes were eventually introduced in Indonesia, South Korea, etc., the BWIs had begun to see that they needed to change their underlying programmatic assumptions. The defining moment came in October 1998 when at the Annual Bretton Woods meeting, the World Bank-IMF Development Committee decided to draft a note on required social policies as a complement to its assistance packages.

Since then, and particularly since the social ramifications of the Asian economic crisis have become much more defined, the UN has had occasion to begin to work closely with the BWIs. In April 1999, for example, for the first time a UN official (Nitin Desai, Under Secretary-General for Economic and Social Affairs) attended a closed-door meeting of the Bretton Woods Development Committee (BWDC). There is also talk of harmonising the UNDAF (pushed for by the UN) with the World Bank's own Common Country Assessment although at the moment this has been bogged down in the intricacies of differing modalities and time frames. There is also a feeling that there continues to remain a sense of competition between the UN and the World Bank[21] and as mentioned in the earlier chapters, the BWIs have tended to turn more to in-house expertise on issues such as gender rather than rely on the UN's own considerably more extensive network of expertise in these areas.

That notwithstanding, prospects for enhanced UN-BWI linkages look more promising than at anytime in their organisational history. The BWIs have come to realise that the UN does have expertise and a deep understanding of the socio-political constraints of development, while the UN has come around to accepting the role of the private sector and the market in enhancement of development. At the upstream policy level, these two entities have been busier than before in sharing ideas. The recent cross-over from the Bank (as Vice President for External Affairs) to UNDP (as Administrator) of Mark Malloch Brown is also considered to be a helpful development in building bridges.

As for the NGOs, while both the UN and the BWIs have included them actively in the downstream programme operational levels, the same cannot be said of the upstream policy planning level. The UN Charter itself is silent on the issue of co-opting the NGOs: the only reference to the work of the NGOs is in Article 71 where it is mentioned that the ECOSOC may make suitable arrangements for consultation with NGOs. The NGOs have to apply to the ECOSOC for consultative status and can then be in association with the UN but they play no major role in policy formulation and programme development at the UN.[22]

For his part, Annan has continually underscored the importance of "civil society" both within nations and globally. As part of his reform proposals, he has, for instance, required all Secretariat units to designate a contact point for NGOs. He has continually highlighted the importance of maintaining the relationship with NGOs, and the UN feels that the relationship between it and civil society now has matured to some extent.

These three issues (i.e., reforms of the General Assembly, of the Security Council, and linkages with the Bretton Woods institutions and NGOs) will then determine to a large extent how the UN will go about meeting its mandates in the years to come. Going by recent trends, with the exception of the final issue (i.e., linkages with the BWIs and the NGOs), however, there does not appear to be much scope for organisational enhancement at the UN.

6.3 SUMMARY AND CONCLUSIONS

There are several conclusions that can be drawn from the analysis conducted so far on the matter of UN reforms. All of them, however, draw from the two central questions that this study has highlighted throughout the analysis here: (a) is there sufficient political will to make and sustain change such that the member states are prepared to give more authority and autonomy to the UN?, and (b) despite all the efforts at reform in the past five decades, why has anything substantive not been done? These are among the questions that frame negotiations among member states and require commitments and answers.

De Marco and Bartolo (1997: 33-35) put forth two main reasons for the inaction among member states despite the spate of reform proposals made to date: (a) that the previous reform efforts asked for major changes, and this was clearly unpalatable to the major powers, and too much to ask of them, and (b) there has always been a lack of political will on the part of member states to implement the daring, and at times utopian, changes. Senarclens (*op cit*: 221-223), on the other hand, highlights nine key reasons why none of the reform efforts see the light of day, primary among them being the unwillingness (and inability) of the member states to subsume their sovereignty to the UN, the independent streak of the UN specialised agencies, a fundamental divergence between the rich and the poor nations on what constitutes reforms, and the lack of strong leaders and personalities at the helm of the UN.

These are valid reasons but they do not tell the entire story, however. To be able to see the totality of the UN reform issue – and in that process, contextualise the Annan Agenda – there is need to bring into the picture the analytical framework used at the beginning of this study to help understand the UN. To recapitulate, the study had posited that the UN could only be understood by using the intellectual underpinnings of both the International Relations (IR) block and the Organisational Theory (OT) block. In that regard, it is obvious that the general steam of available material on what ails the UN has tended to be dominated by explanations centred on the IR block. This study hopes to complement this by putting a commensurate focus on the OT block as well.

In that context then, the following conclusions can be drawn from the analysis presented in this study:

(1) The UN is a constrained organisation, not only by virtue of its origins from a polarised international system (wherein the great powers equipped themselves with the veto power) but also by a confusion on the part of the member states over how the UN should be viewed (as an actor, tool, or arena). As long as there are basically two classes of members, and as long as different members see a different role for the UN, it is difficult to see how the UN can be effective.

(2) The UN is also a constrained organisation given the fact that its constraints are both external and internal in nature. As an externally-constrained organisation, it relies on resources and mandates from its external environment (i.e., member states) and its resource dependence is characterised by a singular inability to control its revenue base (Article 19 is the strongest tool at its disposal and to date the threat of its use has not jolted the powerful delinquent member states). As an internally-constrained organisation, the UN is hobbled by a bureaucracy that spans the globe and that is characterised by arcane and stifling processes and operating procedures. Because recruitment into the bureaucracy is not always based on merit, the capacity of the organisation to meet its mandates in an efficient and effective manner is compromised.

(3) Given (1) and (2) then, there is only one possible result for the UN – and that is incrementalism, or "muddling through" its operations. Various reform efforts at the UN that had promised to be radical were clearly utopian in nature, and there is a clear need to take a more realistic – rather than idealistic – view of how to reform the organisation. For this to happen, reformers should proceed in a more measured manner and start by getting agreements from member states on the very minimum of reform bases. Given the size of the organisation, and vast differences in expectations of it, the end-result of any reform effort is bound to be incremental in nature. To expect anything more would not be realistic, or fair to the Secretary-General.

(4) For all the constraints faced by the UN, Annan has tried to inject some degree of Organisational Learning in the Secretariat, the principal organ of the UN over which he has direct control. Much maligned by critics, the Secretariat, prior to Annan, could be said to have engaged only in adaptation (i.e., responding to stimuli from the external environment rather than being proactive). Annan's decision to institute a Strategic Planning Unit, and his tactical efforts to link up with the Bretton Woods institutions, are but two illuminative instances of an organisation that is riding the learning curve. Unfortunately for Annan, the UN has other organs and other constituents (such as member states with rigid views) that make it difficult for the UN to practice Organisational Learning throughout.

Drawing from the above four conclusions, the following can also be posited:

(1) That reform efforts are nothing new at the UN and that the Annan Agenda will not be the last word in this regard. Annan, however, has succeeded in bringing back a large degree of stability and sanity to the chaos that existed in the waning days of the tenure of Boutros-Ghali. As for his Track I and Track II proposals, while they are realistic in some respects, they also harp on the same bold themes as many other previous ones which appear to be more utopian than practical.

(2) That domestic politics does impact in a substantial way a powerful member state's policy towards the UN. Note, on the one hand, how Gorbachev's rise to power in the former Soviet Union effectuated a new era of cooperation and camaraderie at the UN. On the other hand, the existence of a political tussle between the Democrat President and a Republican Congress in the US has effectively placed a stranglehold on the UN. As long as the Republicans control Congress, the US will continue to show scant attention to the work of the UN, and funding from the US will continue to be a problem. This study has argued that the funding problem at the UN is a subsidiary restraining force and is a function of the negative attitude of the decision-makers in the United States Congress. It is this phenomenon that depicts the externally-constrained characteristic of the UN as an organisation.

(3) That, independent of the feeling of suspicion inherent in the US Congress, the UN itself for quite some time has not necessarily been able to do a very good job selling itself to its customers or responding to its critics. With the strategic changes in the media and communications sphere that Annan has emphasised, it is hoped that this will change. There are some signs that it already has.[23]

(4) That reform measures targeted at the Secretariat address only a small part of the problem. The more important organs to be concentrated for reforms should be the General Assembly and the Security Council.[24] Also to be pursued vigorously are enhanced linkages with the Bretton Woods institutions since that will enable the UN to capture a niche for itself in the economic and development arena at a time when practically all states are undergoing various stages of transition to market economies.

(5) That it serves no purpose for the UN to compare itself to other organisations around the world to demonstrate either that it really is a relatively small organisation or that whatever

organisational inefficiencies it has are normal fare. The UN is <u>not</u> similar to any of the organisations referred to in the comparisons and there is no need to justify the size, form, or the context of the organisation in relation others. Either it is efficient, or it is not.

(6) That, at its core, the UN is an international organisation that is subject to various demands and constraints fuelled almost wholly by the conflicting demands placed on it by its member states. Since that situation will not change, it is extremely difficult for the UN to take the shape or size that would otherwise make it a more efficient organisation.

Hence, in the final analysis, given that the problems in the UN are derived not only from the UN itself but also from world politics of which it is a part, the problem of the reform of the UN is an exercise for which no amount of organisational tinkering alone will improve the situation. Constrained internally by too many – and unclear – mandates, insufficient resources, and cumbersome processes, and externally by uncooperative member states, and divergence of fundamental interests (even in sharing a common premise of what constitutes reforms), any reform in the UN will of necessity tend to be cursory, seemingly superficial, and incremental in nature. Even the staunchest UN supporter agrees that while reforms in the UN are clearly needed on a grand scale, they cannot be done all at once.[25] And Annan, clearly "the best Secretary-General the UN has had in 30 years"[26] is acutely aware of this and has accordingly followed a path of incremental reform.

In the meantime, though, the UN will be a product of drift rather than managed reform: it can only muddle through for the foreseeable future.

Endnotes

[1] The Forcefield Analysis is a simple method for charting change in an organisation. The Analysis facilitates an understanding of the change process by looking at any organisation, or situation, as being held in equilibrium between the forces that are driving – and those that are restraining – change. The resultant diagram then reveals

clearer entry points for the organisation to focus upon in order to minimise the impact of the restraining forces and maximise that of the driving forces. Psychologist Kurt Lewin is credited with coming up with this analysis (see Lewin (1951)).

[2] An implicit assumption made here is that there is consensus on the term "Reformed United Nations". Earlier in the study, the different connotations of the meaning of the term "reformed UN" have been spelt out. For the purposes here, an increase in efficiency and effectiveness at the UN can be cited as the primary end-product of reforms.

[3] Ironically, however, it is this very equality aspect that has also been cited as a key weakness by countries such as the US. There is indeed a fundamental discrepancy in what is maintained in the Charter (that is, the principle of equality among member states as reflected in the one-nation-one-vote system in the General Assembly) and the blunt reality of international relations where nation states are not equal at all in several respects. This dichotomy is a very stark one. In the General Assembly, for example, given the one-nation-one-vote principle, it is possible that a two-thirds majority of countries paying less than three percent of the budget can out-vote one-third of the countries paying 97 percent. As long as this dichotomy continues, and as long as even a few states persist on using it as a crutch for their own anti-UN sentiments, it will be difficult to see the UN moving forward with any degree of commonality of purpose.

[4] Boutros-Ghali was hardly the obstacle to reform that the American conservative legislators – and even the Clinton Administration – made him out to be. In fact, the results of his tenure were quite remarkable given the history of the UN: personnel down by 25 percent, top posts reduced by 40 percent, budget down by $119 million, and institutionalisation of several of the reform measures (see Eric Rouleau, *"Pourquoi Washington veut ecarter M. Boutros-Ghali"* ("Why Washington Wants to Oust Mr. Boutros-Ghali"), *Le Monde Diplomatique*, November 1996). Writing in *The New York Times* on 12 November 1996, the conservative writer, M. L. Rosenthal, asserted that only Dag Hammarskjold earned as much respect as Boutros-Ghali.

[5] This might be changing, however. Barbara Crossette, writing in *The New York Times* (31 December 1999), maintains that Annan is no longer the quiet and gentle personality who took over from Boutros-Ghali in 1997. In the three years in the job, he seems to have grown more "aggressive" and "assertive" and has made many views public (such as on sovereignty) that have taken aback even some UN insiders. Crossette concludes by saying that Annan "is turning out to be one of the most provocative leaders the United Nations has known" (*ibid*).

[6] *The Straits Times* (Singapore), "Annan keeping low profile after criticisms," 18 November 1998.

[7] Many writers have harped on this theme time and again (see, for example, Laszlo (1977), Narasimhan (1988), etc.). Even the former General Assembly President, Razali Ismail, says that he does not see the political will to reform in the UN (remarks made during the symposium on "United Nations Conferences: From Promises to Performances", at American University, Washington, DC, USA, 3 March 1997). Wilenski (1993: 466), for his part, says that because the political will among member states is non-existent, reform at the UN is "extraordinarily difficult".

[8] See also de Marco and Bartolo (1997: 35) for a similar point.

[9] See United Nations Press Release GA/AB/3341, 11 November 1999, for remarks on the OIOS made by the representative of Guyana on behalf of the Group of 77 developing countries and China. The Group argues that the General Assembly never intended to give the OIOS such a large mandate and a big resource base nor have it be treated as a priority activity. In this regard, it needs to be pointed out that a favourite tactic of the Third World nations is to make continual reference to the General Assembly and the decisions made by that body. Since the Assembly is heavily dominated by poor countries, and since no country has veto power, General Assembly resolutions and declarations are usually pro-Third World. Thus, making continual reference to Assembly decisions to thwart the work of agencies such as the OIOS becomes a politically expedient way out for the Third World nations at the UN.

[10] This has been a particularly popular refrain for a long time. Note what Clyde Eagleton said in 1948: "if the UN cannot do more than what it has, the fault lies with the members who made it and operate it, and who, it seems, still prefer the tooth and the fang to international law and order" (1948: 552). What was true in the late 1940s is still very apt!

[11] As a matter of fact, in a *Newsweek* interview at the end of 1997, Annan was quoted as saying that his biggest disappointment for the year was "the reluctance of member states to face issues and accept that we live in a changing world and that if we want to be relevant we too have to change" (29 December 1997-5 January 1998, p. 23).

[12] See Uchida (1999: 69-75) for a concise discussion of the stands taken by various members in the UN on this issue.

[13] There have been several sessions at the UN dedicated solely to discussing the modalities of Security Council reform but to date no progress has been reported (see, e.g., United Nations Press Release GA/9697, 23 December 1999, and the comment by the representative of Sudan that Security Council reforms were still a "mirage"). In the same Release, Turkey proposed the formation of a "small group of wise men" to assist the Working Group in an advisory capacity "to inject fresh thought into the sterile debate" (*ibid*).

[14] For a clear enunciation of this point, see the statement made by Bilahari Kausikan, Permanent Representative of Singapore to the UN, on 4 December 1997 (United Nations Press Release GA/9372). In particular, his concise and very perceptive analysis is breathtakingly honest about the lack of possibilities of reforms in the Security Council anytime soon. Kausikan had a point: the permanent five members of the Council have always defended their veto powers and have now begun to deny even the impasse that was so much a part of UN life for such a long time. There could be no firmer substantiation of this than the remarks made by the representative of the Russian Federation during a debate on Security Council reforms in December 1999. He flatly rejected the claim that the concurring votes of the five permanent numbers almost led to a paralysis of the Council, and then in what clearly appears to be an attempt to re-write history, said: "The veto had proven to be an irreplaceable tool for coordinated Council activities and balanced decisions within its framework" (United Nations Press Release GA/9692, 20 December 1999). It is difficult then to see how fundamental changes in the Security Council can be forthcoming given this type of attitude among the permanent members.

[15] See reactions to this in United Nations Press Release GA/9689, 16 December 1999.

[16] Consider that in the Asian Group, candidacies for non-permanent seats in the Council have already been announced up to the year 2018-2019 (United Nations Press Release GA/9692, 20 December 1999).

[17] This issue will be even more complex in the near future when the European Union (EU), according to the Maastricht Treaty, establishes a common foreign and security policy. At that time, the issue of representation of both France and the UK in the permanent seats of the Security Council will be moot. Complicating that will be the demand of Germany – yet another member of the EU – to be a permanent member of the Security Council.

[18] Mexico probably has come up with the most unique explanation as to why the number of permanent members should not be increased beyond five. The representative from Mexico speaking during deliberations in a meeting in December 1999 said that adding more permanent members would mean including their names in Article 23 of the Charter which, in turn, would mean amending the Charter. Since Charter amendments automatically assume complications, the representative questioned if this was necessary at all (see United Nations Press Release GA/9689, 16 December 1999).

[19] For a concise assessment of the marginalisation of the UN vis-à-vis the BWIs, see Senarclens (1995). The marginalisation of the role of the UN is reflective in the decline of the UNDP as a lead agency in matters of development. Its various mandates are being taken over by other UN agencies (e.g., UNICEF for children, WFP for food, FAO for agriculture, etc.), and while the World Bank backs its interventions in development policy with a US$28 billion budget each year, the UNDP can only muster US$2 billion (see *The Economist*, 10 July 1999, p. 47). Even the UN's own 1992 *Human Development Report* conceded that it only played a peripheral role in global economic management (primarily because the ECOSOC was regarded as unmanageable and unprofessional (UNDP (1992: 76-77, and 82)).

[20] In an address to the World Bank Institute High-Level Workshop on Development in Washington, DC, in June 1999, the Deputy Secretary-General of the UN said that earlier in the 1990s, the debate on development policy was "dominated by sharp differences of emphasis between the Bretton Woods institutions and the United Nations" (see United Nations Press Release DSG/SM/56, 8 June 1999). The BWIs tended to focus on "getting the fundamentals right" (with its consequent reliance on the magic of the market) while the UN appeared to be more interested in "adjustment with a human face" (with its vigorous defence of the role of the State) (*ibid*). She also argued that now, however, there is much greater convergence in policy thinking ("the arguments you hear in the United Nations General Assembly, and in the boards of the Bank and the Fund, are now often so much alike that if you closed your eyes you could not always be sure whether you were in New York or Washington" (*ibid*).

[21] Note once again the Deputy Secretary-General's comments made at the World Bank Institute High-Level Workshop on Development: "At present, our working methods and institutional culture remain quite different, and partnership depends too much on individuals. What we are looking for is real partnership, where we all feel part of the same team rather than competing for leadership" (United Nations Press Release DSG/SM/56, 8 June 1999).

[22] For a lucid explanation of the development of a conceptual and analytical framework for NGO participation vis-à-vis the UN, see, among others, Weiss and Gordenker (eds), (1996). The essays by Antonio Donini, Peter Uvin, and by the editors themselves, are very useful reading.

[23] The UN has lately been taking a vigorous proactive stand on stating its positions and coming up with rebuttals. With cost-cutting at the top of the reform agenda, the question of UN salaries and benefits, and other such cost items, have tended to be raised more frequently. The UN, for its part, has now been quick to respond in many cases. See, for example, the letter to the editor of *Newsweek*, 3 November 1997, by the Information Officer of ESCAP in Bangkok in response to a columnist's remarks in previous issues about "astronomical" UN salaries. Or note the letter to *The Economist* (London) (20 December 1997) by the-then UNDP Administrator himself in response to the perceived negative report on UN reforms in the November 22nd issue. Finally, also note the letter to *Newsweek* (28 September 1998) from the spokesperson of UNHCR over Gupte's report (in the 17 August issue of *Newsweek*) on excesses in that agency and UNHCHR.

[24] Reisman (1997), however, disagrees and says that the problem in the UN is not the Security Council but the General Assembly where, he says, there is no coordination and where the General Assembly is involved in too many things and also does them in an inefficient manner.

[25] Annan himself made this point very evident in his response to the internal policy document prepared by Gert Rosenthal in 1998 on UN system-wide reform. Consider also the personal opinion of the Former President of the General Assembly, Razali Ismail, during the closing meeting of the 51st session. Wilenski (1993: 467), for his part, cites several reasons why radical reforms of the UN are unlikely and concludes that incremental reform is far more likely as the path ahead. See also Bertrand (1993) for an analysis of why the UN – as presently structured – will not be reformed. Finally, note the blunt conclusion by Smouts (1999: 31): "If so many opportunities have been passed by, it is because, in its very essence, the UN is unreformable". Her conclusion rests on her assertion that "all the premises on which the UN rests are false" (p. 37).

[26] This characterisation was made by the US Ambassador to the UN, Richard Holbrooke, in January 2000 after an unprecedented visit to, and address at, the Security Council by one of the staunchest critics of the UN, Senator Jesse Helms (see UN Foundation UN Wire, Monday, 24 January 2000).

Annex One
The Charter of the United Nations (with comments)

The Charter of the United Nations[1] was signed on 26 June 1945 in San Francisco, and came into force on 24 October 1945.

PREAMBLE

WE THE PEOPLES OF THE UNITED NATIONS DETERMINED

to save succeeding generations from the scourge of war, which twice in our lifetime has brought untold sorrow to mankind, and to reaffirm faith in fundamental human rights, in the dignity and worth of the human person, in the equal rights of men and women and of nations large and small, and to establish conditions under which justice and respect for the obligations arising from treaties and other sources of international law can be maintained, and to promote social progress and better standards of life in larger freedom,

AND FOR THESE ENDS

to practice tolerance and live together in peace with one another as good neighbours, and to unite our strength to maintain international peace and security, and to ensure, by the acceptance of principles and the institution of methods, that armed force shall not be used, save in the common interest, and to employ international machinery for the promotion of the economic and social advancement of all peoples,

HAVE RESOLVED TO COMBINE OUR EFFORTS TO ACCOMPLISH THESE AIMS

Accordingly, our respective Governments, through representatives assembled in the city of San Francisco, who have exhibited their full powers found to be in good and due form, have agreed to the present Charter of the United Nations and do hereby establish an international organisation to be known as the United Nations.

Chapter I deals with the purposes and principles of the UN:

Article 1.

The purposes of the United Nations are:

(1) To maintain international peace and security, and to that end: to take effective collective measures for the prevention and removal of threats to the peace, and for the suppression of acts of aggression or other breaches of the peace, and to bring about by peaceful means, and in conformity with the principles of justice and international law, adjustment or settlement of international disputes or situations which might lead to a breach of the peace.

(2) To develop friendly relations among nations based on respect for the principle of equal rights and self-determination of peoples, and to take other appropriate measures to strengthen universal peace.

(3) To achieve international cooperation in solving international problems of an economic, social, cultural, or humanitarian character, and in promoting and encouraging respect for human rights and for fundamental freedoms for all without distinction as to race, sex, language, or religion.

(4) To be a centre for harmonising the actions of nations in the attainment of these common ends.

Comment: Article 1 is used as a basis in the 1978 General Assembly Declaration of Societies for Life in Peace. The Declaration lists eight principles designed to guide states in international relations. Conforti (1997: 7) asserts that this Article denotes a vagueness of the purpose of the United Nations since the list is so all-inclusive and everything can conceivably come within its compass.

Article 2.

The Organisation and its members shall act in accordance with the following principles:

(1) The Organisation is based on the principle of the sovereign equality of all its members.

(2) All members, in order to ensure to all of them the rights and benefits resulting from membership, shall fulfil in good faith the

obligations assumed by them in accordance with the present Charter.

(3) All members shall settle their international disputes by peaceful means in such a manner that international peace and security, and justice, are not endangered.

(4) All members shall refrain in their international relations from the threat or use of force against the territorial integrity or political independence of any state, or in any other manner inconsistent with the Purposes of the United Nations.

(5) All members shall give the United Nations every assistance in any action it takes in accordance with the present Charter, and shall refrain from giving assistance to any state against which the United Nations is taking preventive or enforcement action.

(6) The Organisation shall ensure that states which are not members of the United Nations act in accordance with these Principles so far as may be necessary for the maintenance of international peace and security.

(7) Nothing contained in the present Charter shall authorise the United Nations to intervene in matters which are essentially within the domestic jurisdiction of any state or shall require the members to submit such matters to settlement under the present Charter; but this principle shall not prejudice the application of enforcement measures under Chapter VII.

Comment: Supporters of the United Nations cite Article 2 to respond to critics that the UN is a supra-state. As is clear in this Article, the United Nations is not an organisation that is superior to the members just because they become its members – they are not subsuming their sovereignty to the UN. This then is the basis for Article 2(7) which prohibits the UN from intervening in what are seen as domestic matters. The recent UN involvement in Kosovo and East Timor go to the heart of the matter in Article 2(7). Article 2(6), for its part, is called the "Swiss Clause" (Conforti (op cit: 126) since Switzerland is the most well-known non-member of the UN.

Chapter II focuses on the membership aspects:

Article 3.
The original members of the United Nations shall be the states which, having participated in the United Nations Conference on

International Organisation at San Francisco, or having previously signed the Declaration by 1 January 1942, sign the present Charter and ratify it in accordance with Article 110.

Comment: While 50 states signed the Charter on 26 June 1945 at the founding Conference in San Francisco, Poland did it on 15 October 1945, nine days before the official formation of the United Nations. Hence, there are said to be 51 original members of the UN.

Article 4.

(1) Membership in the United Nations is open to all other peace-loving states which accept the obligations contained in the present Charter and, in the judgement of the Organisation, are able and willing to carry out these obligations.

(2) The admission of any such state to membership in the United Nations will be effected by a decision of the General Assembly upon the recommendation of the Security Council.

Comment: At the beginning, and particularly until the mid-1950s, given the ideological divisions among the superpowers, there was considerable politicising on which new country should become a member. The "package deal" of December 1955 where 16 countries were made members en bloc effectively broke this impasse. These days, however, membership for a new country is virtually automatic and has become a procedural formality, seemingly irrespective of Article 4(1). However, even as far back as 1965, when the US first broached the issue, there have been sentiments expressed that mini-states should be in some kind of an associate membership only, which would enable them to enjoy most of the advantages of membership without the obligations (Conforti (op cit: 27)). The proposal obviously got nowhere.

Article 5.

A member of the United Nations against which preventive or enforcement action has been taken by the Security Council may be suspended from the exercise of the rights and privileges of membership by the General Assembly upon the recommendation of the Security Council. The exercise of these rights and privileges may be restored by the Security Council.

Comment: It is evident here that Article 5 can be weakened considerably since a permanent member of the Security Council – or a member state supported by it – will not be suspended per Article 5 since it will have a veto to stop the recommendation on its own (or the other member's) suspension.

Article 6.
A member of the United Nations which has persistently violated the principles contained in the present Charter may be expelled from the Organisation by the General Assembly upon the recommendation of the Security Council.

Comment: This Article has never been applied. In 1974, a proposal to expel South Africa would have passed through had it not been for the vetoes by the US, UK, and France. Interestingly, expulsion from the United Nations does not automatically mean expulsion from the specialised agencies as well, unless specifically stated by the agency (as UNESCO does, for example).

Chapter III deals with the various organs of the organisation:

Article 7.
(1) There are established as the principal organs of the United Nations: a General Assembly, a Security Council, an Economic and Social Council (ECOSOC), a Trusteeship Council, an International Court of Justice, and a Secretariat.
(2) Such subsidiary organs as may be found necessary may be established in accordance with the present Charter.

Comment: While the ECOSOC and the Trusteeship Council are termed principal organs, in effect they are subordinate in position to the General Assembly since they are "under its authority" (see the wording in Articles 60 and 87 respectively). It also has to be noted that while the General Assembly, the ECOSOC, the Security Council, and the Trusteeship Council are organs made up of states, the International Court of Justice and the Secretariat are organs that are made up of individuals who do not speak on behalf of any state. Subsidiary organs that have been formed can be classified based on four variables (Simma (op cit: 198-200)): composition (by states or by individuals), functions (purely advisory, ad hoc to study specific problems, peacekeeping etc.), duration, and scope of powers.

Article 8.
The United Nations shall place no restrictions on the eligibility of men and women to participate in any capacity and under conditions of equality in its principal and subsidiary organs.

Comment: Towards this end, the UN as an organisation has publicly asserted that it will try to attain gender equality in staffing profiles.

Chapter IV focuses on the composition, functions, procedures, etc., of the General Assembly:

Composition

Article 9.
(1) The General Assembly shall consist of all the members of the United Nations.
(2) Each member shall have not more than five representatives in the General Assembly.

Comment: The General Assembly also includes observers that are allowed to participate in its deliberations, although they are not allowed to vote. There are four types of such observers: non-member states (such as Switzerland), specialised agencies (such as UNIDO), intergovernmental organisations (such as League of Arab States), and national liberation movements (such as PLO).

Functions and Powers

Article 10.
The General Assembly may discuss any questions or any matters within the scope of the present Charter or relating to the powers and functions of any organs provided for in the present Charter, and, except as provided in Article 12, may make recommendations to the members of the United Nations or to the Security Council or to both on any such questions or matters.

Comment: Within the scope of Article 10, there has been in general evidence since the 1960s a greater focus on development – rather than international security – areas spearheaded by the underdeveloped countries.

Article 11.

(1) The General Assembly may consider the general principles of cooperation in the maintenance of international peace and security, including the principles governing disarmament and the regulation of armaments, and may make recommendations with regard to such principles to the members or to the Security Council or to both.

(2) The General Assembly may discuss any questions relating to the maintenance of international peace and security brought before it by any member of the United Nations, or by the Security Council, or by a state which is not a member of the United Nations in accordance with Article 35 paragraph 2, and, except as provided in Article 12, may make recommendations with regard to any such questions to the state or states concerned or to the Security Council or to both. Any such question on which action is necessary shall be referred to the Security Council by the General Assembly either before or after discussion.

(3) The General Assembly may call the attention of the Security Council to situations which are likely to endanger international peace and security.

(4) The powers of the General Assembly set forth in this Article shall not limit the general scope of Article 10.

Comment: Article 11 is seen as being merely supportive of Article 10, and for the General Assembly to exercise some control over setting priorities on what matters get discussed in the UN.

Article 12.

(1) While the Security Council is exercising in respect of any dispute or situation the functions assigned to it in the present Charter, the General Assembly shall not make any recommendation with regard to that dispute or situation unless the Security Council so requests.

(2) The Secretary-General, with the consent of the Security Council, shall notify the General Assembly at each session of any matters

relative to the maintenance of international peace and security which are being dealt with by the Security Council and shall similarly notify the General Assembly, or the members of the United Nations if the General Assembly is not in session, immediately the Security Council ceases to deal with such matters.

Comment: *This Article enables the Security Council to be focused on specific issues without being encumbered by. the General Assembly. The Article is a corollary of the principle brought out by Article 24.*

Article 13.
(1) The General Assembly shall initiate studies and make recommendations for the purpose of: (a) promoting international cooperation in the political field and encouraging the progressive development of international law and its codification, and (b) promoting international cooperation in the economic, social, cultural, educational, and health fields, and assisting in the realisation of human rights and fundamental freedoms for all without distinction as to race, sex, language, or religion.
(2) The further responsibilities, functions and powers of the General Assembly with respect to matters mentioned in paragraph 1 (b) above are set forth in Chapters IX and X.

Comment: *Article 13 provides the starting point for Third World nations in the General Assembly to have the UN be increasingly involved in numerous fields that are dear to them. This accounts for the vast increase in the work of the UN over the years. The section on "progressive development of international law" (under 13(1)) is also said to be "one of the most important, yet least known and understood, functions of the UN" (see Glassner (1998: xi)).*

Article 14.
Subject to the provisions of Article 12, the General Assembly may recommend measures for the peaceful adjustment of any situation, regardless of origin, which it deems likely to impair the general welfare or friendly relations among nations, including situations resulting from a violation of the provisions of the present Charter setting forth the Purposes and Principles of the United Nations.

Comment: While this Article would give the General Assembly some latitude over intervening in applicable matters, for various reasons it has not often been invoked.

Article 15.
(1) The General Assembly shall receive and consider annual and special reports from the Security Council; these reports shall include an account of the measures that the Security Council has decided upon or taken to maintain international peace and security.
(2) The General Assembly shall receive and consider reports from the other organs of the United Nations.

Comment: The only thing this Article does is reaffirm the right of the General Assembly to be informed of what the Security Council did. It does not enable the General Assembly to officially go any further than that. This shows how the General Assembly is constrained in the deliberations of maintenance of international peace and security. Third World critics and reform activists would like to see the General Assembly have a greater say over what transpires at the Security Council.

Article 16.
The General Assembly shall perform such functions with respect to the international trusteeship system as are assigned to it under Chapters XII and XIII, including the approval of the trusteeship agreements for areas not designated as strategic.

Comment: Given that the trusteeship agreements that are deemed strategic are still in the domain of the Security Council (see Article 83), this is further evidence of the domination of the Security Council over the General Assembly.

Article 17.
(1) The General Assembly shall consider and approve the budget of the Organisation.
(2) The expenses of the Organisation shall be borne by the members as apportioned by the General Assembly.

(3) The General Assembly shall consider and approve any financial and budgetary arrangements with specialised agencies referred to in Article 57 and shall examine the administrative budgets of such specialised agencies with a view to making recommendations to the agencies concerned.

Comment: The General Assembly's authority in matters of budget is paramount. However, obligations incurred by the Security Council and others must be honoured by the General Assembly as well. At any rate, it was this predominance of the General Assembly in budget formulation, and the US's consequent lack of control over it, that led to the Kassebaum-Solomon Amendment in 1985 which demanded greater influence in budgetary-making (meaning weighted votes) for the US or else it would hold off on contributions. The issue of financing has been key in the United Nations reform debate.

Voting

Article 18.
(1) Each member of the General Assembly shall have one vote.
(2) Decisions of the General Assembly on important questions shall be made by a two-thirds majority of the members present and voting. These questions shall include: recommendations with respect to the maintenance of international peace and security, the election of the non-permanent members of the Security Council, the election of the members of the ECOSOC, the election of members of the Trusteeship Council in accordance with paragraph 1(c) of Article 86, the admission of new members to the United Nations, the suspension of the rights and privileges of membership, the expulsion of members, questions relating to the operation of the trusteeship system, and budgetary questions.
(3) Decisions on other questions, including the determination of additional categories of questions to be decided by a two-thirds majority, shall be made by a majority of the members present and voting.

Comment: By and large, the vast majority of General Assembly resolutions have been passed by an affirmative vote of 2/3; some have had no vote and have been accepted by acclamation. A few, however, have been passed by a simple majority (such as the issue of representation of China). In relation to Article 18(1), sentiments have been expressed by some in the West that there be introduction of a weighted vote (i.e., one that is proportionate to the weight, in terms of population, economic resources, contributions to the United Nations budget, etc., of each country). Not surprisingly, countries of the Third World have strongly objected to this.

Article 19.
A member of the United Nations which is in arrears in the payment of its financial contributions to the Organisation shall have no vote in the General Assembly if the amount of its arrears equals or exceeds the amount of the contributions due from it for the preceding two full years. The General Assembly may, nevertheless, permit such a member to vote if it is satisfied that the failure to pay is due to conditions beyond the control of the member.

Comment: This is a very relevant Article in today's context of several member states failing to pay their contributions on time. Note that voluntary contributions are not included. Also to note in respect of this Article is the Goldberg Reservation. In 1965, the US stated its position that if some countries could insist on making an exception on financial responsibilities to certain activities, then the US reserved the same right to do so in the future. The US seems now to be applying the Goldberg Reservation in its dealing with the United Nations, although in its blanket refusal to pay arrears to the United Nations, it slightly exceeds it since the latter only applied to exceptions of certain activities. In the meantime, Annan has expressed his opinion that the application of this Article is too lenient and that it has not proven to be the deterrent that it was meant to be.

Regarding the qualifier inherent in this Article, in July 1999, the General Assembly Fifth Committee, upon the recommendation of the Committee on Contributions, accepted that the failure of Moldova, Bosnia & Herzegovina, Comoros, and Tajikistan to pay their dues was due to conditions beyond their control and agreed to extend the payment date to year-end for Moldova, and until June-end 2000 for the others. All in all, as of October 1999, 24 countries were under the provision of Article 19, with 13 of them without an Assembly vote.

Procedure

Article 20.
The General Assembly shall meet in regular annual sessions and in such special sessions as occasion may require. Special sessions shall be convoked by the Secretary-General at the request of the Security Council or of a majority of the members of the United Nations.

Comment: *In 1950, a new category of sessions – emergency special sessions – was introduced (in the Fifth General Assembly). This was in relation to Korea, since the Security Council itself could not agree on anything.*

Article 21.
The General Assembly shall adopt its own rules of procedure. It shall elect its President for each session.

Comment: *Unlike the Secretary-General of the United Nations, the President of the General Assembly can remain a member of his/her national delegation. There is also rotation among the various regions for election as President of the General Assembly session.*

Article 22.
The General Assembly may establish such subsidiary organs as it deems necessary for the performance of its functions.

Comment: *This Article provides the most important legal basis for the complicated organisational structure of the United Nations. While the number of subsidiary organisations can vary over time, there are well over 60 subsidiary units in the General Assembly. In particular, the Fifth Committee – known as the Administrative and Budgetary Committee – has become increasingly more important as the financial and structural crisis of the United Nations places more emphasis on budgetary concerns. The Fifth Committee also draws from a Standing Committee known as the Advisory Committee on Administrative and Budgetary Questions (ACABQ) responsible for the preliminary examination of the United Nations draft budget. Subsidiary organs may be composed of state representatives, experts, or even single individuals. Given the increasing scope of the United Nations activities these days, and given that subsidiary* *organs are created by the General Assembly where Third World countries dominate, there has tended to be a proliferation of organisations within the United Nations.*

Chapter V deals with the Security Council:

Composition

Article 23.

(1) The Security Council shall consist of fifteen members of the United Nations. The Republic of China, France, the Union of Soviet Socialist Republics, the United Kingdom of Great Britain and Northern Ireland, and the United States of America shall be permanent members of the Security Council. The General Assembly shall elect ten other members of the United Nations to be non-permanent members of the Security Council, due regard being specially paid, in the first instance to the contribution of members of the United Nations to the maintenance of international peace and security and to the other purposes of the Organisation, and also to equitable geographical distribution.

(2) The non-permanent members of the Security Council shall be elected for a term of two years. In the first election of the non-permanent members after the increase of the membership of the Security Council from eleven to fifteen, two of the four additional members shall be chosen for a term of one year. A retiring member shall not be eligible for immediate re-election.

(3) Each member of the Security Council shall have one representative.

Comment: The amended version of sub-article (1) was adopted by the General Assembly on 17 December 1963 and came into force on 31 August 1965. The number of members prior to the amendment was 11. Related to Article 23(1), an agreement was reached in Alma Ata (Kazakhstan) in December 1991 wherein the former Soviet Republics agreed to assign the Soviet Union's permanent seat to Russia. The Security Council has always been at the centre of the reform debate since the Third World countries have realised that it is the locus of power within the United Nations. From 1979 to 1990, the question of equitable representation on an increase in the membership was on the Security Council agenda every year but never debated. For any change to take place in the Security Council, the Charter itself would have to be amended. This applies either to taking into account semi-permanent members (as suggested) or for increasing the number of members (as pushed for by the South). Either way, amending the Charter appears to be a difficult task, given that it is bound to go against the interests of specific nations and/or blocs.

<u>Functions and Powers</u>

Article 24.

(1) In order to ensure prompt and effective action by the United Nations, its members confer on the Security Council primary responsibility for the maintenance of international peace and security, and agree that in carrying out its duties under this responsibility the Security Council acts on their behalf.

(2) In discharging these duties the Security Council shall act in accordance with the Purposes and Principles of the United Nations. The specific powers granted to the Security Council for the discharge of these duties are laid down in Chapters VI, VII, VIII, and XII.

(3) The Security Council shall submit annual and, when necessary, special reports to the General Assembly for its consideration.

Comment: *This Article is corollary to Article 12. While the Security Council has been designated as the body with the primary responsibility to deal with issues of peace and security, the General Assembly has also been used at times for that purpose. This was evident during the debate on the Korean War, and also later on in the 1970s when Third World countries decided to assert their voices on these matters. However, the Security Council has now re-established its supremacy on these issues. The General Assembly has also never debated the substance of the Security Council reports it has to receive.*

Article 25.

The members of the United Nations agree to accept and carry out the decisions of the Security Council in accordance with the present Charter.

Comment: *Since the beginning of the 1990s, there has been extraordinary cooperation among the major powers as well as among other countries, and so Article 25 has now become a mere formality. There still are, however, rogue states that have continued to defy the decisions of the Security Council.*

Article 26.

In order to promote the establishment and maintenance of international peace and security with the least diversion for armaments of the world's human and economic resources, the Security Council shall be responsible for formulating, with the assistance of the Military Staff Committee referred to in Article 47, plans to be submitted to the members of the United Nations for the establishment of a system for the regulation of armaments.

Comment: *"Essentially Article 26 has remained a dead letter... the main reason for this has been the lack of unity among the major powers" (Simma (op cit: 428)).*

Voting

Article 27.
(1) Each member of the Security Council shall have one vote.
(2) Decisions of the Security Council on procedural matters shall be made by an affirmative vote of nine members.
(3) Decisions of the Security Council on all other matters shall be made by an affirmative vote of nine members including the concurring votes of the permanent members; provided that, in decisions under Chapter VI, and under paragraph 3 of Article 52, a party to a dispute shall abstain from voting.

Comment: *Article 27 is also called the Yalta Formula (Conforti (op cit: 3)) since it was at the Yalta Conference of February 1945 that the genesis of this Article came into being. The Article is at the very core of what non-permanent members of the United Nations have said is weak about the system. The amended version of Article 27 above was adopted by the General Assembly on 17 December 1963 and came into force on 31 August 1965. The prior version provided that decisions of the Security Council on procedural – as well as on all other matters – would be made by an affirmative vote of seven* *members, including the concurring votes of the five permanent members of the Security Council. On the matter of voting arrangements, it is evident that this is the source of the concerns laid out by non-permanent members. They have put forward numerous proposals to do away with – or to qualify – the use of the veto, but it is highly unlikely that the current veto powers will do anything to dilute their powers. Simma says: "criticism should, therefore, not be directed against the legal existence of the veto right but against its political exercise" (op cit: 467).*

Procedure

Article 28.

(1) The Security Council shall be so organised as to be able to function continuously. Each member of the Security Council shall for this purpose be represented at all times at the seat of the Organisation.

(2) The Security Council shall hold periodic meetings at which each of its members may, if it so desires, be represented by a member of the government or by some other specially designated representative.

(3) The Security Council may hold meetings at such places other than the seat of the Organisation as in its judgement will best facilitate its work.

Comment: *Given the nature of the work that the Security Council has to do, and the fact that it has to respond promptly to situations, the Charter allows for the Security Council to be in continuous session. As for meetings away from headquarters, there have been only a few: in 1948 and 1951-52 in Paris, in early 1972 in Addis Ababa, in March 1973 in Panama City, and in May 1990 in Geneva. Cost concerns are probably the most important reason for the Security Council meetings taking place in New York.*

Article 29.

The Security Council may establish such subsidiary organs as it deems necessary for the performance of its functions.

Comment: *This Article has the same wording as Article 22 but refers to a different organ. The various peacekeeping forces in place* *now around the world derive their existence from this Article. Since the Security Council is more capable than the General Assembly in discharging its own functions, the number of subsidiary organs established by the Security Council is limited compared to the General Assembly. It needs to be noted that the US is in favour of using this Article to enhance cooperation between the Security Council and regional organisations (see Uchida (1999: 70)).*

Article 30.
The Security Council shall adopt its own rules of procedure, including the method of selecting its President.

Comment: To date, the Security Council continues to use "Provisional Rules of Procedure" formulated in June 1946 as its basis of holding meetings. This has stood the test of time and also numerous criticisms. This gives the Security Council more flexibility to bend the procedures as it sees fit.

Article 31.
Any member of the United Nations which is not a member of the Security Council may participate, without vote, in the discussion of any question brought before the Security Council whenever the latter considers that the interests of that member are specially affected.

Comment: Practical application of Article 31 has been extraordinarily liberal in past decades; mere participation has not been discouraged.

Article 32.
Any member of the United Nations which is not a member of the Security Council or any state which is not a member of the United Nations, if it is a party to a dispute under consideration by the Security Council, shall be invited to participate, without vote, in the discussion relating to the dispute. The Security Council shall lay down such conditions as it deems just for the participation of a state which is not a member of the United Nations.

Comment: Article 32 has similar arrangements as those contained in the previous Article except that they apply in this case to non-members of the United Nations as well. Furthermore, while participation in general has not been denied, there have been instances of non-members being refused participation rights, such as for the PLO under opposition by USA.

Chapter VI touches on the principles and modalities concerning pacific settlement of disputes:

Article 33.
(1) The parties to any dispute, the continuance of which is likely to endanger the maintenance of international peace and security, shall, first of all, seek a solution by negotiation, enquiry, mediation, conciliation, arbitration, judicial settlement, resort to regional agencies or arrangements, or other peaceful means of their own choice.
(2) The Security Council shall, when it deems necessary, call upon the parties to settle their dispute by such means.

Comment: While disputes or situations must be of an international character, the Security Council still considers itself empowered to deal with a conflict even when that conflict does not endanger international peace and security. Franck and Nolte (1993: 172) mention that Article 33, along with Article 99, is the legal basis for the "good office" functions of the Secretary-General which are central to the role of that office in the conduct of international affairs.

Article 34.
The Security Council may investigate any dispute, or any situation which might lead to international friction or give rise to a dispute, in order to determine whether the continuance of the dispute or situation is likely to endanger the maintenance of international peace and security.

Comment: In such a case, the state concerned is legally obligated to permit the entry of the investigating authority.

Article 35.
(1) Any member of the United Nations may bring any dispute, or any situation of the nature referred to in Article 34, to the attention of the Security Council or of the General Assembly.

(2) A state which is not a member of the United Nations may bring to the attention of the Security Council or of the General Assembly any dispute to which it is a party if it accepts in advance, for the purposes of the dispute, the obligations of pacific settlement provided in the present Charter.

(3) The proceedings of the General Assembly in respect of matters brought to its attention under this Article will be subject to the provisions of Articles 11 and 12.

Comment: States have a choice of bringing the issue to the attention of either the General Assembly or the Security Council. But due to various compelling reasons (most notably that the Security Council is always in session, and that its decisions are binding on all parties), the Council has more often been chosen as the party to which a member state has addressed its problems.

Article 36.

(1) The Security Council may, at any stage of a dispute of the nature referred to in Article 33 or of a situation of like nature, recommend appropriate procedures or methods of adjustment.

(2) The Security Council should take into consideration any procedures for the settlement of the dispute which have already been adopted by the parties.

(3) In making recommendations under this Article the Security Council should also take into consideration that legal disputes should as a general rule be referred by the parties to the International Court of Justice in accordance with the provisions of the Statute of the Court.

Comment: In a number of Council resolutions based on this Article, the Council has asked other organs of the UN to take further action (e.g., requesting the Secretary-General to intervene on the matter of US hostages in Iran in 1979). Boutros-Ghali in his 1992 Agenda for Peace *report opined that the Council should be more ready to ask member states to use the ICJ as a source of conflict resolution.*

Article 37.

(1) Should the parties to a dispute of the nature referred to in Article 33 fail to settle it by the means indicated in that Article, they shall refer it to the Security Council.

(2) If the Security Council deems that the continuance of the dispute is in fact likely to endanger the maintenance of international peace and security, it shall decide whether to take action under Article 36 or to recommend such terms of settlement as it may consider appropriate.

Comment: In this respect, the role of the Security Council is similar to a mediator but not a court.

Article 38.
Without prejudice to the provisions of Articles 33 to 37, the Security Council may, if all the parties to any dispute so request, make recommendations to the parties with a view to a pacific settlement of the dispute.

Comment: Despite the right of the parties in a dispute to request the Security Council to act under this Article, the Council has discretion as to whether to act at all. In reality, "Article 38 has so far not been applied in practice" (Simma (op cit: 562)).

Chapter VII deals with actions with respect to threats to – and breaches of – the peace, and acts of aggression:

Article 39.
The Security Council shall determine the existence of any threat to the peace, breach of the peace, or act of aggression and shall make recommendations, or decide what measures shall be taken in accordance with Articles 41 and 42, to maintain or restore international peace and security.

Comment: Conforti (op cit: 174) asserts that this Article is very vague and elastic since "it covers a wide range of behaviour by a state". Third World countries have called for reforms in this Article and have argued that the General Assembly should have a say in the decision as well, either in conjunction with the Security Council or independent of it. The Great Powers have obviously resisted these proposals as they would result in a lessening of their own influence. Besides, they argue that the original intent during the San Francisco Conference was to assign these powers to the Security Council and not to the General Assembly.

Article 40.

In order to prevent an aggravation of the situation, the Security Council may, before making the recommendations or deciding upon the measures provided for in Article 39, call upon the parties concerned to comply with such provisional measures as it deems necessary or desirable. Such provisional measures shall be without prejudice to the rights, claims, or position of the parties concerned. The Security Council shall duly take account of failure to comply with such provisional measures.

Comment: Such provisional measures may include suspension of hostilities, troop withdrawal, or adherence to a truce. It is important to note that any decision made under Article 40 does not in any way assign blame for initiating the hostilities.

Article 41.

The Security Council may decide what measures not involving the use of armed force are to be employed to give effect to its decisions, and it may call upon the members of the United Nations to apply such measures. These may include complete or partial interruption of economic relations and of rail, sea, air, postal, telegraphic, radio, and other means of communication, and the severance of diplomatic relations.

Comment: Article 41 is the decisive legal basis for non-military enforcement measures, and the options are not limited to those mentioned here as long as they do not include use of armed force.

Article 42.

Should the Security Council consider that measures provided for in Article 41 would be inadequate or have proved to be inadequate, it may take such action by air, sea, or land forces as may be necessary to maintain or restore international peace and security. Such action may include demonstrations, blockade, and other operations by air, sea, or land forces of members of the United Nations.

Comment: The only time Article 42 has been used as a basis for application of armed force was during the Gulf War. Use of armed forces in the Korean War was based on another Article.

Article 43.

(1) All members of the United Nations, in order to contribute to the maintenance of international peace and security, undertake to make available to the Security Council, on its call and in accordance with a special agreement or agreements, armed forces, assistance, and facilities, including rights of passage, necessary for the purpose of maintaining international peace and security.

(2) Such agreement or agreements shall govern the numbers and types of forces, their degree of readiness and general location, and the nature of the facilities and assistance to be provided.

(3) The agreement or agreements shall be negotiated as soon as possible on the initiative of the Security Council. They shall be concluded between the Security Council and members or between the Security Council and groups of members and shall be subject to ratification by the signatory states in accordance with their respective constitutional processes.

Comment: *However, no member state is obligated to make troops available upon request. Operations can only be carried out with troops provided voluntarily. This lack of a ready force is at the core of some of the reform proposals being made about enhancing the United Nations' capacity to intervene in conflict situations. Both Boutros-Ghali and Annan have called for this availability of forces in order to meet the obligated interventions (the former, in particular, in his* Agenda for Peace *report specifically stated that the option of taking military action was essential to the credibility of the United Nations as a guarantor of international security). Staunch supporters of the UN, such as Brian Urquhart, a one-time senior official of the world body, have also called for the prompt implementation of Articles 43 as well as 47.*

Article 44.

When the Security Council has decided to use force it shall, before calling upon a member not represented on it to provide armed forces in fulfilment of the obligations assumed under Article 43, invite that member, if the member so desires, to participate in the decisions of the Security Council concerning the employment of contingents of that member's armed forces.

Comment: *Since no state has any signed agreement with the United Nations Security Council on placing armed forces at the disposal of the Council, this Article is said to have no practical significance.*

Article 45.

In order to enable the United Nations to take urgent military measures, members shall hold immediately available national air-force contingents for combined international enforcement action. The strength and degree of readiness of these contingents and plans for their combined action shall be determined within the limits laid down in the special agreement or agreements referred to in Article 43, by the Security Council with the assistance of the Military Staff Committee.

Comment: *Article 45 has never been implemented and is not considered to be of practical significance even though Boutros-Ghali in his* Agenda for Peace *report had strongly pushed for the ideas mentioned here.*

Article 46.

Plans for the application of armed force shall be made by the Security Council with the assistance of the Military Staff Committee.

Comment: *Also considered irrelevant now is Article 46 when peacekeeping arrangements are flexible, and also when viewed in relation to the other Articles.*

Article 47.

(1) There shall be established a Military Staff Committee to advise and assist the Security Council on all questions relating to the Security Council's military requirements for the maintenance of international peace and security, the employment and command of forces placed at its disposal, the regulation of armaments, and possible disarmament.

(2) The Military Staff Committee shall consist of the Chiefs of Staff of the permanent members of the Security Council or their representatives. Any member of the United Nations not permanently represented on the Committee shall be invited by the Committee to be associated with it when the efficient

discharge of the Committee's responsibilities requires the participation of that member in its work.

(3) The Military Staff Committee shall be responsible under the Security Council for the strategic direction of any armed forces placed at the disposal of the Security Council. Questions relating to the command of such forces shall be worked out subsequently.

(4) The Military Staff Committee, with the authorisation of the Security Council and after consultation with appropriate regional agencies, may establish regional sub-committees. .

Comment: The Military Staff Committee has been roundly criticised by many as being very ineffective at best, and totally irrelevant at worst. Reform proposals presented have targeted major changes in the Committee. One such proposal to activate the moribund Committee had come from Mikhail Gorbachev, the last leader of the Soviet Union, but the US gave it a cold shoulder. The successor state of the Soviet Union – the Russian Federation – once again called for revitalising the Military Staff Committee in 1993 and 1994 but the US felt that it was "ill-suited to military planning and command" (Uchida (op cit: 67)). Interestingly, the United States Commission on Improving the Effectiveness of the United Nations in 1993 argued that the Committee should indeed be activated. Japan has also voiced its support to this proposal.

Article 48.

(1) The action required to carry out the decisions of the Security Council for the maintenance of international peace and security shall be taken by all the members of the United Nations or by some of them, as the Security Council may determine.

(2) Such decisions shall be carried out by the members of the United Nations directly and through their action in the appropriate international agencies of which they are members.

Comment: Bringing in other specialised agencies to help the Security Council in maintaining international peace and security is unique. The General Assembly itself had tried to institute such a condition in relation to its resolutions on South Africa (on rethinking credit policies) but the World Bank and the International Monetary Fund had refused to comply. Their refusal brings to the fore some unique aspects of their designations as part of the United Nations system which have been discussed earlier.

Article 49.
The members of the United Nations shall join in affording mutual assistance in carrying out the measures decided upon by the Security Council.

Comment: The implication is clear that no member state should attempt to obstruct the application of the Council measures.

Article 50.
If preventive or enforcement measures against any state are taken by the Security Council, any other state, whether a member of the United Nations or not, which finds itself confronted with special economic problems arising from the carrying out of those measures shall have the right to consult the Security Council with regard to a solution of those problems.

Comment: The Article was used by bordering states of the-then Rhodesia to appeal for relief from hardships caused by UN sanctions against the white minority government in that country. During the Gulf War, 20 countries asked for similar relief. In that case, the Security Council merely asked the world community to support the countries in their economic problems without exempting them from participating in the sanctions. But this has been a sore point with the Third World countries. During the Twelfth Ministerial Conference of the Movement of Non-aligned Countries in New Delhi, April 1997, for example, the delegates demanded that there be a mechanism, including a fund, to provide relief to third-party countries affected by the imposition of UN sanctions. Much earlier in 1992, Boutros-Ghali had made a similar plea in his Agenda for Peace *report.*

Article 51.
Nothing in the present Charter shall impair the inherent right of individual or collective self-defence if an armed attack occurs against a member of the United Nations, until the Security Council has taken measures necessary to maintain international peace and security. Measures taken by members in the exercise of this right of self-defence shall be immediately reported to the Security Council and

shall not in any way affect the authority and responsibility of the Security Council under the present Charter to take at any time such action as it deems necessary in order to maintain or restore international peace and security.

Comment: But the right of the state in self-defence is limited in two ways: (1) the response must be proportional, and (2) it has to report to the Security Council immediately of the steps taken in self-defence and discontinue them when the Security Council takes up the matter.

Chapter VIII focuses on regional arrangements and their relation to the United Nations:

Article 52.

(1) Nothing in the present Charter precludes the existence of regional arrangements or agencies for dealing with such matters relating to the maintenance of international peace and security as are appropriate for regional action provided that such arrangements or agencies and their activities are consistent with the Purposes and Principles of the United Nations.

(2) The members of the United Nations entering into such arrangements or constituting such agencies shall make every effort to achieve pacific settlement of local disputes through such regional arrangements or by such regional agencies before referring them to the Security Council.

(3) The Security Council shall encourage the development of pacific settlement of local disputes through such regional arrangements or by such regional agencies either on the initiative of the states concerned or by reference from the Security Council.

(4) This Article in no way impairs the application of Articles 34 and 35.

Comment: There are only three unanimously agreed-to regional agencies (Simma (op cit: 699)): the Organisation of American States (OAS), the Organisation for African Unity (OAU), and the League of Arab States (LAS). It was this Article that Boutros-Ghali was alluding to in 1996 when he opined that the UN should seriously consider using regional organisations to take over many of the functions that it was being asked to be involved in.

Article 53.
(1) The Security Council shall, where appropriate, utilise such regional arrangements or agencies for enforcement action under its authority. But no enforcement action shall be taken under regional arrangements or by regional agencies without the authorisation of the Security Council, with the exception of measures against any enemy state, as defined in paragraph 2 of this Article, provided for pursuant to Article 107 or in regional arrangements directed against renewal of aggressive policy on the part of any such state, until such time as the Organisation may, on request of the Governments concerned, be charged with the responsibility for preventing further aggression by such a state.
(2) The term enemy state as used in paragraph 1 of this Article applies to any state which during the Second World War has been an enemy of any signatory of the present Charter.

Comment: Despite Article 52, the North Atlantic Treaty Organisation (NATO) has also been considered a regional agency since the Security Council in 1992 charged NATO with enforcing specific measures in Bosnia-Herzegovina. Prior to 1992, only once had the Council asked a regional organisation to deal with a local dispute: in 1964, it asked the OAU to attend to the Congo crisis.

Article 54.
The Security Council shall at all times be kept fully informed of activities undertaken or in contemplation under regional arrangements or by regional agencies for the maintenance of international peace and security.

Comment: The purpose of thus informing the Security Council is to ensure that its dispute-resolving activities are integrated into the collective security system of the United Nations.

Chapter IX deals with international economic and social cooperation:

Article 55.
With a view to the creation of conditions of stability and well-being which are necessary for peaceful and friendly relations among

nations based on respect for the principle of equal rights and self-determination of peoples, the United Nations shall promote:
(1) higher standards of living, full employment, and conditions of economic and social progress and development,
(2) solutions of international economic, social, health, and related problems; and international cultural and educational cooperation, and
(3) universal respect for, and observance of, human rights and fundamental freedoms for all without distinction as to race, sex, language, or religion.

Comment: This Article can be considered to be the building block of the link between maintaining international peace and security and encouraging economic and social development. Also, using Article 55, new institutions responsible for enhancing economic development have been formed, including UNCTAD, UNDP, UNCDF, UNIDO, etc. The Universal Declaration of Human Rights also has its origin/basis in this Article (55(3)).

Article 56.
All members pledge themselves to take joint and separate action in cooperation with the Organisation for the achievement of the purposes set forth in Article 55.

Comment: Much as there is great scope that can be attached to Article 56 in the conduct of the affairs of the United Nations, the behaviour of member states over the past five decades has shown this Article to be redundant. Also note that all that has been brought out in the previous Articles assumes this cooperation, and so does not merit specific articulation.

Article 57.
(1) The various specialised agencies, established by intergovernmental agreement and having wide international responsibilities, as defined in their basic instruments, in economic, social, cultural, educational, health, and related fields, shall be brought into relationship with the United Nations in accordance with the provisions of Article 63.
(2) Such agencies thus brought into relationship with the United Nations are hereinafter referred to as specialised agencies.

Comment: This shows the basic concept of the United Nations system: decentralising technical matters of focus to specialised agencies. These agencies issue recommendations/resolutions to member states but they are not binding. Specialised agencies are totally independent and equal with respect to the international organisations as well as with respect to the United Nations. This is why the reform efforts of the Secretary-General are confined primarily to the Secretariat.

Article 58.
The Organisation shall make recommendations for the coordination of the policies and activities of the specialised agencies.

Comment: However, the agencies are under no obligation under the Charter to accept the recommendations. There are also two main areas of coordination – administrative and budgetary (which includes civil service), and programme coordination (e.g., in technical assistance where the dominant role of UNDP is accepted). Some examples of coordination problems are evident in the work of UNESCO and IAEA (on research and technology); of UNIDO and ILO (on industrial development); of FAO, ILO, and UNESCO (concerning rural development), and of FAO and ILO (on land reform, etc.).

Article 59.
The Organisation shall, where appropriate, initiate negotiations among the states concerned for the creation of any new specialised agencies required for the accomplishment of the purposes set forth in Article 55.

Comment: The options for the United Nations are: set up a specialised agency, set up a subsidiary agency of the ECOSOC or the General Assembly, have an existing specialised agency take new functions, or finally have a subsidiary body take the job and become a specialised agency (as happened with UNIDO in 1985). The United Nations also need not enter into the negotiations itself, as evidenced in the creation of the IFC and the IDA as affiliates of the World Bank where the General Assembly passed the initiative to the Bank.

Article 60.
Responsibility for the discharge of the functions of the Organisation set forth in this Chapter shall be vested in the General Assembly and, under the authority of the General Assembly, in the ECOSOC, which shall have for this purpose the powers set forth in Chapter X.

Comment: The ECOSOC is the UN organ of coordination and consultation with respect to specialised agencies. To facilitate this coordination, a subsidiary organ of the ECOSOC – Committee on Programme and Coordination – was formed. The ECOSOC Committee on Coordination consisting of the heads of administration of the specialised agencies and the Secretary-General is known as the Administration Committee on Coordination (ACC). Also included in the ACC are representatives of GATT (now WTO), IAEA, heads of UNDP, UNICEF, UNCTAD and UNIDO. So while ACABQ looks at issues of administration and budget alone, the ACC looks at programme as well. At times, specialised agencies coordinate with each other without going through the United Nations (e.g., World Bank and FAO, UNESCO and WHO, etc.). It is important to note that the ECOSOC is under the authority of the General Assembly and as such is "compelled to follow the directives of the Assembly" (Conforti (op cit: 9)).

Chapter X focuses on the Economic and Social Council (ECOSOC):

Composition

Article 61.
(1) The ECOSOC shall consist of fifty-four members of the United Nations elected by the General Assembly.
(2) Subject to the provisions of paragraph 3, eighteen members of the ECOSOC shall be elected each year for a term of three years. A retiring member shall be eligible for immediate re-election.
(3) At the first election after the increase in the membership of the ECOSOC from twenty-seven to fifty-four members, in addition to the members elected in place of the nine members whose term of office expires at the end of that year, twenty-seven additional members shall be elected. Of these twenty-seven additional

members, the term of office of nine members so elected shall expire at the end of one year, and of nine other members at the end of two years, in accordance with arrangements made by the General Assembly.

(4) Each member of the ECOSOC shall have one representative.

Comment: Article 61 has been amended twice in connection with subsequent enlargements of the Council. The first amended version was adopted by the General Assembly on 17 December 1963 and came into force on 31 August 1965 (this provided the membership of the ECOSOC to be enlarged from the original 18 to 27). A second amendment was adopted by the General Assembly on 20 December 1971, and came into force on 24 September 1973 (this increased the membership of the ECOSOC from 27 to the current 54). Reformers have always targeted the ECOSOC, citing the growing importance of regional economic organisations such as OECD, EU, etc., that has overshadowed the ECOSOC. Third World countries want to give more teeth to the ECOSOC and want to make it as strong in the economic arena as the Security Council is in the security arena. The West has all along argued against expansion on grounds of efficiency.

Functions and Powers

Article 62.

(1) The ECOSOC may make or initiate studies and reports with respect to international economic, social, cultural, educational, health, and related matters and may make recommendations with respect to any such matters to the General Assembly, to the members of the United Nations, and to the specialised agencies concerned.

(2) It may make recommendations for the purpose of promoting respect for, and observance of, human rights and fundamental freedoms for all.

(3) It may prepare draft conventions for submission to the General Assembly, with respect to matters falling within its competence.

(4) It may call, in accordance with the rules prescribed by the United Nations, international conferences on matters falling within its competence.

Comment: The ECOSOC was designed to deal with human development with the same weight the Security Council dealt with strategic concerns. But the ECOSOC cannot adopt resolutions or decisions that are legally binding on member states or specialised agencies. The most that can be expected is that specialised agencies are contractually obliged to at least consider the resolutions.

Article 63.

(1) The ECOSOC may enter into agreements with any of the agencies referred to in Article 57, defining the terms on which the agency concerned shall be brought into relationship with the United Nations. Such agreements shall be subject to approval by the General Assembly.

(2) It may coordinate the activities of the specialised agencies through consultation with and recommendations to such agencies and through recommendations to the General Assembly and to the members of the United Nations.

Comment: Three types of such agreements can be ascertained: (1) with most of the specialised agencies, agreements were reached on a close relationship while maintaining their independence, (2) relationships with old organisations such as the Universal Postal Union (UPU) and the International Telecommunications Union (ITU) are less close, and (3) relationships with the IMF and the World Bank group are relatively loose. The relationship agreements also stipulate that with the exception of the World Bank group, all specialised agencies have to transmit their budgets to the General Assembly. This attempt at harmonisation of budget extends to civil service law and administrative procedures as well (again, with the exception of the World Bank group). Increasingly, the ECOSOC has lost out to the Bretton Woods institutions (BWIs), such as the World Bank, in taking the lead role in development.

Article 64.

(1) The ECOSOC may take appropriate steps to obtain regular reports from the specialised agencies. It may make arrangements with the members of the United Nations and with the specialised agencies to obtain reports on the steps taken to give effect to its own recommendations and to recommendations on matters falling within its competence made by the General Assembly.

(2) It may communicate its observations on these reports to the General Assembly.

Comment: While there is no standard format for these periodic reports, the ECOSOC has increasingly also asked for summaries of such reports and also specific citations of problem areas that it should be aware of.

Article 65.
The ECOSOC may furnish information to the Security Council and shall assist the Security Council upon its request.

Comment: The Article is clearly designed to show two things: (1) that in matters of international peace and security, the Security Council has a dominant role to play, and (2) that there is a clear link between peace and security and economic/social development such that the role the ECOSOC could play would be entirely beneficial. However, in some instances, such as during the Congo crisis, the Security Council has turned directly to the specialised agencies with a request for assistance. Of late, there has been talk of revamping this Article. While these organs have never really made very serious efforts to build on their relationships, in 1998, the President of the ECOSOC made initial contacts with the President of the Security Council building around the theme of poverty eradication (United Nations Press Release ECOSOC/5812, 3 February 1999). One test case was proposed to be Haiti where the security and peace situation was said to tie in inextricably with social and economic problems.

Article 66.
(1) The ECOSOC shall perform such functions as fall within its competence in connection with the carrying out of the recommendations of the General Assembly.
(2) It may, with the approval of the General Assembly, perform services at the request of members of the United Nations and at the request of specialised agencies.
(3) It shall perform such other functions as are specified elsewhere in the present Charter or as may be assigned to it by the General Assembly.

Comment: However, the General Assembly can either turn directly to the ECOSOC or go to the specialised agencies, the Secretary-General, or the member states, keeping the ECOSOC only in the sidelines. If it does go through the ECOSOC, the latter can perform the services either through its own Secretariat or by providing personnel and administrative services to another body.

Voting

Article 67.
(1) Each member of the ECOSOC shall have one vote.
(2) Decisions of the ECOSOC shall be made by a majority of the members present and voting.

Comment: Evidence shows that the majority of decisions taken by the ECOSOC have been adopted unanimously, and that instances when unanimity is not reached, a simple show of hands has sufficed. Roll call votes are very infrequently used.

Procedure

Article 68.
The ECOSOC shall set up commissions in economic and social fields and for the promotion of human rights, and such other commissions as may be required for the performance of its functions.

Comment: Despite the wording of this Article, the responsibility of the UN for international economic and social cooperation is still vested in the General Assembly and only by authority of the General Assembly to the ECOSOC. The General Assembly can require the ECOSOC to set up or dissolve subsidiary organs. Related bodies mean UNDP, UNCTAD, UNITAR, UNHCR, UNICEF, etc., that report to the Council on their activities without being subordinated to its directions.

Article 69.
The ECOSOC shall invite any member of the United Nations to participate, without vote, in its deliberations on any matter of particular concern to that member.

Comment: It needs to be noted that even if a member state has proposed a matter for discussion in the General Assembly, it is not necessarily considered sufficient reason for it to be invited to the ECOSOC for discussion (meaning the state is not entitled automatically to the invitation to attend). Conversely, an invited state is not obliged to participate in the ECOSOC deliberations and occasionally states have declined invitations.

Article 70.
The ECOSOC may make arrangements for representatives of the specialised agencies to participate, without vote, in its deliberations and in those of the commissions established by it, and for its representatives to participate in the deliberations of the specialised agencies.

Comment: Article 70 is designed to enhance coordination of work and policy between the ECOSOC and the specialised agencies. The corresponding attendance at each other's meetings has been a regular affair.

Article 71.
The ECOSOC may make suitable arrangements for consultation with non-governmental organisations which are concerned with matters within its competence. Such arrangements may be made with international organisations and, where appropriate, with national organisations after consultation with the member of the United Nations concerned.

Comment: Article 71 is the only Article in the Charter that refers to NGOs. In light of the increasing role that NGOs currently play in economic and social development, this Article has assumed considerable significance. Note, however, that this is only a consultative relationship, and not a participative one.

Article 72.
(1) The ECOSOC shall adopt its own rules of procedure, including the method of selecting its President.
(2) The ECOSOC shall meet as required in accordance with its rules, which shall include provision for the convening of meetings on the request of a majority of its members.

Comment: However, the provisional agenda of the ECOSOC, as well as its basic programme of work for the year, will be drawn up by the Secretary-General. In addition, the Secretary-General provides certain Secretariat functions for the Council.

Chapter XI focuses on the declaration regarding non-self-governing territories:

Article 73.

Members of the United Nations which have or assume responsibilities for the administration of territories whose peoples have not yet attained a full measure of self-government recognise the principle that the interests of the inhabitants of these territories are paramount, and accept as a sacred trust the obligation to promote to the utmost, within the system of international peace and security established by the present Charter, the well-being of the inhabitants of these territories, and, to this end:

(1) to ensure, with due respect for the culture of the peoples concerned, their political, economic, social, and educational advancement, their just treatment, and their protection against abuses,

(2) to develop self-government, to take due account of the political aspirations of the peoples, and to assist them in the progressive development of their free political institutions, according to the particular circumstances of each territory and its peoples and their varying stages of advancement,

(3) to further international peace and security,

(4) to promote constructive measures of development, to encourage research, and to cooperate with one another and, when and where appropriate, with specialised international bodies with a view to the practical achievement of the social, economic, and scientific purposes set forth in this Article, and

(5) to transmit regularly to the Secretary-General for information purposes, subject to such limitation as security and constitutional considerations may require, statistical and other information of a technical nature relating to economic, social, and educational conditions in the territories for which they are respectively responsible other than those territories to which Chapters XII and XIII apply.

Comment: This Article, and the one that immediately follows, lays down the fundamental regulations of all non-self-governing territories. At the time of the formulation of the Charter, UK and France were, for obvious reasons, vehemently against the international supervision of colonial rule. To them, this was an internal matter. It is this Article, however, that partly forms the basis of what has been considered one of the most successful United Nations interventions since it was created – that of decolonisation.

Article 74.
Members of the United Nations also agree that their policy in respect of the territories to which this Chapter applies, no less than in respect of their metropolitan areas, must be based on the general principle of good-neighbourliness, due account being taken of the interests and well-being of the rest of the world, in social, economic, and commercial matters.

Comment: While this Article has hardly been invoked, it does oblige the colonial powers to keep the interests of the territories at heart.

Chapter XII takes the previous chapter further and focuses on the international trusteeship system:

(A proposal put forth by the Commission on Global Governance (CGG) in 1995 sought to assign new mandates to the international trusteeship system. It asserted that now that the Trusteeship Council had fulfilled its original mandate of administration of trust territories, there was a need for the Council to look into the administration of the Global Commons (thus necessitating a revision of Chapters XII and XIII of the Charter). On the matter of the future of the Trusteeship Council, the Special Committee on the Charter of the United Nations and on the Strengthening of the Role of the Organisation, in April 1999, discussed a range of possibilities, including reconstituting it as a trustee of the global commons, and also abolishing it altogether).[2]

Article 75.
The United Nations shall establish under its authority an international trusteeship system for the administration and

supervision of such territories as may be placed thereunder by subsequent individual agreements. These territories are hereinafter referred to as trust territories.

Comment: The international trusteeship system (ITS) is taken to be the transitory phase from colonial rule to self-government and ultimately statehood. However, with no territories now in trusteeship, the ITS has more academic than practical significance.

Article 76.
The basic objectives of the trusteeship system, in accordance with the Purposes of the United Nations laid down in Article 1 of the present Charter, shall be:
(1) to further international peace and security,
(2) to promote the political, economic, social, and educational advancement of the inhabitants of the trust territories, and their progressive development towards self-government or independence as may be appropriate to the particular circumstances of each territory and its peoples and the freely expressed wishes of the peoples concerned, and as may be provided by the terms of each trusteeship agreement,
(3) to encourage respect for human rights and for fundamental freedoms for all without distinction as to race, sex, language, or religion, and to encourage recognition of the interdependence of the peoples of the world, and
(4) to ensure equal treatment in social, economic, and commercial matters for all members of the United Nations and their nationals, and also equal treatment for the latter in the administration of justice, without prejudice to the attainment of the foregoing objectives and subject to the provisions of Article 80.

Comment: This Article repeats the purposes inherent in Article 1 of the UN Charter and applies the same principles to the administration of trust territories as well.

Article 77.
(1) The trusteeship system shall apply to such territories in the following categories as may be placed thereunder by means of trusteeship agreements:

(a) territories now held under mandate,
(b) territories which may be detached from enemy states as a result of World War Two, and
(c) territories voluntarily placed under the system by states responsible for their administration.
(2) It will be a matter for subsequent agreement as to which territories in the foregoing categories will be brought under the trusteeship system and upon what terms.

Comment: The United Kingdom – as the biggest colonial power – was quite insistent on accepting this Article only after it was made clear that the ITS would be applied exclusively to those territories that were mentioned here.

Article 78.
The trusteeship system shall not apply to territories which have become members of the United Nations, relationship among which shall be based on respect for the principle of sovereign equality.

Comment: Simma (op cit: 951) argues that this Article was added to ensure that Syria and Lebanon – who declared war on Germany in February 1945 and, therefore, became legitimate members of the UN founding Conference – could not be placed under trusteeship.

Article 79.
The terms of trusteeship for each territory to be placed under the trusteeship system, including any alteration or amendment, shall be agreed upon by the states directly concerned, including the mandatory power in the case of territories held under mandate by a member of the United Nations, and shall be approved as provided for in Articles 83 and 85.

Comment: However, the modalities of the trusteeship so defined must be approved by the General Assembly or the Security Council. Hence, the contents of a trusteeship depends on the consent of the administering authority and the United Nations.

Article 80.
(1) Except as may be agreed upon in individual trusteeship agreements, made under Articles 77, 79, and 81, placing each

territory under the trusteeship system, and until such agreements have been concluded, nothing in this Chapter shall be construed in or of itself to alter in any manner the rights whatsoever of any states or any peoples or the terms of existing international instruments to which members of the United Nations may respectively be parties.

(2) Paragraph 1 of this Article shall not be interpreted as giving grounds for delay or postponement of the negotiation and conclusion of agreements for placing mandated and other territories under the trusteeship system as provided for in Article 77.

Comment: This Article was used as a basis for the International Court of Justice's ruling on the responsibilities of South Africa regarding South West Africa.

Article 81.
The trusteeship agreement shall in each case include the terms under which the trust territory will be administered and designate the authority which will exercise the administration of the trust territory. Such authority, hereinafter called the administering authority, may be one or more states or the Organisation itself.

Comment: Simma (op cit: 955) points out that a state, a group of states, and even the United Nations itself, can be administering authorities. It was China's intervention in the San Francisco Conference that added this clause in the Article.

Article 82.
There may be designated, in any trusteeship agreement, a strategic area or areas which may include part or all of the trust territory to which the agreement applies, without prejudice to any special agreement or agreements made under Article 43.

Comment: Strategic areas are trust territories for which the functions of the United Nations are exercised by the Security Council. The Security Council, in turn, is supported by the Trusteeship Council in completing its tasks. Since the Trusteeship Council is not empowered to deal with security matters, the Security Council has to enter into the picture.

Article 83.

(1) All functions of the United Nations relating to strategic areas, including the approval of the terms of the trusteeship agreements and of their alteration or amendment, shall be exercised by the Security Council.

(2) The basic objectives set forth in Article 76 shall be applicable to the people of each strategic area.

(3) The Security Council shall, subject to the provisions of the trusteeship agreements and without prejudice to security considerations, avail itself of the assistance of the Trusteeship Council to perform those functions of the United Nations under the trusteeship system relating to political, economic, social, and educational matters in the strategic areas.

Comment: This Article makes it clear that the Trusteeship Council is subordinate to the Security Council (see also notes on Article 82).

Article 84.

It shall be the duty of the administering authority to ensure that the trust territory shall play its part in the maintenance of international peace and security. To this end, the administering authority may make use of volunteer forces, facilities, and assistance from the trust territory in carrying out the obligations towards the Security Council undertaken in this regard by the administering authority, as well as for local defence and the maintenance of law and order within the trust territory.

Comment: This Article has to be seen in consonance with Article 76(1) since it specifies in more concrete terms what 76(1) refers to.

Article 85.

(1) The functions of the United Nations with regard to trusteeship agreements for all areas not designated as strategic, including the approval of the terms of the trusteeship agreements and of their alteration or amendment, shall be exercised by the General Assembly.

(2) The Trusteeship Council, operating under the authority of the General Assembly, shall assist the General Assembly in carrying out these functions.

Comment: As is evident, the General Assembly then has the ultimate authority over those areas that are not considered strategic; and the General Assembly, in turn, gives the authority to the Trusteeship Council. The Trusteeship Council reports to the General Assembly.

Chapter XIII deals with the Trusteeship Council:

Composition

Article 86.
(1) The Trusteeship Council shall consist of the following members of the United Nations:
   (a) those members administering trust territories,
   (b) such of those members mentioned by name in Article 23 as are not administering trust territories, and
   (c) as many other members elected for three-year terms by the General Assembly as may be necessary to ensure that the total number of members of the Trusteeship Council is equally divided between those members of the United Nations which administer trust territories and those which do not.
(2) Each member of the Trusteeship Council shall designate one specially qualified person to represent it therein.

Comment: The Trusteeship Council was created as the last of the principal organs of the UN. The Council is, furthermore, the only organ of the UN whose size is variable since membership on it is determined by the number of trusteeship areas left around the world. At the moment, that number is zero and so only the five permanent members of the Security Council are part of the Trusteeship Council.

Functions and Powers

Article 87.
The General Assembly and, under its authority, the Trusteeship Council, in carrying out their functions, may:
(1) consider reports submitted by the administering authority,
(2) accept petitions and examine them in consultation with the administering authority,

(3) provide for periodic visits to the respective trust territories at times agreed upon with the administering authority, and

(4) take these and other actions in conformity with the terms of the trusteeship agreements.

Comment: This Article serves as a basis of getting comprehensive information on administered territories. The main activity of the Trusteeship Council is the examination of the regular reports submitted by the administering authority.

Article 88.

The Trusteeship Council shall formulate a questionnaire on the political, economic, social, and educational advancement of the inhabitants of each trust territory, and the administering authority for each trust territory within the competence of the General Assembly shall make an annual report to the General Assembly upon the basis of such questionnaire.

Comment: This Article forms the means by which the UN (through the Trusteeship Council) gets to know what is transpiring in the administered territories. This Article is only applicable for non-strategic areas, however.

Voting

Article 89.

(1) Each member of the Trusteeship Council shall have one vote.

(2) Decisions of the Trusteeship Council shall be made by a majority of the members present and voting.

Comment: Nothing in this Article shows that the Trusteeship Council's decisions are binding on the member states or even, for that matter, on the administering authority.

Procedure

Article 90.

(1) The Trusteeship Council shall adopt its own rules of procedure, including the method of selecting its President.

(2) The Trusteeship Council shall meet as required in accordance with its rules, which shall include provision for the convening of meetings on the request of a majority of its members.

Comment: In this regard, while the Secretary-General prepares the provisional agenda in consultation with the President of the Trusteeship Council, the latter is in no way bound by the provisional agenda and may alter it if he/she deems necessary.

Article 91.
The Trusteeship Council shall, when appropriate, avail itself of the assistance of the ECOSOC and of the specialised agencies in regard to matters with which they are respectively concerned.

Comment: The Trusteeship Council has, in the past, sought the assistance of various specialised agencies. These have included: UNESCO, ILO, WHO, FAO, and the World Bank.

Chapter XIV focuses on the International Court of Justice:

Article 92.
The International Court of Justice shall be the principal judicial organ of the United Nations. It shall function in accordance with the annexed Statute, which is based upon the Statute of the Permanent Court of International Justice and forms an integral part of the present Charter.

Comment: The International Court of Justice (ICJ) consists of 15 judges who are selected in their personal capacities. The Court's activities are governed by this Charter as well as by its own Statute annexed to this Charter. While it is a principal organ of the UN, it is not responsible to any other organ of the UN, including the General Assembly (it only makes annual reports to the General Assembly). Furthermore, the Court is open to all states, even those that are not UN members. The ICJ not only settles disputes between states but also gives interpretations on the Charter to UN organs including the General Assembly and the Security Council. The only other judicial organ in the United Nations is the Administrative Tribunal, which was created by the General Assembly to settle disputes between the organisation and its staff members.

Article 93.

(1) All members of the United Nations are *ipso facto* parties to the Statute of the International Court of Justice.

(2) A state which is not a member of the United Nations may become a party to the Statute of the International Court of Justice on conditions to be determined in each case by the General Assembly upon the recommendation of the Security Council.

Comment: Noteworthy to mention here is that the ICJ is more closely connected to the purposes and principles of the United Nations than its predecessor ever was to the League of Nations.

Article 94.

(1) Each member of the United Nations undertakes to comply with the decision of the International Court of Justice in any case to which it is a party.

(2) If any party to a case fails to perform the obligations incumbent upon it under a judgement rendered by the Court, the other party may have recourse to the Security Council, which may, if it deems necessary, make recommendations or decide upon measures to be taken to give effect to the judgement.

Comment: Article 94(1) has not always been complied with. Countries have taken political expediency by rejecting the opinions of the ICJ (not that they are legally bound by the decisions). The US's refusal in 1986 to accept the Court's ruling in favour of Nicaragua on the matter of the harbour mining is a strong case in point. The Security Council still drew up a draft resolution as per Article 94(2) but it was inevitably vetoed by the US. It needs to be mentioned here that it is not only members of the UN that fall under this Article, several of the specialised agencies as well have accepted the supremacy of the ICJ.

Article 95.

Nothing in the present Charter shall prevent members of the United Nations from entrusting the solution of their differences to other tribunals by virtue of agreements already in existence or which may be concluded in the future.

Comment: *Member states then do not have to subject their disputes to the ICJ if other avenues already exist (such as treaties governing their relations).*

Article 96.
(1) The General Assembly or the Security Council may request the International Court of Justice to give an advisory opinion on any legal question.
(2) Other organs of the United Nations and specialised agencies, which may at any time be so authorised by the General Assembly, may also request advisory opinions of the Court on legal questions arising within the scope of their activities.

Comment: *While the ICJ may provide legal interpretations, none of its advisory opinions are binding, unless the Statutes of the specialised agencies clearly specify so. In 1992, Boutros-Ghali in his* Agenda for Peace *report specifically called on the member states to make more use of the ICJ as a means of conflict resolution. It is interesting to note that a proposal was made at the San Francisco Conference to give the ICJ "a kind of control over the legitimacy of UN acts" (Conforti (op cit: 14)) but the proposal was strongly opposed by the participants.*

Chapter XV focuses on the Secretariat:

Article 97.
The Secretariat shall comprise a Secretary-General and such staff as the Organisation may require. The Secretary-General shall be appointed by the General Assembly upon the recommendation of the Security Council. He shall be the chief administrative officer of the Organisation.

Comment: *The selection of the Secretary-General by the Security Council is considered to be a non-procedural matter and, therefore, the Permanent Five are eligible to veto any candidate. All members of the Secretariat derive their position and authority directly from the Secretary-General. The Secretariat is a centralised agency and is at the disposal of all the other principal organs. The Secretary-General is involved in administrative as well as political functions. It is interesting to note that nowhere in this Article, or indeed the*

Chapter, is there mention made of the term limit of the Secretary-General. The current practice of a five-year term (almost always extended to a second one of similar tenure) has evolved by convention and has tended to be institutionalised since the stewardship of Waldheim who was appointed in 1972. One of the issues for reforms at the United Nations has been a proposal to limit the tenure of the Secretary-General to one single seven-year term. There has not been much progress on this, however.

Article 98.

The Secretary-General shall act in that capacity in all meetings of the General Assembly, of the Security Council, of the ECOSOC, and of the Trusteeship Council, and shall perform such other functions as are entrusted to him by these organs. The Secretary-General shall make an annual report to the General Assembly on the work of the Organisation.

Comment: This is the Article that is the central provision of the Charter that delimits the functions of the Secretary-General. These functions are of general administrative and executive nature, including technical, financial, political, representational, and organisation and administration of the Secretariat. Cuellar has put this Article in its proper context by stating that "this is not meant to be a mere rapporteur's job" (Cuellar (1993: 129)). He further opines that the submission of the annual report "is one of the ways in which the (Secretary-General) can act as a initiator and can galvanise the efforts of the other parts of the United Nations" (ibid).

Article 99.

The Secretary-General may bring to the attention of the Security Council any matter which in his opinion may threaten the maintenance of international peace and security.

Comment: This Article enables the Secretary-General to take the political initiative in maintaining international peace and security. The Security Council may have dominant domain over this, but the Secretary-General also has a certain degree of latitude in advocacy. This was evident during the 1979 Teheran takeover of the US Embassy, and the Secretary-General invoked his powers under this Article to urgently draw the Security Council's attention to it. All

Secretary-Generals have at one time or another invoked this Article to exercise certain political powers. Many authors have argued that for the UN to be made more effective, the Secretary-General would have to take recourse to Article 99 more vigorously. The first Secretary-General of the League of Nations, Sir Eric Drummond, is reported to have said that had he had at his disposal Article 99 then, "the position of his office – and by implication the influence of the League on events – would have developed differently" (Cuellar (op cit: 129)). Finally, Boutros-Ghali also accorded considerable emphasis to this Article in his Agenda for Peace *report.*

Article 100.

(1) In the performance of their duties the Secretary-General and the staff shall not seek or receive instructions from any government or from any other authority external to the Organisation. They shall refrain from any action which might reflect on their position as international officials responsible only to the Organisation.

(2) Each member of the United Nations undertakes to respect the exclusively international character of the responsibilities of the Secretary-General and the staff and not to seek to influence them in the discharge of their responsibilities.

Comment: *This Article brings out the true extent of the character of an international civil servant in the Secretary-General. This independence is key if all member states are to place their trust in the head of the UN. This independence also has implications for non-national considerations in matters of recruitment of senior Secretariat staff. However, in practice, this independence in recruitment is rather infrequently evident (many senior positions continue to be filled/replaced by strong considerations of an individual nation's interests). As a matter of fact, Secretary-Generals have repeatedly complained of political pressures from member states in filling senior positions.*

Article 101.

(1) The staff shall be appointed by the Secretary-General under regulations established by the General Assembly.

(2) Appropriate staffs shall be permanently assigned to the ECOSOC, the Trusteeship Council, and, as required, to other

organs of the United Nations. These staffs shall form a part of the Secretariat.

(3) The paramount consideration in the employment of the staff and in the determination of the conditions of service shall be the necessity of securing the highest standards of efficiency, competence, and integrity. Due regard shall be paid to the importance of recruiting the staff on as wide a geographical basis as possible.

Comment: The issue of fairness of geographical distribution is, however, difficult to settle; the UN itself says that the developing countries are under-represented in the senior ranks of the Organisation. On a related matter, the Secretary-General's political authority in the UN has as one of its bases the fact that he/she has powers to select staff members to work in the Secretariat. The organisation's personnel policy is then in the domain of the Secretary-General. However, in the context of the General Assembly having legislative powers in the UN, the Secretary-General's organisational powers are subject to the approval of the General Assembly, and in the 1980s, the General Assembly took in its own hands the reform of the organisation's personnel matters, creating its own committees and study groups. The Secretaries-General have, for obvious reasons, objected to this. All in all, Article 101 is the core of the personnel system of the UN.

Chapter XVI focuses on the miscellaneous provisions related to the organisation:

Article 102.
(1) Every treaty and every international agreement entered into by any member of the United Nations after the present Charter comes into force shall as soon as possible be registered with the Secretariat and published by it.
(2) No party to any such treaty or international agreement which has not been registered in accordance with the provisions of paragraph 1 of this Article may invoke that treaty or agreement before any organ of the United Nations.

Comment: The purpose of Article 102 is to ensure that there is cohesion among the applications of the various treaties and agreements, and that international diplomacy can proceed in public view with no hidden agreements.

Article 103.

In the event of a conflict between the obligations of the members of the United Nations under the present Charter and their obligations under any other international agreement, their obligations under the present Charter shall prevail.

Comment: This Article then reaffirms the supremacy of the agreements among member states within the context of the Charter. Article 103 is considered essential if the Charter is to be recognised as a global constitution since all other agreements – if in conflict with the stipulations of the Charter – are subsumed under it.

Article 104.

The Organisation shall enjoy in the territory of each of its members such legal capacity as may be necessary for the exercise of its functions and the fulfilment of its purposes.

Comment: This extends, among other things, into areas that deal with purchase of assets in the fulfilment of UN duties (such as land for buildings), use of air space (in times of relief operations), etc.

Article 105.

(1) The Organisation shall enjoy in the territory of each of its members such privileges and immunities as are necessary for the fulfilment of its purposes.

(2) Representatives of the members of the United Nations and officials of the Organisation shall similarly enjoy such privileges and immunities as are necessary for the independent exercise of their functions in connection with the Organisation.

(3) The General Assembly may make recommendations with a view to determining the details of the application of paragraphs 1 and 2 of this Article or may propose conventions to the members of the United Nations for this purpose.

Comment: Critics have charged that UN staff members in member countries have considerable privileges and immunities. While UN officials do have the luxury of several privileges in many duty stations around the world, it is not true, as alleged, that all UN officials have diplomatic immunity (only very senior officials do). One of the most serious and recent incidents exemplifying the provision inherent in Article 105 occurred in Ethiopia in July 1998 when the Government declared as persona non grata 38 locally recruited UN staff members all of whom were of Eritrean origin. The UN protested this treatment citing the violation of Article 105.

Chapter XVII deals with transitional security arrangements:

Article 106.
Pending the coming into force of such special agreements referred to in Article 43 as in the opinion of the Security Council enable it to begin the exercise of its responsibilities under Article 42, the parties to the Four-Nation Declaration, signed at Moscow, 30 October 1943, and France, shall, in accordance with the provisions of paragraph 5 of that Declaration, consult with one another and as occasion requires with other members of the United Nations with a view to such joint action on behalf of the Organisation as may be necessary for the purpose of maintaining international peace and security.

Comment: Simma (op cit: 1151) says that so far Article 106 has not attained any practical significance, and that it has rarely been called into practice.

Article 107.
Nothing in the present Charter shall invalidate or preclude action, in relation to any state which during the Second World War has been an enemy of any signatory to the present Charter, taken or authorised as a result of that war by the Governments having responsibility for such action.

Comment: This Article has to be seen, however, in light of the fact that with the granting of membership to all former enemy states, its utility was considerably curtailed. Furthermore, the Article is even more of academic importance only given the conclusion and ratification of the Treaty on the Final Settlement with Respect to Germany when the two Germanys united.

Chapter XVIII touches upon the issue of amendments to the Charter:

Article 108.

Amendments to the present Charter shall come into force for all members of the United Nations when they have been adopted by a vote of two thirds of the members of the General Assembly and ratified in accordance with their respective constitutional processes by two thirds of the members of the United Nations, including all the permanent members of the Security Council.

Comment: The Charter has only been amended three times – all on the basis of Article 108. They were only used to increase the membership levels in the Security Council and the ECOSOC. But the Article wording also shows how difficult it would be to change the Charter in the event that any one permanent member does not agree to it.

Article 109.

(1) A General Conference of the members of the United Nations for the purpose of reviewing the present Charter may be held at a date and place to be fixed by a two-thirds vote of the members of the General Assembly and by a vote of any nine members of the Security Council. Each member of the United Nations shall have one vote in the conference.

(2) Any alteration of the present Charter recommended by a two-thirds vote of the conference shall take effect when ratified in accordance with their respective constitutional processes by two thirds of the members of the United·Nations including all the permanent members of the Security Council.

(3) If such a conference has not been held before the tenth annual session of the General Assembly following the coming into force of the present Charter, the proposal to call such a conference shall be placed on the agenda of that session of the General Assembly, and the conference shall be held if so decided by a majority vote of the members of the General Assembly and by a vote of any seven members of the Security Council.

Comment: An amendment to this Article (which relates to the first paragraph) was adopted by the General Assembly on 20 December

1965 and came into force on 12 June 1968. This amendment provided that a General Conference of Member States for the purpose of reviewing the Charter may be held at a date and place to be fixed by a two-thirds vote of the members of the General Assembly and by a vote of any nine members of the Security Council. Unlike Article 108, this one allows for a more comprehensive review of the Charter. Annan's proposal on a ministerial committee to review the Charter falls under the domain of this Article. But Article 109 has never been formally invoked. Conforti (op cit: 17) argues that Articles 108 and 109 together imply that the UN Charter is very rigid.

Finally, Chapter XIX focuses on issues of ratifications and signature:

Article 110.

(1) The present Charter shall be ratified by the signatory states in accordance with their respective constitutional processes.

(2) The ratifications shall be deposited with the Government of the United States of America, which shall notify all the signatory states of each deposit as well as the Secretary-General of the Organisation when he has been appointed.

(3) The present Charter shall come into force upon the deposit of ratifications by the Republic of China, France, the Union of Soviet Socialist Republics, the United Kingdom of Great Britain and Northern Ireland, and the United States of America, and by a majority of the other signatory states. A protocol of the ratifications deposited shall thereupon be drawn up by the Government of the United States of America which shall communicate copies thereof to all the signatory states.

(4) The states signatory to the present Charter which ratify it after it has come into force will become original members of the United Nations on the date of the deposit of their respective ratifications.

Comment: *The number of such original members is 51 with Poland signing the Charter a mere nine days before the formal opening of the United Nations on 24 October 1945. The other 50 states had signed it on 26 June 1945 immediately at the end of the San Francisco Conference.*

Article 111.
The present Charter, of which the Chinese, French, Russian, English, and Spanish texts are equally authentic, shall remain deposited in the archives of the Government of the United States of America. Duly certified copies thereof shall be transmitted by that Government to the Governments of the other signatory states.

Comment: While five official languages are mentioned in the Article, only English and French are considered UN working languages for the organisation as a whole. In the General Assembly, Arabic is also now considered an official as well as a working language. For the ICJ, English and French are considered official languages as well.

Endnotes

[1] There is currently in the UN a Special Committee on the Charter of the United Nations and on the Strengthening of the Role of the Organisation that is involved in looking at various ways of improving specific aspects of the Charter. The Committee has made numerous suggestions on amendments to specific Articles and Chapters within the Charter, including reviewing proposals related to assistance to third states affected by sanctions (Article 50), the future of the Trusteeship Council (Chapter 13), and strengthening the competence of the International Court of Justice (Chapter 14) (see United Nations Press Release L/2923, 23 April 1999).
[2] *Ibid.*

Annex Two
The Components of the United Nations System

The Official WEB Site Locator for the United Nations System of Organisations classifies the UN system as consisting of the following:[1]

(1) programmes of the United Nations,
(2) specialised agencies,
(3) autonomous organisations,
(4) convention secretariats, and
(5) the inter-agency coordination mechanism.

(1) The Programmes of the UN include the following:

Offices located in New York, USA:
(a) Advisory Committee on Administrative and Budgetary Questions (ACABQ),
(b) International Civil Service Commission (ICSC),
(c) Panel of External Auditors of the United Nations, the Specialised Agencies, and the International Atomic Energy Agency (IAEA),
(d) United Nations Board of Auditors,
(e) United Nations Children's Fund (UNICEF),
(f) United Nations Development Fund for Women (UNIFEM) (programmatically under UNDP),
(g) United Nations Development Programme (UNDP),
(h) United Nations Headquarters (UN),
(i) United Nations Joint Staff Pension Fund (UNJSPF),
(j) United Nations Office for Project Services (UNOPS), and
(k) United Nations Population Fund (UNFPA).

Offices located in Geneva, Switzerland:
(a) Economic Commission for Europe (ECE),
(b) International Trade Centre UNCTAD/WTO,
(c) Joint Inspection Unit (JIU),
(d) Office of the United Nations High Commissioner for Human Rights (UNHCHR),
(e) Office of the United Nations High Commissioner for Refugees (UNHCR),

(f) United Nations Compensation Commission (UNCC),
(g) United Nations Conference on Trade and Development (UNCTAD),
(h) United Nations Institute for Disarmament Research (UNIDIR),
(i) United Nations Institute for Training and Research (UNITAR),
(j) United Nations Office at Geneva (UNOG), and
(k) United Nations Research Institute for Social Development (UNRISD).

Offices located in Vienna, Austria:
(a) Office for Outer Space Affairs (OOSA),
(b) United Nations Commission on International Trade Law (UNCITRAL),
(c) United Nations International Drug Control Programme (UNDCP),
(d) United Nations Office at Vienna (UNOV), and
(e) United Nations Postal Administration (UNPA).

Offices located in Rome, Italy:
(a) United Nations Interregional Crime and Justice Research Institute (UNICRI), and
(b) World Food Programme (WFP).

Offices located in Nairobi, Kenya:
(a) United Nations Centre for Human Settlements (UNCHS (Habitat)), and
(b) United Nations Environment Programme (UNEP).

Offices located elsewhere in the world:
(a) Economic and Social Commission for Asia and the Pacific (ESCAP), located in Bangkok, Thailand,
(b) Economic and Social Commission for Western Asia (ESCWA), located in Beirut, Lebanon,
(c) Economic Commission for Africa (ECA), located in Addis Ababa, Ethiopia,
(d) Economic Commission for Latin America and the Caribbean (ECLAC), located in Santiago, Chile,
(e) International Court of Justice (ICJ), located in The Hague, The Netherlands,

(f) International Research and Training Institute for the Advancement of Women (INSTRAW), located in Santo Domingo, Dominican Republic,

(g) United Nations Common Supply Database (UNCSD), located in Oslo, Norway,

(h) United Nations Relief and Works Agency for Palestine Refugees in the Near East (UNRWA), located in Gaza, Gaza Strip & Amman, Jordan,

(i) United Nations Staff College (UNSC), located in Turin, Italy,

(j) United Nations University (UNU), located in Tokyo, Japan, and

(k) United Nations Volunteers (UNV), located in Bonn, Germany (programmatically under UNDP).

(2) The Specialised Agencies of the UN include the following:

Offices located in Geneva, Switzerland:

(a) International Bureau of Education (IBE) (programmatically under UNESCO),

(b) International Labour Organisation (ILO) (formulates policies and programmes to improve working conditions and employment opportunities, and defines international labour standards as guidelines for Governments),

(c) International Telecommunication Union (ITU) (fosters international cooperation for the improvement and use of telecommunications, coordinates usage of radio and TV frequencies, promotes safety measures, and conducts research),

(d) World Health Organisation (WHO) (coordinates programmes aimed at solving health problems and the attainment by all people of the highest possible level of health; works in areas such as immunisation, health education, etc.),

(e) World Intellectual Property Organisation (WIPO) (promotes international protection of intellectual property and fosters cooperation on copyrights, trademarks, and industrial designs and patents),

(f) World Meteorological Organisation (WMO) (promotes scientific research on the atmosphere and on climate change, and facilitates the global exchange of meteorological data and information), and

(g) World Trade Organisation (WTO) (promotes international trade; replaces the General Agreement on Trade and Tariffs).

Offices located in Rome, Italy:
(a) Food and Agriculture Organisation of the United Nations (FAO) (works to raise levels of nutrition and standards of living, to improve agricultural productivity and food security, and to better the conditions of rural populations), and
(b) International Fund for Agricultural Development (IFAD) (mobilises financial resources for better food production and nutrition among the poor in developing countries).

Offices located in Washington, DC, USA:
(a) International Monetary Fund (IMF) (facilitates international monetary cooperation and financial stability, and provides a permanent forum for consultation, advice and assistance on financial issues),
(b) Multilateral Investment Guarantee Agency (MiGA) (programmatically under IBRD), and
(c) World Bank (IBRD) (provides loans and technical assistance to developing countries to reduce poverty and advance sustainable economic growth).

Offices located elsewhere:
(a) International Centre for Science and High Technology (ICSHT), located in Trieste, Italy,
(b) International Civil Aviation Organisation (ICAO), located in Montreal, Canada (sets international standards necessary for the safety, security, efficiency and regularity of air transport, and serves as the medium for cooperation in all areas of civil aviation),
(c) International Maritime Organisation (IMO), located in London, UK (works to improve international shipping procedures, encourages the highest standards in marine safety, and seeks to prevent marine pollution from ships),
(d) International Training Centre (ITC), located in Turin, Italy (acts as a part of ILO; related to training activities),
(e) United Nations Educational, Scientific and Cultural Organisation (UNESCO), located in Paris, France (promotes education for all, cultural development, protection of the world's natural and cultural heritage, press freedom, and communication),

(f) United Nations Industrial Development Organisation (UNIDO), located in Vienna, Austria (promotes the industrial advancement of developing countries through technical assistance, advisory services, and training), and

(g) Universal Postal Union (UPU), located in Berne, Switzerland (establishes international regulations for the organisation and improvement of postal services, provides technical assistance and promotes cooperation in postal matters).

(3) The Autonomous Organisations of the UN include the following:

(a) International Atomic Energy Agency (IAEA), located in Vienna, Austria, and

(b) World Tourism Organisation, located in Madrid, Spain.

(4) The Convention Secretariats of the UN include the following:

(a) United Nations Convention to Combat Desertification (UNCCD), located in Bonn, Germany, and

(b) United Nations Framework Convention on Climate Change (UNFCCC), located in Bonn, Germany.

(5) The Inter-Agency Coordination within the UN System includes the following:

Offices located in New York, USA:
(a) ACC Subcommittee on Statistical Activities,
(b) ACC Subcommittee on Water Resources,
(c) Administrative Committee on Coordination (ACC),
(d) Inter-agency Committee on Sustainable Development (IACSD),
(e) Inter-agency Meeting on Language Arrangements, Documentation, and Publications (IAMLADP),
(f) Joint United Nations Information Committee (JUNIC), and
(g) Organisational Committee of ACC.

Offices located in Geneva, Switzerland:
(a) ACC Subcommittee on Nutrition,
(b) Consultative Committee on Administrative Questions (Financial and Budgetary Questions) (CCAQ(FB)),

(c) Consultative Committee on Administrative Questions (Personnel and General Administrative Questions) (CCAQ(PER)),

(d) Consultative Committee on Programme and Operational Questions (CCPOQ),

(e) Information Systems Coordination Committee (ISCC),

(f) International Computing Centre (ICC),

(g) Joint Inter-agency Meeting on Computer-assisted Translation and Terminology (JIAMCATT), and

(h) Joint United Nations Programme on HIV/AIDS.

Offices located elsewhere:

(a) ACC Subcommittee on Drug Control, located in Vienna, Austria,

(b) ACC Subcommittee on Oceans and Coastal Areas, located in Paris, France,

(c) ACC Subcommittee on Rural Development, located in Rome, Italy, and

(d) Inter-Agency Procurement Services Office (IAPSO), located in Copenhagen, Denmark.

Endnotes

[1] Official Web Site Locator for the United Nations System of Organisations (http://www.unsystem.org/), ref. index 8, 11 February 2000.

Annex Three
UN Secretaries-General

Name	Country	Tenure	Remarks[1]
Trygve Lie	Norway	February 1946 to November 1952	Former Foreign Minister of Norway; resigned as UN Secretary-General two years into his three year extension after the first five-year term; appointed in 1959 as a mediator in the dispute over Somalia involving Italy and Ethiopia.
Dag Hammarskjold	Sweden	April 1953 to September 1961	Son of a former PM of Sweden; PhD in Economics from University of Stockholm; held honorary degrees from several top universities in the US, Canada, and Europe; died in a plane crash while on mission to the Congo; faced the brunt of Cold War rivalries in the organisation; described as the most respected Secretary-General in the history of the UN
Sithu U Thant	Myanmar	September 1961 to December 1971	The only Asian to hold the post; served previously as Ambassador to the UN; served on several occasions as Advisor to Prime Ministers of Myanmar; received honorary degrees from over 35 top universities around the world.
Kurt Waldheim	Austria	January 1972 to December 1981	Doctor of Jurisprudence from University of Vienna; Ambassador to various countries as well as to the UN; former Foreign Minister of Austria; would have been SG for an unprecedented third term if China had not used the veto; accused of Nazi past; elected Chancellor of Austria after his tenure as SG.

Name	Country	Tenure	Remarks
Javier Perez de Cuellar	Peru	January 1982 to December 1991	Lawyer and career diplomat; former Ambassador to various countries as well as to the UN; served as Professor of International Law in Peru; received several honorary degrees from around the world; as SG, instrumental in bringing an end to several conflicts; headed the UN at the point of the end of the Cold War; ran for President of Peru but did not succeed.
Boutros Boutros-Ghali	Egypt	January 1992 to December 1996	Former Foreign Minister of Egypt; PhD in International Law from Paris University; Professor of International Law in Egypt; recipient of several honorary degrees; only SG not to serve more than five years; fell out with the Americans for being too independent; in November 1997, elected General Secretary of *Organisation Internationale de la Francophonie*.
Kofi Annan	Ghana	Since January 1997	Management degree from MIT; varied UN career prior to being SG; only career UN bureaucrat to be SG; background in the UN includes posts in management and peacekeeping; submitted radical reform proposals; said to be very engaging and soft-spoken.

Endnotes

[1] The information in this Annex is adapted from the official UN source on Secretaries-General (http://www.un.org/Overview/SG/former_sgs.html), 1999, as well as from other newspaper and magazine reports, including appropriate United Nations Press Releases.

Annex Four
United Nations Membership

As of February 2000, there were 188 member states in the United Nations. Kiribati, Nauru, and Tonga were the latest additions to the UN in September 1999. The Pacific island of Tuvalu (originally part of Kiribati) was in February 2000 recommended for membership to the UN by the Security Council but a date has yet to be set for the General Assembly to formalise this recommendation. There were 51 original members (Poland signed nine days before the Charter came into force even though it had signed the Declaration in 1942).

Year	Members
As of 1945	Original members: Argentina, Australia, Belgium, Bolivia, Brazil, Byelorussia,[1] Canada, Chile, China,[2] Colombia, Costa Rica, Cuba, Czechoslovakia,[3] Denmark, Dominican Republic, Ecuador, Egypt,[4] El Salvador, Ethiopia, France, Greece, Guatemala, Haiti, Honduras, India, Iran, Iraq, Lebanon, Liberia, Luxembourg, Mexico, The Netherlands, New Zealand, Nicaragua, Norway, Panama, Paraguay, Peru, Philippines, Poland, Saudi Arabia, South Africa, Soviet Union,[5] Syria,[6] Turkey, Ukraine, UK, USA, Uruguay, Venezuela, Yugoslavia[7]
1946	Afghanistan, Iceland, Sweden, Thailand
1947	North Yemen,[8] Pakistan
1948	Burma[9]
1949	Israel
1950	Indonesia[10]
1955	Albania, Austria, Cambodia,[11] Ceylon,[12] Finland, Hungary, Ireland, Italy, Jordan, Laos,[13] Libya, Nepal, Portugal, Romania, Spain
1956	Japan, Morocco, Sudan, Tunisia
1957	Ghana, Malaya[14]
1958	Guinea
1960	Cameroon, Central African Republic, Chad, Congo (Brazzaville), Congo (Léopoldville)[15], Cyprus, Dahomey,[16] Gabon, Ivory Coast,[17] Madagascar, Mali, Niger, Nigeria, Senegal, Somalia, Togo, Upper Volta[18]
1961	Mauritania, Mongolia, Sierra Leone, Tanganyika[19]
1962	Algeria, Burundi, Jamaica, Rwanda, Trinidad and Tobago, Uganda
1963	Kenya, Kuwait, Zanzibar[20]

1964	Malawi, Malta, Zambia
1965	Bulgaria, The Gambia, Maldives, Singapore
1966	Barbados, Botswana, Guyana, Lesotho
1967	Democratic Yemen (Aden)[21]
1968	Equatorial Guinea, Mauritius, Swaziland
1970	Fiji
1971	Bahrain, Bhutan, Oman, Qatar, United Arab Emirates
1973	Bahamas, East Germany, West Germany[22]
1974	Bangladesh, Grenada, Guinea-Bissau
1975	Cape Verde, Comoros, Mozambique, Papua New Guinea, São Tomé and Príncipe, Suriname[23]
1976	Angola, Seychelles, Western Samoa[24]
1977	Djibouti, Vietnam
1978	Solomon Islands
1979	Dominica, Saint Lucia
1980	Saint Vincent and the Grenadines, Zimbabwe
1981	Antigua and Barbuda, Belize, Vanuatu
1983	Saint Kitts and Nevis
1984	Brunei Darussalam
1990	Liechtenstein, Namibia
1991	Estonia, North Korea (DPRK), South Korea (PRK), Latvia, Lithuania, Marshall Islands, Federated States of Micronesia
1992	Armenia, Azerbaijan, Bosnia and Herzegovina, Croatia, Georgia, Kazakhstan, Kyrgyzstan, Moldova, San Marino, Slovenia, Tajikistan, Turkmenistan, Uzbekistan
1993	Andorra, Eritrea, Macedonia, Monaco
1994	Palau
1999	Kiribati, Nauru, Tonga

Endnotes

[1] From September 1991, the country has been known as Belarus.
[2] Chiang Kai-Shek's Republic of China (Taiwan) represented China until 1971 when the UN voted to have China represented by the People's Republic of China.
[3] Czechoslovakia was bifurcated in January 1993 into the Czech Republic and Slovakia. Both are now considered to be new members.

[4] Egypt and Syria, while original members, formed a union in February 1958 and were considered as one member (United Arab Republic (UAR)). The UAR was nullified in October 1961, and the two became separate members again.

[5] The Soviet Union was dissolved in December 1991, and since then, the Russian Federation has succeeded to the Soviet seat. However, the Russian Federation is still considered to be an original member since it took over all the obligations of the former Soviet Union.

[6] See note 4 above.

[7] Yugoslavia broke up in 1992 into six constituent republics; rump Yugoslavia was denied UN membership.

[8] Yemen (i.e., North Yemen, capital: Sana) was admitted as a member in 1947 while its southern counterpart (i.e., Democratic Yemen, capital: Aden) was admitted in 1967. In 1990, the two countries united, and have since then been included as one UN member under the name Yemen.

[9] Burma from 1989 has been known as Myanmar.

[10] In January 1965, Indonesia voluntarily withdrew from the UN. It rejoined of its own accord in September 1966.

[11] Now known by the name Democratic Kampuchea.

[12] From 1972, Ceylon has been known as Sri Lanka.

[13] Laos is now listed in the UN roster as Lao PDR.

[14] From 1963, Malaya has been known as Malaysia.

[15] From 1966 to 1971, and later from 1997 on, known as Congo (Kinshasa); between 1971 and 1997, the name used was Zaire.

[16] From 1975, the country has come to be known as Benin.

[17] Since 1986, known as Côte d'Ivoire.

[18] In 1984, the country's name was changed to Burkina Faso.

[19] Tanganyika (which became a member in December 1961) and Zanzibar (which became a member in December 1963) merged in 1964 to form Tanzania. From April to November 1964, the union was named United Republic of Tanganyika and Zanzibar which was then subsequently changed to its current name: United Republic of Tanzania.

[20] See note 19 above.

[21] See note 8 above.

[22] East Germany (the German Democratic Republic) and West Germany (the Federal Republic of Germany) united in October 1990, and the united country has been known simply as Germany.

[23] The former name was Surinam.

[24] From 1997, the country has been known as Samoa.

Annex Five
United Nations Salary and Pension Scales

1. UN Salary Scale

Salary Scale for Professional and Higher Categories
(Annual Gross Salaries and Net Equivalents)
(in US Dollars; effective 1 March 1999)

Level	Steps ➔	I	II	III	IV	V	VI	VII
USG	Gross	151,440						
	Net D	104,662						
	Net S	94,190						
ASG	Gross	137,683						
	Net D	95,995						
	Net S	86,926						
D2	Gross	112,824	115,311	117,797	120,283	122,768	125,256	
	Net D	80,334	81,901	83,467	85,033	86,599	88,166	
	Net S	73,801	75,114	76,427	77,739	79,052	80,365	
D1	Gross	99,848	101,948	104,047	106,142	108,243	110,346	112,476
	Net D	72,068	73,410	74,751	76,090	77,432	78,773	80,115
	Net S	66,615	67,793	68,970	70,146	71,324	72,493	73,617
P5	Gross	88,099	89,975	91,875	93,775	95,674	97,571	99,471
	Net D	64,545	65,759	66,973	68,187	69,401	70,613	71,827
	Net S	59,963	61,075	62,142	63,208	64,273	65,337	66,403
P4	Gross	72,631	74,438	76,257	78,085	79,917	81,743	83,573
	Net D	54,516	55,701	56,883	58,066	59,251	60,433	61,617
	Net S	50,767	51,856	52,940	54,024	55,111	56,194	57,279
P3	Gross	59,386	61,057	62,731	64,400	66,088	67,782	69,477
	Net D	45,777	46,888	48,001	49,111	50,224	51,335	52,447
	Net S	42,730	43,752	44,776	45,798	46,821	47,843	48,865
P2	Gross	47,805	49,265	50,721	52,180	53,636	55,098	56,594
	Net D	37,953	38,949	39,942	40,937	41,930	42,925	43,920
	Net S	35,598	36,501	37,401	38,302	39,202	40,105	41,021
P1	Gross	36,422	37,791	39,157	40,525	41,891	43,258	44,627
	Net D	30,044	31,001	31,956	32,912	33,867	34,822	35,779
	Net S	28,341	29,222	30,102	30,983	31,863	32,743	33,625

contd...

Net D = Net salary rate applicable to staff members with dependents
Net S = Net salary rate applicable to staff members with no dependents

Note: The cells with thick borders show the bar (qualifying period) currently consisting of two years for the top step of level P-2, above step XIII of level P-3, above step XII of level P-4, above step X of level P-5, above step IV of the D-1 level, and for all steps at the D-2 level.

317

Salary Scale for Professional and Higher Categories...
(in US Dollars; effective 1 March 1999)

Level	Steps →	VIII	IX	X	XI	XII	XIII	XIV	XV
USG	Gross								
	Net D								
	Net S								
ASG	Gross								
	Net D								
	Net S								
D2	Gross								
	Net D								
	Net S								
D1	Gross	114,605	116,732						
	Net D	81,456	82,796						
	Net S	74,741	75,864						
P5	Gross	101,371	103,269	105,169	107,067	108,966	110,878		
	Net D	73,041	74,254	75,468	76,681	77,894	79,108		
	Net S	67,469	68,534	69,600	70,665	71,730	72,773		
P4	Gross	85,403	87,232	89,060	90,898	92,756	94,606	96,459	98,31
	Net D	62,801	63,984	65,167	66,349	67,536	68,718	69,902	71,08
	Net S	58,364	59,448	60,533	61,594	62,636	63,674	64,713	65,75
P3	Gross	71,174	72,867	74,564	76,275	77,994	79,711	81,430	83,14
	Net D	53,560	54,671	55,784	56,895	58,007	59,118	60,230	61,34
	Net S	49,888	50,909	51,932	52,951	53,970	54,989	56,008	57,02
P2	Gross	58,087	59,585	61,080	62,573	64,071			
	Net D	44,913	45,909	46,903	47,896	48,892			
	Net S	41,934	42,851	43,766	44,680	45,596			
P1	Gross	46,018	47,418	48,820					
	Net D	36,734	37,689	38,645					
	Net S	34,494	35,359	36,226					

Source: ICSC, United Nations Common System of Salaries, Allowances and Benefits, Annex I, May 1997 (http://www.un.org/Depts/icsc/sad/sab/index.htm)

Net D = Net salary rate applicable to staff members with dependents
Net S = Net salary rate applicable to staff members with no dependents

Note: The cells with thick borders show the bar (qualifying period) currently consisting of two years for the top step of level P-2, above step XIII of level P-3, above step XII of level P-4, above step X of level P-5, above step IV of the D-1 level, and for all steps at the D-2 level.

2. UN Pension Scale

Pensionable Remuneration for
Professional and Higher Categories
(in US Dollars; effective 1 November 1999)

Level	I	II	III	IV	V	VI	VII
USG	189,701						
ASG	175,336						
D2	145,798	149,111	152,424	155,734	159,047	162,360	
D1	129,131	131,779	134,426	137,069	139,717	142,497	145,334
P5	114,283	116,679	119,074	121,470	123,866	126,259	128,655
P4	94,487	96,825	99,159	101,493	103,832	106,166	108,502
P3	78,640	80,648	82,656	84,660	86,670	88,676	90,682
P2	64,516	66,315	68,108	69,904	71,698	73,494	75,289
P1	50,238	51,968	53,691	55,416	57,142	58,865	60,594

contd...

Level	VIII	IX	X	XI	XII	XIII	XIV	XV
USG								
ASG								
D2								
D1	148,171	151,004						
P5	131,052	133,444	135,841	138,236	140,638	143,205		
P4	110,839	113,174	115,509	117,843	120,185	122,518	124,853	127,191
P3	92,692	94,793	96,989	99,182	101,377	103,571	105,764	107,961
P2	77,081	78,880	80,674	82,468	84,265			
P1	62,317	64,041	65,768					

Source: ICSC, United Nations Common System of Salaries, Allowances and Benefits, Annex XII, May 1997 (http://www.un.org/Depts/icsc/sad/sab/index.htm)

Note: Pensions are calculated on the basis of the staff member's final average remuneration, which is the average of pensionable remuneration for the highest 36 months of the last five years of service. The current rate of contribution to the Fund is 23.7 per cent of pensionable remuneration, with two thirds paid by the UN and one third by the staff member. For the UN-designated mid-point salary scale (i.e., Net D at P-4, Step VI), the annual pension amount as of 1 November 1999 came to US$25,161 (23.7% of US$106,166).

Select Bibliography

Abbott, John. *Politics and Poverty, A Critique of the Food and Agriculture Organisation of the United Nations*. London: Routledge, 1992.

Abi-Saab, Georges (ed). *The Concept of International Organisation*. Paris: UNESCO, 1981.

Addo, Herb, et al. *Development as Social Transformation: Reflections on the Global Problematique*. London: Hodder & Stoughton for UN University, 1985.

Akehurst, Michael. *The Law Governing Employment in International Organisations*. Cambridge, UK: Cambridge University Press, 1967.

Aldrich, Howard. *Organisations and Environments*. New Jersey: Prentice-Hall, 1979.

Alger, Chadwick (ed). *The Future of the United Nations System: Potential for the Twenty-First Century*. Tokyo: United Nations University Press, 1998.

Alger, Chadwick. "Thinking about the Future of the UN System." *Global Governance*. 2, 3 (1996): 335-60.

Alger, Chadwick, Gene Lyons, and John Trent (eds). *The United Nations System: The Policies of Member States*. Tokyo: United Nations University Press, 1995.

Amerasinghe, C. F. *The Law of the International Civil Service (as applied by International Administrative Tribunals)*, 2 volumes. Oxford: Clarendon Press, 1988.

Ameri, Houshang. *Politics of Staffing the United Nations Secretariat*. New York: Peter Lang, 1996.

Ameri, Houshang. *Politics and Process in the Specialised Agencies of the United Nations*. UK: Gower Publishing Co., 1982.

Annan, Kofi. "Two Concepts of Sovereignty." *The Economist* (18 September 1999): 49-50.

Archer, Clive. *International Organisations*. London: George Allen & Unwin, 1983.

Baehr, Peter, and Leon Gordenker. *The United Nations in the 1990s*. Basingstoke: Macmillan Press, 1992.

Baehr, Peter, and Leon Gordenker. *The United Nations: Reality and Ideal*. New York: Praeger, 1984.

Baratta, Joseph Preston (compiler). *United Nations System*. New Brunswick, NJ: Transaction Publishers, 1995.

Baratta, Joseph Preston (compiler). *Strengthening the United Nations: A Bibliography on UN Reform and World Federalism*. New York: Greenwood Press, 1987.

Barnaby, Frank (ed). *Building a More Democratic United Nations.* Proceedings of the First International Conference on a More Democratic UN. London: Frank Cass, 1991.

Bedeian, Arthur. *Organisations: Theory and Analysis.* Second edition. New York: Dryden Press, 1984.

Behanan, Kovoor Thomas. *Realities and Make-Believe: Personnel Policy in the United Nations Secretariat.* New York: The William-Frederick Press, 1952.

Beigbeder, Yves. "The Continuing Financial Problems of the United Nations: Assessing Reform Proposals," (pp. 201-226), in Taylor, et al (eds), 1997(a).

Beigbeder, Yves. *The Internal Management of United Nations Organisations: The Long Quest for Reform.* London: Macmillan Press, 1997(b).

Beigbeder, Yves. "Reforming the Economic and Social Sectors of the United Nations: An Incomplete Process," (pp. 239-256), in Hufner (ed), 1995.

Beigbeder, Yves. *The Role and Status of International Humanitarian Volunteers and Organisations.* Dordrecht, The Netherlands: Martinus Nijhoff, 1991.

Beigbeder, Yves. "Administrative and Structural Reform in the Organisations of the United Nations Family," (pp. II.4/1-31), in de Cooker (ed), 1990.

Beigbeder, Yves. *Threats to the International Civil Service: Past Pressures and New Trends.* London: Pinter, 1988.

Beigbeder, Yves. *Management Problems in United Nations Organisations: Reform or Decline?* London: Frances Pinter, 1987.

Bennett, A. Le Roy. *Historical Dictionary of the United Nations.* Lanham, Md.: Scarecrow Press, 1995(a).

Bennett, A. Le Roy. *International Organisations: Principles and Issues.* Sixth edition. New Jersey: Prentice-Hall, 1995(b).

Bennis, Phyllis. *Calling the Shots: How Washington Dominates Today's UN.* New York: Olive Branch Press, 1996.

Berridge, G. R., and A. Jennings (eds). *Diplomacy at the UN.* London: Macmillan Press, 1985.

Bertrand, Maurice. *The United Nations: Past, Present and Future.* The Hague: Kluwer Law International, 1997.

Bertrand, Maurice. "The Historical Development of Efforts to Reform the UN," (pp. 420-436), in Roberts and Kingsbury (eds), 1993.

Bertrand, Maurice. *The Third Generation World Organisation.* Dordrecht, The Netherlands: Martinus Nijhoff Publishers, 1989.

Bertrand, Maurice. "Can the United Nations be Reformed?" (pp. 193-208), in Roberts and Kingsbury (eds), 1988.

Bertrand, Maurice. *The UN in Profile: How its Resources are Distributed.* New York: UNA-USA, 1986.

Bertrand, Maurice. *Some Reflections on Reform in the United Nations.* Report of the Joint Inspection Unit, JIU/REP/85/9, Geneva, October 1985.

Bertrand, Maurice, and Daniel Warner. *A New Charter for a Worldwide Organisation?* The Hague: Kluwer Law International, 1997.

Boulding, Kenneth. *The World as a Total System.* Beverly Hills, CA: Sage, 1985.

Bourantonis, Dimitris, and Jarrod Wiener (eds). *The United Nations in the New World Order: The World Organisation at Fifty.* London: Macmillan Press, 1995.

Boutros-Ghali, Boutros. "Global Leadership After the Cold War." *Foreign Affairs.* 75, 2 (March/April 1996): 86-98.

Boutros-Ghali, Boutros. "A New Departure on Development." *Foreign Policy.* 98 (Spring 1995): 44-49.

Boutros-Ghali, Boutros. *An Agenda for Development.* Report of the Secretary-General. Document A/48/935. New York: United Nations, 6 May 1994.

Boutros-Ghali, Boutros. "Empowering the United Nations." *Foreign Affairs.* 71 (1992/93): 89-102.

Boutros-Ghali, Boutros. *An Agenda for Peace: Preventive Diplomacy, Peacemaking and Peacekeeping.* Document S/24111, A/47/277. New York: United Nations, 17 June 1992.

Boyle, Francis. *World Politics and International Law.* Durham, NC: Duke University Press, 1985.

Browne, Marjorie Anne. *United Nations Reform: Issues for Congress.* Washington, DC: Congressional Research Service, Library of Congress, 6 September 1988.

Bulkeley, J. Russell. "Depoliticising United Nations Recruitment: Establishing a Genuinely International Civil Service," (pp. 267-304), in Taylor, et al (eds), 1997.

Bull, Hedley. *The Anarchical Society: A Study of Order in World Politics.* London: Macmillan Press, 1977.

Butler, Stuart, and Kim Holmes (eds). *Mandate for Leadership IV: Turning Ideas into Actions.* Washington, DC: The Heritage Foundation, 1997.

Carlsson, Ingvar. "The UN at 50: A Time to Reform." *Foreign Policy.* 100 (Fall 1995): 3-18.

Carlsson, Ingvar. "A New International Order Through the United Nations." *Security Dialogue.* 23, 4 (1992): 7-11.

Chebeleu, Traian. "The Administrative and Financial Reform of the United Nations: Some Reflections." *Revue Roumaine d'Etudes Internationales.* 22 (1989): 533-553.

Childers, Erskine, and Brian Urquhart. "Renewing the United Nations System: The International Civil Service." *Development Dialogue.* 1 (1994): 159-70.

Childers, Erskine, and Brian Urquhart. "Towards a More Effective United Nations." *Development Dialogue.* 1, 2 (1991): 11-40.

Claude, Inis. "Peace and Security: Prospective Roles for the Two United Nations." *Global Governance.* 2, 3 (1996): 289-98.

Claude, Inis. *Swords into Plowshares: The Problems and Progress of International Organisation.* Fourth edition. New York: Random House, 1971.

Claude, Inis. *The Changing United Nations.* New York: Random House, 1967.

Cleveland, Harlan, Hazel Henderson, and Inge Kaul (eds). *The United Nations: Policy and Financing Alternatives – Innovative Proposals by Visionary Leaders.* Washington, DC: The Global Commission to Fund the United Nations, 1995.

Coate, Roger (ed). *US Policy and the Future of the United Nations.* New York: The Twentieth Century Fund Press, 1994.

Collins, P. "Administrative Reforms in International Development Organisations." *Public Administration and Development.* 7 (1987, Special Issue): 125-142.

Commission on Global Governance. *Issues in Global Governance.* The Hague: Kluwer Law International, 1995(a).

Commission on Global Governance. *Our Global Neighbourhood: The Report of the Commission on Global Governance.* Oxford: Oxford University Press, 1995(b).

Conforti, Benedetto. *The Law and Practice of the United Nations.* The Hague: Kluwer Law International, 1997.

de Cooker, Chris (ed). *International Administration: Law and Management Practices in International Organisations.* Dordrecht, The Netherlands: Martinus Nijhoff Publishers, 1990.

Cosgrove, Carol, and Kenneth Twitchett (eds). *The New International Actors: The United Nations and the European Economic Community.* London: Macmillan Press, 1970.

Cot, Jean-Pierre, and Alain Pellet. *La Charte des Nations Unies.* Paris: Economica, 1991.

Cox, Robert, and Harold Jacobson. *The Anatomy of Influence: Decision-Making in International Organisation.* New Haven, CT: Yale University Press, 1973.

de Cuellar, Javier Perez. "Reflecting on the Past and Contemplating the Future." *Global Governance*. 1, 2 (1995): 149-70.

de Cuellar, Javier Perez. "The Role of the UN Secretary-General," (pp. 125-142), in Roberts and Kingsbury (eds), 1993.

Dadzie, Kenneth. *Report of the Special Advisor and Delegate of the Secretary-General on Reform of the Economic and Social Sectors*. New York: United Nations, 1993.

Dag Hammarskjold Foundation. *The 1968 Dag Hammarskjold Seminar on the Structure, Role, and Functions of the UN Systems*. Parts I and II. Uppsala, Sweden, January 1969.

Davidson, Nicol, and John Renninger. "The Restructuring of the United Nations Economic and Social System: Background and Analysis." *Third World Quarterly*. 4, 1 (1982): 74-92.

Deldique, Pierre-Edouard. *Le Mythe des Nations Unies: L'ONU Apres la Guerre Froide*. Paris: Hachette, 1994.

Deutsch, Karl. *The Analysis of International Relations*. Third edition. Englewood Cliffs, NJ: Prentice Hall, 1988.

Dijkzeul, Dennis. *The Management of Multilateral Organisations*. The Hague, The Netherlands: Kluwer Law International, 1997.

Dirks, Gerald, et al. *The State of the United Nations, 1993: North-South Perspectives*. Providence, RI: The Academic Council on the United Nations System, 1993.

Donini, Antonio. "The Bureaucracy and the Free Spirits: Stagnation and Innovation in the Relationship Between the UN and NGOs," (pp. 83-102), in Weiss and Gordenker (eds), 1996.

Downs, Anthony. *Inside Bureaucracy*. Boston: Little, Brown & Company, 1966.

Eagleton, Clyde. *International Government*. Revised edition. New York: Ronald Press, 1948.

Easton, David. "Categories for the Systems Analysis of Politics," (pp. 189-201), in Susser (ed), 1992.

Easton, David. *A Systems Analysis of Political Life*. New York: Wiley, 1965.

Eban, Abba. "The UN Idea Revisited." *Foreign Affairs*. 74, 5 (1995): 39-55.

Elmandjra, Mahdi. *The United Nations System: An Analysis*. Hamden, CT: Archon Books, 1973.

European Union. *Proposals of the European Union for Reform of the United Nations System in the Economic and Social Areas*. Brussels: European Union, 28 January 1997.

Evans, Gareth. *Cooperating for Peace: The Global Agenda for the 1990s and Beyond*. St. Leonards: Allen & Unwin, 1993.

Ewing, A. F. "Reform of the United Nations." *Journal of World Trade Law*. 20, 2 (1986): 131-41.

Falk, Richard. "Contending Approaches to World Order." *Journal of International Affairs* (New York). 31 (Fall-Winter 1977): 171-98.

Farley, Lawrence. *Change Processes in International Organisations.* Cambridge, Massachusetts: Schenkman Publishing Co., Inc., 1981.

Fawcett, Eric, and Hanna Newcombe (eds). *United Nations Reform: Looking Ahead After Fifty Years.* Toronto: Science for Peace, 1995.

Felix, David. "The Tobin Tax Proposal: Background, Issues, and Prospects," (pp. 195-208), in Cleveland, et al (eds), 1995.

Finger, Seymour Maxwell. *American Ambassadors at the United Nations: People, Politics, and Bureaucracy in the Making of Foreign Policy.* New York: UNITAR, 1992.

Finger, Seymour Maxwell. "Jeanne Kirkpatrick at the United Nations." *Foreign Affairs*, 62, 2 (1983): 445-447.

Finger, Seymour Maxwell, and Arnold Saltzman. *Bending with the Winds: Kurt Waldheim and the United Nations.* New York: Praeger Publishers, 1990.

Finkelstein, Lawrence (ed). *Politics in the United Nations System.* Durham: Duke University Press, 1988.

Fomerand, Jacques. "UN Conferences: Media Events or Genuine Diplomacy?" *Global Governance.* 2, 3 (1996): 361-75.

Foreign Affairs Committee. *The Expanding Role of the United Nations and the Implications for UK Policy: Report and Proceedings.* London: House of Commons, 1992-93.

Forum on the Future of the United Nations. *Reforming the United Nations: A View from the South.* Geneva: South Centre, March 1995.

Franck, Thomas. *Nation Against Nation: What happened to the UN Dream and what the US can do about it.* New York: Oxford University Press, 1985.

Franck, Thomas. "Of Gnats and Camels: Is There a Double Standard at the United Nations?" *American Journal of International Law.* 78 (1984): 811-33.

Franck, Thomas, and Georg Nolte. "The Good Offices Function of the UN Secretary-General," (pp. 143-182), in Roberts and Kingsbury (eds), 1993.

Fromuth, Peter (ed). *A Successor Vision: The United Nations of Tomorrow.* Maryland, USA: UNA-USA, 1988.

Fromuth, Peter. *The UN at 40: The Problems and the Opportunities – UN Management and Decision-Making Project.* New York: UNA-USA, 1986.

Fromuth, Peter, and Ruth Raymond. *UN Personnel Policy Issues, UN Management and Decision-Making Project.* New York: UNA-USA, 1987.

Galen, Ted (ed). *Delusions of Grandeur: The United Nations and Global Intervention.* Washington, DC: Cato Institute, 1997.

Galtung, Johan. *The United Nations Today: Problems and Some Proposals.* Princeton, NJ: Princeton University, Centre for International Studies, 1986.

de Gara, John. *Administrative and Financial Reform of the United Nations: A Documentary Essay.* Hanover, NH: Academic Council on the United Nations System, 1989.

Gati, Toby Trister (ed). *The US, the UN, and the Management of Global Change.* New York: New York University Press, 1983.

Gerbet, Pierre. "Rise and Development of International Organisations: A Synthesis," (pp. 27-49), in Abi-Saab (ed), 1981.

Glassner, Martin Ira (ed). *The United Nations at Work.* Westport, Connecticut: Praeger, 1998.

Goodrich, L., E. Hambro, and A. Simons. *Charter of the United Nations: Commentary and Documents.* Third edition. New York: Columbia University Press, 1969.

Gorbachev, Mikhail. *The River of Time and the Imperative of Action.* Fulton, Missouri: Westminster College, 1992.

Gordenker, Leon. "The NGOs and the UN in the Twenty-First Century," (pp. 141-49), in United Nations University, 1995.

Gordenker, Leon, and Paul Saunders. "Organisation Theory and International Organisation," (pp. 84-107), in Taylor and Groom (eds), 1978.

Gordenker, Leon, and Thomas Weiss. "NGO Participation in the International Policy Process," (pp. 209-222), in Weiss and Gordenker (eds), 1996.

Gordon, Wendell. *The United Nations at the Crossroads of Reform.* New York: M. E. Sharpe, 1994.

Graham, N., and R. Jordan (eds). *The International Civil Service: Changing Roles and Concepts.* New York: Pergamon Press, 1980.

Gregg, Robert. *About Face: The United States and the United Nations.* Boulder, CO: Lynne Rienner Publishers, 1993.

Griesgraber, Jo Marie. "Rethinking Bretton Woods," (pp. 240-246), in Cleveland, et al (eds), 1995.

Groom, A. J. R., and Paul Taylor. *Functionalism.* New York: Cross Russack, 1975.

Gurstein, Michael, and Josef Klee. "Towards a Management Renewal of the United Nations." *Public Administration and Development.* Part 1 in 16, 1 (1996): 43-56, and Part 2 in 16, 2 (1996): 111-122.

Haas, Ernst. *When Knowledge is Power: Three Models of Change in International Organisations.* Berkeley: University of California Press, 1990.

Haas, Ernst. *Why We Still Need the United Nations: The Collective Management of International Conflict, 1945-1984.* Berkeley: University of California, 1986.

Haas, Ernst. *Beyond the Nation State: Functionalism and International Organisation.* Stanford: Stanford University Press, 1964.

Haas, Ernst. "A Functional Approach to International Organisation." *Journal of Politics.* 27 (1960): 499-517.

Haas, Peter, and Ernst Haas. "Learning to Learn: Some Thoughts on Improving International Governance of the Global *Problematique*," (pp. 295-332), in Commission on Global Governance, 1995(a).

Hall, Richard. *Organisations: Structures, Processes, and Outcomes.* Fourth edition. New Jersey: Prentice-Hall, 1987.

Hancock, Graham. *Lords of Poverty.* London: Macmillan Press, 1989.

Harrod, Jeffrey. "United Nations Specialised Agencies: From Functionalist Intervention to International Cooperation," (pp. 130-44), in Jeffrey Harrod and Nico Schrijver (eds), *The UN Under Attack,* Aldershot, England: Gower, 1988.

Helms, Jesse. "Saving the UN: A Challenge to the Next Secretary-General." *Foreign Affairs.* 75, 6 (Sept/Oct 1996): 2-7.

Heritage Foundation. *Setting Priorities at the United Nations.* Backgrounder No. 952, Washington, DC, July 1993.

Heritage Foundation. *The United Nations: Its Problems and What to Do About Them – 59 Recommendations Prepared in Response to GA Resolution 40/237.* Washington, DC, 16 September 1988.

Heritage Foundation. *How the United Nations can be Reformed: The Recommendations of Four Former Ambassadors to the UN.* The Heritage Lectures. Washington, DC, 1986.

Heritage Foundation. *A UN Success Story: The World's Fattest Pensions.* Backgrounder No. 378, Washington, DC, 11 September 1984.

Hoffman, Walter. *United Nations Security Council Reform and Restructuring.* Livingston, NJ: The Centre for UN Reform Education, 1994.

Hufner, Klaus (ed). *The Reform of the United Nations: The World Organisation Between Crisis and Renewal.* Opladen: Leske+Budrich, 1994.

Independent Commission on the Future of the United Nations. *Toward Common Goals.* Ottawa, Canada, 1993.

Independent Working Group on the Future of the United Nations. *The United Nations in its Second Half-Century.* New York: Ford Foundation, 1995.

Inoguchi, Takashi. "Envisioning the United Nations in the Twenty-first Century: The United Nations as Actor, Arena, and Tool," (pp. 34-39), in United Nations University, 1995.

Jackson, Richard. *The Non-Aligned, the UN, and the Superpowers.* New York: Praeger, 1983.

Jonsson, Christer. "Inter-organisation Theory and International Organisation." *International Studies Quarterly.* 30, 1 (March 1986): 39-57.

Kanninen, Tapio. *Leadership and Reform: The Secretary-General and the UN Financial Crisis of the Late 1980s.* The Hague: Kluwer Law International, 1995.

Kaplan, Morton. *System and Process in International Politics.* New York: Wiley, 1957.

Kasto, Jalil. *The United Nations: A Global Organisation – Its Evolution, Achievements, Failure, and Reconstruction.* Hounslow, UK: 1995.

Kaufmann, Johan, Dick Leurdijk, and Nico Schrijver. *The World in Turmoil: Testing the UN's Capacity.* Hanover, NH: Academic Council on the United Nations System, 1991.

Kaul, Inge. "Beyond Financing: Giving the United Nations Power of the Purse." *Futures.* 27, 2 (1995): 181-188.

Kay, David. *The United Nations Political System.* New York: John Wiley & Sons, 1967.

Kennedy, Paul, and Bruce Russett. "Reforming the United Nations." *Foreign Affairs.* 74, 5 (1995): 56-71.

Kolosovsky, Andrei Igorevich. "UN Mirrors the Whole World." *International Affairs* (Moscow). 36, 2 (February 1991): 21-29.

Laszlo, Ervin. "Global Goals and the Crisis of Political Will." *Journal of International Affairs.* 31 (1977): 199-214.

Lemoine, Jacques. *The International Civil Servant: An Endangered Species.* The Hague, The Netherlands: Kluwer Law International, 1995.

Lewin, Kurt. *Field Theory in Social Science.* London: Harper and Row, 1951.

Lindblom, Charles. "The Science of 'Muddling Through'." *Public Administration Review.* 19, 2 (Spring 1959): 79-88.

Lyons, Gene. "Competing Visions: Proposals for UN Reform," (pp. 41-88), in Alger, et al (eds), 1995.

Mailick, Sidney. "A Symposium: Towards an International Civil Service." *Public Administration Review.* 30, 3 (May/June 1970): 206-63.

de Marco, Guido, and Michael Bartolo. *A Second Generation United Nations: For Peace in Freedom in the 21st Century.* London and New York: Kegan Paul International, 1997.

Matanle, Emma. *The UN Security Council: Prospects for Reform.* London: Royal Institute of International Affairs, 1995.

Mathiason, John. "Who Controls the Machine? The Programme Planning Process in the Reform Effort." *Public Administration and Development.* 7 (1987): 165-180.

Maynes, Charles, and Richard Williamson (eds). *US Foreign Policy and the United Nations System.* New York: W. W. Norton & Company, 1996.

McLaren, Robert. "The UN System and its Quixotic Quest for Co-ordination." *International Organisation.* 34, 1 (1980): 139-148.

Meltzer, Ronald. "Restructuring the United Nations System: Institutional Reform Efforts in the Context of North-South Relations." *International Organisation.* 32, 4 (Autumn 1978): 993-1018.

Melvern, Linda. *The Ultimate Crime: Who Betrayed the UN and Why.* London: Allison and Busby, 1995.

Mendez, Ruben. "Financial Reform for the International Sector," (pp. 185-199), in Taylor, et al (eds), 1997.

Menon, Bhaskar. "The Image of the United Nations," (pp. 175-193), in Commission on Global Governance, 1995(a).

Meron, Theodor. "Staff of the United Nations Secretariat: Problems and Directions." *American Journal of International Law.* 70, 4 (October 1976): 659-93.

Michelmann, Hans. *Organisational Effectiveness in a Multinational Bureaucracy.* Farnborough, England: Saxon House, 1978.

Miller, Lynn. *Global Order: Values and Power in International Politics.* Boulder, CO: Westview, 1985.

Mitrany, David. *A Working Peace System: An Argument for the Functional Development of International Organisations.* London: Royal Institute of International Affairs, 1943.

Mitrany, David. *The Progress of International Government.* New Haven: Yale University Press, 1933.

Morgan, Gareth. *Images of Organisations.* California: Sage Publications, 1986.

Morgenthau, Hans. *In Defence of the National Interest.* New York: Knopf, 1951.

Morgenthau, Hans. *Politics among Nations.* New York: Knopf, 1948.

Moynihan, Daniel with Suzanne Weaver. *A Dangerous Place.* Boston: Atlantic, Little Brown, 1978.

Muller, Joachim (ed). *Reforming of the United Nations: New Initiatives and Past Efforts.* The Hague: Kluwer Law International, 1997.

Muller, Joachim. *The Reform of the United Nations.* Volumes I and II. New York: Oceana, 1992.

Myers, Patrick. *Succession Between International Organisations.* London: Kegan Paul International, 1993.

Myrdal, Gunnar. *Realities and Illusions in Regard to Inter-Governmental Organisations.* London: Oxford University Press, 1955.

Narasimhan, C. *The United Nations: An Inside View.* New Delhi: Vikas, 1988.

Nerfin Marc. *The Future of the UN System – Some Questions on the Occasion of an Anniversary.* Uppsala, Sweden: Dag Hammarskjold Foundation, 1985.

Nicholas, Herbert. *The United Nations as a Political Institution.* Fifth edition. New York: Oxford University Press, 1975.

Nicol, David, and John Renninger. "The Restructuring of the United Nations Economic and Social System: Background and Analysis." *Third World Quarterly.* 4, 1 (1982): 74-92.

Nordic UN Project. *The United Nations in Development: Reform Issues in the Economic and Social Fields.* Final Report of the Nordic UN Project. Stockholm: Almquist & Wiksell International, 1991.

Ogata, Shijuro, Paul Volcker, et al. *Financing an Effective United Nations: A Report of the Independent Advisory Group on UN Financing.* New York: The Ford Foundation, 1993.

Ostrower, Gary. *The United Nations and the United States.* New York: Twayne Publishers/Simon & Schuster, Macmillan Press, 1998.

Otunnu, Olara. "The Peace and Security Agenda of the United Nations: From a Crossroads into the Next Century," (pp. 2-23), United Nations University, 1995.

Park, Sang-Seek. "Reform of the United Nations System." *Korea and World Affairs.* 20, 2 (Summer 1996): 272-295.

Pfeffer, Jeffrey, and Gerald Salancik. *The External Control of Organisations: A Resource Dependence Perspective.* New York: Harper & Row, 1978.

Pines, Burton Yale (ed). *A World Without the United Nations: What Would Happen if the United Nations Shut Down.* Washington, DC: The Heritage Foundation, 1984.

Pitt, David, and Thomas Weiss (eds). *The Nature of United Nations Bureaucracies.* London: Croom Helm, 1986.

Puchala, Donald, and Roger Coate. *The Challenge of Relevance: The United Nations in a Changing World Environment.* New York: Academic Council on the United Nations System, 1989.

Rajiv Gandhi Memorial Initiative for the Advancement of Human Civilisation. *Reform of the United Nations Organisation.* New Delhi: Rajiv Gandhi Foundation, 1994.

Rasgotra, M. (ed). *UN in the 21st Century.* New Delhi: Rajiv Gandhi Foundation, 1995.

Reisman, Michael. "Redesigning the United Nations." *Singapore Journal of International and Comparative Law.* 1 (1997): 1-27.

Renninger, John. "Improving the UN System." *Journal of Development Planning.* 17 (1987(a)): 85-111.

Renninger, John. "The International Civil Service Commission and the Development of a Common Personnel Policy in the United Nations

System." *Public Administration and Development.* 7 (1987(b)): 181-194.

Reymond, Henri, and Sidney Mailick. *International Personnel Policies and Practices.* New York: Praeger Publishers, 1985.

Righter, Rosemary. *Utopia Lost: The United Nations and World Order.* New York: The Twentieth Century Fund Press, 1995.

Rivlin, Benjamin, and Leon Gordenker (eds). *The Challenging Role of the UN Secretary-General: Making 'The Most Impossible Job in the World' Possible.* Westport, Connecticut: Praeger, 1993.

Roberts, Adam, and Benedict Kingsbury. *Presiding over a Divided World: Changing UN Roles, 1945-1993.* Boulder, Colorado: Lynne Rienner, 1995.

Roberts, Adam, and Benedict Kingsbury (eds). *United Nations, Divided World: The UN's Roles in International Relations.* Second edition. Oxford: Clarendon Press, 1993 (first edition: 1988).

Rochester, J. Martin. *Waiting for the Millennium: The United Nations and the Future of World Order.* Columbia, South Carolina: University of South Carolina Press, 1993.

Ruggie, John. "The United States and the United Nations: Toward a New Realism." *International Organisation.* 39, 2 (Spring 1985): 343-56.

Ruggie, John. "On the Problems of 'the Global *Problematique*': What Roles for International Organisations?" *Alternatives.* 5 (1979-80): 517-50.

Russett, Bruce. "Ten Balances for Weighing UN Reform Proposals," (pp. 24-31), United Nations University, 1995.

Saksena, K. *Reforming the United Nations: The Challenge of Relevance.* New Delhi: Sage Publications, 1993.

Schaefer, Brett, and Thomas Sheehy. "Reforming and Working with the United Nations," (pp. 701-732), in Butler and Holmes (eds), 1997.

Schechter, Michael (ed). *Innovation in Multilateralism.* Tokyo: United Nations University, 1999.

Schiavone, Giuseppe. *International Organisations: A Dictionary.* Fourth edition. London: Macmillan Press, 1997.

Schlensinger, Stephen. "Can the United Nations Reform?" *World Policy Journal,* 14, 3 (Fall 1997): 47-52.

Senarclens, Pierre de. "Reforming the United Nations: A Necessity and an Illusion," (pp. 211-228), in Hufner (ed), 1995.

Shanks, Cheryl, Harold Jacobson, and Jeffrey Kaplan. "Inertia and Change in the Constellation of International Governmental Organisations, 1981-1992." *International Organisation.* 50, 4 (1996): 593-627.

Simma, Bruno (ed). *The Charter of the United Nations: A Commentary.* New York: Oxford University Press, 1994.

Simon, Herbert. *Administrative Behaviour.* Second edition. New York: Macmillan Press, 1961.

Simons, Geoff. *UN Malaise: Power, Problems, and Realpolitik.* New York: St. Martin's Press, 1995.

Simons, Geoff. *The United Nations: A Chronology of Conflict.* London: Macmillan Press, 1994.

Smouts, Marie-Claude. "United Nations Reforms: A Strategy of Avoidance," (pp. 29-44), in Schechter (ed), 1999.

Soroos, Marvin. *Beyond Sovereignty: The Challenge of Global Policy.* Columbia, SC: University of South Carolina Press, 1986.

South Centre. *Reforming the United Nations: A View from the South.* Geneva/Dar es Salaam: South Centre, 1995.

Stanley Foundation. *The UN Security Council and the International Criminal Court: How Should They Relate?* Twenty-ninth UN Issues Conference, 1998; Muscatine, IA, 1998.

Stanley Foundation. *Beyond Reform: The United Nations in a New Era.* Thirty-second UN of the Next Decade Conference, 1997; Muscatine, IA, 1997(a).

Stanley Foundation. *Making UN Reform Work: Improving Member State-Secretariat Relations.* Twenty-eighth UN Issues Conference, 1997; Muscatine, IA, 1997(b).

Stanley Foundation. *The United Nations and the Twenty-First Century: The Imperative for Change.* Thirty-first UN of the Next Decade Conference, 1996; Muscatine, IA, 1996.

Stassen, Harold. *United Nations: A Working Paper for Restructuring.* Minneapolis, Minnesota: Lerner Publications, 1994.

Steele, David. *The Reform of the United Nations.* London: Croom Helm, 1987.

Susser, Bernard (ed). *Approaches to the Study of Politics.* New York: Macmillan, 1992.

Taylor, J. P., and A. J. R. Groom (eds). *International Organisation: A Conceptual Approach.* London: F. Pinter, 1978.

Taylor, Paul, Sam Daws, and Ute Adamczick-Gerteis (eds). *Documents on Reform of the United Nations.* Aldershot, UK: Dartmouth, 1997.

Thakur, Ramesh (ed). *Past Imperfect, Future UNcertain: The United Nations at Fifty.* New York: St. Martin's Press, 1997.

Thakur, Ramesh. "The United Nations in a Changing World." *Security Dialogue.* 24, 1 (1993): 7-20.

Touval, Saadia. "Why the UN Fails." *Foreign Affairs.* 73, 5 (1994): 44-57.

Uchida, Takeo. "Northern Perspectives for Peace and Security Functions of the United Nations," (pp. 61-110), in Schechter (ed), 1999.

UNA-USA. *A Successor Vision: The United Nations of Tomorrow.* New York: UNA-USA, 1987.

UNDP. *Human Development Report, 1994.* New York: UNDP, 1994.

UNDP. *Human Development Report, 1992.* New York: UNDP, 1992.

UNIDO. *UNIDO Reform Bulletin, October 1995.* Vienna, Austria: UNIDO, 1995.

United Nations. *Preventing War and Disaster: A Growing Global Challenge.* 1999 Annual Report on the Work of the Organisation. New York: United Nations, September 1999.

United Nations. *Renewing the United Nations: A Programme for Reform.* Document A/51/950. New York: United Nations, 14 July 1997(a).

United Nations. *The World Conferences: Developing Priorities for the 21ˢᵗ Century.* New York: United Nations, Department of Public Information, 1997(b).

United Nations. *UN 21: Accelerating Managerial Reform for Results.* Document A/51/873. New York: United Nations, 1997(c).

United Nations. *A Vision of Hope: The Fiftieth Anniversary of the United Nations.* London: The Regency Corporation Ltd., 1995.

United Nations University. *Envisioning the United Nations in the 21ˢᵗ Century: UN21 Project Annual Report.* The Proceedings of the Inaugural Symposium on the United Nations System in the 21ˢᵗ Century. Tokyo: UNU, 1995.

United States Commission on Improving the Effectiveness of the United Nations. *Defining Purpose: The UN and the Health of Nations.* Final Report. Washington, DC: US Government Printing Office, September 1993.

Urquhart, Brian. "Selecting the World's CEO: Remembering the Secretaries-General." *Foreign Affairs.* 74, 3 (1995): 21-26.

Urquhart, Brian. "The United Nations in 1992: Problems and Opportunities." *International Affairs.* 68, 2 (1992): 311-19.

Urquhart, Brian. "Problems and Prospects of the United Nations." *International Journal.* 44, 4 (1989(a)): 803-22.

Urquhart, Brian. "The United Nations System and the Future." *International Affairs.* 68 (1989(b)): 225-31.

Urquhart, Brian, and Erskine Childers. *A World in Need of Leadership: Tomorrow's United Nations – A Fresh Appraisal.* Revised second edition. Uppsala, Sweden: Dag Hammarskjold Foundation, 1996 (first edition: 1990).

Uvin, Peter. "Scaling Up the Grassroots and Scaling Down the Summit: The Relations Between Third World NGOs and the UN," (pp. 159-176), in Weiss and Gordenker (eds), 1996.

Weiss, Thomas George. "International Bureaucracy: The Myth and Reality of the International Civil Service." *International Affairs* (London). 58, 2 (1982): 286-306.

Weiss, Thomas George. *International Bureaucracy: An Analysis of the Operation of Functional and Global International Secretariats.* Lexington, Massachusetts: Lexington Books, 1975.

Weiss, Thomas George, David Forsythe, and Roger Coate. *The United Nations and Changing World Politics.* Boulder, Colorado: Westview Press, 1994.

Weiss, Thomas, and Leon Gordenker (eds). *NGOs, the UN, and Global Governance.* Boulder, CO: Lynne Rienner, 1996.

Wells, Robert, Jr. (ed). *Peace by Pieces: United Nations Agencies and Their Roles.* Metuchen, NJ: Scarecrow, 1991.

Werner, J. Feld, Robert Jordan with Leon Hurwitz. *International Organisations: A Comparative Approach.* Third edition. Connecticut: Praeger, 1994.

Wilenski, Peter. "The Structure of the UN in the Post-Cold War Period," (pp. 437-467), in Roberts and Kingsbury (eds), 1993.

Wiletts, Peter (ed). *The Conscience of the World: The Influence of Non-Governmental Organisations in the UN System.* London: Hurt & Company, 1996.

Williams, Douglas. *The Specialised Agencies and the United Nations: The System in Crisis.* New York: St. Martin's Press, 1987.

Yeselson, Abraham, and Anthony Gaglione. *A Dangerous Place: The United Nations as a Weapon in World Politics.* New York: Grossman, 1974.

Index

References from endnotes are indicated by 'n' after page numbers